Principles of Human Communication

Fourth Edition

Robert E. Smith
Purdue University

. . . .
With exercises by
R. E. Smith and Suzanne Collins
. . . .

KENDALL/HUNT PUBLISHING COMPANY
4050 Westmark Drive   Dubuque, Iowa 52002

Photograph by
    Bob Coyle, Dubuque, IA
    Nancy Ann Dawe, Decatur, GA
    Center for Instructional Services, Purdue University
    The Purdue Exponent

ISBN 0-7872-4230-6

Printed in the United States of America
10 9 8 7 6 5

Quick Reference Contents

Contents
· · · ·

Study Materials and Exercises Contents
· · · · ·

Preface

· · · · ·

Unlike other works such as novels, plays, and film, textbooks are always in the process of being revised. The effectiveness of a textbook depends on how well it reflects the tradition of a field and the latest ideas and information. Its effectiveness also depends on how well it adapts to its ever changing audience of students.

This Fourth Edition is another step in the evolution of *Principles of Human Communication*. The text retains its broad focus on the field of communication and introduces students to several significant areas of communication: communication theory, interpersonal communication, small group communication, and public speaking. Major revisions have been made in the areas of theory, interpersonal communication, and small group. The public speaking section follows the same format as the third edition, but the material has been completely rewritten.

In addition to the changes in the text, the Fourth Edition is cast in a new format. Previously, we have provided a workbook to accompany the text. With the Fourth Edition, the text and workbook materials have been combined into one volume. Each chapter in the text is followed by study questions, exercises, response sheets, and assignment sheets pertinent to the unit. This arrangement eliminates the need for teachers and students to shift back and forth between the separate books.

Audience

This book is written for the beginning college student who may have only a vague knowledge of communication, a person, for example, who may think of communication as limited to public speaking or who may think that common sense is all we need to know about communication. The book has four goals:

1. To introduce the reader to communication and communication studies,
2. To provide an understanding of the process of communication in various contexts (interpersonal, small group, public speaking),
3. To supply practical knowledge useful in improving communication skills in interpersonal, small group, and public speaking contexts,
4. To provide a solid foundation in communication for those wishing to go beyond the basic course in formal or individual study.

Organization

The book is divided into four main sections. The first is an introduction to communication.

Chapter One confronts a common question asked by many students in a communication class, "Why should I study communication?" The answer is that communication and communication study is an inevitable part of our existence and its study informs and improves our lives.

Chapter Two defines and discusses the process of communication. The chapter provides an overview of the field of communication to introduce students to the breadth of communication study and to create an awareness of the universality of communication.

Chapter Three looks at the combination of elements that create each of us as communicators: culture, language, and nonverbal communication.

Chapter Four discusses the ethics of communication. Having introduced the idea of communication and choices in the earlier chapters, we discuss the nature of those choices in this chapter. Guidelines are given for ethical communication.

The second major division of the book is interpersonal communication.

Chapter Five addresses interpersonal communication. The chapter deals with the nature of interpersonal communication and the skills needed in three major areas of interpersonal communication: conversation, comforting, and conflict resolution.

The third major division of the book is small group communication.

Chapter Six provides an overview of small group communication. It discusses types of groups, groups and context, task and relationships in groups, creative activities of group members, group tensions, and group development.

Chapter Seven looks at roles and leadership in small groups. Positive and negative activities of group members are discussed as well as leadership responsibilities and planning meetings.

Chapter Eight looks at the ineffective and effective ways small groups can approach problem solving. The rational model of small group problem solving is discussed as are methods of decision making and dealing with conflict.

The last major division of the text is public speaking. The two types of speaking addressed in this section are informational speaking and persuasive speaking.

Chapter Nine looks at basic factors inherent in most speaking situations. Of particular interest is its discussion of creativity as it pertains to public speaking. Other important topics in the chapter are analyzing the speaking situation, finding and narrowing topics, and patterns of organization.

Chapter Ten builds on the preceding chapter and discusses further organization of a speech such as how to create introductions, transitions, and conclusions. The chapter provides two ways of organizing materials: traditional outlining and speechmapping. As practice is an important part of creating a speech, the chapter discusses effective techniques for rehearsal.

Chapter Eleven deals specifically with informational speaking. The chapter details several ways in which topics may be approached as well as the principles and skills necessary for good informational speaking.

Chapter Twelve addresses performance concerns, how speakers can coordinate the elements of a speech to good effect. Notes, visual aids, the speaking voice, and physical communication are discussed, as is communication apprehension.

Chapter Thirteen deals with persuasive speaking. It provides a definition and discussion of persuasion as well as the ethics of persuasion. It also details the process of decision making.

Chapter Fourteen provides the procedures for composing a persuasive speech. It discusses audience analysis, styles of persuasive speaking, persuasive thesis statements, and organization. The chapter includes the important areas of evidence and speaker credibility.

Chapter Fifteen deals with the arguments and lines of reasoning speakers might use in persuasive speaking. Deductive reasoning, inductive reasoning, and fallacious reasoning are discussed with examples provided of each.

Special Features

Beyond the basics in communication, the book offers several features which may be of special interest. It begins with a topic which should be of major interest to students, themselves, then moves into ever widening patterns of communication. Its discussion of culture as a factor in communication provides students with a basis for understanding the communication patterns of others as well as their own.

The overall view of the text is not so much on the products of communication as it is on the process of communication. The public speaking section is notable for not approaching public speaking from the standpoint of "giving a speech." Instead, it emphasizes the creative process that links ideas, composition, and performance.

Other features include a section on voice, which is missing from many textbooks, and a discussion of speechmapping in addition to the usual section on outlining. Each chapter is followed immediately by study questions that reinforce chapter concepts and provide review material for exams.

The text-workbook format combines factual material with exercise material into one package. The arrangement of materials is easy to follow and provides concepts and reinforcement of those concepts.

Acknowledgments

When working on a project such as this textbook, it is gratifying to have available friends and colleagues upon whom one can call for assistance and expertise. I have numerous people to thank for their help with this volume:

▶ The Department of Communication at Purdue for its support

▶ My department head, Charles J. Stewart, for his encouragement, support, and trust

▶ The Assistant Directors, past and present, of the basic course whose initiative and industry have lightened my load considerably: Derek Arnold, Craig Booth, Jacquelyn Buckrop, Suzanne Collins, Paula M. E. Mendenhall, Lisa Goodnight, and Ron Sandwina

▶ Special thanks to Suzanne Collins for her work on the study materials

▶ My colleagues for their contributions of time and expertise: Brant Burleson, Chris Nelson, Robert Ogles, Linda Putnam, William Rawlins, Cynthia Stohl, Glen Sparks, Leon Trachtman

▶ Omar Swartz for his work on the persuasion and reasoning chapter

▶ Scott Mandernack for his preparation of the material on research in communication

▶ Darla Williams for her work on the small group portion of the text

▶ Mary Keehner for her review of the text;

▶ My 1993 Summer School Module One Com. 114 class for their help and willingness to share materials

▶ The Department of Communication office staff: Diana Cable, Beverly Robinson, Carolyn Parrish, and Bonnie Parker

▶ Finally, Pauletta Smith, my wife, for her support throughout.

1

The Study of Communication

Key Concepts

Communication as a Human Activity
The Import of Communication Study

• • • • • • • • • • •

It is one of the best known stories from the ancient world, a story of conflict, strategy, and a famous message.

In 490 BC, the fate of Athens and the other free city-states of Greece hung in the balance. Seeking to extend the Persian empire, a large army of Persians landed on the plain of Marathon about twenty-five miles from Athens. Facing them was an outnumbered force of Athenians. Defeat looked inevitable.

The Athenian general, however, struck a bold plan. Instead of concentrating his forces at the center, he concentrated them in the flanks. Then, instead of waiting in a defensive position, he charged.

The Persians were routed. Herodotus, the Greek historian, reports that the Persians lost 6,200 men to the Athenians' 192 (6, 117).

As soon as it was clear that Athens was saved, the general sent a message as swiftly as he could. He selected a runner, Phidippides, to carry the news to Athens. Phidippides set off at his best pace, eager to let the Athenians know the outcome of the battle.

He ran the long distance from Marathon to Athens, reached the city, shouted the notable words, "Victory! We conquer!" then collapsed and died from exhaustion.

The story remarks on numerous ideas: the bravery of the Greeks, their dedication to preserving their freedom, the bold stroke that may wrench victory from impending doom, and the importance of communication.

The ability to respond to a story such as the one above speaks to the multiplicity of talents we have as human beings to link ourselves to others. The original story was carried word of mouth, yet somehow it has been preserved into other forms so that it is available to us today. The story has had an existence in oral form, writing, printing, film, and video. Even though it happened over twenty-four hundred years ago, we are still able to recall it. That our communicative abilities allow us to move between time periods is itself something of a marvel.

Beyond the transmission of the story, we discover that communication begets more communication. We not only receive the story, but we respond to it. We may recount the tale to someone else. We may muse on the story to de-

cide its application to our situations. Based on this story, the Olympic committee created the modern long distance race, the marathon, in 1896 (Benyo 6). Hearing one story, we may feel motivated to tell a story of our own, a phenomenon known as the "Canterbury Effect." We might add, in a poetic note to history, that the first Olympic marathon was won by a Greek, Spiridon Louys (Guttman 19). We may subject the story to a variety of critiques and analyses. One historian notes, for example, that "Herodotus' account is far from being above criticism" (Hart 91).

Interestingly enough, analyses of the above story show that, while it is widely accepted, major portions of it are probably false. Indeed, the Athenians defeated the Persians at Marathon in 490 BC. No runner, however, breathlessly staggered into Athens, proclaimed victory, and collapsed. Once again, what appear to be the facts are not as entertaining as their embellishment.

Herodotus tells of Phidippides, a courier, but his role was to run to Sparta, not to Athens. He ran before the battle, not after, and his mission was to secure reinforcements (6, 105–106). The Spartans delayed because they were engaged in a religious festival. When they eventually arrived, as one historian puts it, "They inspected the field, complimented the Athenians, and went home" (Evans 97).

Knowing the second version, however, makes the story more fascinating. How and why was the story preserved in the first place? Why do we have two versions of the story? Have we, perhaps, lost other versions? How did the original events become embroidered? Why is the first version more dramatic than the second? What different ideas and values does each version carry? How do we judge that the second version is closer to the truth than the first?

Communication as Human Activity

These questions point to one of our most human characteristics. Not only do we possess communicative abilities that are magnitudes beyond those of other creatures, we are the

▲ **Figure 1.1.** The study of communication, formally or informally, is a lifetime process. (Dawe and Coyle)

only creatures who can communicate about communication itself. We possess not only the ability to send and receive messages but also the ability to create, analyze, and change our own patterns of communication.

The process of communicating, analyzing communication, and changing our patterns of communication is at the heart of this textbook. In short, it is a study of communication with the goal of providing both knowledge about communication and improving communication skills.

The study of communication is an inevitable part of life. That people are able to read this page, decipher the symbols on the page, and to comment on the ideas is testimony to our abilities to learn language, to process symbols, and to respond to others. Training in communication is a mixture of informal and formal study. We do not, for example, go to class to learn how to speak our first language. We learn from a process of imitation, trial and error. To learn to read, however, we attend school.

This book and the class it accompanies are a more formal way of approaching the study of communication. Instead of learning through imitation, learning takes places through an examination of the nature of communication as a human endeavor and analyses of communication in a variety of settings: interpersonal, small groups, and public speaking. Coupled with the exercises in communication, the course will provide us with a combination of knowledge and practice.

The Importance of Communication Study

Communication study is important because *communication is a decidedly human activity*. Through communication we create and sustain all our endeavors. Like art, play, aggression, and relationships, communication is woven into our very beings. Because it is a part of being human, communication demands our attention.

Communication study is important because *it is a fascinating study of human activity*. To look at communication is to look at ourselves. The life process is shaped by communication. How we see ourselves and others, how we perform at work, and how we relate to our families are all shaped by the ways in which we communicate. Through communication study we become aware of our behavior and the behavior of others and begin to see why we act as we do. Why, for example, is it common in the United States for us to stand one-and-a-half to two feet apart when we converse? Why do we feel threatened when someone moves closer than that? How are we persuaded to move from one opinion to another? How do we structure our organizations? If we ever wonder why we behave as we do, communication study can supply some of the answers to our questions.

Communication study is important because *it provides us with insights and skills* necessary to understand and solve the problems we face in our lives. To live is to confront problems, and inherent in the solution of those problems is the use of communication.

Some of the problems we face are simple. Daily we decide how to greet people, make requests, or respond to a conversational opener. Other problems are more complex. How do we resolve a conflict within our families or at work? How do we persuade people to accept our view? How do we function effectively within an organization? How do we respond to someone who is distraught over personal problems? How do we function effectively in a small group?

These kinds of situations are ones that we will face whether or not we study communication. Having studied communication, we will be better able to respond.

In our highly technological world, the temptation is to think that problems will be solved by better technology. We will have better businesses when we have improved equipment. We will have more leisure time and easier lives if we invent time saving machines. We will communicate better when we have better computer networks. We will all speed down the information superhighway into ultimate knowledge.

The technological is certainly part of human endeavors, but technology is not the only part. No matter how much technology we deal with, we ultimately deal with people. As one has astutely observed, "Today there are no problems with strictly technological solutions" (Ringel). Any significant effort will have implications for humans.

▲ **Figure 1.2.** Communication study provides us with insights and skills necessary to relate to others constructively. (Dawe)

An engineer may have excellent training in materials, mathematics, and methods, but as one engineering professor succinctly put the matter, "If you can't talk to your clients, you won't be a good engineer" (Satterly).

In the 1960s, three counties in the San Francisco area initiated what was to have been a state of the art transportation system, the Bay Area Rapid Transit system, commonly known as BART. It involved the best and newest computer technology, the best and newest trains and tracks, and it hired a staff of experts in engineering, transportation, computer science, and other relevant fields.

From the beginning, however, the project was hampered by numerous problems. When it finally opened, it was "many years after it was originally scheduled, at a cost well in excess of its original estimates, and in a context of genuine and widespread dissatisfaction . . . ." (Anderson, et. al. 256).

A study of the system discovered interesting data. The problems were due to several factors, one of the most important being the communication environment. Examined as individuals, those involved in the project were doing their jobs in good faith. The failure was not in the technology, but in the relationships between people.

One problem was external in that BART had difficulty persuading its clientele to support the system (Anderson, et. al. 341–43). Another problem, and perhaps the most important, was the manner in which the system was organized. Work was contracted to outside organizations in a way that placed BART employees in a secondary role in directing the work. Selection of the board of directors cast the board in the role of interest group advocates instead of a deliberative body. The organizational and administrative structure was such that people were forced into roles "almost predestined to create conflict and dysfunctional communication" (Trachtman).

Further, the system was set up to encourage "narrow specialization of roles" (Anderson, et. al. 352) which meant that the various elements of the project could not or did not communicate well with each other. As long as the computer programers saw their programs running

Figure 1.3. Common sense does not always give us the right answers. Common sense would indicate that these two would fall at different speeds. They do not.

well, they saw no problem. That the trains were stopping a hundred yards before loading platforms was somebody else's concern. As long as the rolling stock kept rolling, engineering was fine no matter the financial difficulties. The lack of communication created a lack of cooperation which undercut the success of the venture. The problem with BART lay not so much in its technology, as in its failure to create and foster an environment of productive communication.

Another common mistake is to think that communication is simple. "All you need is common sense," some claim. The view is that simply by existing we have acquired enough knowledge and judgment to be able to function competently in all situations. The problem with this view is that common sense grows out of knowledge and experience. Given that we all have limited knowledge and experience, we will not know what to do in all situations without study, either formal study or study from long experience.

How should one behave in a typical interpersonal situation, say a job interview? Any number of interviewing books will provide guidelines: one should dress appropriately, be on time, create answers to typical questions, learn about the company, provide positive nonverbal responses, and prepare questions to ask the interviewer. These behaviors make sense in the interview situation and become part of the "common sense" of interviewing.

Yet when one passes a placement center and reads the remarks of the interviewers, their complaints mirror the above advice. Potential employees do not dress properly, they show up late, they know nothing of the company, the questions they ask are shortsighted and self-centered. Somehow, these interviewees missed the "common sense" of interviewing. We do not simply *know* how to respond; we must *learn* how to respond. When something strikes us as "common sense," it does not necessarily mean the idea is trivial. What we may be observing is a process in which "common sense makes clear that which I think I already know" (Yoder).

Finally, the study of communication is important because *it is one of the few areas of learning that is transferable from one situation to another, from job to job, and from relationship to relationship.* Graduating college seniors face the challenge of securing a first job, but that is only the beginning. Ten years ago, a study concluded that "today's workers will change jobs five times before they are forty and that they will change careers three times before they retire" ("Involvement in Learning . . ." 43.) Years later, the pattern continues. A more recent study concludes that "on the average, a student leaving college today can be expected to have three, four, or five careers and ten, eleven, or twelve jobs during a work life that will last 40/50 years" (Birch 40). Job-related skills learned for one career may have little meaning in a subsequent career.

Within all the change, however, certain skills and attributes will always be needed. These will be necessary no matter what professions we enter, no matter what jobs we work, no matter the rate of change or the type of change. Among these skills are critical thinking, mathematics, language skills, and "people skills." Whatever professions we pursue, whatever situations we find ourselves in, we will need some abilities in these areas. The study of communication supplies us with an education in three of the areas. We must use critical thinking skills to appropriately interpret communication situations. We must use language skills to create, send, and interpret messages. We must use "people skills" to work effectively with others.

Communication is not only something we use, but it is something that makes us, even as we use it. We not only respond to relationships with communication, we build the very relationships by the patterns with which we communicate. The study of communication commends itself to us because communication is integral to our natures and to our lives. Through the study of communication we gain insight into ourselves as human beings, and we learn how to function better in the variety of roles we play in life. Learning and using communication is a process that extends from the beginning of our lives to the end. To study communication is to study ourselves, and this is the fundamental basis of education.

• • • Discussion Questions

1. What instances of informal communication training can you think of?

2. What instances of formal communication training can you think of?

3. Why is communication an integral part of our humanity?

4. What kind of situations have you observed that would have been improved by better communication?

5. How might technological innovations such as the telephone, television, and e-mail affect our communication?

6. Why would skills such as mathematics, critical thinking, language, and communication be important in our lives?

• • • Sources and References

Anderson, Robert M., Robert Perucci, Dan E. Schendel, and Leon E. Trachtman. *Divided Loyalties: Whistle-Blowing at BART.* West Lafayette, Indiana: Purdue University Office of Publications, 1980.

Benyo, Richard. *Masters of the Marathon.* New York: Atheneum, 1983.

Birch, David L. "The Coming Demise of the Single-Career Career." *Journal of Career Planning and Employment.* Winter (1990).

Evans, J. A. S. *Herodotus.* Boston: Twayne Publishers-G. K. Hall and Company, 1982.

Guttman, Allen. *The Olympics: A History of the Modern Games.* Urbana: University of Illinois Press, 1992.

Hart. John. *Herodotus and Greek History.* London: Croom Helm Ltd., 1982.

Herodotus. *The History of Herodotus.* Trans. David Green. Chicago: The University of Chicago Press, 1987.

"Involvement in Learning: Realizing the Potential of American Higher Education." *Chronicle of Higher Education* 24 October 1984. 43.

Ringel, Robert L. Commencement Address. University of Missouri, Columbia, Missouri. 10 December 1988.

Satterly, Gilbert. Professor of Civil Engineering, Purdue University. Conversation with the author.

Trachtman, Leon E. Note to the author. 29 April 1994.

Yoder, Don. Central States Communication Association Convention. Oklahoma City, Oklahoma. 7 April 1994.

Name _____ Section _____ Date _____

The Study of Communication

1. Describe the Canterbury Effect.

   _____

   _____

2. Animals have been shown to be able to communicate. List at least two things related to communication which distinguish human communication from animal communication.

   1. _____

   2. _____

3. Why is a formal study of human communication important?

   _____

   _____

Preface To Supplemental Materials

The material following each chapter supplements the ideas and concepts of the text. Whereas the emphasis in the text is on presenting the theory and underlying principles of communication, the supplementary material provides an application for those ideas. Through completing the exercises and speaking assignments explained in them students will develop their communication skills.

The full **course schedule** provides an overview of what will be covered in the course. You can read ahead if necessary to adapt course demands to your own time blocks.

Each assignment begins with a clearly defined **purpose**. It explains the skills that will be mastered when the assignment is completed. Assignments are arranged for progressive skill building. With each assignment you build upon previously learned material by adding new speaking skills.

Basic requirements listing minimum criteria for successful completion of the assignment are listed next. These make it easy for you to clearly understand what is expected. You can check off each requirement as it is met to ensure success on the assignment.

Sometimes the most difficult part of speech writing is selecting a speech topic. **Suggested topics** for speaking assignments are listed to serve as a springboard for your own creative thinking. Success is further ensured because you choose a topic of personal interest.

Worksheets are included to serve as a centralized record for brainstorming and topic development. They include a skeleton speech outline to fill in which aids in organization and speech development.

Grading criteria specify what an instructor will be looking for when evaluating the finished product. These criteria make the evaluation process less subjective and more objective for all parties.

Two important aspects of a speech class are learning speaking techniques by watching speeches delivered by classmates and offering constructive observations about them. **Student evaluation sheets** encourage students to focus on construction techniques as well as delivery skills. Feedback should be positive, specific and practical. Student evaluation sheets provide feedback which supplements the instructor's evaluation.

Each unit has **exercises** designed to illustrate concepts from the text readings. They are a hands-on way to learn theoretical concepts.

Sample exam questions enable you to spot-check your comprehension of the textbook material. Answers are provided for self-assessment.

Library Research in Communication provides you with basic procedures to identify and locate information and resources across a broad spectrum of fields to aid in speech development.

While course policies, grading scales and the development of the sixteen week course schedule are specific to the needs of the basic communication course at Purdue University, they can easily be adapted for use in any university's one semester course. They have proven workable when used by the 5,000 students who annually take this class, and are thus included for consideration.

Assignments and Grading

There are six major graded assignments in this course: a small group presentation, a written analysis of the small group process, three speeches, and one examination. Due to the nature of this course, a great deal of learning takes place during in-class exercises. They constitute a lab for this course. Therefore, in addition to the major assignments, students will be graded on attendance and class participation.

Assignments are weighted for computing the final class grade. Each completed assignment is evaluated and assigned a letter grade by the instructor, which is then converted to a point value by the student. Uncompleted assignments will receive an F/00.00.

The following chart should be filled out to maintain an unofficial record of class grades.

Directions for Maintaining a Class Grade Record

1. After each assignment record the appropriate letter grade in the blank under column 1.
2. Using the scale for "individual assignment point value," record the appropriate point value in column 2.
3. Multiply the number entered in column 2 by the number in column 3, and enter the total in column 4, or see the tables on page 13 for the appropriate number.
4. At the completion of the semester add the figures in column 4 and enter the sum in blank 5.
5. Using the scale for "course letter grade," convert the course final point total to the course final letter grade, and enter it in blank 6.

The student, not the instructor, is responsible for the accuracy of the calculations entered in the chart and any decisions made as a result of those calculations.

Falsification of Information

This course works on the assumption that students are acting in good faith when they interact with university staff and submit materials. Should that, however, not be the case, falsification of information constitutes grounds for failure of the assignment, failure of the course, and disciplinary action by the university. Falsification of information would include such actions as citing sources that do not exist, forging absence excuses, or misrepresenting yourself or your situation.

Plagiarism

Plagiarism is the unauthorized or inappropriate use of the words or ideas of others. Plagiarism occurs when written or spoken material is borrowed, in whole or in part, and passed off as original by another writer or speaker. Plagiarism includes, but is not limited to, presenting someone else's speech, paper, or outline as original. It also includes not documenting the source of word-for-word or PARAPHRASED material in speeches or papers.

The following examples illustrate possible plagiarism situations for this class: using someone else's outline for a speech; working with a friend on a topic and both using the same outline or giving the same speech; failing to cite during a speech or paper the source of information, ideas, or statements taken from material found during research.

It is course policy to pursue plagiarism cases vigorously, to fail the plagiarist on the assignment in question, to fail the plagiarist in the course as a whole, and to report cases to the dean of students for possible further action.

	Individual Assignment Point Value Scale	**Course Letter Grade Scale**

Individual Assignment Point Value Scale

A+	=	4.25
A	=	4.00
A−	=	3.75
B+	=	3.25
B	=	3.00
B−	=	2.75
C+	=	2.25
C	=	2.00
C−	=	1.75
D+	=	1.25
D	=	1.00
D−	=	.75
F	=	.00

Course Letter Grade Scale

3.51 to 4.25	= A
2.51 to 3.50	= B
1.51 to 2.50	= C
.51 to 1.50	= D
.50 and below	= F

Assignment	**Letter Grade**		**Point Value**	**Weighting**		**Final Value**
			(From Left scale above)			
	1.		2.	3.		4.
Exam	_____	=	_____	× .20	=	_____
Sm. Gp. Project	_____	=	_____	× .10	=	_____
Sm. Gp. Analysis	_____	=	_____	× .10	=	_____
Speech 1	_____	=	_____	× .12	=	_____
Speech 2	_____	=	_____	× .18	=	_____
Speech 3	_____	=	_____	× .23	=	_____
Attendance/Part.	_____	=	_____	× .07	=	_____

Course Final Point Total   5. _____

Course Final Letter Grade   _____

(from Right scale above)   6. _____

Calculations for Exam

.20 × A+   (4.25) = .85
.20 × A   (4.00) = .80
.20 × A−   (3.75) = .75
.20 × B+   (3.25) = .65
.20 × B   (3.00) = .60
.20 × B−   (2.75) = .55
.20 × C+   (2.25) = .45
.20 × C   (2.00) = .40
.20 × C−   (1.75) = .35
.20 × D+   (1.25) = .25
.20 × D   (1.00) = .20
.20 × D−   (.75) = .15
.20 × F   (.00) = .00

Calculations for Small Group

.10 × A+   (4.25) = .43
.10 × A   (4.00) = .40
.10 × A−   (3.75) = .38
.10 × B+   (3.25) = .33
.10 × B   (3.00) = .30
.10 × B−   (2.75) = .28
.10 × C+   (2.25) = .23
.10 × C   (2.00) = .20
.10 × C−   (1.75) = .18
.10 × D+   (1.25) = .13
.10 × D   (1.00) = .10
.10 × D−   (.75) = .08
.10 × F   (.00) = .00

Calculations for Speech I

.12 × A+   (4.25) = .51
.12 × A   (4.00) = .48
.12 × A−   (3.75) = .45
.12 × B+   (3.25) = .39
.12 × B   (3.00) = .36
.12 × B−   (2.75) = .33
.12 × C+   (2.25) = .27
.12 × C   (2.00) = .24
.12 × C−   (1.75) = .21
.12 × D+   (1.25) = .15
.12 × D   (1.00) = .12
.12 × D−   (.75) = .09
.12 × F   (.00) = .00

Calculations for Speech II

.18 × A+   (4.25) = .77
.18 × A   (4.00) = .72
.18 × A−   (3.75) = .68
.18 × B+   (3.25) = .59
.18 × B   (3.00) = .54
.18 × B−   (2.75) = .50
.18 × C+   (2.25) = .41
.18 × C   (2.00) = .36
.18 × C−   (1.75) = .32
.18 × D+   (1.25) = .23
.18 × D   (1.00) = .18
.18 × D−   (.75) = .14
.18 × F   (.00) = .00

Calculations for Speech III

.23 × A+   (4.25) = .98
.23 × A   (4.00) = .92
.23 × A−   (3.75) = .86
.23 × B+   (3.25) = .75
.23 × B   (3.00) = .69
.23 × B−   (2.75) = .63
.23 × C+   (2.25) = .52
.23 × C   (2.00) = .46
.23 × C−   (1.75) = .40
.23 × D+   (1.25) = .29
.23 × D   (1.00) = .23
.23 × D−   (.75) = .17
.23 × F   (.00) = .00

Calculations for Attendance

.07 × A+   (4.25) = .30
.07 × A   (4.00) = .28
.07 × A−   (3.75) = .26
.07 × B+   (3.25) = .23
.07 × B   (3.00) = .21
.07 × B−   (2.75) = .19
.07 × C+   (2.25) = .16
.07 × C   (2.00) = .14
.07 × C−   (1.75) = .12
.07 × D+   (1.25) = .09
.07 × D   (1.00) = .07
.07 × D−   (.75) = .05
.07 × F   (.00) = .00

Course Schedule

Following is a schedule of activities and assignments for the semester. Note that the readings listed are TO HAVE BEEN COMPLETED by the day noted, and are NOT assignments given that day for the completion by the next class.

Day	Text Assignment	Activities
Day 1	The Study of Communication (Chapter One)	orientation
Day 2	Field of Communication (Chapter Two)	lecture/discussion
Day 3	You as a Communicator (Chapter Three) The Ethics of Communication (Chapter Four)	lecture/discussion
Day 4		culture inventory
Day 5		culture inventory
Day 6	Interpersonal Communication (Chapter Five)	lecture/discussion
Day 7		interpersonal exercises
Day 8	Small Group Assignments Nature of Small Groups (Chapter Six)	explain small group assignment
Day 9	Working in Small Groups: Roles and Leadership (Chapter Seven)	lecture/discussion
Day 10	Working in Small Groups: Problem Solving Procedures (Chapter Eight)	lecture/discussion
Day 11		small group exercises
Day 12		small group workshop
Day 13		small group workshop
Day 14		GROUP 1 PRESENTATION
Day 15		GROUP 2 PRESENTATION
Day 16		GROUP 3 PRESENTATION
Day 17		GROUP 4 PRESENTATION
Day 18		GROUP 5 PRESENTATION
Day 19	Intro to Public Speaking	assign first speech
Day 20	Beginning Public Speaking (Chapter Nine)	lecture/discussion
Day 21	Selecting a Topic/Thesis Statements	
Day 22	Developing your Speech (Chapter Ten)	lecture/discussion
Day 23	Informational Speaking (Chapter Eleven, Chapter Twelve)	
Day 24		INFORMATIVE SPEECH I
Day 25		INFORMATIVE SPEECH I
Day 26		INFORMATIVE SPEECH I
Day 27		INFORMATIVE SPEECH I
Day 28		INFORMATIVE SPEECH I

Day 29		INFORMATIVE SPEECH I
Day 30	Improvement Review Day	
Day 31		INFORMATIVE SPEECH II
Day 32		INFORMATIVE SPEECH II
Day 33		INFORMATIVE SPEECH II
Day 34		INFORMATIVE SPEECH II
Day 35		INFORMATIVE SPEECH II
Day 36		INFORMATIVE SPEECH II
Day 37	Why We Believe (Chapter Thirteen)	lecture/discussion
Day 38	Developing Presentational Speeches (Chapter Fourteen)	lecture/discussion
Day 39	Evidence and Credibility; Persuasion and Reasoning (Chapter Fifteen)	lecture/discussion
Day 40		PRESENTATIONAL SPEECH
Day 41		PRESENTATIONAL SPEECH
Day 42		PRESENTATIONAL SPEECH
Day 43		PRESENTATIONAL SPEECH
Day 44		PRESENTATIONAL SPEECH
Day 45		PRESENTATIONAL SPEECH
Day 46	EXAM	

The "I Am" Speech

As one of your first speaking assignments, you may be asked to present a short speech about yourself. The speech will be, very loosely, a three part speech. This is an informal presentation to introduce yourself to the class and to introduce you to the speaking situation.

In the speech, you should discuss topics such as the following:

Your Past	where born
	brothers and sisters
	early childhood
	pets
	interesting places you have lived, etc.
Your Present	favorite subjects
	activities
	hobbies
	sports, etc.
Your Future	plan of study
	plans after graduation

Your instructor may give you added suggestions.

Adapted from: Corey, James W. "The 'I Am' Speech." *The Speech Communication Teacher II*, iv (Summer 1988): p. 1. Used by permission of Speech Communication Association.

Exploring Perceptions

These lists of questions will be used as part of an in-class exercise in perception. Answer the first set as they pertain to you. Leave the second set blank for use in class.

1. What is your favorite color?

2. What is your favorite food?

3. What is your favorite type of music?

4. What city in the U.S. would you most like to visit?

5. What is your favorite hobby?

6. What is your favorite pastime?

7. What is your favorite sport?

1. What is your favorite color?

2. What is your favorite food?

3. What is your favorite type of music?

4. What city in the U.S. would you most like to visit?

5. What country in the world would you most like to visit?

6. What is your favorite hobby?

7. What is your favorite pastime?

8. What is your favorite sport?

Adapted from: Hanks, Gail Armstead. "Don't Judge a Book By Its Cover." *The Speech Communication Teacher* V, iv (Summer 1991): p. 8. Used by permission of Speech Communication Association.

2

··

The Field of Communication

··

Key Concepts

· · · · · · · · · · · ·

As we have pointed out, communication permeates and shapes our lives. To pursue the study of communication, we need to know what communication is and how communication influences our learning and our practice. Let us begin by offering a definition of communication.

Defining Communication

Defining communication is not an easy task since it is a complex blend of numerous entities. We will incorporate major areas of the concept by defining it as: *Communication is the process of sending, receiving, and interpreting messages through which we relate to each other and to our larger world as well.*

Process

The first important concept in this definition is "process." By process, we mean that communication is not a single act but a series of interconnected acts moving through time. This means, first of all, that communication is *ongoing*. It begins when two or more parties (senders and receivers) come into contact with each other and continues until the parties break contact. The parties may be two people, a group of people, a large audience and a speaker, or even individuals communicating with themselves via "intrapersonal communication."

Because it exists in time, communication is *irreversible*. Once the process begins, it cannot go back to its beginnings and start all over. A common experience is that we, from time to time, say things we wish we had not said. Perhaps the words slipped out in the heat of an argument, perhaps we said something as a joke that turned out to be more hurtful than funny. Much as we would like to recall the message, to counteract its negative effect, we cannot. We can try to reframe the message, but we cannot "erase the tape."

Since communication is ongoing and irreversible, it is also an activity in which the elements are *interdependent*. Each part of an interchange influences what follows. Each portion builds on what went before it.

Communication is more like a game than it is like a play in which the lines are all known in

▲ **Figure 2.1.** Senders and receivers are necessary for communication to occur. How many senders and receivers are seen or implied in this situation? (Dawe)

advance. In tennis, for example, player A serves the ball to player B. Player B attempts to return the serve. Where and how B hits the ball will be determined by where and how A served and what kind of player B is. Player A's volley will respond to B's return of the serve, and they will continue reacting to each other until one of them fails to return the ball over the net.

In communication, one person makes a statement, sends a greeting, answers the phone, or calls a meeting to order. Others respond to that initiation. That response calls forth another response and that response, yet another. What each party contributes to the interchange adds to the situation and at the same time changes it. The final result and shape of the interchange is not known until the very end.

Messages

What passes between the parties in communication are *messages*. Messages are signals sent with the intent of creating understanding in the receiver. While the concept of messages is familiar to us, we need to realize the wide variety of messages that exist.

On a personal level, we send verbal and nonverbal messages through our voices and our bodies. The number of ways we have created to communicate is testimony to human ingenuity. We send written transmissions through a wide variety of communication channels: letters, faxes, newspapers, magazines, advertising brochures, etc.. We send aural messages through telephones, radios, and various types of musical devices. We reach one person through conversation; we reach millions through mass communication. Some even communicate through the use of drums, flags, fireworks, mirror flashes, waggling airplane wings, and firing shots across the bow.

Interpretation

Interpretation is the act of bringing to understanding. Whatever messages we receive, we try to make sense of them. As long as sender and receiver use the same language and operate in familiar settings, responses are easy to make. When the context of communication begins to include the unfamiliar, then interpretation is more difficult and, in some cases, impossible.

One would think that people speaking English could readily understand each other. Americans, for example, have general agreements on the meanings of words such as "napkin," "dear," and "lavatory." The first is something we put in our laps when we eat; the second is someone or something toward which we feel affection; the third is a sink. Should one be travelling in the British Isles, however, one might discover to one's embarrassment that those terms in British English are interpreted as "diaper," "expensive," and "commode."

As meaning is not automatic and as interpretation is necessary in communication, misunderstanding is always a possibility in communication. Both sender and receiver may be thoroughly convinced that they have done all that is necessary for effective communication

▲ **Figure 2.2.** In responding to messages, interpretation if necessary. (Dawe)

yet discover later that the messages are still garbled and confusion exists.

Relationships

Communication is a linking of selves in some ways, be those ways serious or superficial. The quality and type of our relationships are highly dependent on the quality and type of our communication.

Saying "good morning" to someone and having that person respond with "good morning" seems simple enough. When we think, though, of the number of "good mornings" that occur in a university housing unit, a family, or a huge industrial complex such as IBM or General Motors, the number becomes staggering. Each of those greetings adds another strand to the web of relationships in those organization. The thousands of messages that pass back and forth between thousands of people create their environments, the worlds in which they will function as individuals or groups. When we move from simple greetings to all the social communication, conflicts, group discussion, and decision making that occurs in a family, much less a corporation, we have a mind boggling amount of communication to consider. All of the communication contributes to the nature of that unit.

Communication also shapes our relationship to our larger world, be it local or international. As children, our parents communicate to us what kinds of behavior are acceptable or not acceptable, including how our communication should be patterned. Friends and institutions such as schools, clubs, athletic teams, and religious organizations further shape our consciousness and foster patterns of interaction.

When we move beyond the personal, we rely on mass media. Our perceptions and judgments of events are often dependent on how newspapers, radio, and television communicate an event. The naive conception of these media is that they simply report the facts of a case. Upon closer inspection, we discover that the stories communicate a viewpoint, one of the many possible viewpoints available to observers.

A school closes in a town. The local newspaper and television station cover the story. As they cannot report every aspect of the event, reporters pick and choose which elements they wish to feature. They put their information into a format appropriate for print or broadcast and the composition process involves another set of choices.

One approach to the story would be to show how the school building is aging, how it needs repairs. The superintendent is quoted about the need to save money and to provide educational opportunities for students. Pictures are shown of the new, more modern building that the children will attend next year. The report portrays the school closing as an improvement in educational quality for all concerned.

Another approach would be to show teachers boxing up materials, hugging children goodbye for the last time, and sadly leaving the old building. Parents are quoted on how much they dislike the fact that their children can no longer walk to school but will be bussed far from home. Long time residents of the neighborhood talk about how the school has added to the neighborhood. Pictures of the new school emphasize how large, cold, and impersonal it seems. The second version of the story shows the school closing to be destructive to relationships and educational quality.

Which story is the truth? Neither one and both. All the elements, both good and bad, are part of the story. The selection and organization of those elements into a message will convey a viewpoint. Dependent as we are on others for information, the viewpoint communicated will shape our perceptions and hence the way we react to the world.

The communicative process of sending, receiving, and interpreting involves us at all levels, from the intimacy of our private lives to the world view of our political lives. Messages do not simply come to us. They are shaped by their senders, and we, in turn, shape them through our perceptions.

Areas of Communication Study

As an essential part of human activities, communication invites study, study which provides us with insights into ourselves as human beings. The complexities of the field, as do the complexities of any area, lead us to divide it into smaller units. These divisions are made more for convenience, though, than in recognition of any clear-cut boundaries. When we speak of "areas of communication," we are talking about the different contexts in which communication may occur.

The following are not an exhaustive listing of areas of communication study, but they provide a survey of the different ways in which we may approach the study of communication.

Public Communication

Perhaps the best known area of communication, and certainly one of the first one studies, is *public communication* or *public speaking*. This communication is marked by an individual addressing an audience which may number from several to thousands. Examples of public speaking include political speakers and speakers at service organizations, convocations, lectures, religious services, and dedication ceremonies.

Public speaking was a topic of high importance to the Greeks twenty-four hundred years ago, and the people who wrote then are still studied today for what they can tell us about the process of communication. Plato and Aristotle were the most important of these people, but they were only two of a number of people talking about talk and how we influence each other through communication. One of their main concerns was how cases should be argued in courts of law. Aristotle provided us with a classic description of *rhetoric* when he labelled it as "the faculty of discovering in any given case the available means of persuasion" (*Rhetoric*, 1355b). Another way of phrasing this idea is to say that rhetoric is "finding all the available means of persuasion in a given situation." The study of communication and rhetoric has extended in an unbroken line from that time to this.

Public speaking is an integral part of our lives. Most professions, be they technical or artistic, will demand that we make presentations to audiences. Architects show plans to clients. Agronomists tell farmers of developments in seeds. Financial officers diagnose their company's fiscal health. The study of public communication puts us in front of audiences, develops confidence, and makes us aware of the importance of organizing our thoughts well for effective communication.

Scholars in rhetoric and public communication look, naturally enough, at public discourse. These may be examined from an historical context in which one studies the forces that produced the speech, or they may be studied from other viewpoints such a style, type, or philosophy. In looking at speeches and speaking, rhetorical scholars look at the processes by which we accommodate ourselves to our changing political and intellectual environments. Rhetorical scholars are interested in what one calls "adjusting ideas to people and people to ideas" (Bryant 413). This view of rhetoric allows us to examine such diverse areas as presidential rhetoric, ceremonial rhetoric, and social movements.

Interpersonal Communication

When we deal with people individually or in small groups, we engage in what is generally designated *interpersonal communication*. Interpersonal communication could include such situations as talking with a friend, going through a job interview, arguing with a roommate, negotiating with sales personnel, and comforting a friend or family member. Interpersonal communication is often labelled *dyadic* (from the Greek word for "two") communication since much of it is between two people. Three people communicating would, naturally enough, be *triadic* communication.

Numerically, the next step in interpersonal communication is small group communication. Small groups may form for a number of purposes. Some, such as social groups, exist for the sake of the relationships within the group, while other small groups exists primarily for the accomplishment of tasks. Sales meetings, quality circles, board meetings, study groups, bridge foursomes and even tailgate parties would qualify as small groups.

Interpersonal communication research examines how we respond to each other in various settings and under varying conditions. Studies might detail the kind of communication that goes on between friends, between married couples, between superiors and subordinates, and between parents and children. Studies might also look at how we communicate through the way we use our bodies or the

▲ **Figure 2.3.** We spend much of our lives in interpersonal communication. (Coyle)

way in which we learn how to take turns in conversations. Those interested in small groups might study the life cycles of groups as they form, function, and then disband. Others examine the patterns of communication within groups or how groups contribute to a larger whole such as a business or organization, an approach closely linked to organizational communication.

Organizational Communication

Organizational communication centers on the process of sending, receiving, and interpreting messages within and between organizations. As W. Charles Redding has observed, organizations consist of interdependent, goal-oriented activities of people who work together within a system or rules, norms, and routines. People band together in organizations to accomplish their purposes: businesses make money and service organizations relieve problems. Goals, however, are not always singular or explicit. To achieve their objectives, organizational members perform a variety of tasks that are linked to the activities of other members. The size of organizations may range from small, such as a neighborhood day-care center, to a multinational corporation.

Another important aspect about organizations is that they are formed and maintained through communication. In effect, an organization has a life of its own. The activity of organizing continues even when particular individuals leave or retire from a company. Organizations rely on communication and the coordination of activities to form work units that change over time. Large corporations such as Ford, Exxon, RCA, and Beatrice have employed thousands of people and experienced many changes in their operations, but these businesses typically survive despite the inflow and outflow of people. Hence, organizations are dynamic activities rather than static collections of people.

Studies in organizational communication focus on many elements of the organizing process. Areas of study include modes and channels of communication, interaction between superior and subordinates, and formal and informal relationships among organizational members. Other researchers look at the use of communication to socialize new members, to make decisions, to resolve conflicts, and to shape the environment and climate of organizations. Other areas of study include who uses written communication and who uses face-to-face communication and for what type of messages? With the proliferation of personal computers and computer networks, researchers now also study the influence of computer interaction on the communication patterns of an organization.

Organizations require constant adjustments of people, resources, and goals. Thus, mediation and conflict management are a large part of the study of organizational communication. Communication in organizations also establishes a sense of "culture" through sharing stories of organizational events, using particular language patterns such as military or technical jargon, and telling tales of company history. This culture may reflect an atmosphere or climate which casts an organization as "a big happy family," "a dull sweatshop," or even "a strange zoo." Communication is also an integral part of the process organizations go through as they shape and adapt to their external environments.

Mass Communication

Another major area of communication and communication study is *mass communication*. Two major considerations determine whether or not communication is considered mass communication. The first, and most obvious, is that mass communication involves large numbers of people. Instead of a personal audience or a small group, or even a large audience for a public speech, mass communication reaches far more people and its audience is dispersed, rather than collected in one place. While hundreds or even thousands of people may come together for a public speech, thousands more can watch a newscast without leaving their homes.

The second major characteristic of mass communication is that it is mediated communication. Something comes between the sender and the final receiver of the message. Rather than the firsthand directness of interpersonal communication, mass communication distances senders and receivers. The "something" that comes between sender and receiver is both mechanical and human. Mass communication is dependent on both senders and receivers possessing the appropriate technology such as cameras, tape, film, editing equipment, and receiving equipments (radios, television sets, etc.). Mass communication also imposes the shaping consciousness of a third party between the event and the receiver.

We can see the mediation process in mass communication by following a typical story. A reporter attends a meeting to report the University's board of trustees' decision on an important issue such as raising tuition. The television tape of the meeting is edited, the reporter writes the commentary, and the board's decision is recounted in a minute or so of the evening news. People watching the program receive the news of the meeting but do it through a television set rather than obtaining the information directly from the reporter. Further, the account of the meeting has been shaped by the perceptions of the reporter and the format of television news. This is not to say that the reported story is untrue, but that, rather, the story will necessarily reflect one viewpoint of the many available.

A great deal of discussion has been generated in the study of mass communication on the influence of the medium on its audience and on society. Numerous studies have been done, for example, on the effects of television violence on people who watch such programming. Other researchers examine how people use mass communication and what needs it satisfies in people's lives. Others look at how messages are shaped by the media. Some study the effect of mass media on society. Studies, for example, have indicated that the more people watch television, the more they think they are likely to be the victim of a crime (Ogles and Sparks "Question Specificity . . ." and "Television Violence . . .").

On a broader scale, Marshall McLuhan's well known claim that "the medium is the message" suggests that the advent of electronic mass communication in our society has had more impact on us that all the individual messages communicated through the medium. Other scholars focus on the impact of these individual messages. For example, many claim that much of the opposition to the Vietnam war arose because the American public saw the gore and bloodshed of the fighting in color on the evening news.

Public Affairs and Issue Management

Coming into prominence is another area of communication studies, *public affairs and issue management.* The field is allied to public relations but is much larger than the techniques of running campaigns and writing press releases. Issue management is an outgrowth of the traditional study of rhetoric.

Public affairs and issue management investigates how organizations affect and are, in turn, affected by aspects of the communicative environment. Some of these aspects include government regulatory agencies, politicians, consumers, competitors, and other organizations. The area studies how organizations seek to adjust to the demands of their publics and how

they seek to adjust the public's views of the organizations. Organizations may be for-profit or not-for-profit and in corporate, political, and private contexts.

An oil tanker runs aground in Alaska and dumps thousands of gallons of crude oil into the ocean, polluting the ocean, destroying wildlife, and fouling the beaches. The oil company responds to the situation as do the municipal, state, and federal governments and environmental groups. Issue management would examine the ways in which each of these groups defines the situation and how each group argues for and counterargues to convince the public of the rightness of its stance.

While much of the work in public affairs and issue management is in reaction to crises of various kinds, not all is reactive. One aspect of issue management involves planning ahead to help shape public opinions in the direction desired by the organization. A hospital, for example, might foresee a need for a routine raise in revenue because of projected increases in salaries, maintenance costs, supplies, and equipment. Prior to raising fees, the hospital would make a strong effort to explain its situation to the community via press releases, seminars, speeches, and newsletters. The communication could stress the high quality of the hospital's care, its dedication to maintaining high standards, and the rising cost of providing quality health care. If the campaign were successful, the public would be more accepting of the increased charges than if the charges were put into effect with no explanation.

Performance Studies

The last area of study we will discuss is *performance studies* which, like public speaking, is one of the oldest areas of communication. Besides writing the *Rhetoric*, Aristotle also wrote a *Poetics* in which he examined how we are emotionally moved when we watch stories being enacted. "Performance" in the sense of "performance studies" means those ways of behaving that are set apart from ordinary communication (Bauman, 9) and are "preceded by rehearsal or preparation" (Scheckner 2, 36). Theatre is, of course, an area of performance study, but performance goes much further than the formalities of the stage. We perform in various ways in our own lives. We tell jokes. We recount our experiences and imitate people to make a point about how our day went. Religious life is permeated by performance be it in sermons, testimonials, or the celebration of the mass.

One area of performance study is oral interpretation, the performance of literature. The performer studies and empathizes with a poem, an essay, or a work of fiction. The performer then reads or recites the literature in a way that the audience understands the ideas and emotions of the piece.

Research in performance studies may examine how performers approach different kinds of literature and the demands of different types of literature. Others in the field examine how performance is used in daily life, how gender affects performance, and how folklore is created and transmitted.

Conclusion

Communication is a wide ranging field that permeates our lives and creates relationships. Communication is the sending, receiving, and interpreting of messages. The study of commu-

Figure 2.4. Performance study looks at how we behave when we take on roles such as storytellers or actors.

nication includes a number of areas: public communication and rhetoric, interpersonal communication, organizational communication, mass communication, issue management, and performance studies, among others. Research and study in communication investigate the patterns of communication in our personal and professional lives and encompasses a wide spectrum of behavior from business to art. Understanding communication allows us to know ourselves better and to understand better how we function as individuals and as a society.

• • • Discussion Questions

1. How do you see communication influencing your view of the world?

2. When is communication a process and when is communication a product?

3. What examples can you think of that illustrate sending and receiving in communication?

4. What kinds of communication would you classify as public communication or public speaking?

5. What does it mean when it is said that the function of rhetoric is to "adjust ideas to people and people to ideas"?

6. What types of communication would be classified as interpersonal?

7. What examples of organizational communication can you see functioning in a university?

8. Do you think that mass communication shapes the ideas of society or does it simply reflect the ideas of society?

9. How would rhetoric function as a part of issue management?

10. How do you see performance at work in daily life?

• • • Sources and References

Aristotle. *The Rhetoric and Poetics of Aristotle.* Trans. W. Rhys Roberts and Ingram Bywater. New York: The Modern Library, 1954.

Bauman, Richard. *Verbal Art as Performance.* Rowley, Massachusetts: Newbury House Publishers, 1977.

Berlo, David. *The Process of Communication: An Introduction to Theory and Practice.* New York: Holt, Rinehart and Winston, Inc., 1960.

Bryant, Donald. "Rhetoric: Its Function and Scope." *The Quarterly Journal of Speech* 29 (1953): 401–24.

Dominick, Joseph R. *The Dynamics of Mass Communication.* 4th ed. New York: McGraw-Hill, 1993.

Littlejohn, Stephen W. *Theories of Human Communication.* 4th ed. Belmont, California: Wadsworth Publishing Company, 1992.

McLuhan, Marshall. *Understanding Media: The Extensions of Man.* New York: McGraw-Hill Book Company, 1964.

Ogles, Robert M. and Glen G. Sparks. "Question Specificity and Perceived Probablity of Criminal Victimization." *Mass Comm Review* 20 (1993): 51–61.

———. "Television Violence and Perceptions of Crime: The Cultivation Effect." *Mass Comm Review* 16 (1989): 2–11.

Putnam, Linda L. and George Cheney. "Organizational Communication: Historical Development and Future Directions." *Foundations of Organizational Communication.* Eds. Steven R. Corman, Stephen P. Banks, Charles R. Bantz, and Michael E. Mayer. New York: Longman Publishers, 1990. 44–61.

Redding, W. Charles. *Communicating Within the Organization.* New York: Industrial Communication Council, Inc., 1972.

Ruben, Brent, D. *Communication and Human Behavior.* 2nd. ed. New York: Macmillan Publishers, 1988.

Scheckner, Richard. *Essays on Performance Theory 1970–1976.* New York: Drama Books Specialists (publishers), 1977.

Tompkins, Philip K. *Communication as Action: An Introduction to Rhetoric and Communication.* Belmont, California: Wadsworth Publishing Company, 1982.

Name _____ Section _____ Date _____

The Field of Communication

1. How does the text define communication?

   _____

   _____

2. How does dyadic communication differ from small group communication?

   _____

   _____

3. What would a communication researcher in interpersonal communication study?

   _____

   _____

4. What are areas of interest for research in organizational communication?

   _____

   _____

5. What two characteristics separate mass communication from other forms of communication?

   A._____

   B._____

6. What is public affairs and issue management?

   _____

   _____

7. What are some instances in which you perform as part of communication?

   _____

   _____

8. Develop your personal definition of communication.

   _____

   _____   _____

   _____

Photo Analysis

Turn to page 20.

Analyze the picture on that page on the basis of the following questions.

1. What types of communication are being demonstrated in this picture?

2. How many senders and receivers are being implied in the situation?

3. How might the presence of the various audience affect what the interviewers say and do? How might they affect what the interviewee says and does?

4. How does the television reporting of the interview affect the message received by the viewing audience?

The Nature of Communication

Key Concepts

We are not born independent of history nor do we grow unsullied by societal forces. First, we come into the world with a set of commands buried in our DNA, genes, and chromosomes that determine a number of factors about us. As a result of those commands, we are male or female, tall or short, light skinned or dark skinned, athletic or klutzy, intelligent or stupid, and a great deal more.

Beyond being a unique assemblage of biological components, we are, at any point in our lives, the result of forces that have shaped us. The amount and type of food we eat determines how healthy we are. Our families, friends, and society influence what we become psychologically. Similarly, our communication is shaped by a variety of influences.

Communication, by its very nature, implies connection with other human beings. Through communication, we are taught the nature of the world, and through communication we, in turn, give shape to our worlds. To understand how we go about creating the process of communication, several important aspects need to be understood.

Culture

In realizing the influence our social world has on us, one of the first things we need to recognize is the importance of culture. We all develop and function within a culture or even within various cultures. A culture is *a set of assumptions held by a large number of people about how things should be done, what values are prized, and how people should behave.* These assumptions are not focused on isolated incidents but cover the full range of our lives from birth to death. The cycle of human life is almost unvaryingly uniform and in reaction to it, we have developed a broad range of activities which move from birth to death, from how we treat newborn babies to how we dispose of corpses.

Culture is something we pick up as we live and grow. The learning process is both conscious and unconscious with much of it so subtle that we seem to absorb our cultural norms rather than learn them. When we look at others, we can often readily identify and describe important aspects of their cultures.

▲ **Figure 3.1.** Culture is a major determinant in our development and shapes much of our communication patterns. (Dawe)

For example, let us note how some societies react to the passages we make through the stages of life. The Kota people of the Congo mark the transition from adolescence to adulthood by having boys paint their faces blue. The "masks of blue . . . signify the phantom of their childhood" (*Circles* 66). To prepare for marriage, young Balinese women have their teeth filed. The tooth filing is to reduce the intensity of the six human passions: lust, anger, greed, stupidity, intoxication, and jealousy (*Circle* 132). In the final transition, the passing from life to death, people also exhibit a range of customs. In Papua New Guinea, the Kuku-kuku honor the dead by a ceremony in which they "mummify their deceased relatives by smoking them over a fire" (*Circles* 217).

When we turn the cultural microscope upon ourselves, however, things often go out of focus. To view our own cultural practices is difficult for several reasons. For one, our society is a complex one. Not only do we function within local and regional cultures, but we possess a national culture as well. The United States, for example, is a constitutional democracy. We change governments by voting people into and out of office rather than by staging armed coups. We look to a written document for the final word on legal matters. We place a high premium on individual rights. To us, these practices appear to be the norm, but even a cursory review of international news shows that in many societies these principles are not the norms but aberrations.

Besides participating in a national culture, we also participate in local cultures and subcultures. Even in a small town one can find a mixture of cultures as people divide along social lines, religious lines, professional lines, and economic lines.

The major obstacle to perceiving our culture is ourselves. Consider what is an important rite of passage for many people. On a designated spring night, those in late adolescence dress in a style of clothing radically different from their regular dress. Families will even undergo financial hardship to provide the appropriate costume for their offspring. The participants are paired off male-female. The couples eat a sumptuous meal together but not in their residences. After the meal, they go to a site selected beforehand. Between the meal and the site, they may change costumes. Their transportation should be in the most impressive vehicle available, preferably an expensive rented one. The chosen site is a large room, decorated beforehand, in a public building. At the site, loud music is played, and they spend the majority of their time engaging in two forms of dance: they either clench together or independent of each other, improvise free style body movements.

After a number of hours of this activity, the large gathering breaks up. Smaller groups assemble at residences or less formal settings than the original dancing site. They again change costumes. In place of their formal attire, they put on play clothes and play games and continue dancing. They are not allowed to sleep for the remainder of the night. In the morning, they are fed breakfast and they return to their residences. The event signals their anticipated freedom from their homes. Through a mock marriage which lasts only the one night and the breaking of curfews, a last reminder of childhood, they indicate their readiness to participate in the adult realm.

A strange ritual from an exotic land? Only if you perceive your home town and high school to be exotic and the annual senior prom to be strange.

Children at an early age presume that their family's way of doing things is the only correct way to behave (Swensen 28). As they grow up, they begin to see that other families behave in

ways different from their own. They eat differently. They provide discipline and approval in different ways. They talk to each other differently. One of the tasks of maturation is to make sense of these kinds of differences.

As adults, we may make the same kind of mistake but on a larger scale. We presume that what we consider, consciously and unconsciously, to be norms are norms for everyone. Everything we do seems so natural that we feel that whatever differences exist between people are only superficial differences (Hall, Hidden Dimension 183). As long as we stay within our own set of values and assumptions, we will experience little conflict or discord with our presumptions. When we contact other cultures, we start to discover conflicts and differences.

One of the interesting areas where we see our cultural preferences at work is in the world of sports. A sport or game, by its definition, is an activity engaged in for its own sake and has no import beyond itself. Yet, we load onto games a great deal of emotional weight and involve ourselves deeply with them. We fail to see how anyone could not appreciate a sport so interesting as the one we like to watch. Basketball, for example, is a sport that has traditionally commanded a great deal of attention in the Midwest. The madness of the state high school basketball tournament in Indiana is described as "Hoosier Hysteria." The Big Ten Conference produces leading teams. People discuss the outcomes of games as if they were confrontations between global superpowers instead of school athletic teams. Why such value on ten people exhausting themselves trying to put an air-filled spheroid through a metal hoop?

The value placed on basketball—or any other sport, for that matter—is a matter of culture. One reason that basketball became such an integral part of midwestern society is that it fit into the patterns of midwestern agriculture. Players, isolated on farms, could still, by themselves, hone their skills. All they had to do was hang a basket on the side of the barn or a utility pole. Before consolidation, schools were small. Because basketball is an inexpensive sport (as compared to football) and requires few players, even the smallest school could field a team. The basketball season came after fall harvest and before spring planting. With free time in the winter, families could attend games, and because it fit easily with societal conditions, the sport became an integral part of the culture.

In an interesting reverse twist, basketball has become a popular urban sport for a different set of reasons. Again, cultural conditions come into play. Cities are crowded and space is at a premium. A sport that can be played by a large number of people in a small area fits well into the societal conditions. Twenty people can play two half-court games in about the same area that a maximum of four people can play tennis. Other regions developed sports based on similar combinations of economics, convenience, and practicality. Northern states, for obvious reasons, play ice hockey more than southern states.

The same ready assumptions we make about the import of popular games in our area carries over into our feelings about other aspects of our lives. We grow accustomed to certain foods and new diets strike us as strange. Someone raised on meat and potatoes finds it difficult to see how anybody could enjoy eating bean sprouts, tofu, and brown rice. Conversely, a person raised on this diet may find it difficult to understand how anybody could eat so much grease, fat, and starch.

In the same way that we grow accustomed to ways of eating and playing, we grow accustomed to ways of communicating. We learn the norms of our societies. We learn how to function within the framework of complicated rules by being part of a culture. We learn how we are to address our parents, our siblings, our elders, co-workers, superiors, and so on. We learn how to behave in a variety of situations such as games, meetings, religious services, funerals, weddings, classes, dates, and family gatherings.

A person growing up on the south side of Chicago in an almost totally black urban setting will see the world differently and communicate differently than someone growing up on a farm in predominantly white southern Indiana. In between the two, an upper class black living in Indianapolis will have a different set of perceptions and ways of behaving and communicating.

The main point about culture is that our lives and our communication grow out of an entire set of values, beliefs, and behavior we have learned. To recognize this fact is not to make a value judgment about any system over another or to denigrate any beliefs we hold. We may still hold and defend our beliefs. To communicate clearly about those beliefs, or any other topic, we must be as aware as possible of our own culture and how it has shaped us, and we must be aware of the culture and assumptions of the people with whom we communicate.

Language: Our Linguistic Heritage

Within our cultures, we communicate in a number of different ways. Basic to almost all our communication is the use of language.

As we have noted, we "grow into" our culture by observing and imitating those around us. We "grow into" language in much the same way, acquiring language skills by imitation, trial and error. Contact with other language users is a necessity for learning how to speak. The Romantic view of feral children, children who grow up apart from human company, is that they develop a sensitivity that enables them to communicate with animals. Like Mowgli, in Kipling's *The Jungle Book,* or Tarzan they come to possess a wisdom beyond that of civilization. Actual cases of feral children show them to be severely retarded in language usage and living on the barest of survival levels (see, for example, Lane).

In the manner of animals, human beings are born with the ability to make sounds and make them in reaction to their circumstances. Cries indicate discomfort; coos indicate comfort, etc. Then we move beyond sounds as a reaction to the present situation. As perceptive powers and muscular control develop, human beings then make a leap of truly momentous proportions. We assign sounds to an object, we name something and become able to consider that object whether it is present or not.

Language Is a Symbol System

The leap to naming moves us into a realm of sophisticated thought. Human beings can be characterized in many ways, but one way is to use the label applied to the species by a twentieth century philosopher, Kenneth Burke. Burke's description of humans is that we are "the symbol using animal" (Burke 3).

A *symbol is something that stands for something else by association or connotation.* Symbols may be physical in nature. Be they of countries, organizations, or events, flags are typically symbolic. Religious emblems such as the cross, the Star of David, the Crescent, and the wheel all have meanings beyond their physical characteristics. Schools have mascots. Jewelry serves symbolic purposes when people wear wedding rings, class rings, or lapel pins.

Beyond the physical, symbols take other forms. In language, sounds constitute the primary form of the symbols. Language begins with the association of sounds with objects or concepts. Combinations of sounds come to stand for the object or idea to be discussed. Instead of referring directly to a flower or a body of water or combustion, we can say "rose," "ocean," or "fire" and be sure that most English speakers will understand us even if no rose, ocean, or fire can be seen.

From the association of sounds with objects and ideas, the next step is to link the object or ideas to a marking system, the alphabet. Marks come to stand for sounds which stand, in turn, for the objects of discussion. Writing emerges and changes the shape of communication. The invention of the alphabet makes possible the creation of messages that can exist outside the direct presence of their creators. No longer does a message have to be passed orally from one person to the next. The message can be set down and left for others to discover.

Language Is an Arbitrarily Chosen Symbol System

The sounds and markings of words pass into our culture. As they are used by a large number of people, they seem to take on a life of their own. We do not usually make up our own language as we grow up. We appropriate the language of those around us. Thus, the learning process seems to be one of discovering tools that already exist.

That sense of discovery may mask one of the chief characteristics of language, that it is an *arbitrary* symbol system. By "arbitrary," we

mean that no direct correspondence exists between a word and the sounds or letters that make it up. This is not an easy concept to grasp at first since, as one linguist points out, "It is generally difficult to make a complete divorce between objective reality and our linguistic symbols of reference to it" (Sapir 9). Still, should enough language users decide that a certain combination of sounds signified a given object, that would be the object's name. As Shakespeare reminds us, "A rose by any other name would smell as sweet," but we should note that with another name, the flower would no longer be a rose.

The attribution of meaning becomes abundantly clear when one sets out to learn a second language. One may, for example, describe the relationship with a male sibling by calling that person "brother," "bruder," "hermano," "brat," or "otoko no kyodai." The relationship remains the same but the words, the combinations of sound specifying the person, change from English to German to Russian to Spanish to Japanese.

Communication Depends on Shared Meanings

The arbitrariness of language points to the true source of the meanings of words. Language does not give meaning to its users so much as its users give meaning to it. The meanings of words reside not in the words themselves, but in the people who use the words.

One way of understanding the process of meaning in words is to put the process into a three point scheme as did C. K. Ogden and I. A. Richards, two noted linguists (8–13). At one point, we place the symbol, the word or words that must be interpreted. At the top of the triangle, we place the perceiver who receives and interprets the message. At the third point, we place the referent, what the perceiver assumes the word to mean (Figure 3.2).

The meaning of the word, the referent will be dependent on the perceptions of the user or interpreter. For a readily recognized word, like "dog," the relationship would look like this (Figure 3.3).

Even with a word like "dog," though, the referents will differ among perceivers. Some will see a miniature poodle, others a pit bull, others

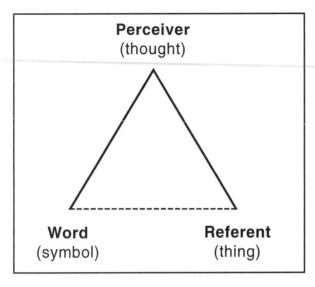

▲ Figure 3.2.

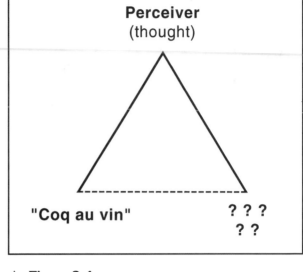

▲ Figure 3.4.

Lassie. For a word that is unfamiliar or a word that is being used in an unfamiliar context, the process is even more complicated.

Let us presume a case in which the person hearing or seeing the word is a customer in a French restaurant and is trying to impress the person he is with. Let us further presume that the perceiver is a monolingual North American who speaks only English. He opens the menu and sees "coq au vin" is one of the items listed on the menu. Unable to make any connection between the sounds and a referent, the perceiver will have no meaning to attach to the sounds (Figure 3.4).

Afraid of what he might have to swallow if he does not swallow his pride, the customer asks the waiter for a definition of "coq au vin." The waiter supplies him with a definition: "coq au vin" is a chicken cooked in wine. The customer now has a referent for the item (Figure 3.5).

Another possibility is that the perceiver sees or hears enough similarities in the sounds that he attaches a meaning from his world of experience. Embarrassed at his problems in ordering an entree, our diner looks for something familiar for dessert. He sees "a la mode" on the menu. That, of course, means a dessert with ice

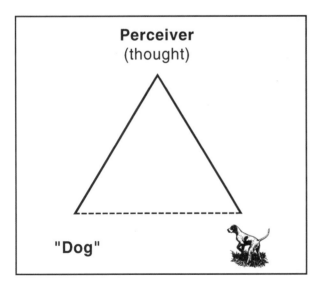

▲ Figure 3.3.

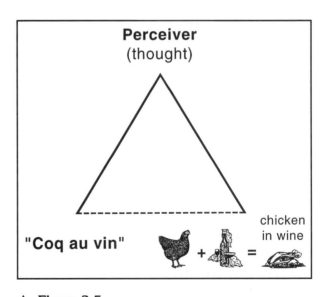

▲ Figure 3.5.

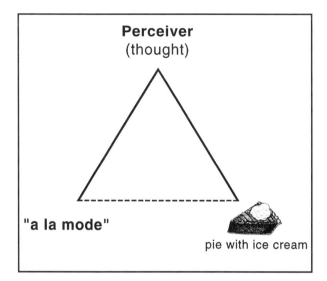

▲ Figure 3.6.

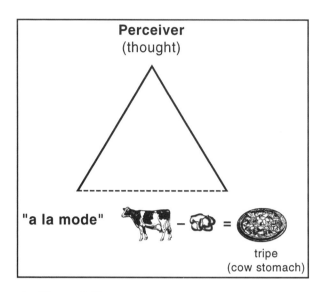

▲ Figure 3.7.

cream on top, as in "apple pie a la mode." Everyone knows that (Figure 3.6).

The customer orders the dish, "tripes a la mode de Caen," to finish the meal. Unfortunately, the diner does not realize that while "a la mode" is a French term, it does not necessarily mean "with ice cream." The waiter's perception of the term is quite different. "A la mode" for him means "in the style or fashion of."

Instead of a piece of apple pie with ice cream on top, the customer's referent, the waiter places in front of the customer the waiter's referent (Figure 3.7), a steaming bowl of cow's stomach cooked in the style of Caen, a city in Normandy, France (Child 243).

Even then, once our perceiver learns that in this context "a la mode" designates a tripe dish, the process of meaning attribution is not over. The meanings of the word may still differ due to the experiences of the users. If one likes tripe as a dish, "tripes a la mode de Caen" will mean "tasty, delicious, a true delicacy." If one dislikes tripe, "tripes a la mode de Caen" will mean "yukky, repulsive, no way I'm going to eat that."

Meanings and Communication

As the meanings of words are not inherent in a combination of sounds nor in the combinations of markings on a page, communication is not a simple process. Rather than one person

sending meanings to another, meanings are created between the two parties. The meanings will be dependent on the referents and experiences of the two parties. The process may result in a total lack of understanding between parties; it may result in full accord; or it may result in some stage in between.

To be effective as a communicator, one must be sensitive to the nature of language and the numerous possibilities for differing interpretations between senders and receivers. One must also be adaptive to ensure that senders and receivers are using the same set of meanings. Language is not so much a toolbox of words as it is an interactive process, wherein the perceptions of one person or party must join with the perceptions of another.

Nonverbal Communication

We are creatures who occupy space and live in time, and thus, it should be no surprise that we communicate by the manner in which we utilize these dimensions. Certainly language provides the basis for our communication, but we indicate through a number of different actions how those words are to be interpreted. In other cases, we manage to communicate without words at all. Nonverbal communication, simply put, is the "communication besides the spoken or written words" (Knapp 21; Mettaetal and Benjamin-Leiter 77). The number of ways that

40 *Principles of Human Communication*

people communicate nonverbally shows us a fascinating combination of nature and culture.

The impact of nonverbal communication on a communication situation is often crucial. For one thing, people trust nonverbal communication more than they trust verbal communication. If the words say one message, and the sender's facial expression contradicts the verbal message, most will rely on the facial expression to interpret the true intent of the sender. How socially attractive we are depends, to some degree, on how we communicate nonverbally. Persons showing positive nonverbal communication are judged more credible by those with whom they are speaking (Burgoon, "Nonverbal Behaviors . . ." 140). Nonverbal communication may also determine how much time one spends in jail. In one study, defendants showing moderate levels of anxiety were most likely to receive low credibility ratings and a high number of guilty votes. Defendants showing low levels of anxiety received the highest credibility ratings and the lowest number of guilty verdicts. High anxiety defendants were ranked in the middle (Pryor and Buchanan 96).

Types of Nonverbal Communication

Communicating with the Body

Our bodies provide a starting point for nonverbal communication. The way in which we occupy space may signal a number of reactions. Standards of beauty and attractiveness vary from place to place, and from time to time, so that the very shapes of our bodies may help or hinder us socially. Both anecdotal evidence and research indicate that the height of males influences how they are perceived in our society. No romantic western star is described as riding "short in the saddle." In presidential elections since 1900, the taller candidate has won with the exception of Jimmy Carter in 1976 (Knapp and Hall 112). Tall males are often given higher ratings than shorter males in a variety of situations (Elman; Lechelt; Lester and Sheehan). Moving beyond the shape of our bodies, how we employ our bodies is a major ingredient of our communication.

Facial Expressions. Facial expressions are one of the major ways in which we communicate nonverbally. The first way we communicate with

facial expressions is to show our emotions. Before they speak words, babies reveal their feelings by facial expressions, and this process continues throughout life. While we combine facial expressions into a wide range of variations, we have a small number of basic expressions: surprise, fear, anger, disgust, happiness, and sadness (Knapp and Hall 272; Burgoon et. al. 353). To these others add interest and distress-pain (Camras, et. al. 80).

Beyond the primary function of communicating emotions, facial expressions also serve to indicate how verbal messages are to be interpreted. If someone answers a question with "Right!" and a smile, the presumption is that the answer is correct. If the response is "Right!" with a scowl, the presumption is that the speaker is being ironic and that the true message is exactly the opposite of the word used. Facial expressions may also take the place of words. A look of disgust or interest may signal disapproval as readily as words to that effect.

When a symbol was needed to warn children away from poisonous substances, the most effective approach was not to use words nor to use the old symbol for poison, a skull and cross bones. The most effective and direct way to communicate "Leave this alone!" was to create a cartoon face that immediately communicated disgust. "Mr. Yuk" communicates the same message even to sophisticated adults.

Posture and Gestures. Besides the small movements of facial expressions, we communicate through the larger medium of our bodies by the use of posture and gestures. Posture is the way people hold their bodies. People indicate how nervous or at ease they are by the amount of rigidity in their bodies. Interest in a speaker is

◀ **Figure 3.8.** Facial expressions can communicate powerfully even in an abstract form such as "Mr. Yuk," a poison warning symbol for children. Permission to reproduce Mr. Yuk given by Children's Hospital of Pittsburgh.

indicated by leaning forward or leaning away from the person.

Gestures are movements made by our extremities: our hands, arms, heads, and legs. Rather than something added to verbal communication, gestures appear to be inextricably linked with talk. One study brought pairs of students together to talk about movies. One set of pairs could see each other; the second set could not see each other. Both sets made the same kinds of gestures. As the authors state. "merely pronouncing words thus seems to give rise to some degree of body movement" (Rime and Schiaratura 239).

The meanings of many gestures are situational in that their meanings are created from their interaction with the communication situation and language. In a conversation, someone flings out an arm. The person could be indicating a direction or the person could be urging the conversational partner to leave. To interpret the gesture correctly, one would need to know the words accompanying it.

Other gestures, though, are independent of language and have taken on their own symbolic meanings. "Thumbs up" and "thumbs down" signal approval or disapproval. The hitchhiker's extended thumb is instantly recognized as a request for a ride.

Clothing. In addition to using our bodies as direct instruments of communication, we also drape or display things on our bodies which communicate messages of different kinds. The first use of coverings for the body was probably for protection, and that function still remains an important element of choice of clothing. In winter, we wear heavy coats, caps, gloves, and earmuffs. In summer, we resort to wide-brimmed hats, sunglasses, and beach wraps. Certain professions such as welders, blast furnace attendants, and firefighters call for protective clothing as well.

Clothing also serves as a mean of identification. Formal uniforms may designate a number of professions such as postal workers, flight attendants, pilots, ministers, nurses, and mechan-

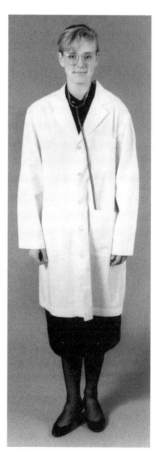

▲ **Figure 3.9.** Clothing and artifacts may carry a variety of messages about the wearer.

ics. Clothing also identifies people in more informal ways. A person's membership in a social group or social class may be indicated by dress. In one of life's many ironies, some groups of people who see themselves as independent often exhibit high standards of conformity in dress so that the "independents" can tell who is in the group and who is out. The American West created the cowboy as a symbol of the rugged individualist, but it is hard to recognize a person as a cowboy if he is not wearing jeans, a western hat, and boots. Similarly, some groups of motorcycle riders are recognizable because of their preference for boots, black clothing, leather jackets, chains, and their scorn of crash helmets.

Artifacts. Additions to our clothing also signal other people about our roles and intentions. Some artifacts are evidently identifiers. Workers in large organizations often wear clip-on identification to show they belong on the premises and that they are not to be treated as clients, patients, or customers. Police officers wear or carry a badge to show that the bearer is authorized to behave in certain ways. Police officers also carry weapons and other equipment which serve as tools of the trade but also readily identifies the wearer's purpose.

In a more subtle fashion, jewelry may tell people about a person's job, income, place identification, or how the person wishes to be perceived. A person wearing an ornate Navajo squash blossom necklace will create a different impression from a person wearing a single gold chain or a strand of pearls. A Mickey Mouse watch on an adult sends a message that the person is fun loving, perhaps even juvenile, while a Rolex may communicate money or ostentation.

Communicating with Space

Distance and Communication. How we use the space we inhabit may also communicate. The distances maintained by people in different situations carry meanings as does the behavior initiated once people are within touching distance.

One specialist in nonverbal communication noted that Americans divide distance into four principle ranges, each of which signals a different relationship. The study was based on observations of middle-class, educated people primarily from northeastern United States, but the conclusions still seem to apply in much of our culture. Public distance starts at twelve feet and moves further away. At this distance, people see each other's entire body. Relationships and communication are formal. Social distance is from four feet to twelve feet. This distance is used for business and more formal personal interactions. Personal distance ranges from eighteen inches to four feet. Here people maintain personal relationships which may range from close to cool. When people enter this range, they begin to approach each other on personal terms. Intimate distance is from zero to eighteen inches. Within this distance, we feel as though the other person is contacting us physically even though the person may not be touching us (Hall, The Hidden Dimension 116–25).

Within the intimate range, people experience the "fight or flight" response. They respond with hostility—fight—or move away—flight. A third option is to embrace, to hug, kiss, dance, etc. Intimate distance is so close that people have difficulty allowing people to exist within that space without relating to them.

Touch and Communication. Within personal space, touching behaviors come into play. Who touches whom and when and where may carry a variety of messages. Touch is obviously part of intimacy. As one observer puts the matter, "numerous studies . . . show that as the relationship between the individuals becomes more intimate, the level of nonverbal involvement increases" (Patterson, "A Functional Approach . . ." 477). Among the nonverbal behaviors that increase are intimate distance and the frequency and intimacy of touch.

Touch, though, can also signal power and social role. Typically, the more powerful engage in non-reciprocal touching behavior within lower positions. The boss may clap employees on the back as a greeting, but the employees risk affronting the boss if they use the same greeting. "Higher rank can provide a person with the power to touch, gaze, or stand close to a lower-rank person" (Patterson, "Social Influence . . ." 212). The assumed permission to invade the personal space of the subordinate may be charitable, as in the case of a physician and patient, or it may be aggressive, as in the case of a military drill instructor chewing out a recruit.

Communicating with Time

The temporal aspect of our lives comes into play in communication in several ways. Time is a construct that human being have thrust upon the world. Seconds, minutes, months, seasons, and other divisions of time do not exist in nature any more than mathematics or philosophy exists in nature. Animals may have a sense of time but only in a rudimentary sense such as their migrating in a given season. They do not, however, check their watches or look at their calendars.

Different parts of the world use different calendars such as the Gregorian, Jewish, Muslim, Chinese, etc. Each gives time a different dimension or perspective. The reason that different peoples begin their new year at different times is due to the way their calendars calculate time. The Gregorian or western calendar is a solar calendar that divides the year according to the number of days. The Chinese calendar, and most other Asian calendars, is a lunar calendar that divides the year according to the cycles of the moon.

Even when we use the same calendar and set our watches to the same standard (for most of the world Greenwich mean time), we still react to time differently. North Americans tend to be very time conscious. American television, for example, is programmed, literally, to the second, and "dead air" is to be avoided at all costs. Programs start and conclude at exact hour and half hour divisions. Other countries broadcast with much less regard for precision. Programs may start at a variety of times other than the hour or half–hour. While a Norwegian program may start on the hour, it may only run forty minutes. In earlier times, the station simply pointed the camera at a fish tank and showed the fish swimming until time for the next program to begin. Now they run previews of their upcoming programs.

North Americans usually regard punctuality as a virtue. A person kept waiting in an office for fifteen minutes begins to fidget. A half–hour wait is considered long. Much longer, and the person may consider walking out. Latin American countries regard time much more leisurely. When told to arrive at eight, a person may come a half–hour before or after.

Recognition of how the other party regards time will make communication much easier. A long wait for one person does not necessarily signal disinterest on the part of the other person. A waiting period before a decision may mean a proposal is rejected or it may mean that the deciding parties are giving the matter full consideration. Social affairs may be regulated in different ways when it comes to time. Among many in the South and Southwest, "dinner at seven" means that one is expected to arrive at seven and the meal will be served as close to seven as possible. In the Northeast, "dinner at seven" means one is expected to arrive no earlier than seven-thirty, have drinks and appetizers, and the party may not sit down to dinner until nine or ten o'clock.

Paralinguistics

The form of nonverbal communication most closely linked to verbal communication is that of paralinguistics. Paralinguistics is the inflections and tonalities we give to words as we pronounce them. Among these vocal characteristics would be the pitch, rate, volume, and quality of the voice along with the use of pauses and accents, the product of articulation.

The importance of paralinguistics has been testified to in several interesting ways. In an interview, Margaret Thatcher, former prime minister of England, has talked about the value of having a translator sensitive to paralinguistics (Thatcher). In diplomatic discussions and negotiations, with the Russians, for example, it was important to her that the other parties received her messages in a form as close to the original as possible. Thus, she made sure she had a translator who not only translated the words but paid close attention to the rises and falls of pitch and the use of volume to highlight words. Then, when presenting the Russian version of her statement, he would attempt to reproduce the same emphasis she placed on the words. The result was that the Russian version came as close as possible to its English origin.

Closer to home, former president Richard Nixon became involved in the Watergate scandal which eventually forced his resignation. One of the key elements of that scandal was tape recordings he made of conversations in the presidential office. When they were called into evidence, a question arose in what form they should be presented. The United States Supreme Court ruled unanimously that "Richard Nixon's taped Oval Office conversations were better evidence of what transpired there than were typewritten transcripts of the same conversations" (Ellyson and Dovido 4).

Different languages and cultures employ paralinguistics in different ways. Japanese is characterized by being a mono-pitch language. One speaking Japanese correctly speaks always at the same pitch level with no rises or falls. Volume may increase or decrease as may the speaking rate, but the pitch remains constant. Another oriental language, Chinese, is quite different. Chinese employs at least four different pitch levels to distinguish the meaning of words: a high pitch, a low pitch, a rising pitch, and a descending pitch.

American English falls in between the two in the use of pitch. A rising inflection characterizes a word or phrase as a question or an indecisive statement. A falling pitch designates a command, decision, or affirmation. "You are going to take this class" spoken flatly is ambiguous. If the speaker places a rising inflection at the end of the sentence, it is heard as "You are going to take this class?" A falling inflection causes the sentence to be heard as an order.

The rate of utterance may indicate the nature of statements as well. Rapidly spoken phrases denote excitement, agitation, or fear. Slowly spoken phrases can signal a casual attitude or thoughtful consideration of a matter.

Loudness usually designates importance. Matters of personal concern often arouse one to show their importance by a rise in volume when speaking of them. On a small scale, the stressing of a word or phrase with added volume highlights that word or phrases and can decide the meaning of a sentence. Consider what emerges when different words are stressed in the same sentence:

▶ "*I* will pay the bill tomorrow." (You will not have to pay it.)

▶ "I *will* pay the bill tomorrow." (I promise to take care of the matter.)
▶ "I will *pay* the bill tomorrow." (I am giving up trying to get out of paying it."
▶ "I will pay the *bill* tomorrow." (I am ignoring the credit card statement but not the bill.)
▶ "I will pay the bill *tomorrow*." (I will take immediate action, almost.)

The quality of the voice is determined by how the voice is resonated in the body. Different vocal qualities affect us in different ways. When exaggerated, vocal qualities call forth stereotyped characters. Since *The Wizard of Oz* movie, cackling voices have been associated with witches. Breathy voices designate sexiness in women. The old timer prospector speaks with a cracked and nasal voice.

The more subtle forms of quality also elicit responses. Social attractiveness, intelligence, and credibility can all be enhanced or diminished by the quality of one's voice.

Accents are combinations of the several characteristics of voice. Pitch, rate, quality, and articulation all combine to produce a distinctive manner of speaking. Like other aspects of nonverbal communication, accents may signal characteristics as social standing, roles, credibility, professions, and one's region.

Accents usually characterize the population of a region. As people learn to speak by imitation, they perpetuate the patterns of their families and area. When they contact people from a different region, the differences in speech then become apparent. Perhaps the most important thing to remember about accents is that everyone has one. "Accent-less" speech is simply that speech to which we are accustomed.

Is Nonverbal Communication the Result of Nature or Culture?

As we have seen, nonverbal communication is tied closely to our bodies, the nature of which each individual shares with all humanity. Because of this universal tie, we may wonder about the source of nonverbal communication, whether it is something that comes from human nature or if it is culturally bound. The short answer to the question is "yes."

Some portions of nonverbal communication are evident across cultures. Facial expressions are probably the most universal form of nonverbal communication. They are also the most persistent in that "emotional expression patterns for infants are similar to those described for adults. . . ." (Camras, et. al. 100). One study compared the facial expressions of male university students in Tokyo and Berkeley, California. The results showed that the Japanese and American shared the same facial reactions to the same videotape (Ekman and O'Sullivan 176).

Other portions of nonverbal communication are more culturally bound. Even the facial expressions mentioned above came in for cultural control. The observers noted while the Japanese and Americans in the study shared facial reactions, they displayed those facial expressions differently when in the presence of an authority figure. The Japanese masked more of their feelings.

It has also been noted that congenitally blind people do not exhibit the same range of facial expressions as sighted people (Rinn 16). One explanation is that those blind from birth do not have the opportunity to observe and imitate the facial expressions of those around them.

Even though they seem a natural part of us, the elements of nonverbal communication are learned just as verbal communication is learned. Through a process of imitation and trial and error, people learn the norms for behavior and follow them.

Some of the learning may have such a long history that it seems an integral part of human nature. In southern Italy, the natives use a head toss for negation. Interestingly enough, the gesture is not common to the rest of Italy. Investigation reveals that the gesture is used only in that part of Italy settled by Greeks three thousand years ago. The lineage of the gesture is long but is still the result of cultural education (Bitti and Poggi 437).

In practice, the cultural background of nonverbal communication means that to be an effective communicator, one must be sensitive to differences of meaning and the norms of different cultures. In terms of space, for example, distances between people are not a constant from one place to another. Arab cultures, for example, stand much closer to each other than do Europeans or North Americans. Moving back may signal the other person that you are cold or aloof. Table sharing is common in European restaurants while North Americans feel invaded when a stranger sits at their table.

Nonverbal communication includes numerous elements of space and time, elements which are used in different ways by different peoples to communicate. Understanding the ways in which people utilize space, time, gestures, facial expressions, clothing and artifacts, and paralinguistics provides us with a sensitivity which can enhance our abilities to communicate.

Implications for Communication

This chapter has examined three major factors—culture, language, and nonverbal behaviors—that shape our practice of communication. Awareness of these three factors is a critical part of effective communication. We need to be aware of our own practices and their effects, and we need to be aware of the practices of the other party or parties with which we communicate.

One way of understanding communication is through the use of a *communication model,* a schematic representation of the communication process. Sketching a model helps us clarify the process. At the same time, we need to remember that "however we may choose to draw a diagram of human communication, . . . the process itself is more complicated that any picture or description of it which we are likely to put down" (Schram 24).

When we engage in communication, we bring to the communication situation a combination of elements. Among these elements would be our physical characteristics, our cultural training, our language training and skills, our nonverbal training and skills, our experience, our education, and other factors which contribute to our makeup. The other party or parties do the same.

Drawing on one's backgrounds, desires, interests, understandings, and abilities, one person creates a message to be sent. The message is then put into a symbol system which the sender

▲ **Figure 3.10.**

hopes will convey to another what the first person is thinking or feeling. The symbol system may be words, nonverbal behaviors, print, electronic impulses, or some combination of elements. The process of creating the message is *encoding*.

The first person then transmits the message to another person via some *channel* of communication. A channel is the medium which carries the message. In interpersonal communication, the channel is usually the air which carries the sounds of the voice from one person to another. One could also see the various forms of nonverbal communication such as gestures and space as channels also. For other forms of communication, the channels could be broadcast signals, wires, or print media. The person receiving the message attempts to interpret it. The process of interpreting the message, making sense of it, is *decoding*.

Having decoded the message, the second person responds. As with the first person's message, the response will be shaped into some form of symbols. It is then the first person's task to make sense of the message. Thus, in communication, both parties play the roles of sender and receiver and engage in encoding and decoding. The work of encoding and decoding continues until the parties break apart.

Another concept informing our conception of communication is *feedback*. Feedback occurs in a system—mechanical, interpersonal, or oth-

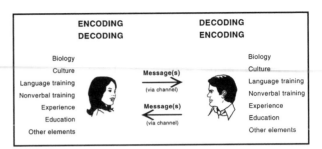

▲ **Figure 3.12.**

erwise—when a portion of the system's product is monitored and the results influence subsequent production. A simple example of a mechanical feedback system is the thermostat. The furnace system produces a product, heat. Part of that product, the air temperature around the thermostat, is monitored. Depending on the temperature of the air, the thermostat starts the furnace, lets it continue, or shuts it off.

In communication, the system consists of the senders and receivers who are linked together. The product of the system is the reactions they make, both intentional and unintentional. Feedback occurs when the communicators note the nature of their communication and react to it.

We can engage in feedback because, as one scholar has pointed out, "the message is, at some point in the process, separate from both the sender and the receiver" (Schram 26). This characteristic may be most obvious when we have mailed a letter that we wish we could recall and change (Schram 15). Like the letter, spoken words and nonverbal communication also have an existence separate from their creators and receivers.

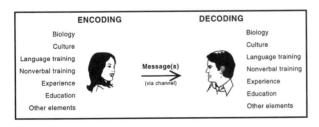

▲ **Figure 3.11.**

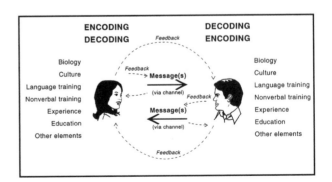

▲ **Figure 3.13.**

Be it large or small, this distance between senders and messages, and receivers means that we can regard and judge our efforts at communication and the efforts of others. We can, in essence, step back and see how we are doing. Whether we have written a letter, produced a video, or spoken a phrase, we can look at it and decide how closely it came to being what we wanted. We can also note the reactions of the receiver and judge how closely our message comes to accomplishing our goals. Having seen the effect of our past communication, we can try to frame future communication to be as effective as possible.

For example, let us look at Lanie Wilson, a graduating senior, who is at the university placement center interviewing for her first major job. She wants a position in international business and to that end is interviewing with Narwell Incorporated, an international finance company.

After introductions, the interviewer asks her how much experience she has had travelling outside the United States. She responds that because of financial reasons, she has not been able to travel much at all and has not been abroad. The interviewer says, "uh-huh," frowns a little, looks down, and writes a note on the interview form.

She notes his response and quickly adds that while she has not travelled overseas, she has read widely about international business. She mentions also that she has studied German and Japanese and has conversational skills in both.

The interviewer looks up, smiles, and nods.

Wilson then elaborates on some of the major works on international business that she has read. By monitoring both her messages and their effect, she has directed the interview in a positive direction.

The more complicated the communication, the more complex will be the feedback process. In situations such as counseling, negotiations, and small groups, problems in feedback may have disastrous consequences while sensitive monitoring of feedback can be highly rewarding.

Conclusion

As communicators, we bring to each communication situation a number of factors. Our cultural backgrounds provide us with ways of seeing the world and ways of reacting to that world. Language allows us to deal with the world through the use of symbols while nonverbal communication may reinforce or, in some instances, replace, verbal communication.

Though communication often seems spontaneous, uninhibited, and easy, communication is not inevitable when we contact others. The assumptions people make about language and nonverbal aspects such as space, time, gestures, and clothing are not necessarily the same assumptions made by others, even others from our own background. To communicate well, people need to be aware of themselves as communicators and how they function. They need also to be aware of how forces such as culture, language, and nonverbal training impinge on others. Self-knowledge and sensitivity are major ingredients in effective communication.

• • • Discussion Questions

1. How would you describe your own culture? What are some of its main features? What are some of its main beliefs?

2. Why may different sounds carry the same meanings in different languages?

3. Look at what you are wearing? Why are you wearing it? What do you think it communicates to others?

4. Why do we wear artifacts?

5. What is a comfortable distance for you when engaged in a conversation? Why is this distance comfortable? How do you think you would react if someone stood closer or farther away than your comfortable distance?

6. What kind of touching behaviors have you observed in your culture?

7. Why do North Americans see punctuality as important?

8. What are some examples of learned nonverbal behavior?

• • • Sources and References

Bitti, Pio Enrico Ricci and Isabella Poggi. "Symbolic Nonverbal Behavior: Talking Through Gestures." *Fundamentals of Nonverbal Behavior.* Eds. Robert S. Feldman and Bernard Rime. Cambridge, England: Cambridge University Press, 1991. 433–57.

Burgoon, Judee, William A. Donohue, and Mike Allen. "Nonverbal Behaviors, Persuasion, and Credibility." *Human Communication Research* 17 (1990): 140–69.

Burgoon, Judee, Douglas L. Kelley, Deborah A. Newton, and Maureen Keeley-Dyreson. "The Nature of Arousal and Nonverbal Indices." *Human Communication Research* 16 (1989): 217–54.

Burgoon, Judee K. and Joseph B. Walther. "Nonverbal Expectancies and the Evaluative Consequences of Violations." *Human Communication Research* 17 (1990): 232–63.

Burke, Kenneth. *Language as Symbolic Action: Essays on Life, Literature, and Method.* Berkeley: University of California Press, 1966.

Camras, Linda A., Carol Malatesta, and Carroll E. Izard. "The Development of Facial Expressions in Infancy." *Fundamentals of Nonverbal Behavior.* Eds. Robert S. Feldman and Bernard Rime. Cambridge, England: Cambridge University Press, 1991. 73–105.

Child, Julia and Simone Beck. *Mastering the Art of French Cooking.* Vol. 2. New York: Alfred A Knopf, 1970.

Circle of Life, The: Rituals from the Human Family Album. Ed. David Cohen. San Francisco: Harper, 1991.

Ekman, Paul and Maureen O'Sullivan. "Facial Expressions: Methods, Means, and Moues." *Fundamentals of Nonverbal Behavior.* Eds. Robert S. Feldman and Bernard Rime. Cambridge, England: Cambridge University Press, 1991. 163–99.

Ellyson, Steve L. and John F. Dovidio. "Power, Dominance, and Nonverbal Behavior: Basic Concepts and Issues." *Power, Dominance, and Nonverbal Behavior.* Eds. Steve L. Ellyson and John F. Dovidio. New York: Springer-Verlag, 1985. 1–28.

Elman, Donald. "Physical Characteristics and the Perception Masculine Traits." *Journal of Social Psychology* 103 (1977): 157–58.

Griffin, Em. *A First Look at Communication Theory.* 2nd ed. New York: McGraw-Hill, Inc., 1994.

Hall, Edward T. *The Hidden Dimension.* New York: Anchor-Doubleday, 1990.

———. *The Silent Language.* New York: Anchor-Doubleday, 1973.

Harper, Robert G. "Power, Dominance, and Nonverbal Behavior: An Overview." *Power, Dominance, and Nonverbal Behavior.* Eds. Steve L. Ellyson and John F. Dovidio. New York: Springer-Verlag, 1985: 29–48.

Hawking, Stephen. *A Brief History of Time: From the Big Bang to Black Holes.* New York: Bantam Books, 1990.

Henley, Mary M. and Sean Harmon. "The Nonverbal Semantics of Power and Gender: A Perceptual Study." *Power, Dominance, and Nonverbal Behavior.* Eds. Steve L. Ellyson and John F. Dovidio. New York: Springer-Verlag, 1985. 151–64.

Joseph, Nathan. *Uniforms and Nonuniforms: Communication through Clothing.* New York: Greenwood Press, 1986.

Knapp, Mark L. and Judith A. Hall. *Nonverbal Communication in Human Interaction.* 3rd ed. Fort Worth: Holt Rinehart and Winston, Inc., 1992.

Lane, Harlan. *The Wild Boy of Aveyron.* Cambridge, Massachusetts: Harvard University Press, 1976.

Lasswell, Harold D. "The Structure and Function of Communication in Society." *The Process and Effects of Mass Communication.* Eds. Wilbur Schram and Donald F. Roberts. Revised ed. Urbana, Illinois: University of Illinois Press, 1977. 84–99.

Lechelt, Eugene C. "Occupational Affiliation and Ratings of Physical Height and Personal Esteem." *Psychological Reports* 36 (1975): 943–46.

Lester, David and Donald Sheehan. "Attitudes of Supervisors Toward Short Police Officers." *Psychological Reports* 47 (1980): 462.

Lieberman, Devorah, Thomas G. Rigo, and Robert F. Campain. "Age-Related Differences in Nonverbal Decoding Ability." *Communication Quarterly* 36 (1988): 290–97.

Littlejohn, Stephen W. *Theories of Human Communication.* 3rd ed. Belmont, California: Wadsworth Publishing Company, 1989.

—. *Theories of Human Communication.* 4th ed. Belmont, California: Wadsworth Publisihing Company, 1992.

Lonergan, Bernard L. *Insight: A Study of Human Understanding.* San Francisco: Harper and Row, Publishers, 1978.

Odgen, C. K. and I. A. Richards. *The Meaning of Meaning: A Study of the Influence of Language Upon Thought and of the Science of Symbolism.* New York: Harcourt Brace Jovanovich, n.d.

Patterson, Miles L. "A Functional Approach to Nonverbal Exchange." *Fundamentals of Nonverbal Behavior.* Eds. Robert S. Feldman and Bernard Rime. Cambridge, England: Cambridge University Press, 1991. 458–95.

___. "Social Influence and Nonverbal Exchange." *Power, Dominance, and Nonverbal Behavior.* Eds. Steve L. Ellyson and John F. Dovidio. New York: Springer-Verlag, 1985. 207–18.

Pryor, Bert and Raymond W. Buchanan. "The Effects of a Defendant's Demeanor on Juror Perceptions of Credibility and Guilt." *Journal of Communication* 34 (1984): 92–99.

Rime, Bernard and Lois Schiaratura. "Gesture and Speech." *Fundamentals of Nonverbal Behavior.* Eds. Robert S. Feldman and Bernard Rime. Cambridge, England: Cambridge University press, 1991. 239–84.

Rinn, William E. "Neuropsychology of Facial Expression." *Fundamentals of Nonverbal Behavior.* Eds. Robert S. Feldman and Bernard Rime. Cambridge, England: Cambridge University Press, 1991. 3–30.

Sapir, Edward. *Culture, Language and Personality:* Selected Essays. Ed. David G. Mandelbaum. Berkeley: University of California Press, n.d.

Schram, Wilbur. "The Nature of Communication Between Humans." *The Process of Effects of Mass Communication.* Eds. Wilbur Schram and Donald F. Roberts. Revised Ed. Urbana, Illinois: University of Illinois Press, 1977. 3–54.

Thatcher, Margaret. Interview. *Book Talk.* C-Span. 9 December 1993.

Whitehurst, Teresa C. and Valerian J. Derlega. "Influence of Touch and Preferences for Control on Visual and Subjective Responses." *Power, Dominance, and Nonverbal Behavior.* Eds. Steve L. Ellyson and John F. Dovidio. New York: Springer-Verlag, 1985. 165–82.

Name _____ Section _____ Date _____

The Nature of Communication

1. What is culture?

    _____

    _____

2. How do people become aware of their cultures?

    _____

    _____

3. In language, what are the symbol systems used?

    _____

    _____

4. What is meant by, "Language is an arbitrarily chosen symbol system?"

    _____

    _____

5. Where do the meanings of words reside, in the words themselves or outside of the words? If outside, where is that?

    _____

    _____

6. How can you be an effective communicator despite the complexities involved in the communication process?

    _____

    _____

7. What is nonverbal communication?

    _____

    _____

8. How important is nonverbal communication in relation to verbal communication when trying to communicate with someone?

    _____

    _____

9. Facial expressions can convey at least two types of information. What are they?

   1. _____

   2. _____

10. In what way can meanings associated with gestures be situational?

    _____

    _____

11. What messages can clothing communicate?

    _____

    _____

12. In the communication sense, what are artifacts?

    _____

    _____

13. How can space be used to communicate a message?

    _____

    _____

14. What are the characteristics of how North Americans view time?

    _____

    _____

    Is this the same way all other cultures view it? _____

    If not, what are some differences?

    _____

    _____

15. What is paralinguistics?

    _____

    _____

16. Is nonverbal communication derived from human nature, or is it culturally bound? Explain your response.

_____

_____

17. What is a communication model?

_____

_____

18. What is encoding?

_____

_____

19. In reference to communication, what is a channel?

_____

_____

20. Describe decoding.

_____

_____

21. How does feedback work in communication?

_____

_____

Culture Analysis

Listed below are some items which are components of your culture, and consequently, you as a communicator. Answer the questions with information pertinent to you. This information will not be collected, but will serve as the basis for a class discussion on how these areas have influenced your view of yourself, your family, your community, and the world. How do you think your world would be different if some of these items were changed?

The information may also serve as the basis of an introductory speech exercise in which you would identify the three major influences on you from your culture or explain a significant aspect of your culture.

As with all assignments in this course, you will not be asked to reveal any information you are uncomfortable disclosing.

Family

► Do you live in an extended family, relative nearby, or an isolated family?
► What is your parents' marital status? (always married, separated or divorced, divorced and remarried, single parent, one or both parents deceased)
► How many brothers and sisters do you have?
► Where in the birth order were you born? (only child, oldest, middle, youngest)
► Do you have half or step brothers and/or sisters?

Education

► How much formal education do your parents have?
► How much formal education do your grandparents have?
► What attitudes toward education does your family have? Your friends?
► Did you attend public or private secondary schools?
► How large was your high school?
► What was the atmosphere there?
► What percentage of your graduating class went on to college?

Home Setting

► What kind of area do you live in? (urban, suburban, town, village, rural)
► How stable is your neighborhood? (most residents have been there for years, some residents have been there for years, generally there is a large turnover in residents)
► How many times has your family moved since you've been born? How many different states have you lived in?
► Is your family's home in another country? If yes, where?
► Is your neighborhood dominated by one ethnic background? If yes, are you a part of the majority?
► How do you feel about living in your area?
► What kind of housing does your family have? (single family, duplex, multi-family) If your parents live in separate homes, do you live primarily in one, or do you spend significant time in each home?

Religion

► What is your religious background, if any?
► How strongly are you affiliated with your religious group?

▶ What are the major beliefs of your religious group?
▶ Are both your parents from the same religious upbringing? If not, how has this affected your religious choices?

Politics

▶ What is your party affiliation, if any?
▶ How would you classify yourself politically? (extreme right, conservative, moderate, liberal, extreme left, disinterested in politics)
▶ How did you develop your political beliefs?
▶ Have you taken an active part in campaigning for a law or candidate?

Business Life

▶ What working experience have you had?
▶ How much money are you contributing to your education?
▶ What are your parents' jobs?
▶ What are the most respected jobs in your community?
▶ What are the least respected jobs in your community?
▶ If you have decided on a major, what most influenced in making that choice?

National Concerns

▶ Of what country are you a citizen?
▶ How would you describe the values of people in your part of this country?
▶ If you're a citizen of another country, how do its values differ from those in the United States?
▶ Have you traveled outside the U.S.? Where?
▶ Have you lived outside the U.S. for more than six months? Where?

Foods

▶ What would be a typical evening meal in your family?
▶ What are your favorite foods?
▶ If you wanted to introduce somebody from a different area to the foods of your area, what would you serve them?

Ethnic Heritage

▶ What is you ethnic background? How much contact with other ethnic groups or races have you had in your community?
▶ How much contact with other ethnic groups or races have you had in your school?

Language

▶ What is your first language?
▶ What is your second language?
▶ What is your third language?
▶ Do your family members normally communicate with each other in English? If not, what language do they use?
▶ Were your high school classes bilingual? What languages were used?

4

The Ethics in Communication

Key Concepts

Communication is one of the most basic of human activities, a process by which we engage ourselves with others for understanding, for cooperation, and the accomplishment of a variety of goals. To exist as a human being is to interact with others, to influence others, and to be subject to their influence upon ourselves. We are, as one has observed, "a persuading and persuaded animal" (Johnstone, Henry 306.) The interaction may be as complex as that of a family with a complicated web of relationships that extends over the lifespans of its members. The interaction may be as simple as a request for information from a stranger on the street whom we will never see again.

However complex or simple our interactions, we impinge on each other in multiple ways. It is a short jump from recognizing that we influence each other through communication to recognizing that communication is not a neutral activity. We do not simply influence each other; we influence each other in positive and negative ways, for good and for bad. Phrases from our daily rounds of communication indicate the kind of judgments we make about the worth and value of the communication: "She should never have told me that;" "He was very helpful;" "The government is engaged in another cover-up;" "She said what needed to be said;" "He's lying'" "She told it like it was."

▲ **Figure 4.1.** Questions of ethics arise because we influence each other for good or ill. (Dawe)

When communicating, we do not simply choose words; we choose words for the effect they will have on our audiences, on ourselves, and ultimately, on society. Thus, when we communicate, we cannot escape ethical questions, questions which ask how helpful or harmful our actions are. An awareness of the ethical dimensions of communication provides us with a deeper understanding of ourselves and of our potential as human beings. Communicating ethically is important because it has the greatest positive impact for others and, ultimately, ourselves. This chapter examines the subject of communication and ethics by looking at the nature of ethics, how communication and ethics interlock, and at some guidelines for making ethical choices in communicating.

The Nature of Ethics

Ethics is the discussion of the judgments we make about the appropriateness, the right or wrong, of our actions and policies be those actions communicative, political, social, personal, or a mixture of areas. Ethics is the study of what, ultimately, is the best course of action: How should we behave to have the most positive effect upon society and to become the best individuals we can?

The question is certainly not a new one; the search for answers is both ancient and cross-cultural. With its text dating back to 2,400 BC, The Egyptian *Book of the Dead* contains a kind of creed or standard of behavior which the virtuous were expected to recite to pass successfully from the world of the living to the realm of the dead. Among the statements, the virtuous are asked to affirm that "I have not oppressed the members of my family," "I have not defrauded the oppressed one of his property," and "I have not cut a cutting in a canal of running water," an important consideration in an arid land (Budge 360–71). In ancient India, in its religion and philosophy, "truthfulness means more than a moral obligation to avoid deceit. It is revered as one of the greatest of human accomplishments and the greatest service one person can render another" (Kirkwood 213).

Both the Jewish and Christian scriptures have clear indications of how one is to behave.

The Ten Commandments (Exodus 20: 1–17) and the Sermon on the Mount (Matthew 5–7), for example, both contain guidelines for religion, marriage, treatment of others, honesty, and respect for the truth. The Confucian codes of China, dating from the sixth century, AD, detail how one should behave in a benevolent and virtuous way.

In his *Nicomachean Ethics*, circa 325 BC, Aristotle discusses what contributes to the creation of a good and just society. His view is that ethics is a kind of "practical philosophy," the application of good judgment when faced with decisions about courses of action. Through the use of our rationality, we seek a virtuous path, one that avoids the extremes of overreaction. For example, Aristotle views generosity as a virtue which consists of giving "to the right people, the right amount, at the right time . . . ." By practicing generosity, one avoids the vices of extravagance, spending too much on oneself, and stinginess, spending too little on others (1120a). By seeking the mean, one creates "happiness," a term which for Aristotle meant "living well," leading a rewarding and fulfilling life (Ostwald xxi).

The discussion of ethics has continued to be an area of discussion and research from its earliest beginnings until the present time. Even a quick search of listings in a university library will yield a lengthy list of materials ranging from a general discussion of ethics in society to discussion of ethics in specific fields such as medicine, education, and law.

Ethics as an Integral Part of Communication

In contemporary society, when we consider questions of ethics, we often turn immediately to the world of politics, not without reason. The administrations of presidencies in this half century have all faced, and in some cases bungled, questions of truthfulness.

The most famous case of presidential truth or consequences was that of Richard Nixon. In 1972, during the election campaign, an attempt was made to burglarize the Democratic National Headquarters located in the Watergate Building. The Congressional hearings, judicial investigations, revelations, and public outcry stemming from that incident forced Nixon to become, on 8 August 1974, the first president to resign from office.

By its very nature, the democratic process creates decisions that are often difficult for its participants if they subscribe to a high ethical standard. How should a candidate behave in order to be elected? How does a voter choose between two candidates, neither one of whom is particularly desirable? How do elected officials balance the often conflicting needs and desires of their constituencies?

When we turn to non-political questions, we sometimes think that ethics is a matter of debating major issues such as euthanasia, war, or capital punishment (Williams 196). These are certainly significant matters, but the "major ethical issues" that most of us will face will be matters of how to behave in our daily lives and in our relationships with those with whom we have personal contact at home, at school, or at work.

Because it is relational, communication brings us face to face with questions that contain ethical judgments. We must decide what is the purpose or purposes of a relationship in which we find ourselves. We must decide how to behave. We must choose how to respond in that situation. Our responses will be based on how we regard the other party or parties and what the consequences of our actions will be. All of these are basic ethical questions in that they involve our deciding what is the "best" course of action.

▲ **Figure 4.2.** Deciding on courses of action in our communication involves us in ethical decisions. (Dawe)

Discovering the ethical element in our communication does not mean that we go through a complete ethical inventory every time we engage in communication. Rather, we make basic assumptions about the nature of people and our responsibilities to them and then act on the basis of those assumptions.

It does not take long, however, before we find ourselves in situations in which we must attempt to satisfy conflicting demands. Then we come consciously face to face with the ethical issues in communication. How do you respond when a friend comes to you and asks, "How do you like this shirt?" and you think the shirt is hideous? How do you balance the conflict between sparing the person's feelings and saving the person from public embarrassment? What do you say or do?

A friend reveals to you that she has a six pack of beer hidden in her dormitory room, and you both know alcohol is prohibited by regulation on campus. Later, the resident counselor comes to you and asks if you know of anyone on the floor who has alcohol in her room. What would you say or do in response? How would you frame your communication with your friend and the counselor?

What if, in a more serious case, your friend insisted that she was not drunk and was perfectly capable of driving her car, but you could tell that she was completely intoxicated and a threat to herself and others on the road? How would you persuade her to stay off the road? Would it be ethical to lie to her to separate her from her car keys? If she proved unresponsive to your persuasion and drove off, would you call the police to alert them to a dangerous driver? If she were arrested for "driving while under the influence," how much of your role in the affair would you reveal? In what ways, if any, would your reactions differ if your friend were a "he" instead of a "she"? How would you respond if the person involved were a family member, a parent or grandparent?

In a more public setting, let us imagine that you are part of a committee presenting a proposal to your housing unit about parking facilities. Close to the time you are to present your proposal, you discover that a key piece of evidence is outdated and the latest information is damaging to your case. Do you simply present the evidence? Do you present the data with a qualifier about its timeliness? Do you leave it out entirely?

While the answers to these kinds of questions may be difficult, we have to make decisions and live by the consequences. The decision to communicate and the decisions made within the communication event carry with them ethical implications.

Ethical Communication

To make the best decisions in our communication, to communicate ethically, we must give thought to the manner in which we communicate. Formulating a list of rules to be applied in the different communication situations in which we find ourselves would be a futile endeavor. The situations are too vast and too varying. Rather, we would do better to suggest guidelines for ethical communication, considerations which should shape communicating practice.

Ethical Communicators Are Respectful of Their Audiences

Communication is a two way process. Communication implies a party other than ourselves and an attempt on our part to influence that person or party in some way. As one scholar has put the matter, "A *communicator*, with particular *motives*, attempts to achieve a specific *end* with a specific *audience* by employ-

▲ **Figure 4.3.** Ethical communicators respect their audiences. (*The Purdue Exponent*)

ing (*intentionally or unintentionally*) communicative *means* or techniques to influence that audience" (Johanssen 16).

The nature of the influence we have on others will depend to a large extent on our attitudes towards our audiences. As several have observed, an ethical communicator is one who regards other persons as possessing inherent dignity and worth (Jaska and Pritchard 81; Nilsen 14). Human beings are to be regarded not as means to ends but rather as valued participants whose welfare is a significant and considered part of the interaction.

In terms of practice, this principle means that audience analysis is an important part of communication. We cannot respond appropriately if we are ignorant of the people with whom we communicate.

Respect for audiences includes respect for the ideas and feelings of the people with whom we interact. If people possess dignity and worth, then they need to be treated as such even when we may disagree with them strongly. One student was addressing an issue which some saw as racially charged. His response to those opposing his ideas was, "Get a life." His reaction demeaned not only those disagreeing with him but his own ideas as well.

Ethical Communicators Consider the Consequences of Their Communication

We do not communicate in vacuums. Our communication endeavors are never isolated one from the other. How we respond at school influences how we respond at home, and that in turn affects how we respond in our public lives. Having considered the natures of our audiences, we need to consider further the effect of our communication on them and upon ourselves.

Sam is chairing the planning committee for the Outing Club's spring break trip to Isle Royale. Committee members are all doing their work except for Larry who has missed several meetings and has not had his committee reports ready on time. Larry is slowing down the committee's progress and threatening the success of the trip. Sam has to talk to Larry about the problem and is frustrated enough to bawl him out about his poor work. Telling Larry off in loud and uncertain terms may make Sam

feel better, but if Sam is an ethical communicator, he will consider the possible outcomes of his communication with Larry.

If Larry's work is late because he has been sick, an outburst may leave Larry resentful and even less willing to perform the necessary work. Relations will be strained more. The trip may be further endangered. Whatever the situation, Sam's best choice will be an approach that encourages Larry to be a contributing member, reduces the possibility of conflict, and ensures the success of the projected trip rather than just venting his feelings.

Ethical Communicators Respect Truth

A great deal of the ethics of communication involves a respect for truth. Indeed, as one has put it, the assumption of truth undergirds the very concept of communication itself: "an inherent end of speech is the communication of belief" (Kupfer 118). If we cannot trust the other party, we cannot accurately judge how to respond. If we cannot accurately judge how to respond, then our communication becomes increasingly ineffective. If the lack of trust is pervasive enough, it is destructive finally to society. As one person has observed, "This is why some level of truthfulness has always been seen as essential to human society, no matter how deficient the observance of other moral principles" (Bok 18).

Let us say that an instructor receives a call from a student just before the student is scheduled to make a presentation in class. The student tells the instructor that he cannot make his presentation because he is sick. He says that he has a fever and has been up all night with nausea. His voice sounds hoarse and tired. The instructor is sympathetic and offers to let the student make up the presentation later. Two hours later, the instructor goes to lunch and across the restaurant, sees the same student. The student is active, lively, and in animated conversation with his friends. It is apparent that he is not the least bit sick.

The student has created trouble for himself, but he has also created trouble for other students. Once deceived, the instructor will be less likely in the future to accept reasons for missed work. Rather than accepting the word of the student, the instructor may demand proof of the illness and move the relationship toward a more legalistic level.

Instructors are not immune to disrespect for truth. An instructor assigns a five page paper due in two weeks and lists the penalties for turning in the paper later. You work hard and hand your paper in on the day it is due. After collecting the papers, the instructor says that he put the deadline and penalties on the assignment to get them in so he would have time to grade them, but he will not enforce any penalty if the work is late. Several people turn in their work the next week and receive the same grade as you. Given another week, you might have made your paper even better. You would probably feel that you have, to some degree, been cheated. The instructor not only gave different people different deadlines but deceived the class as to the true nature of the assignment. The instructor's credibility has been damaged so that you will probably be leery of anything the instructor says. In short, you will have increased difficulty making your judgments about the intent of what is said and what course of action you should follow.

Ethical Communicators Use Information Properly

Adequate Information. As an ethical communicator, a respect for truth means being informed on a topic before posing as any kind of authority on the subject. Certain professions such as law, medicine, and education have formal standards of expertise and knowledge that must be met before one can be a practitioner. We would be appropriately appalled to discover that the physician who just treated us had never attended medical school.

The same principle applies in communication situations. If we are going to provide information to people, much less persuade them, we need to be well prepared for the occasion. To talk about "How Students Can Handle Their Finances" with little or no background would be giving limited, if not false, information. To speak with any authenticity on the subject, we would need to look into such items as educational costs, credit card use, banks and credit unions, and work opportunities.

▲ Figure 4.4. Ethical communicators use adequate and accurate information. (Coyle)

Accurate Information. In addition to securing information, we also need to consider the accuracy of the information and the accuracy with which we use it. When we communicate, we expect people to react in some way to what we say and do. When we use inaccurate information to influence others, we cause difficulty for them and for ourselves.

Accurate information is information that is timely, up to date, and applicable to the situation. In making a presentation on where to attend college, a speaker might quote a reference work that listed information about schools such as tuition, majors, and academic standing. If the reference book, though, were ten years old, the information would be of little use. Out of date information about other significant topics such as the environment, drug use, or crime rates would be just as useless.

Along with finding timely and adequate information, an ethical speaker will use quotations, facts, ideas, and figures accurately. Quotations will, for example, reflect the intent of the larger passage from which they are taken.

A recent *Consumer Reports* article evaluates commercial diet plans. Several of the statements made in the article could be used to persuade people of the merits of the plans. A psychologist specializing in eating disorders says, "*Weight Watchers* is the only place I ever send anyone" ("Losing Weight" 355). In another place, the article evaluates a well know program by saying, "People who tried *Optifast* lost 45 pounds on average . . .("Losing Weight" 357).

These quotations sound like endorsements of the plans until one sees their larger context. The psychologist is characterized as someone who "generally warns clients away from the very idea of dieting." The information on the success of the customers of *Optifast* adds that the customers "had gained back 15 pounds six months later." The article's conclusion? "Despite their sales pitches, there is no evidence that commercial weight-loss programs help most people achieve significant, permanent weight loss. If you want or need to lose weight, you would probably do well to try to reduce on your own, or through a free hospital-based program, before spending money on a commercial weight-loss center" ("Losing Weight" 357). Misquoting could give a very biased view of the information.

Ethical Communicators Do Not Falsify Information

Worse than the distortion of information is falsifying information. Failing to find information useful to our goals, we make it up. Lena Guerrero, a person active in Texas politics was appointed to an important state commission by the governor. Part of Guerrero's credentials were notations of her graduation from the University of Texas and membership in Phi Beta Kappa, a prestigious honorary society. As the featured speaker at a college graduation, she waxed sentimental about her own graduation, saying, "Now, I remember well my own commencement, and I think I can guess what you're feeling about now" (Burka 125). Investigative reporters discovered some important facts about her college years: Guerrero attended college but fell nineteen hours short of the required minimum. She had no college degree; she never graduated. Nor was she ever a member of Phi Beta Kappa. She had lied about the situation. Such invention of information is highly unethical.

Another way of falsifying information is through *plagiarism.* Plagiarism is a kind of theft, intellectual theft. We plagiarize when we use the words or ideas of another and fail to credit the source. Instead of attributing the material to its original creator, we pretend the words or ideas are our own. When writing, we acknowledge sources by the use of quotation marks and include a citation of the source. When speaking, we acknowledge sources by naming them in the context of the speech.

If one were speaking, for example, about the problem of dealing with aging pets, one could make the problem vivid for the audience by describing the behavior of an old beloved dog. The loyalty, affection, and trust of the dog and the owner's conflicting feelings could be poignantly pictured by a phrase such as "putting 'their kids' old dogs to sleep, friends that drool and quiver and stumble hobbling to our hands'." If ethical, the speaker, though, would give credit where credit is due by acknowledging the author: "As Walter McDonald aptly describes in his poem . . ." (McDonald 24).

The most blatant form of plagiarism is appropriating the entire work of another. This type of plagiarism occurs when instead of composing their own speeches, students give speeches created by people other than themselves: their roommates, their friends, family members, or even professional writers. Besides constituting a lie about the true composer, such plagiarism subverts the educational process. We do not learn to communicate by using a stand-in any more than we learn to swim by having someone else take swimming lessons for us.

Ethical Communicators Respect the Rights of Others to Information

A respect for truth and an ethical consideration of others also means respecting the rights of others in regard to information and access to information. Collecting information is an integral part of the research process, but stealing information is theft, taking something that does not belong to us. Beyond the personal act of theft, stealing information is unethical because it prevents other people from securing information and unnecessarily makes their lives more difficult.

For example, a periodical article may be useful to our speech, but we should either take notes on the material or photocopy it rather than tearing it out of the magazine. Tearing out the article robs others of the opportunity to read it and creates added expense for the library which must replace it. That expense, along with similar expenses, adds to the financial burden of the school and eventually, its students, including the person who tore out the article.

Conclusion

For the sake of our audiences, ourselves, and the people affected by our interactions we need to recognize the ethical component of our communication. Ethics is not just a matter of political or social policy but is a part of our personal policies as well, an integral part of our behaviors and our regard for others. Ethical communication will incorporate a respectful view of its audiences, a consideration of the consequences of the communication for all parties involved, and a respect for truth. Such a view is both a challenge and a reward.

• • • Discussion Questions

1. Why does our communication have ethical implications?

2. How can communicators show respect for their audiences or co-communicators?

3. How does a respect for truth shape our communications? What happens in communication when we cannot believe the other party?

4. How would falsifying information affect communication?

5. How might communicators use information improperly?

6. What would you do if your were involved in the case described in this chapter about beer in the dormitory or a case where someone you know is drinking and driving? How would you choose to communicate?

7. What problems are created when people destroy information such as tearing out periodical articles or stealing books from the library?

• • • Sources and References

Anderson, Kenneth E. "Communication Ethics: The Non-Participant's Role." *The Southern Speech Communication Journal* 44 (1984): 219–228.

Aristotle. *Nicomachean Ethics*. Trans. Martin Ostwald. Indianapolis: Bobbs-Merrill Company, Inc., 1962.

Arnett, Ronald C. "The Practical Philosophy of Communication Ethics and Free Speech as the Foundation for Speech Communication." *Communication Quarterly* 38 (1990): 208–17.

———. "The Status of Communication Ethics Scholarship in Speech Communication Journals from 1915 to 1985." *Central States Speech Journal* 38 (1987): 44–61.

Bok, Sissela. *Lying: Moral Choice in Public and Private Life*. New York: Vintage Books, 1989.

Bormann, Ernest G. "Ethical Standards for Interpersonal/Small Group Communication." *Communication* 6 (1981): 267–85.

Budge, E. A. Wallis. *The Book of the Dead: An English Translation of the Chapters, Hymns, etc., of the Theban Recension, with Introduction, Notes, etc.* 2nd ed. 1923. Surrey, England: Unwin Brothers Limited, 1977.

Burka, Paul. "Honesty is the Best Politics." *Texas Monthly* Nov. 1992: 122+.

Condon, John. "Values and Ethics in Communication Across Cultures: Some Notes on the North American Case." *Communication* 6 (1981): 255–65.

Confucius. *The Analects.* Trans. D. C. Lau. New York: Penguin Books, 1979.

Deetz, Stanley. "Reclaiming the Subject Matter as a Guide to Mutual Understanding: Effectiveness and Ethics in Interpersonal Interaction." *Communication Quarterly* 38 (1990): 226–43.

Garver, Eugene. "Essentially Contested Concepts: The Ethics and Tactics of Argument." *Philosophy and Rhetoric* 23 (1990): 251–70.

Grisez, Germain. "The Concept of Appropriateness: Ethical Consideration in Persuasive Argument." *The Journal of the American Forensic Association* 2 (1965): 53–58.

Hoff, Christina Hoff. "Moral Education in America." *The American Scholar* 53 (1984): 381–89.

Holy Bible.

Jaska, James A. and Michael S. Pritchard. *Communication Ethics: Methods of Analysis.* Belmont, California: Wadsworth Publishing Company, 1988.

Johannesen, Richard L. *Ethics in Human Communication.* 3rd ed. Prospect Heights, Illinois: Waveland Press, Inc., 1990.

Johnstone, Christopher Lyle. "Ethics, Wisdom, and the Mission of Contemporary Rhetoric: The Realization of Human Being." *The Central States Speech Journal* 32 (1981): 177–88.

Johnstone, Henry W., Jr. "Towards an Ethics of Rhetoric." *Communication* 6 (1981): 305–14.

Kirkland, William G. "Truthfulness as a Standard for Speech in Ancient India." *The Southern Communication Journal* 54 (1989): 213–34,

Kupfer, Joseph. "The Moral Presumption Against Lying." *Review of Metaphysics* 35 (1982): 103–26.

"Losing Weight: What Works. What Doesn't." *Consumer Reports* 58 (1993): 347–52.

McDonald, Walter. *After the Noise of Saigon.* Amherst, Massachusetts: The University of Massachusetts Press, 1988.

McGuire, Michael. "The Ethics of Rhetoric: The Morality of Knowledge." *The Southern Speech Communication Journal* 45 (1980): 133–48.

Nicotera, Anne Mayden and Donald P. Cushman. "Organizational Ethics: A Within-Organization View." *Journal of Applied Communication Research* 20 (1992): 437–62.

Nilsen, Thomas. *Ethics of Speech Communication.* 2nd ed. Indianapolis: Bobbs-Merrill Company, Inc., 1974.

Ostwald, Martin. Introduction. *Nicomachean Ethics.* By Aristotle. Indianapolis: Bobbs-Merrill Company, Inc., 1962. xi–xxiv.

Perelman, Chaim. "The Rhetorical Point of View in Ethics." Trans. D. Raymond Tourville. *Communication* 6 (1981): 315–20.

Rives, Stanley G. "Ethical Argumentation." *The Journal of the American Forensic Association* 1 (1964): 79–85.

Williams, Clifford. "Teaching Virtues and Vices." *Philosophy Today* 33 (1989): 195–203.

Name _____ Section _____ Date _____

Ethics in Communication

1. What is ethics?

    _____

    _____

2. Why is communicating ethically important?

    _____

    _____

3. In what way do we incorporate ethics into communicating with others?

    _____

    _____

4. How is the statement, "Ethical communicators are respectful of their audiences," actually put into practice?

    _____

    _____

5. How does the communicator use information ethically?

    _____

    _____

6. What is plagiarism?

    _____

    _____

5

Communicating with Others One-to-One

Key Concepts

• • • • • • • • • • •

Interpersonal Communication

Having discussed the nature of communication in general, we want now to look at the nature of communication in several different settings. The first of these is interpersonal communication which you may recall from its brief introduction in an earlier chapter.

What Is Interpersonal Communication?

Interpersonal communication is the sending and receiving of messages between two parties, usually in close visual and aural proximity which allows for immediate feedback and close attention to verbal and nonverbal cues.

Number of People

The concept of interpersonal communication involves several key ideas. The first is a small number of participants. Often, interpersonal communication is referred to as *dyadic* communication, a term from "dyo," the Greek word for two. The two parties involved in interpersonal communication may be two individuals such as two friends or a husband and wife. The two parties may involve more than two people, however. A couple talking to a real estate agent about a house, for example, would involve three people but two parties, the potential buyers and the agent. The number of parties may be enlarged to three—triadic communication—but when we move beyond three, the people involved begin to take on the characteristics of yet another communication configuration, the small group.

Proximity

Another important element in the creation of interpersonal communication is that the parties are in close proximity. Their communication is usually unmediated. Interpersonal communication, at its fullest, is characterized by being face-to-face communication: a teacher and student talk at the teacher's desk, a physician discusses a set of symptoms with a patient in an examining room, two friends talk over their day's classes across a table in the Student Union snack bar.

This small number of people involved and the close proximity affect the nature of the *language* used in interpersonal communication. In interpersonal communication we usually use language that is less formal that than of written discourse or public speaking (Tannen). We use more pauses, string together more phrases, and use a simpler vocabulary. We also adapt our language very specifically to our audiences. One moment, a person may be babbling nonsense to a child or a pet, and the next moment, the person is discussing the grocery bill with the spouse. Males talking to males will use a different kind of language than they will talking to females or mixed-gender groups, and females

▲ **Figure 5.1.** Interpersonal communication is the sending and receiving of messages between two parties, usually in close visual and aural proximity which allows for immediate feedback and close attention verbal and nonverbal cues." (Dawe)

will employ a different kind of language depending on whether they are talking to another woman, a male, or a mixed-gender group (Pearson 174–209).

As interpersonal communication takes place between a small number of people who can easily see and hear each other, *feedback* has high importance. Details that may be meaningless in the larger context of a public speech may have great impact on interpersonal communication. If a back row audience member at a public speech yawns, shifts position, or checks a watch, the speaker may not even see the movement. In an interpersonal situation, those small gestures may convey volumes because they are easily seen and noted.

A person, for example, may be involved in what seems to be an engaging conversation. At one point, though, the conversational partner rolls her wrist a quarter turn and directs her glance downward for half a second. Instead of continuing to lean forward, the first speaker straightens up several inches. The partner picks up her books. The first speaker sits all the way back in his chair. The partner stands and they move into leave-taking phrases. Through a series of small movements and gestures, they have signalled each other that their need or desire to continue the conversation is ending.

Close proximity also means that physical contact is easily made and is often expected. Here a range of activities may be appropriate. Business interviews almost universally open with a handshake, a throwback to an earlier nonverbal gesture when men grasped each other's sword hand to signal that they came in peace. Children may want to be held while a parent comforts them. Latin Americans may give each other a "brazo," a hearty hug as a greeting or parting gesture.

The key elements of small numbers and close proximity with immediate feedback may be modified in some interpersonal situations. A phone conversation is a form of interpersonal communication, but while it involves a small number in close aural proximity, it eliminates all nonverbal cues with the exception of paralinguistics. When one moves to written form of communication—letters, e-mail, computer bulletin boards, notes on the refrigerator—one has eliminated both proximity and immediate feedback. These types of communication fall out of the category of interpersonal communication as it is discussed here.

Contexts of Interpersonal Communication

Interpersonal communication occurs in all the contexts of communication. Within families, interpersonal communication occurs between parents, between parents and children, between children, and between other relations. Throughout our lives, we create, sustain and leave friendships, or relationships which display a pattern of communication different from other forms of interpersonal communication. When we have health problems, we find ourselves communicating with a variety of people involved in health professions—patient service personnel, laboratory technicians, nurses, physicians, orderlies, and finally, accountants.

Professionally, our success may be due largely to the interpersonal relationships we establish within and without our organizations. In a typical day, an office worker will move through a series of greetings, leave-takings, conversations, information interviews, persuasive interviews, and telephone calls. The success at these various activities will depend largely on the person's interpersonal skills.

Interpersonal Communication Skills

Listening

Definition of Listening

When we think of interpersonal communication, we most often think of what we need to do as senders rather than as receivers. Before we can respond appropriately to others, we need to judge the sender, the message, and our possible responses. To do that, we need to exercise good listening skills. Listening, as we define it, is *paying thoughtful attention to the verbal and nonverbal cues of others.*

Listening for Ideas

In listening for ideas, we are trying to gather facts or follow a line of logical thinking. Listening for ideas is the kind of listening that students do as part of the learning process, the kind of listening patients do when doctors explain ailments and medications, and the kind of listening customers do as a mechanic details what is wrong with the car. Here the main goal is the comprehension and retention of information.

To aid the process and listen well, one can *concentrate on the message.* Distractions to good listening are many. We may be thinking of an upcoming vacation rather than attending to the professor's lecture. We may work in an environment with high noise levels. In crowded offices, the conversations around us may distract us. The best course of action in these cases is

not to think of the distractions but rather to devote full attention to the message. Concentrating on eliminating the distractions will only create yet another distraction.

Another hindrance to good listening is when a person tries to take in an extended message word for word. Instead, the person should *listen for major ideas.* The major ideas are the foundations of messages. In attending to a lecture, one should pay attention to the main points. In listening to directions about how to reach a given destination, the turns and landmarks become the heart of the message. When the major points are not comprehended, the message will not make sense.

One helpful way to retain information is to *link new knowledge with old knowledge.* If one knows how a carburetor works, it will be easy to learn the functions of a fuel injection system by looking at the similarities and differences between the two systems. If one can transfer the concept of "trump" from one card game to another, the learning time is shortened for the new game.

Tying ideas together can work in other ways as well. One can *use memory devices* to aid the retention of information. People tend to remember visual images more readily than words. Hence, one way to remember a word or concept is to connect the words with an image. The communication term, "feedback," could be recalled by, say, the picture of a small child pushing away his plate. The child would be giving his "feed back" and at the same time illustrating the verbal and nonverbal responses that allow a communicator to adjust future communica-

▲ **Figure 5.2.** An easy way to improve listening for facts is to take notes. (Dawe)

tion. Admittedly, the idea is obvious, even silly, but oftentimes the sillier or more bizarre the image, the easier it is to remember.

Some memory aids require the receiver to provide feedback to the sender. One simple act is to *ask for a repetition of an idea or ask for clarification.*

For accurate listening, one must also be careful not to be too hasty in responding. Often, it is a good idea to *hear the person out* before reacting. Pouncing on the information without hearing the complete message may reduce the amount of information conveyed and unnecessarily complicate the communication.

In talking with her financial aid counselor, Sandy Hargrave heard the counselor say that Hargraves's student loan might be reduced. Hargrave immediately began to object. After several interchanges, the counselor was finally able to follow up the original remark by telling Hargrave that other and better funding was now available.

A final aid to listening for ideas may sound simple, but *taking notes* provides the listener with a concrete collection of information that can be referred to for reference and memorization.

Listening for Feelings

Besides being attentive to facts, good listening is also attentive to feelings. Here comprehension of details is not so important as recognizing what the other person is going through. "My car won't start" may be a statement of fact, but it is also the kind of statement that will carry an emotional message as well. The feeling could be frustration if the intent is "So I missed my French exam, and I'll have to go through the hassle of talking to the instructor and setting up another time." The statement could convey amusement if it means "I now have the excuse I wanted so I don't have to go to work." Other possibilities would include despondency ("Everything else is going wrong in my life, why not my car as well?") or contemplation ("Maybe I should think about buying a new car.").

To respond effectively, one must pay close attention not only to the words but also to the nonverbal cues. The rise, fall, and inflections of pitch may signal the speaker's feelings as may the volume and speed of the statement. Physical cues may also indicate a person's state. A smile can contradict a seemingly serious statement. Eye blinking, hand movements, or fidgeting may signal the true emotional state of a person who claims, "I don't mind talking about this at all."

Verbal responses will, of course, also signal a person's state. Often though, a person may not come out with a direct statement of feeling such as "I am having a bad semester." Instead, the person may make an observation or indirect statement such as "I wish I could start this semester all over again." In some cases, the purported source of distress may have only the slightest connection with the true problem.

Karl Harper was studying in his room when his roommate came in, threw his coat on the bed, looked around, and began complaining, "Why do you always have to have the window closed? You can't even breathe in this place, it's so stuffy." Karl waited until his roommate had finished talking, then began asking questions about how his day had gone. It turned out that the roommate had been in a car accident and then, when asked to produce his driver's license, discovered that he had lost his wallet. The closed window simply happened to be the nearest target for his anger.

Sorting out the messages a person is sending may be a difficult task. A useful question to ask in these situations is "What would I be feeling if I were saying and doing these things?" (Bolton 57). This response allows people to begin with a known entity, themselves, and apply what they know to an unknown entity, the other person. Even if the first interpretation is not totally accurate, this approach may at least start someone in the right direction. After that, the person can adjust and work toward the most accurate interpretation.

Listening for facts and feelings provides us with a basis for interacting with other people. Good listening skills enhance communication in a variety of settings: in conversation, in comforting, and in conflict resolution.

Conversation

The Nature of Conversation

Conversation is the *informal exchange of opinions and information in which a major component of*

▲ **Figure 5.3.** Conversation is communication for the enjoyment of the interchange. (Dawe)

the process is the pleasure derived from the communication. Conversation is, in some ways, communication for its own sake. Conversations may impart information or allow the parties to express their feelings, but the primary goal of conversation is the pleasurable exchange of talk, no matter what the topic. As such, conversation is a major ingredient of any number of relationships. One former F.B.I, agent even said that he used conversation as a way of encouraging confession or disclosure of information. In an investigative interview, he said, the first thing to do with the interviewee is to "get him talking about anything" (Wilt).

While at first glance, conversation seems to be only "making small talk," we discover on a closer examination that it is a form of communication that involves a number of subtleties. Opening and maintaining conversations demands that we find appropriate ways to approach other people and that together we find a pattern of talk that is mutually acceptable. Having opened the conversation, we must find ways to keep it going. Not only does this process demand attention to the responses of conversational partners, but it also demands our creativity as we phrase responses. Finally, we need to find ways to break off the conversation and part company.

Beyond the basics, our conversational style may indicate not only our thoughts and feelings but may also provide cues as to how our remarks are to be interpreted by our conversational partners.

Person A: "I left my keys in the car."

How is Person B to respond to this remark? The response will depend on a number of contextual factors. A may be recounting a bad incident during the day. In this case, B's response would probably be along the lines of, "What did you do to get into your car?" On the other hand, A's hands may be full with packages and is making a request of B so that B's best response is, "I'll get them for you" (Jacobs and Jackson). Whether the statement is interpreted as a report or a request is determined by the context.

Another of the subtleties we must master is turn-taking, a kind of communicative dance that determines who will speak when and what will be the relationship between the conversational partners. How turn taking is managed may determine who controls the direction of the conversation, how we are perceived in the conversation, and how topics will be treated (Lerner; Palmer; Drummond; Mandelbaum).

Through a series of different cues, we may also signal a conversational partner that our remarks are not to be interpreted at face value, but rather taken to be a form of verbal play (Glen and Knapp).

> **Person A:** "Did you remember that we are running together today at noon?"
> **Person B:** "I had forgotten. Thanks for jogging my memory."

When we engage in conversation, we involve ourselves in a process of communication that can be not only entertaining but also subtle. Conversation is a basic ingredient of relationships and mastering conversational skills is an important part of becoming a competent communicator.

Conversational Skills

The basic conversational skills upon which the subtleties rest are the abilities to initiate, maintain, and close a conversation. How well we master these activities may have a major impact on our lives. One researcher has found, for example, that people with strong feelings of loneliness have difficulty engaging in conversation and "may be perceived as poor candidates for friendship" (Bell 231).

Initiating Conversation. Opening a conversation, getting the other person to talk, is not always easy. Most of us have been in some social situation in which we wanted desperately to say something but could find no words, or if words came, they were the wrong ones and only deepened the misery or heightened the tension. At other times, though, we may find ourselves in the midst of a pleasant conversation almost without realizing it. How "openers" are phrased can set the tone for what follows.

In opening conversations, it is often helpful to remember the purpose of the opener. It is not intended to convey important information, disclose significant feelings, nor to launch a person into a long term, rewarding relationship. The purpose of a conversational opener is (1) to recognize the other party and (2) to say something that will prompt an appropriate response.

As such, *we do not need to worry about using cliches.* The subject matter of a conversational opener is oftentimes of little importance (Adler 153). Some may refrain from attempting a conversation because they can think of nothing to say that is original or significant. The truth of the matter is that most conversational openers are trite and stereotypical. Realizing that frees us to begin from what is at hand rather than trying to find unique ways to approach each individual we meet.

It is also helpful to remember that in opening conversations, *we have three basic options for topics.* People typically open conversations with remarks about themselves, about the conversational partner, or about the situation (Carnes 70). For example,

Themselves
"Hi, my name is . . . I'm a political science major."
"You won't believe what my math TA did today . . ."
"Man, am I feeling good. I finally got my schedule worked out."

The Other Person
"Whatcha up to?"
"How did you do on the chemistry exam?"
"That's a nice jacket. Where did you get it?"

The Situation
"How about this weather we're having?"

"This stuff tastes pretty good."
"Gee, Toto, this sure doesn't look like Kansas."

The three can, of course, be combined into variations which include two or even all three possibilities as in "What do you think I should do about the English paper we have to write for Thursday?"

Another helpful triad to remember in phrasing conversational openers is the subject matter of the opener. *We can state a fact, give an opinion, or express a feeling* (Adler 154–55). People can phrase these in the form of a statement or the form of a question.

Themselves—facts:
"I'm from . . ." or "Where do you think I'm from?"
The other person—opinions
"I really like the color of your jacket."
The situation—feelings
"I feel lost in a class this size", or "How do you feel about being in a class this big?"

It may also be helpful in starting conversations to remember that failures do not necessarily mean that we are poor conversationalists. Some people are less responsive than others. Some may be unavailable to talk because of the press of other demands. If a conversational opener is unsuccessful, then we should try another approach or try another person. No matter how tempting the bait, not every cast catches a fish.

Maintaining Conversation. Shortly after conversation is initiated, the first major transition arrives. After we have recognized the presence of the other person and made an opening statement or two, we shift the talk to a topic or topics which will allow us to continue, or we break off the conversation and move to a conclusion. If we wish to prolong the conversation, we have a number of avenues available to us.

One useful practice for maintaining conversation occurs before we interact with others. *We become better conversationalists by becoming more knowledgeable and potentially more interesting.* We communicate from our experiences, both personal and vicarious, and if we limit our experiences, we limit our potential areas of discussion. Being informed is a major help to our conversational skills.

Knowledge can come from general reading or specific studies. Being informed about current events, be they international, national, or local, can easily provide material for talk. Staying informed on controversies and issues allows us to make intelligent responses and to ask good questions. We can also do background study for talking with specific people. Perhaps we have been invited to a dinner party and we know one of the guests is a nuclear engineer. Perhaps we will be asked to entertain a campus visitor from Indonesia. Perhaps we have a first date with someone we know is from a rural area and we are urbanites. A few minutes in the library reading encyclopedia or magazine articles about "Nuclear engineering," "Indonesia," or "Agriculture" will provide us with a source of comments and questions.

Another practice useful for maintaining conversations is *paying attention to the stories we hear.* One of our basic human impulses is to recount events in a way that engages the attention of others. Stories may be jokes, but they do not have to be. Some stories are sobering, others scary, and still others whimsical. People enjoy hearing a well told story, even if it is only a minute or two in length. Honing our story-telling skills provides us with another element to add to our conversations.

Once conversation is engaged, it can be sustained by *making responses appropriate to what is being said.* When one person responds to another with a *non sequitur,* the conversation is likely to come to an abrupt halt.

Person A: What do you think we should do about our communication class small group project?"

Person B: "I have always hated lima beans."

or

Person A: "I am from Jakarta, the capitol of Indonesia."

Person B: "How do you think the Cowboys will do in their game against the Giants?"

Besides listening for ideas and tying our responses to them, we need also to be sensitive to the feelings expressed by conversational part-ners. Conversations are far more likely to be successful when people show themselves sympathetic to what the other person is expressing.

Person A: "I just broke up with my boyfriend."

Person B: "Splitting up can really hurt."

or

Person A: "I sometimes find it hard to understand the English you speak here."

Person B: "Having to take notes in a strange language in addition to learning the material must be difficult."

One of the ingredients of conversation—and other relationships as well—is that of self disclosure. We reveal facts about ourselves, our opinions, and our observations. If the revelations are well timed, they can be an encouragement to deepening the relationship whether the relationship be a first meeting or a long term relationship. We encourage conversational partners to communicate more freely when *we reveal appropriate information about ourselves.* By "appropriate information," we mean those personal facts which are in keeping with the level of the relationship. Obviously, we would not tell someone we are meeting for the first time the same kind of personal information we would reveal to our best friend.

Often, when one person reveals personal information, the other party will respond in kind. This kind of pattern is often observed in the early stages of conversations.

Person A: "I live in Owens Hall."

Person B: "I live in Earhart Hall."

or

Person A: "I did not realize how big this campus was until I started walking to all my classes."

Person B: "I think I have a quarter mile hike from my biology class to my PE class."

Another way conversations can be maintained is *by directing it into new areas.* When we have reached the limits of a topic, we introduce a second, much in the same way we would open a conversation initially. If two people have been talking about sports and have said all they wish to say about the school's football team, they switch and begin talking about the basketball team. Having talked about the industry of a country, the topic could switch to urban life, agricultural practices, the educational system, or scenic places.

A useful technique for discovering new areas of conversation and to explore established areas is to *practice question linking*. In this procedure, one listens to what the conversational partner says, then "links" the response, in the form of a question, to information the conversational partner has revealed. The first person recognizes what the partner has disclosed and uses that as the core of the response. A well phrased question acknowledges what the partner has said and suggests a continuance of the thought presented.

Person A: "I'm a junior."
Person B: "What are you majoring in (as a junior)?"
Person A: "English."
Person B: "What kind of English courses do you like best?"
Person A: "I take mostly literature courses."
Person B: "What kind of literature courses are your favorites (or least favorites)?"
Person A: "It may sound funny, but I like medieval literature."
Person B: "What kind of things did they write about in the medieval period?"

In addition to the way language is employed in a conversation, *conversations can also be encouraged by the use of nonverbal behavior*. Maintaining interpersonal distance shows that a person is interested in continuing the exchange. One can make encouraging nonverbal responses such as leaning forward, nodding, maintaining eye contact as a listener, and reflecting facially the mood of the exchange. These signal an interest in what the partner has to say and encourage continuation of the interchange.

By being attentive, both verbally and nonverbally, we can create and maintain conversations. The final part of skillful conversations is bringing them to a close.

Closing Conversations. Conversations, short or long, eventually reach ending points. The partners may have reached the end of mutually interesting topics, they may have run out of time, or their attention may be attracted in other directions. Whatever the case, the conversation is ready to be terminated. One way to finish a conversation is for both partners to stop talking and to turn and walk away. Abrupt endings, however, are seldom satisfactory. As we ease into conversation with openers, we ease out of conversation with a variety of closing techniques.

Recognizing the conversation is one way in which people may signal that they wish to move the conversation to a close. A recognition statement would be a remark along the lines of "It's been nice talking to you" or a kind of summary statement such as "You've certainly had some interesting experiences", or "I'm glad things worked out for you." These remarks bring a topic to a close and can indicate a person's desire to stop talking whereas an encouraging response such as a question or reflective comment would indicate a desire to continue.

To finish a conversation, people may also *present a pressing claim*. Here one discloses another commitment or interest that should be met, one ostensibly competing for attention with the conversation. Remarks of this kind would be statements such as, "Well, I need to be getting home," or "I guess I'd better go back to the office and deal with some more paperwork" or "You'll have to excuse me now. I have another appointment." The statement indicates diminishing attention to the conversation at hand and hence, a reason for breaking off the interchange.

Finally, *conversations often finish with some kind of farewell*. Like greetings and openers, they acknowledge the presence and significance of the partner and signal a step in the conversational process. Also like openers, their significance is not so much in the information they carry as it is in the transition they supply. "Goodbye," "See you later," or "Thanks for everything" are obvious farewells. Other kinds of statement such as admonitions or best wishes can also serve as farewells. Responses such as "Hope your car starts," "Take it easy," "Take care," and "Good luck at the store" can serve to provide the finishing touch for a conversation.

In addition to verbal signals, nonverbal signals can also provide a transition out of the conversation. We mention above nonverbal behaviors that encourage interaction. Reversing those cues can have the effect of discouraging further interaction and serve as a way for conversational partners to bring their talk to a halt.

Shifting position away from the conversational partner may indicate that a person is starting to move out of the situation. Instead of leaning forward, the person sits back in the chair or instead of facing the partner, turns sideways.

Larger scale movements such as *increasing distance* between partners may show that participants are moving away from the interchange, both literally and figuratively. The farther apart people are, the more difficult it becomes to maintain the intimacy necessary for conversation. Some may back up a few inches, finish the conversation, then walk away. Others may move through a series of retreats until they are so far apart they can communicate only by shouting, then bring the talk to a halt.

Breaking eye contact can also signal the end of a conversation. Shifting one's gaze to papers on the desk, to activity outside a window, to a passerby, or to one's watch can also signal that the conversation holds less and less attention of a participant.

Leave taking behaviors are another way in which we indicate our readiness to terminate a conversation. By "leave taking behaviors" we mean those actions which we do in preparation for exiting. We pack up our belongings; we put on our coats; we take out our car keys.

Successful conversation requires that we pay close attention to our partner's responses and that we choose verbal and nonverbal actions which supply appropriate responses. By doing so, we can engage in satisfying social communication. When the intensity of an interchange moves into realms of strong feelings, the demands on our listening and response skills increase. A common situation in which we may find ourselves called upon to respond to heightened feelings is when we are called upon to engage in comforting communication.

▲ **Figure 5.4.** Comforting is an important interpersonal communication skill.

Comforting

We are already well acquainted with comforting behavior. It is what we asked for and received as children when we were hungry, hurt, frightened, or distressed in some way. Disappointments and distress, however, do not end with childhood nor with adolescence nor with middle age. We may fail to achieve an important goal such as passing an exam, winning a scholarship, or being hired for a particular job. Our relationships may go awry. A romance comes to an end; our parents or children are having problems; we have to deal with an abrasive boss or co-workers. Our daily rounds can be the source of frustration when cars don't start, bank balances dip too low, or appliances break down.

When we encounter people in these situations, we may be called upon to provide comforting. *Comforting communication is communication "having the goal of alleviating or lessening the emotional distress felt by others"* (Burleson, "Comforting as Social Support . . ." 68).

One interesting finding from research on comforting is that in helping others, we may be helping ourselves. People who are skilled in providing comfort to others appear to be better liked and more sought after as companions than those unskilled in comforting (Burleson, "Comforting as Social Support . . ." 78; Samter and Burleson 322–23). The comforting skills of parents have implications for their children. Children raised by parents with good comforting skills are less likely to be rejected by classmates and are more prosocial than their counterparts from homes in which parents had poor comforting skills (Burleson, "Comforting Communication . . ." 93; Burleson, "Comforting as Social Support . . ." 80.)

Some people seem to have a knack for saying the right thing while others need to work to begin to offer assistance to others. Wherever people fall on the spectrum, they can still improve their skills. What we offer here are some points that may help us begin to respond to others in helpful ways.

One of the most important elements in comforting is the ability to empathize. *Empathy* is a "feeling with," an awareness of what someone else is experiencing. Empathy is not so much an intellectual awareness that another person is happy or depressed or frustrated as it is an emotional awareness of what is happening with another person. We empathize with people when we tune into their feelings and let them know that we understand what they are experiencing.

The listening done in comforting situations, then, is much more listening for feelings than listening for ideas. We may need to make sure of the facts of a situation so that we can respond better, but the most important thing is to discover what are the emotions of the other person. At times, we may have to respond to a number of different feelings and in different degrees. After a car accident, a person may feel anger at the other driver, frustration at the loss of transportation, and depression because the situation creates additional financial and emotional burdens.

Nonverbal communication can show empathy in comforting situations. Eye contact and a posture that shows attention can indicate concern for another. Facial expressions can mirror, to some extent, what the other is feeling. Touching can also communicate comfort. A hug, a pat, or a handshake can all show understanding.

In phrasing reactions to those who need comforting, it is helpful to keep in mind three goals. Effective comforting will involve communicating in a way that *acknowledges, elaborates, and legitimizes* the feelings of the other person (Burleson, "Comforting as Social Support . . ." 70).

By "acknowledge," we mean that a comforting situation calls upon a person to recognize what the partner is going through. Appropriate remarks would be along the lines of "I can see you are angry," or "You look really down," or "You seem to be under a lot of pressure."

By "elaborating," we mean that the comforter moves beyond labelling the emotion felt by the other and describes the situation in a way that demonstrates empathy and understanding. Here one might say "Considering you were kept waiting for an hour and half and then didn't even get to see the doctor, it's no wonder you're upset." One might venture "You look depressed and sad about your grandfather's illness." In responding to someone upset about the pressing number of commitments, one might say "You have a lot on your shoulders: term papers, exams, and the possibility of losing some financial aid. That's a lot to have to carry."

By "legitimizing," we mean that one comforting another communicates that it is all right to be experiencing what the partner is going through. When one offers comforting communication, one accepts the other's problem as significant. Rather than brushing the other person off, one shows interest in the partner and communicates that what the other person is experiencing is significant.

Acknowledging, elaborating, and legitimizing the feelings of another can be done in several ways. One of the first and simplest is to *show that we are available to talk.* The immediate presence of another who is willing to listen can in itself by a comfort. Sometimes a person can provide an opening to talk by describing the partner's physical state. "You look beat" may be all it takes for someone to begin talking about the rough day at work. Another useful technique is to invite the other person to talk. An obvious invitation would be "Do you want to talk about the situation?" but invitation can also be indirect, "Let's go get a cup of coffee." The interest in the problem is provided by giving "the other person time to decide whether to talk and/or what to talk about" (Bolton 41).

When the partner begins talking, *avoid attempting to argue or cajole the person out of the feelings* of the moment. Inappropriate responses would be those which fail to recognize the significance of the situation for the other person. These reactions would be such as :

▶ "I know you had a wreck, but you're not really angry or frustrated."

▶ "So you broke up after two years. You'll find somebody else and forget all about him."

▶ "Okay. You flunked the exam. That's no big deal."

If issues exist that must be decided, it is best to postpone them until the other person feels more like discussing the matter. The time to worry about filing an accident report and notifying a friend's insurance company is after the friend is over the first shock and anger of having a wreck.

Perhaps the most useful technique to use in comforting communication is to *reflect what the other person is saying*. Reflecting may sound easy at first, but in reality it is a skill that takes effort to do well. Reflecting is playing back what the other person is saying or feeling, mirroring for them what they are experiencing. To reflect is to respond in kind to what the person says of does.

Some reflecting is done nonverbally. Head nods can communicate an affirmation of what the person is saying. By saying "yes" nonverbally, a person also says, "I can see that is bad" or "I know that must hurt."

Reflecting verbally calls upon a person to empathize with the feeling and to make a statement parallel to what the other person has said. The cliché of reflection is to say, "I see. You feel (label the feeling)." While the phrase may have become something of a cliché, the basic direction is still valid. In fact, if one cannot think of anything to say, the formula works well as a starter. As one's skills increase, the reflective statement will become more sophisticated, but the basic goal is still to recognize and describe the other's feelings. The point of

reflecting is to help the other person "recognize and clarify the emotions which he feels" (Rogers 27).

Some examples of reflective responses are these:

Person A: "I don't know what I am going to do."

Person B: "You feel trapped with no outlet."

Person A: "This is awful."

Person B: "You really feel bad."

Person A: "I have to go home for my grandmother's funeral."

Person B: "It sounds like a bad time for you."

One problem to avoid with reflection is parroting rather than reflecting. Parroting is when, instead of rephrasing and clarifying a feeling, a person just says back what the partner said originally.

Person A: "I don't know what I'm going to do."

Person B: "You don't know what you are going to do."

Person A: "This is awful."

Person B: "Your situation is awful."

Dealing with someone in need of comfort may be uncomfortable at first. Wanting to do something but unsure of what to do, people may be motivated more by discomfort than charity. The above ideas will make comforting an easier process. The presence of another willing to listen is in itself a comfort. When that person can listen empathically and encouragingly, a great deal will be accomplished.

Conflict Resolution

Not all our communication situations place us in the position of being sympathetic or sharing common goals with others. Conflict is a given in human relationships. One roommate is neat and tidy while the other is messy. Parents have different views on how to discipline the children. The teachers in a school system want one set of conditions in the contract; the school board wants another. A customer buys an appliance which fails to function properly, but the dealer says the repair is not covered under the warranty.

▲ **Figure 5.5.** Handling conflict constructively is the mark of a good communicator. (Dawe)

Nature of Conflict

Conflict occurs when the feelings, interests, or ways of behaving of one person interfere with the feelings, interests, or ways of behaving of another person.

Approaching Conflict

As conflict is inevitable in human relations, the question is not whether or not to eliminate it, but rather how to deal with it in the most positive way. Depending on how it is handled, the presence of conflict in a relationship can be constructive or destructive. Resolved conflict can strengthen and maintain a relationship while ongoing, unresolved conflict can weaken and possibly destroy the relationship.

In approaching conflict, people have several options. Which option is the best will depend on a number of factors such as the people involved, the importance of each person's goals in the conflict, the amount of time available to solve the conflict, and influences from outside the relationship.

Approaches to Conflict

At one end of the spectrum is *avoidance.* Here the party or parties stay away from conflict if at all possible. When bothered by what another person says or does, they keep their feelings to themselves or leave the scene.

Beth Donaldson is from a small town in Indiana. At lunch one day, her roommate introduces her to Sarah White who is from New York City. Throughout their conversation, Sarah describes her impressions of life in the Midwest stressing how provincial and boring it must be to live in a small town. Beth is offended at the attacks on her background, but rather than saying anything to contradict her, Beth remains silent through the meal.

Like all approaches to conflict management, avoidance may be appropriate in some situations, inappropriate in others. At a family holiday gathering, parties may stay off topics such as religion or politics which they know will be divisive. Instead, they look for points of mutual agreement. At other times, avoidance leads to deteriorating relationships. One study of couples in therapy revealed that "avoidance, indirectness, and decreased involvement" characterized the behavior of couples unable or unwilling to maintain their marriages (Courtright et. al., 429).

Capitulation is another approach to conflict similar to avoidance. Here one states one's views, but then gives up the effort for a variety of reasons. Since little accommodation is made to the views and feelings of the capitulating party, the solution may cause resentment further along.

Phil Adams stops at the grocery store with his three year old son. As they go through the checkout line, the son spots the candy bars and asks for one. Phil says, "No, it's almost dinner time." The child continues to plead and beg. Phil continues to say, "No." The child finally starts to whine and cry loudly. "Oh, all right," Phil says and hands the child a candy bar. When Phil gets home, he gets into an argument with his wife over his giving the child the candy.

Often closely linked to capitulation is *coercion.* Here one party is forced into a course of action that one does not want to take. Coercion involves the threat, real or implied, of harm that will come to a person if that person does not submit to the requests of the other party. As might be imagined, coercive resolutions to conflicts leave the coerced party feeling misused and resentful and hinder the creation of a satisfactory solution (Tutzauer 429).

One of the most famous of coercive strategies to resolve a conflict occurs in the book and movie, *The Godfather.* The Godfather, a Mafia crime boss, Vito Corleone, is having a disagreement with a band leader who has a friend of

Corleone's under contract. Corleone wants the band leader to sign a contract releasing his friend from the terms of the old contract. The band leader refuses. Corleone then makes him "an offer you can't refuse." He takes out a pistol and tells the band leader, "In one minute, either your signature or your brains are going to be on that contract." The band leader signs (Puzo 42).

Another approach to conflict in relationships is *fighting*. Here both parties may make clear their viewpoints, but instead of working toward a mutually acceptable goal, they maintain their positions without giving ground and hammer at each other until one gives up or they separate. Again, little accommodation is made for the feelings and ideas of the parties, and the final outcome may be only a temporary stay to hostilities.

Larry and Jessica McGovern are arguing about their finances and whether or not to buy a new car. She wants to wait for a year and buy a mid-priced car. He wants to buy a luxury car now. He argues that he needs the car to impress his real estate clients. She argues that the money is better invested. One afternoon, without telling or asking her, he comes home driving a brand new Lincoln Town Car. The next day, she transfers to their checking account a sum equal to the cost of the car. She goes to a jewelry store and uses the money to buy two diamond rings.

Sometimes, the best approach to handling a conflict is *separation*. Here the parties "agree to disagree." Realizing that they cannot find a mutually satisfying solution to the present situation, they part company.

After graduating from college and working for a while, Patrick Larson agrees to go to work in the family business, a small furniture manufacturing plant. He rapidly takes on more and more responsibility. As his role becomes more important in the company, he increasingly finds himself in conflict with the president of the company, his mother. Finally, it becomes clear that they have different ideas on directions for the company and both want to have the final word in major decisions. They argue at work, and their personal relationship is becoming more and more distant. Finally, Larson de-

cides that his personal relationship with his mother is more important than his work in the company. He leaves the family business and finds employment elsewhere.

By far the best approach handling conflict is *cooperative conflict resolution*. Here the parties maintain contact instead of breaking apart. Through *negotiation*, they explore the situation and discover a mutually satisfying solution to the conflict. Negotiation is communication in which the parties confer with each other "so as to arrive at the settlement of some matter" (Webster's Seventh New Collegiate Dictionary, 1967). The "some matter" may be as trivial as "which child sits in which seat" on a family trip or may be an international problem such as nuclear disarmament.

Sometimes, the solution involves *compromise* in which each party accomplishes some of its original goals while giving up others. ("I'll let you sit by the window if you give me your comic book.") At other times, no compromise may be needed as the parties discover ways for each party to accomplish its goal. ("On the way to Indianapolis, I'll sit by the window and you get the comic book, and coming back, we'll switch.")

Conflict Negotiation

When involved in a conflict, people can resort to any of the methods discussed above. If, though, one wishes to negotiate a cooperative resolution to the conflict, communication research indicates some helpful guidelines.

Perhaps the hardest part of engaging in cooperative conflict resolution is to *realize that we are part of the problem*. The tendency—indeed, the almost inevitable reaction—is to see the other person as the sole source of the problem. People in conflict situations are inclined to attribute the source of the conflict to the conflict partner (Sillars 191) and to judge themselves the more competent communicator in the situation (Canary and Spitzberg 146). Seeing a conflict as a two person problem rather than a one person problem can help negotiation start and continue profitably.

Another temptation is to phrase the problem in terms of the other person's personality or a character flaw. "You're the messiest person I have ever know. Your family is messy. Your brother is messy. And now I have to live with all your mess. Can't you even take your dirty dishes to the sink?"

A more productive approach is to *look to behavior, not personality* (Donohue 10). Concentrating on the behavior we would like to see changed moves the conflict into a realm in which change is more easily accomplished. Finding a new personality is an impossibility. Picking up a dirty dish and carrying it to the sink is a feat that is easily accomplished.

Related to looking to behavior is the suggestion that people in conflicts *talk to the issue, not the person.* Instead of labelling the conflict partner negatively, a person talks about what is personally bothersome in the situation.

Greg Wilson's girlfriend is supposed to pick him up after his last class on Friday and drive him to the body shop where his car is being repaired. She is a half–hour late. Worse, the agreed meeting spot is in the open, and it is raining. By the time he sees her car, he is really angry.

To express his anger, he could say, "Where have you been? You're always late. Did it ever occur to you that I would be soaking wet waiting in the rain? Why can't you ever do what you say you're going to do?"

He could also react, "I am really angry I had to wait for thirty minutes in the rain." His statement is a strong expression and addresses what he sees as the main point of contention, her tardiness. At the same time, though, it does not attack the other person and it leaves her room to respond. Their chances of a quick resolution to the conflict are much greater if he takes the second course of action.

It is also helpful in conflicts to *describe how you see the issue affecting you* (Bolton 221–22; Adler 187–90, 219–27). Here the person talks about the situation in personal terms instead of directing accusations or commands at the other person. One also brings out the consequences of the other person's action, consequences that the person might not realize. In Greg's case, he might add, "Now I'm going to have to wear wet clothes for the next hour."

One would also hope that in addition to describing his feelings, Greg would also work to *see the other person's position in the contested matter*

(Fisher and Ury 24; Bolton 220–24). Seeing the other person's position is not just a courtesy. Those people in conflict situations who can see the other person's perspective are more efficient negotiators (Pappa and Pood 418). In Greg's case, it would involve two different approaches. Before she arrived, he could consider what reasons she might have for being late: car problems, traffic jams, a late customer at work. Once she picks him up, he could listen while she tells her side of the story.

To find out more information about the situation, people may do well to *ask questions instead of making statements* (Tutzauer and Roloff 376). Instead of making judgments about the situation, here one explores the conflict situation by allowing the other party to express himself. Questions also soften a request and sound less threatening than commands. Instead of "Tell me why you were late," one would do better to ask, "Why were you late?" While "I want to know why you bought that child a candy bar just before dinner," gets at the point, "Why did you buy him a candy bar just before dinner?" does not sound as demanding nor as argumentative.

As conflicts give rise to strong emotions, it is also a good idea in conflict resolution to *allow for feelings.* Partners in a conflict must find some way to control their own emotions and to deal with outbursts of the other. One good rule of thumb is, "If it feels good, don't do it." An emotional outburst may be very enjoyable. To cut loose and tell the other person off may be a great release, but it is also likely to be shortlived and counterproductive. Anger, typically, begets anger. A better approach to the situation is the old adage, "A soft answer turns away wrath."

Ways can be found for handling emotions likely to get out of hand. One way is simply to declare a break. If a situation is so hot that everyone is angry and the communication unproductive, a time out may be in order. After a pause, a walk around the block, or some refreshment, people may be better equipped for productive negotiation.

Another approach is for a person to vent emotions but outside of the conflict situation. A third party who can be sympathetic and not become upset at what one says can be a big help (Bolton 24).

Feelings can be channeled by conflict partners setting guidelines for the conflict (Fisher and Ury 31–32). Football players know that they will batter each other up and down the field, but they also know the limits of the battering. Clipping, grabbing facemasks, "crackback" blocks, and other assaults are illegal and will result in punishments for the offender's team. Similarly, in conflict situations, people may establish what is acceptable behavior and what is not: "Shouting is all right, but we do not call each other names" or "We don't bring up problems until we have had dinner and a chance to unwind from the day."

In the search for a solution to a conflict, it may be helpful to *separate the solution from the decision* (Fisher and Ury 62–63). If one person takes a stand, it is likely the other person will take just as strong a stance. A more productive approach would be to put forth tentative solutions and discuss those. The approach is to say, "Here is one possibility; here is another; here is a third. Let's talk about them and see which one will work best for us."

Arriving at a solution may involve a great deal of communication, and implicit in communication is give and take. In searching for a way out of a conflict, people must *be prepared to compromise.* Each may need to give up some of its original goals or ideas. The starkest kind of compromise is a sales situation in which the dealer wants $X for a car, the customer is prepared to pay $Y, and the final price is $Z, halfway between $X and $Y. The "split the difference" approach is not, though, the only way to compromise. The dealer may offer more money for the customer's trade-in, may offer options or delete options to meet a price, or may offer special financing or a rebate. The customer may change the list of desired options, settle for a different model, or sell the present car instead of trading it in.

Successful conflict resolution is not always easy. It demands self-control, imagination, and consideration for the other party, none of which are simple matters. Our personal involvement in conflicts makes the task even more difficult as we are not third party bystanders but participants with our own feelings and desires. By understanding the nature of conflict and by communicating productively, we can ease the task of finding good solutions.

Conclusion

Interpersonal communication involves us with others on a personal level. Our verbal and nonverbal behavior, used in a variety of ways, create and sustain our relationships. Four of the major skills we use to foster relationships are listening, conversation, comforting, and conflict resolution. Conversation is communication for the pleasure of exchanging views and feelings with others. Comforting is using communication to alleviate the problems of another. Conflict resolution is working through a situation in which we find ourselves at odds with others.

Guidelines exist for all these activities, but practice is necessary to do them well. Sensitivity and judgment are needed to know when and how to use different styles of communication. Capable communicators are those who can respond with insight, empathy, and clarity. Communication offers challenges in even daily contacts, but when met, the challenges lead us to enriched and rewarding lives.

• • • Discussion Questions

1. What situations can you think of that would be classified as interpersonal communication?

2. How would you think that language in an interpersonal situation would differ from language in a public setting? How would it differ from the language in a magazine or newspaper article? Why would the language of interpersonal communication be different from that of other modes of communication?

3. What kinds of actions contribute nonverbally in interpersonal communication?

4. What situations have you been in where listening for ideas was important?

5. How does listening for feelings differ from listening for ideas?

6. In what instances have you found it difficult to carry on a conversation?

7. What kind of person do you want to talk to when you are having problems? What makes you want to talk with this person?

8. What kind of conflict situations have you found yourself in? How were the conflicts handled badly? How were the conflicts handled well?

• • • Sources and References

Adler, R. A. *Confidence in Communication: A Guide to Assertive Social Skills.* New York: Holt, Rinehart and Winston, 1977.

Alberts, J. K. "Perceived Effectiveness of Couples' Conversational Complaints." *Communication Studies* 40 (1989): 280–92.

Beach, Wayne. "Forward: Sequential Organization of Conversational Activities." *Western Journal of Speech Communication* 53 (1989): 85–90.

Bell, Robert A. "Conversational Involvement and Loneliness." *Communication Monographs* 52 (1985): 218–35.

Berryman-Fink, Cynthia and Claire C. Brunner. "The Effects of Sex of Source and Target on Interpersonal Conflict Management Styles." *The Southern Speech Communication Journal* (1987): 38–48.

Bies, Robert J., Debra L. Shapiro, and Larry L. Cummings. "Causal Accounts and Managing Organizational Conflict: Is It Enough to Say It's Not My Fault?" *Communication Research* 15 (1988): 381–99.

Bulton, R. *People Skills*. Englewood Cliffs, New Jersey: Prentice-Hall, 1979.

Burleson, Brant R. "Comforting as Social Support: Relational Consequences of Supportive Behaviors." *Personal Relationship and Social Support*. Ed. Steve Ducks. London: Sage Publications, 1990.

Burleson, Brant R. "Comforting Communication." *Communication by Children and Adults: Social Cognitive and Strategic Processes*. Eds. Howard E. Sypher and James L. Applegate. Beverly Hills, California: Sage Publications, 1984.

Burleson, Brant R. "Social Cognition, Empathic Motivation, and Adults' Comforting Strategies." *Human Communication Research* 10 (1983): 295–304.

Burleson, Brant R. and Wendy Samter. "Consistencies in Theoretical and Naive Evaluations of Comforting Messages." *Communication Monographs* 52 (1985): 103–23.

Burleson, Brant R. and Wendy Samter. "Individual Differences in the Perception of Comforting Messages: An Exploratory Investigation." *Central States Speech Journal* 36 (1985): 39–50.

Burleson, Brant R. "The Production of Comforting Messages: Social-Cognitive Foundations." *Journal of Language and Social Psychology* 4 (1985): 253–73.

Burrell, Nancy A., William A. Donohue, and Mike Allen. "Gender-Based Perceptual Biases in Mediation." *Communication Research* 15 (1988): 447–70.

Canary, Daniel J. and Brian H. Spitzberg. "Attribution Biases and Associations between Conflict Strategies and Competence Outcomes." *Communication Monographs* 57 (1990): 139–51.

Canary, Daniel J., Ellen M. Cunningham, and Michael J. Cody. "Goal Types, Gender, and Locus of Control in Managing Interpersonal Conflict." *Communication Research* 15 (1988): 426–46.

Courtright, John A., Frank E. Millar, L. Edna Rogers, and Dennis Bagarozzi. "Interaction Dynamics of Relational Negotiation: Reconciliation versus Termination of Distress Relationships." *Western Journal of Speech Communication* (1990): 429–53.

Donohue, William A., Mike Allen, and Nancy Burrell. "Mediator Communicative Competency." *Communication Monographs* 55 (1988): 104–19.

Drummond, Kent. "A Backward Glance at Interruptions." *Western Journal of Speech Communication* 53 (1989): 150–166.

Ewbank, H. L. "The Rhetoric of Conversation in America: 1776–1828." *The Southern Speech Communication Journal* 53 (1987): 49–64.

Fisher, Roger and William Ury. *Getting to Yes: Negotiating Without Giving In*. New York: Penguin Books, 1983.

Garner, Alan. *Conversationally Speaking*. New York: McGraw-Hill, 1981.

Glenn, Phillip J. "Initiating Shared Laughter in Multi-Party Conversations." *Western Journal of Speech Communication* 53 (1989): 127–49.

Glenn, Phillip J. and Mark L. Knapp. "The Interactive Framing of Play in Adult Conversations." *Communication Quarterly* 35 (1987): 48–66.

Hopper, Robert. "Speech in Telephone Openings: Emergent Interaction v. Routines." *Western Journal of Speech Communication* 53 (1989): 178–94.

Infante, Dominic A., Teresa Chandler, Jill E. Rudd, and Elizabeth A. Shannon. "Verbal Aggression in Violent and Nonviolent Marital Disputes." *Communication Quarterly* 38 (1990): 361–71.

Jacobs, Scott and Sally Jackson. "Strategy and Structure in Conversational Influence Attempts." *Communication Monographs* 50 (1983): 285–304.

Jones, Tricia S. "Phase Structures in Agreement and No-Agreement Mediation." *Communication Research* 15 (1988): 470–95.

Knapp, Mark L., Roderick P. Hart, Gustav W. Friedrich, and Gary Shulman. "The Rhetoric of Goodbye: Verbal and Nonverbal Correlates of Human Leave-Taking. *Communication Monographs* 60 (1973): 182–98.

Lerner, Gene H. "Notes on Overlap Management in Conversation: The Case of Delayed Completion." *Western Journal of Speech Communication* 53 (1989): 167–177.

Mandelbaum, Jenny. "Interpersonal Activities in Conversational Storytelling." *Western Journal of Speech Communication* 53 (1989): 114–27.

Maynard, Douglas M. "Perspective-Display Sequences in Conversation." *Western Journal of Speech Communication* 53 (1989): 91–114.

Millar, Frank E., L. Edna Rogers, and Janet Beavin Bavelas. "Identifying Patterns of Verbal Conflict in Interpersonal Dyads." *Western Journal of Speech Communication* 48 (1984): 231–46.

Palmer, Mark T. "Controlling Conversations: Turns, Topics and Interpersonal Control." *Communication Monographs* 56 (1989): 1–18.

Papa, Michael and Elizabeth J. Natalie. "Gender, Strategy Selection, and Discussion Satisfaction in Interpersonal Conflict." *Western Journal of Speech Communication* 53 (1989): 260–72.

Papa, Michael and Elliott A. Pood. "Coorientational Accuracy and Differentiation in the Management of Conflict." *Communication Research* 15 (1988): 400–425.

Patterson, C. H. *Theories of Counseling and Psychotherapy.* Fourth ed. New York: Harper and Row, Publishers, 1986.

Pearson, Judy Cornelia. *Gender and Communication.* Dubuque, Iowa: William C. Brown, Publishers, 1985.

Putnam, Linda L. and Joseph Folger. "Communication, Conflict, and Dispute Resolution: The Study of Interaction and the Development of Conflict Theory." *Communication Research* 15 (1988): 349–59.

Rawlins, William K. *Friendship Matters: Communication, Dialectics, and the Life Course.* New York: Aldine de Gruyter, 1992.

Rawlins, William K. "Openness as Problematic in Ongoing Friendships: Two Conversational Dilemmas." *Communication Monographs* 50 (1983): 1–13.

Rogers, Carl A. *Client-Centered Therapy: Its Current Practice, Implications, and Theory.* Boston: Houghton Mifflin Company. 1951.

Samter, Wendy and Brant R. Burleson. "Cognitive and Motivational Influences on Spontaneous Comforting Behavior." *Contemporary Perspectives on Interpersonal Communication.* Eds. S. Petronio, J. K. Alberts, M. L. Hect, and J. Buley. Madison, Wisconsin: Brown and Benchmark (1993): 297–316.

Samter, Wendy and Brant Burleson. "Evaluations of Communication Skills as Predictors of Peer Acceptance and a Group Living Situation." *Communication Studies* 41 (1990): 311–25.

Samter, Wendy, Brant R. Burleson, and Lori Basden Murphy. "Comforting Conversations: The Effects of Strategy Type on Evaluations of Messages and Message Producers." *The Southern Speech Communication Journal* 52 (1987): 263–84.

Sereno, Kenneth K., Melinda Welch, and David Braaten. "Interpersonal Conflict: Effects of Variations in Manner of Expressing Anger and Justification for Anger Upon Perceptions of Appropriateness, Competence, and Satisfaction." *Journal of Applied Communication Research* 15 (1987): 128–43.

Sillars, Alan L. "Attributions and Communication in Roommate Conflicts." *Communication Monographs* 47 (1980): 180–201.

Tannen, Deborah. "Spoken and Written Narrative in English and Greek." *Coherence in Spoken and Written Discourse.* Ed. Deborah Tannan. Norwood, New Jersey: Ablex Publishing Corp., 1984. 21–41.

Tutzauer, Frank and Michael E. Roloff. "Communication Processes Leading to Integrative Agreements: Three Paths of Joint Benefits." *Communication Research* 15 (1988): 360–80.

Waln, Virginia G. "Questions in Interpersonal Conflict: Participant and Observer Perceptions." *The Southern Speech Communication Journal* 49 (1984): 277–89.

Wilt, Frederick. Conversation with the author.

Witteman, Hal. "Interpersonal Problem Solving; Problem Conceptualization and Communication Use." *Communication Monographs* 55 (1988): 336–59.

Name _____ Section _____ Date _____

Interpersonal Communication

1. How is interpersonal communication defined?

   _____

   _____

2. What is dyadic communication?

   _____

   _____

3. When communicators are in close proximity, what does that mean?

   _____

   _____

4. What is characteristic of the language used in interpersonal communication?

   _____

   _____

5. How important is the role of feedback in interpersonal communication versus in public speaking?

   _____

6. What is listening?

   _____

   _____

7. While listening for facts or ideas, it is advisable to practice good listening skills. List seven suggestions for good listening.

   1. _____

   2. _____

   3. _____

   4. _____

   5. _____

   6. _____

7. _____

8. How can you listen for feelings?

   _____

   _____

9. How is conversation distinguished from other types of communication?

   _____

   _____

10. What is the two-fold purpose of a conversational opener?

    1. _____

    2. _____

11. What are the three basic options for topics in conversational openings?

    1. _____

    2. _____

    3. _____

12. In what three ways can subject matter be treated in openings?

    1. _____

    2. _____

    3. _____

13. Seven suggestions are given for helping to maintain a conversation once it has been initiated. List those suggestions.

    1. _____

    2. _____

    3. _____

    4. _____

    5. _____

    6. _____

    7. _____

14. What is question linking?

   _____

   _____

15. Suggest four different ways you can close a conversation.

   1. _____

   2. _____

   3. _____

   4. _____

16. What is comforting communication?

   _____

17. What is empathy?

   _____

18. How is comforting communication distinguished from conversation?

   _____

   _____

19. What is meant by elaborating?

   _____

20. What is meant by legitimizing?

   _____

21. What three things can you do to meet the goals of acknowledging, elaborating and legitimizing in comforting conversation?

   1. _____

   2. _____

   3. _____

22. When does conflict occur?

   _____

23. The text lists five reactions to conflict which are generally not productive in solving the conflict. What are they?

    1. _____

    2. _____

    3. _____

    4. _____

    5. _____

24. Cooperative conflict resolution can be achieved through negotiation. What is negotiation?

    _____

    _____

    _____

25. Communication research indicates some helpful guidelines for cooperative resolution to conflict. What are the nine suggestions listed?

    1. _____

    2. _____

    3. _____

    4. _____

    5. _____

    6. _____

    7. _____

    8. _____

Name _____ Section _____ Date _____

Conversation Stoppers Exercise

The conversational remarks below are followed by inappropriate responses: 1) tell what is wrong
with the inappropriate response, and 2) phrase a better response.

1. "Tell me about yourself."
   "There's not much to tell."

2. "What happened at school today?"
   "Nothing much."

3. "I'm from _____."
   "I went through there once. It looked real run down."

4. "I just bought a Fiat."
   Why did you buy a loser like that?"

5. "Boy, do I feel good. I got an *A* in my Shakespeare class."
   "Big deal."

6. "I have to get a good job this summer."
   "My family has enough money that I don't have to work."

7. "I think that's the best Chinese restaurant in town."
   "Chinese food—yuk!"

8. "What are you majoring in?"
   "High level nuclear physics. It's not something you could understand."

9. "Hot enough for you?"
   "No. I'm seriously thinking of moving to Death Valley."

10. "What did you think about last night's game?"
     "I don't go to the games. I think basketball is dumb."

11. "That was a great movie, wasn't it?"
     "If you say so."

12. "Pretty day, isn't it?"
     "It's supposed to rain this afternoon."

13. "Look at my engagement ring."
     "That's a small stone."

14. "I lost ten pounds."
     "You still look chunky."

15. "How do you like my new shoes?"
     "I don't think that style looks good on feet as large as yours."

People Search

Find someone in this class who meets one of the criteria. Write down the person's name. Then discover something you have in common with this person other than attending college and being in this class. You may not use the same person for more than one item. Find Someone Who

1. knows the capital of Venezuela:
   We have in common:

2. has blue eyes:
   We have in common:

3. knows how to ride a horse:
   We have in common:

4. is from Illinois:
   We have in common:

5. has sung in a choir:
   We have in common:

6. likes Mexican food:
   We have in common:

7. can juggle:
   We have in common:

8. was in a high school dance troupe:
   We have in common:

9. can't stand professional wrestling:
   We have in common:

10. traveled outside the U.S. this past year:
    We have in common:

11. can drive a tractor:
    We have in common:

12. knows the chemical formula for sulphuric acid:
    We have in common:

Name _____ Section _____ Date _____

Comforting Responses Exercise

For each of these statements choose what you think would be the most comforting response. Tell why you think that response is the best. If none of the responses seem appropriate, write one of your own.

1. "I just got my grades. My GPA isn't high enough to get into the program I want."
   A. You need to study harder.
   B. Some people are smart enough for that field, and others aren't.
   C. How high a GPA do you need?
   D. That's tough to deal with.

2. "My car broke down in the middle of a busy intersection. Everyone was honking and shouting at me. I had to have the car towed to a shop. Then they told me it would cost eight hundred dollars to have it fixed."
   A. I kept telling you to have that funny noise checked.
   B. What did the shop say was wrong with it?
   C. You've really had a bad day.
   D. It could be worse.

3. "I feel so nervous about giving this speech."
   A. Getting up in front of a group can be intimidating.
   B. Just cool it. Chill out.
   C. Why do you think you're so nervous?
   D. Giving speeches is easy. I've never had any problems with them.

4. "I don't know how I'm going to get all this work done."
   A. You need to develop better time management skills.
   B. You sound as if you're really feeling the pressure.
   C. Why have you let yourself get so behind?
   D. Is there anything I can do to help you?

5. "I feel so stupid. The cashier shortchanged me and I just stood there and took it."
   A. It's only money.
   B. You have eyes. You have a brain. Count it yourself next time.
   C. I've done the same thing. I felt dumb, too.
   D. How much did you come up short?

6. "My folks just called and told me my dog died."
   A. Dogs' life expectancies are shorter than humans'. You just have to be prepared for these things.
   B. You feel as if you just lost an old friend?
   C. Dogs are dogs. You can always get another one.
   D. You haven't lived at home for three years. What's the big deal?

7. "_____ said something to me that really hurts my feelings."
   A. Just remember, "Sticks and stones may break my bones, but words can never hurt me."
   B. Call him up and tell him off.
   C. Really stabbed you, huh?
   D. What did he say?

8. "I let my group down in our presentation"
   A. The way you've been acting lately, I'm not surprised.
   B. You feel you failed them?
   C. From what you've told me, they're all idiots anyway. Don't worry about it.
   D. You never were much good at making presentations.

9. "You would never understand."
   A. Of course I would. I have taken a communication class.
   B. If you're going to be secretive, we're not going to get anywhere.
   C. Maybe I will, maybe I won't.
   D. Try me.

10. "My roommate is the most incredible slob. I can't stand living with her."
    A. Sounds as if you have a real mess to contend with.
    B. You're just compulsive.
    C. Use better judgment the next time you pick a roommate.
    D. You could solve the problem easily enough. Just clean up for both of you.

Name _____ Section _____ Date _____

Communication and Conflict Exercise

Following are descriptions of three situations, each viewed from two different perspectives. You will be assigned one case version to role play. In class discussion, describe the communication problem that is a source of the conflict. How do you think people involved would act? How could the conflict have been prevented? How can the conflict be resolved?

Conflict Roles I

Case 1 You are a twenty-two year old student, a senior living at home while you complete the student teaching requirement for your degree. As you leave in the morning, you tell your parents, "My co-operating teacher and I are going to a workshop after school." Following school you drive the seventy-five miles to the workshop, after which you and your cooperating teacher have a late dinner and drive back. You arrive home at about midnight.

Case 2 You have a dental appointment at 3:00 p.m. When you try to start your car, you discover that the battery is dead. You go back to your apartment building to seek your neighbor's help. You and your neighbor are good friends. You knock, but nobody answers. However, you discover that the door is unlocked. You remember that this is the hour that your neighbor jogs. You have borrowed your neighbor's car before, so you go in, take the car keys off the counter and borrow the car. You come back an hour later, your jaw full of novocaine and knock on your neighbor's door to return the keys.

Case 3 It is your night to cook. It is nearing the end of the month, so you and your roommate are short on cash. You have already planned what you are going to fix. You come home at the end of the day, tired and hungry, but ready to do your part. That is when you discover that you forgot to take the meat out of the freezer. Instead of a potential dinner, you have a frozen block of meat.

Name _____ Section _____ Date _____

Conflict Roles II

Case 1 You are middle-aged parent whose twenty-two year old son/daughter is living at home while completing student teaching requirements for an education degree. You expect your son/daughter home in time for dinner. Dinner comes and goes, no return. Early evening comes and goes, no son/daughter. You are becoming increasingly worried because he/she is very dependable and predictable. You call the cooperating teacher but get only an answering machine. You call the school principal where the student teaching takes place, but the principal cannot tell you anything. You are about to call the police at midnight when your son/daughter walks in the door.

Case 2 You have been in the apartment laundry center and are walking back to your apartment to leave for a job interview. You really want this position and don't want to be late. As you return you notice that your car is missing from the parking lot. You reach your apartment, find the door unlocked and your car keys missing from the counter. The time to leave for your interview comes and passes. You start to panic. You hear a knock on the door and open it to find your neighbor from across the hall standing there with your keys.

Case 3 It is not your night to cook. Your roommate is handling that chore tonight. As it is nearing the end of the month and you are short on cash, you are looking forward to eating at home. You arrive home at the usual hour, tired and hungry, but nothing is on the stove, nothing is on the table.

6

The Nature of Small Groups

Key Concepts

It is the lunch hour at the Midwest Chemical Company, a medium sized corporation. In the cafeteria, eight people sitting at the same table begin to talk among themselves and discover that in the past week each one has lost at least a dollar in the soft drink and snack vending machines on their floor. They decide something needs to be done about the problem.

At another table four secretaries are playing bridge, just as they do every noon hour.

At yet another table, four people have their notes and books in front of them as they prepare to take an exam in an in-service course. This is a course offered by the company to help employees improve their skills and knowledge in job-related ways.

In the infirmary, six people recently identified as drug users, are talking about ways to kick their habits.

In the recreation area, representatives from the various divisions and levels are meeting with the newly hired corporate fitness instructor about the best way to set up a company-wide program.

Four people, representatives of different divisions in the company, are meeting to go over final plans for presenting their report on competing accident insurance plans.

The workers' contract negotiation team is holding a quick session to set up a time for a meeting after work in response to the latest offer from management. The management team is meeting to decide what possible responses they may have to meet from the employees' negotiating team.

Small groups are a natural activity of human beings. Even in primitive conditions, humans join themselves to others to fulfill two of our most basic needs: the need for mutual help and the need for socialization. By banding together, people accomplish, or accomplish more efficiently, tasks they could not accomplish alone whether that be finding food, fighting off enemies, raising structures, or other activities necessary for simple survival. Beyond survival, people also band together for the pleasure they derive from contact with others through talk, games, rituals, stories, and affection. Whether we call them committees, bridge foursomes, task forces, *ad hoc* committees, boards, commissions, car pools, families, clubs, fact-finders, gangs, or patrols, small groups are a major feature of our communication landscape.

Knowing something of the nature of small groups, what they are, how they function, and how we contribute to their success or failure, better prepares us for dealing with life's problems. Whether the situation be professional or private, if we can function well in small group settings, we will find both our problem solving skills and our social skills enhanced.

What Is a Small Group?

A small group is obviously a collection of people, but it is more than people thrown together by coincidence. People sitting at one of the lunch tables at the Midwest Chemical Company would not constitute a small group unless they exhibit other characteristics as well.

One characteristic would be the *number of people*. As the term is usually used in communication, a small group is a collection of people larger than a dyad yet small enough that all members can interact readily with other members. The maximum for a small group is usually about twelve to fifteen people. Beyond this size, the group tends to fracture into subdivisions, small groups within a larger group, so that the element of direct interaction is lost or sorely hampered.

To be a small group, the *three to twelve people* must also *share some common goal* toward which they are willing to work. The goal must be one which they cannot accomplish individually. The eight people sitting at the same lunch table can all eat their meals by themselves. If the same eight people decide that they are all fed up with the malfunctioning soft drink and food machines and want the situation remedied, they have taken their first step as a small group.

Finally, a small group is a collection of people who share a common goal which they attempt to *articulate and accomplish through the process of communication*. If the people at the lunch table continue talking among themselves about the concession situation at the company, then formulate a plan of action to correct the situation, they have become a functioning small group.

To summarize, then, *a small group is a collection of people, usually three to twelve, who attempt through communication to accomplish a common goal.*

Types of Small Groups

Problem Solving Group

The people at the lunch collecting themselves into a group represent one type of group, the *problem-solving group*. Other problem solving groups would be the committee meeting to create a fitness program and the four discussing how best to make their presentation. *A problem-solving group is one whose chief reason for existence is the removal or lessening of a difficult situation.*

Problem solving groups may be short-lived or ongoing. An *ad hoc* (Latin for "to this") group is one created to respond to a specific problem and nothing beyond that problem. Once the problem is solved, the group disbands. A rash of accidents in the parking lot might call forth an *ad hoc* committee charged with investigating the situation and making recommendations to the physical plant. After its report is submitted, the committee breaks up. More permanent problem solving groups would be those with an ongoing task or mission such as the Medical Benefits Committee, the Affirmative Action Committee, or the Sales Directors. Committees such as these deal with ongoing problems, and the group continues despite changes in its membership.

▲ **Figure 6.1.** A common type of group is the problem solving group. (Coyle)

Therapy Group

The former drug users meeting in the infirmary for mutual help constitute a *therapy* group. *A therapy group is one whose primary aim is to assist the members in overcoming their personal problems.* Usually, the members have the same problem in common, be it drug addiction, eating disorders, grief, or marital problems. The group may be led by a professional counselor or the leadership may be provided by one of the group members. When the group members talk among themselves without the guidance of a professional, it is often called a *support group*, that is one in which the members offer each other empathic understanding and encouragement.

Study Group

The people reviewing for their exam constitute a *study group*. Here the emphasis is on *assisting each other to learn material.* Members help each other by posing questions, sharing notes and readings, offering corrections, and clarifying concepts for each other. Together they can create a more comprehensive view of material than each could singly.

Social Group

The bridge foursome that plays every lunch hour would be a *social group*. Their *primary goal is the enjoyment of each other's company* which they achieve by sharing in an activity they all find entertaining. Other social groups might include softball and bowling teams, golf foursomes, after-work beer drinkers, various clubs, or even people who make a point of taking their coffee break together every afternoon.

Bargaining Group

Bargaining groups are those groups which *negotiate with another group or a person to arrive at a settlement acceptable to both parties.* Both sides in a bargaining situation are represented by a small group. Bargaining groups, however, differ significantly from the other groups listed above. Bargaining groups arise out of conflict and are created in opposition to pressures from another group. Each group arrives at the negotiating situation with its own set of demands and wishes. The negotiation is characterized by communication which attempts to convey the wishes of the party together with an attempt to influence the other party (Putnam and Jones 263).

What begins in opposition, though, must end in agreement if the negotiating process is to be a success. To achieve this success, the two sides must find common interests which form the basis for agreement. If at Midwest Chemical the two sides of the contract negotiation cannot discover enough commonality to reach accord, the discussions will fail (Putnam and Jones 275). The successful negotiating situation begins with two separate groups and ends with a blending of the groups' viewpoints.

Groups and Context

As individuals do not exist untouched by other influences, neither do small groups exist in isolation. Even though a small group constitutes a unit of relationships, the relationships in a small group are influenced by forces both within the group and outside the group such as the history of the group and members' loyalties to other relationships.

Group History

One of the most important factors in determining how a group will function is the history of the group. Is the group newly formed or has it been in existence for a long time? The distinction is an important one.

When a group is newly constituted, it is a "*zero history group*" (Bormann and Bormann 98). A zero history group is one that must move through all the stages of group formation. It must select leaders, develop norms, and define its task. It must work out the relationships among its members and relationships between the group and entities outside the group. It is a group that must begin at "square one" as its members bring with them little or no knowledge of each other or of how they will function in the work of the group.

At Midwest Chemical, the people who discover they are all upset about the same thing, the faulty drink machine, could well be a zero history group. Similarly, the drug therapy group might also be a zero history group if the members do not know each other beforehand. In both these cases, the groups would have to make basic decisions about how they are to function, and those decisions would shape the nature of the group as it progresses.

A person joining a zero history group might experience the same atmosphere as one the workers at Midwest Chemical: Phil Homais has had a drinking problem and has finally acknowledged it. He has decided to take advantage of the therapy program offered at Midwest Chemical and has responded to the flier distributed by the therapist. At the announced day, he goes to the infirmary for the first session. As he enters, he notices about ten people sitting around the room. He finds an empty seat and sits down. He thinks he may know one person from production, but the others are strangers. They sit uncomfortably, nobody speaking. Homais debates whether or not to say anything. Finally, the therapist enters.

At the other end of the spectrum from zero history groups are *ongoing* small groups which have been in existence for a some time and thus take on a life of their own. A new member arriving to participate in the group would soon discover a number of factors have already been decided. Norms may be well developed and firmly established, and new members must adjust to the existing situation.

For a new member, the first meeting of an established group might be like this: Jane Keppler, an accounting executive, has been assigned to the safety committee, a committee that has been in existence for years at Midwest Chemical. It is charged with reviewing accident reports and making recommendations. She enters the first meeting and finds an empty chair. "That's Charlie's place," another member tells her. Keppler elects to move to a different seat. Even after the group is fully assembled, they carry on conversations for several minutes before beginning the business of the day. Once the business begins, Keppler notices that the group is reviewing the reports according to the date when they were filed, not by the date of the accidents. When she asks about the procedure, she is told, "That's the way we've always done it."

Groups and Relationships

Another important factor influencing the functioning of small groups is the *context of relationships*, both internal and external, that the group must deal with. Small groups usually exist within the context of a larger organization. All the groups at Midwest Chemical are part of the corporation and will be influenced by the atmosphere of that corporation. In a university, a departmental committee charged with directing the undergraduate education will, naturally, exist within a department, but the department is also part of a greater whole. It exists within a school which exists within a university. The committee will be influenced by its place in the department, the department's place in the school, and the school's place in the university, and even the school's place in the state system of universities.

The influence of the group's context can be shown by a decision made by the Midwest Chemical accident insurance committee: In discussing the personal accident insurance, the committee has reviewed a variety of plans and is satisfied that four offer good coverage at acceptable cost. The first three plans, however, allow Midwest Chemical workers to buy coverage for their families in addition to themselves. The fourth plan, that of Acme Insurance, is the cheapest. While its coverage for workers is as good as the first three plans, it does not allow Midwest Chemical workers to purchase coverage for their families. Coverage is extended only to those employed by Midwest Chemical.

In discussion, the committee recalls that Midwest Chemical has long had a policy of supporting family activities and that a major portion of the company's health care plan is devoted to the care of family members. Further, when the workers last voted on accidental insurance plans, they overwhelmingly turned down a plan similar to that of Acme Insurance.

Because of the influence of company policy and worker sentiments—forces from outside the committee—the committee places Acme's plan at the bottom of their list of four companies.

Besides relations with outside entities, small groups will also be affected by the relationships of its members to other people, both inside and outside of the group. If group members are answerable to those outside the group, that relationship will exert influence on their activities. If in addition to their relationships within the group, members also sustain relationships with each other outside of the group, those outside relationships will influence what transpires within the group as well.

The study group at Midwest Chemical is about to break up early, but John Torres suggests one final review of the material. The other members go along. "You really must want to pass this test," one of the members says. "You're right," Torres responds. "If we pass the test, it means a higher rating, and that means we have a better chance of promotion and a raise in pay. My kids are both going to need braces, and we could use the money."

In the group making the presentation about the personal accident insurance, one of the members is Rosalie Lindowski, a senior accountant in the company. She supplies most of the financial information about Midwest Chemical. Another member is Harold Mishima a junior executive from production. He suspects that Lindowski's information does not always reflect the total picture but is biased toward efficiency over human concerns. Lindowski, though, is also on the company grievance committee, a committee that investigates complaints. Mishima has had a grievance filed against him, a grievance which he sees as totally unfounded but which, nevertheless, will be heard by the grievance committee. Mishima is careful when choosing his words and is reluctant to create conflict with Lindowski as she will sit in judgment on him later.

While a group will create an identity of its own, the nature of a given small group will be strongly influenced by how that group fits into its context and how members balance their relationships both within and without the group.

Group Climate

As group members interact with each other, they create a "climate" for the group. Just as "climate" indicates the nature of our geographic environment—cold, rainy, sunny, or cloudy with a thirty percent chance of precipi-

▲ **Figure 6.2.** Group climate influences a group for good or bad.

tation—"climate" in the context of small groups will indicate the group's environment.

Some groups seem to be characterized by ill will and tension. No leadership arises. The members dislike each other, and the more they attempt to communicate, the more angry, hateful, and upset they become. In other groups, members are congenial, supportive, and creative, and the group is highly successful in accomplishing its goals.

The creation of group climate is not the work of one person. It is the work of all group members, even the person who says nothing and does little or nothing. The various ingredients of the group, the members and their actions, create something that is greater than simply the sum of the individual group members.

Group climate is pervasive. It is not the matter of a few minutes or a few interactions. Climate is something that characterizes the group for a relatively long period of time. Two group members may become upset and argue loudly. The climate of the group is not determined by that one argument but by the interaction which preceded it and the interaction which follows it. If the group climate is one of distrust and antagonism, the argument will be another black cloud on the group's horizon. If the group constructively handles conflict, the argument can be a plus for the group.

Group climate is also pervasive in that the climate is perceived by more than one or two group members. Climate characterizes the group as a whole. All members experience the

tension, the cooperation, the distrust, or the mutual support of the group.

Bringing these two main ideas together, we can define "climate" as *"the relatively enduring quality of the group situation that (a) is experienced in common by group members, and (b) arises from and influences their interaction and behavior"* (Folger and Poole 84).

Tasks and Relationships

Every group must balance two sets of demands if the group is to survive. Whether the group be formal or informal, professional or recreational, problem solving or therapeutic, the group must effectively manage the relationships between its members, and it must do the work necessary for the group to accomplish its purpose. These two aspects are often called the *relational side* and the *task side* of small group processes.

One can imagine a group in which the members do not see each other outside of the group meetings, a group in which the total focus appears to be on accomplishing a given piece of work. The members address each other coolly, and it is clear little affection exists between the members. Relationships would appear to be of little importance in this group. Yet, upon closer inspection it is clear that the group has answered a number of questions such as "How will we talk to each other?" "What is the reason we are here?" "How can we accomplish our task with a minimum of socializing?" In short, the group has defined the style of relationships that will exist between its members. Had the group not been able to create patterns for relationships, the group could not function.

At the other end of the scale, one can picture a group that has little work to accomplish and exists strictly for the enjoyment of its members. The lunch time bridge foursome would appear to be such a group as would a tailgate party, a wine tasting club, or four people who regularly attend the theatre together.

Despite its strong emphasis on socializing, such a group still has tasks which it must perform if it is to exist. The bridge foursome must decide who is to bring the cards, when they will meet, where they will meet, how much talking is allowed, and what topics are acceptable. The theatre foursome still has work to do. The four must decide on what nights to attend, how to purchase and pay for the tickets, how to handle transportation and parking.

Groups as Self-Sustaining and Self-Directing Units

In accomplishing their tasks, small groups display an interesting pattern of creation and self-regulation. For a group to function, its members must work out a pattern of interaction acceptable to the group. Having worked out a pattern that allows them to interact, they are then able to change that pattern through the very interaction it allows. Thus, groups define themselves and, by their defining, open the way to changes in that definition.

The bridge foursome at Midwest Chemical has met now for two years. As only four can play the same game of bridge at a time, they have closely defined the borders of their group. The pattern that has emerged is that any changes in the regular procedures—an absence, a change in the time to play—are to be discussed openly. A new person appears at work, someone who has the same lunch hour as the foursome, is a pleasant person, and is an excellent bridge player. The newcomer asks about finding a game.

Since the four have constituted themselves as a group, they are able to discuss what to do about the newcomer. They have three choices. They can exclude the person and maintain the tight boundaries of their group. They can ask the per-

son to join them on a regular basis so that one of the group would sit out every game. They could partially include the newcomer by, say, asking the person to be available as a substitute when one of the regular players is unable to play.

Whatever the decision, the bridge foursome will be a different group than it was before the decision was made. The group will have redefined itself to some extent, and the members' new vision of the group will influence its future action. If, for example, they elect to exclude such a likely candidate as the newcomer, the group will probably be even more strongly opposed to new members in the future.

Creative Activities of Groups

The decision of whether or not to admit a newcomer is only one of the many activities in which groups must engage (Putnam and Stohl 258; Poole, Seibold, and McPhee 84). Whatever its main goal, in the course of its existence, a group will need to do a number of things if it is to continue.

A group will engage in *problem solving*. It will confront difficulties and discover effective ways to deal with them.

While planning its first session with the management negotiating team, the workers' team discovered that it lacked recent data about inflation rates. The statistics were necessary because they would provide a basis for the workers' wage demands. Until the figures were available, the work was at a standstill. One member volunteered to find the information and bring it to the next meeting. The group took up the next topic on the agenda.

Groups will engage in *decision making*. They will discover or create ways to choose courses of action. Groups must confront a wide range of issues. Some of these might be procedural such as how best to arrange the meeting. Other decisions may concern what information is acceptable and what is not. Still other decisions may address which issues to take up, what stances to take, and even such seemingly trivial matters as whether or not to have refreshments and who is to supply them.

Groups will also practice *boundary maintenance*. Boundaries separate members from non-

▲ **Figure 6.3.** Each small group has a task side and a relational side. (Coyle)

members. Groups must have some way of telling who is a member and who is not. If it is impossible to tell who is a member of a given group, then the group has no identity. If it does not define itself, create a sense of purpose for itself and find a way to distinguish those who share that purpose, it will fade away rapidly.

The eight upset about the faulty food and drink machines decide that they want to band together to attack the problem. Then they pick a name for their committee. They decide on "The Snack Pack." Having given themselves an identity, they now have a way of determining who is part of the project and who is not.

Similar to boundary maintenance is another group activity, *inclusion and exclusion*. The group must decide who is to be admitted and who is not, who is to continue working with the group and who is to be expelled. In some groups, the process is done by appointment and membership is for a fixed term. The appointment may be made by an administrator, a nominating committee, or a legislative body. With other groups, it is the group members themselves who decide who will be recruited or admitted. Selection is done by such methods as self-selection, screening, and elections.

Self-selection takes place when people volunteer for positions or roles. Screening is when candidates for a position are evaluated by interviews, tests, or other means, and selections are based on the evaluations. Elections are when people are selected by voting.

To exist, small groups must also *provide support* for their members. The support may come in a variety of ways. The accomplishments of the group may provide a sense of accomplishment for members, and they will find their goals reinforced. The social climate of the group—how positive or negative the group's relationships seem—may be a major factor in members' willingness to participate. Group members must provide each other with enough positive responses that the members are willing to respond and interact so that the group can accomplish its business.

At Midwest Chemical Paula Krupskaya has been appointed to the corporate fitness planning committee. She is overweight, out of condition, and out of her element. She is on the committee not by any personal choice but because her position in the company as supervisor of services demands it. She approaches the first meeting with trepidation. Sure enough, everyone else in the group looks healthy and fit. She sits down at the edge of the group.

The meeting starts, but she says nothing. As the members talk of those who are overweight with bad diet habits and those who need exercise, she feels the group looking at her from the corner of their eyes. Finally, the fitness coordinator says to her, "You have been very quiet. What observations do you have?"

Krupskaya says, "I'm just here to help the program fit into our range of services."

"I know that you and I have talked about that," the coordinator says, "But why don't you describe that process for the rest of the group."

Krupskaya begins explaining her role as supervisor of services. As she explains the organization of her division, she sees members nodding their heads. Later in the discussion, they ask her for more information and for her advice on making the program successful.

She leaves the meeting chatting with one of the members. She returns to the second meeting feeling more comfortable and participates more.

As groups come into existence and begin their work, it is important that they create a sense of themselves as a group. The group must also create places for its members. Members establish identities for themselves based on their relationships to others in the group, the task of the group, and their relationships outside of the group. One of the activities of a group is the *creation of identities*. What roles will the group members play?

The study group at Midwest Chemical has come into existence informally. After the first class, four of the class members began talking over coffee. As they discussed their concerns and hopes for the class, they decided that they would meet before each class to review materials. Darlene Jensen suggested a time and place for the next meeting. The others agreed. At the second meeting, she suggested that they agree to guidelines: each reads all the assigned material and each writes four questions on the material. The other three agree.

By the third meeting, it is obvious that Jensen is the group's leader in decisions concerning the group's goals and approaches to those goals. Her identity in the group has been established. Other group members will also take on identities within the group. John Torres establishes himself as the persistent one who wants to continue working until all the material is mastered. The other two will take on roles that allow them to fit in as well.

It should be noted, though, that the manner in which Jensen and Torres behave in this group does not mean that they will take on the same identities in other groups. Their roles in other groups will depend on the dynamics of those groups, and hence, their places in those groups may be entirely different than they are in their study group. Should Torres not believe in the group's goal or see little reward in the group's activities, he might become a detractor rather than a strong supporter. If Jensen is in a group in which she does not know how best to approach a problem, she may defer to someone else as an agenda setter for the group. Should she try to play the same leadership role in a second group as she does in her study group, the second group may not accept her in the position, and she would find it impossible to perform in the same way in both groups.

Finally, groups must also engage in *self-regulation* if they are to be successful. Groups must create ways of accomplishing their goals that are compatible with their purposes and that are accepted by group members. Each group will decide how it will do business and what are acceptable standards for behavior in the group. These in-group standards are called "*norms*": norms measure and determine what is correct and incorrect for the group. Written or unwritten, they belong to the group as the "property of a social system that is created and sustained by practice" (Poole, Seibold, and McPhee 87). Behavior according to the norms helps group processes go smoothly; behaving contrary to norms introduces disturbance and conflict into the group.

Norms may regulate a number of things. They may deal with details of behavior such as dress, who cleans up after the meeting, and how members are to be addressed: by first name, by last name, by title and last name, or by nickname. Norms will also determine how the work of the group is accomplished, for example, how proposals are made, how punctual members are expected to be, how tasks are to be divided, and how expenses are to be met.

When Jane Keppler arrives at the accident investigation committee and discovers that members all have their specified seats and that they begin each meeting with small talk, she is encountering the norms of that group. As she continues to meet with them, she will contribute to the evolution of the group's norms. Some, such as the seating patterns, she accepts. Others she might attempt to change. She might suggest, for instance, that preliminary investigation of the reports be done by individuals or sub-committees. If the group accepts her suggestion for ways of acting, the new pattern will become the norm.

Group Tensions

As we have noted above, groups are collections of individuals and exist within the context of members' relationships. We also noted that groups often exist within the context of a larger organization. This relationship indicates that group members may be pulled in several directions by their loyalties to themselves, to others in their lives, to the group, and to the organization. Every group will thus find itself having to deal with some tensions created by the pull of these different loyalties. To function, groups must find effective means of dealing with the various tensions and different levels of commitment among individual members.

One of the tensions may be between the *personal desires* of a group member and the *desires of the group*. A group member's actions will, to some extent, be determined by how compatible the member feels with the goal, norms, or directions of the group.

A group member's incompatibility with the sentiments of the group may even lead to the members pushing a "*hidden agenda.*" A hidden agenda is *a plan for action pursued by one or more group members but is never openly acknowledged in the group.* Usually the hidden agenda works against the goals of the group. The group's charge may be "find the best person for this job" while a group member's hidden agenda may be "hire my friend." The articulated purpose of the group may be to achieve a high grade on its small group presentation in class, but one member's hidden agenda may be, "I want to spend the least possible time on this project."

In the drug therapy group, a hidden agenda is at work. The six state in the opening meeting that they have a problem with drugs and want to quit using the drugs. Five want to put their habits behind them because of the problems their drug usage is causing in their families and on their jobs. The goal of the sixth group member, Roy Frank, is to obtain a letter certifying that he has been through the program. With the letter he can keep his probated sentence and avoid jail time. Frank just wants to find enough of the right things to say in the meetings to get him through.

Another pressure of tension that groups must deal with is that between the *internal demands* the group places on its members and the *external demands* placed on members by their relationships outside of the group.

Paul Li is on the negotiating team for the workers and is caught between internal and external demands. Besides the meetings during work time, the group also has to meet in the evenings to plan. Besides his commitment to his fellow workers, Li is also strongly committed to his family. He tries to bring meetings to an end in time for him to be home before his children go to bed. He also skips the post-meeting sessions when the group stops in at a local tavern for drinks and misses out on some of the social aspects of the group.

Groups are collections of individuals, yet they are more than the sum of their parts. Group members must also maintain a balance between their *individuality* and their *conformity* to group norms and pressures from other group members. If people assigned to a group strictly maintain their individuality, the group will never become a group in the true sense. It will remain a collection of people arguing their separate viewpoints. On the other hand, if group members are too eager to agree with each other, the group process will still be thwarted. If all agree upon every suggestion,

they will find themselves settling for untested and contradictory courses of action. Also the group misses out on the unique contributions individuals can make.

Groups must also maintain a balance between *concentration* and *relaxation*. Studies of small groups have discovered that group work is not a matter of unwavering attention to a task with relaxation then following the accomplishment of the task (Poole, "Decision Development . . ." 222). Rather, groups move toward their goals by an oscillation between concentration and relaxation. They will give full attention to a phase of the task, such as defining a key term or settling a conflict, then they will release some of tension by emotional expression such as jokes and comments. Following that, they will then pick up another aspect of the task.

The accident insurance committee has finished its report. The meeting has been tiring. The last part of the meeting is devoted to planning the presentation. The group decides on how to organize the presentation, who is responsible for which parts, and how visual aids are to be handled. "What should we wear?" one member asks.

"How about a leg cast?" another responds.

"I think I'll go for an eye patch," another says.

The group chuckles and then resumes the discussion. The pace picks up and they finalize their plans.

Group Development

Small groups have their own histories as they begin, exist, and disband. Each group will face its challenges and respond to the various influences, both internal and external, that shape the group and create its distinct character. That process of coming into being and the continued activity constitute what we call small group development.

It is customary to think of group development as a continuous process that always moves forward. As humans, for example, we begin as small helpless infants and increase in size and mental capacity. Upon closer inspection, however, we find that development may not be the straightforward, unwavering progression it appears at first glance. Economies swing between recessions and expansions. Diseases are stopped or arrested. Buildings are not simply built but are also maintained, remodelled, refurbished, and razed. Emotionally, we have our good days and our bad days. In our education, we do not master a topic for all time; we are either learning or forgetting.

Development in groups follows along the lines of our development in other areas. In some cases, it is a straightforward progression; in other cases, groups develop in a circular pattern of looping back to earlier stages then resuming forward motion.

The groups that will usually show the most straightforward motion are the zero history leaderless groups. Beginning at the initial point of group formation and with no roles assigned, members of zero history leaderless groups must accomplish all the tasks facing groups. Since they are beginning at the most basic starting point, these groups have no place to go but forward.

People joining groups which are already formed and functioning will discover that much of the group work has been accomplished. That does not mean, however, that the group has little left to accomplish. The group will need to engage in a number of activities to sustain itself. Some of these will be the same as those done by a zero history group just starting. Instead of being a straightforward progression, though, these groups may find themselves returning to tasks accomplished earlier.

With zero history leaderless groups, the first step in group development is *orientation*. In travel, "orientation" means getting our bearings or figuring out where we are in relation to the points of the compass. In small groups, orientation means much the same thing in that the group has to figure out some primary way of organizing itself and discovering a direction for itself.

In this stage, the relationship aspect of the group will be foremost. Finding themselves in a strange, unknown set of relationships, group members will try to sort out how they will behave in the group environment. Once members find their places in the group, the group can begin to move on to other tasks.

It is in this early stage that the group's first leader or leaders will emerge. The process of leadership selection is two fold. The group's first task is to select those people unsuited to the job. Once the untalented or unwilling are removed from consideration, the group accepts the remaining person or goes through the throes of conflict as it tries to decide between two or more contenders for leadership (Bormann and Bormann 100).

As the "Snack Pack" discusses how to go about solving its decided problem, a conflict develops between three members who want to start with a letter to the concession company and two who want to confront the manager of concessions. Sara Colvino and James Rutledge begin to summarize what is being said and to mediate between the two factions. It is apparent that the five arguing are not interested in mediating and that Colvino and Rutledge are putting themselves forward as mediators. The group is already, at this first meeting, discovering to whom it can turn to work through conflicts and who is not likely to play that role well.

With established groups, orientation will not be as obvious as it is in the beginning stages of zero history leaderless groups, but it will still be a necessary function. Changes in the pattern of the group will necessitate adjustments in its operation. The introduction of new members, the exit of old members, a change in purpose, the introduction of a specific problem, even a change of meeting room may necessitate members turning inward to establish new relationships or re-establish old patterns.

The second stage is the *sorting out*. Here members have some feel for how they will relate to each other, and their task now is to decide how they will do business. In this phase, the group places primary importance on task. It is in the process of sorting out that groups create norms for themselves by setting up written or unwritten guidelines for how they will behave and function within the group.

Zero history groups will probably have to devote more effort to the sorting out stage than will established groups. Established groups will still have to go through sorting out periodically as relationships and tasks change within the group. Decisions made earlier will not always fit the present situation.

The next stage is *to settle down to work*. While relational aspects were foremost in the orientation stage, here task aspects are foremost. The group has decided, for the most part, questions of who is to do what and how it is to be done. What remains now is for the group to attack its assigned problem and to marshall its forces in working toward a solution.

Whether groups accomplish the work of orientation, sorting out, and settling down to work in a straightforward or a circular way, the stages must be accomplished if the group is to exist. Like individuals, if groups do not solve basic problems such as orientation, the later problems of the group will be that much harder to solve. Also, like individuals, groups often operate by moving "two steps forward and one step back." What appears at first glance to be regression is often a necessary step to forward progress.

The workers' negotiating team is almost finished with its work when Patricia Desmond, one of its key members, suffers an attack of appendicitis. Hospitalized, she is unable to continue her committee work. The first alternate, Hank Souder, is asked to fill in for her. He has not attended previous meetings, and the first time he meets with the team, Souder is critical of the list of demands and the committee's plan for presentation. He wants the matter reconsidered. The group has a lengthy meeting arguing with Souder. Rachel Hempstead takes the lead in arguing for the group's present position. Souder

gradually backs down. The group has reoriented its relationships and moves back to its original task, polishing the fine points of the presentation.

Conclusion

We form ourselves into groups to accomplish those things which would be difficult or impossible to accomplish on our own. In doing so, we play out two long term needs of people: the need for assistance and cooperation and the need for socialization. Every small group will need to meet these needs though in varying ways.

Small groups exist in numerous forms: therapy groups, social groups, study groups, and problem solving groups. Whether groups are at their beginning points as zero history leaderless groups or are existing groups with a long history, they will still be self-creating and self-sustaining. They will create the framework for their communication and with that communication alter that framework as they see necessary.

Groups will engage in a number of creative activities as they go about their business. Some of the activities small groups will engage in are problem solving, decision making, boundary maintenance, inclusion and exclusion, support, the creation of identities, and self-regulation.

Groups will also need to find ways to balance the tensions and pressure upon them. These tensions arise from the divided loyalties group members may have. Some of these relationships are the personal desires versus group desires, internal loyalties versus outside loyalties, task emphasis as opposed to relational emphasis, and concentration versus relaxation.

To exist groups will also need to accomplish the work of group development. Groups must work through orientation, sorting out, and settling down to work as they start up and as they continue their existence.

Groups are a fascinating and useful part of human communication. Knowing something of their nature and function will be an aid to us in the range of collective activities in which we find ourselves.

▲ **Figure 6.4.** When a group has oriented itself and sorted out its roles, it settles down to work. (Dawe)

• • • Discussion Questions

1. What kind of small groups have you participated in or have observed working?

2. How could a group's history or lack of a history affect its performance?

3. Why are task and relational work necessary for small groups to function?

4. How would task and relational roles function in, say, a study group? In a bargaining group? In a social group?

5. Why is it necessary for groups to practice boundary maintenance and find ways to include and exclude members?

6. Why do groups create identities for themselves and their members?

7. What are group norms? How can they function positively in a group? How can they function negatively in a group?

8. How could a hidden agenda affect group process?

9. Why may group members feel the pull of tensions such as individuality/conformity or personal desires/group desires?

10. Why do groups go through stages of development?

11. What might happen if a group does not progress through the stages of development?

• • • Sources and References

(The references cited here are those cited specifically in this chapter. A fuller bibliography of small group material influencing this chapter appears at the end of Chapter Eight.)

Bormann, Ernest G. and Nancy C Bormann. *Effective Small Group Communication.* 4th ed. Edina. Minnesota: Burgess Publishing Company, 1988.

Folger, Joseph P. and Marshall Scott Poole. *Working Through Conflict: A Communication Perspective.* Glenview, Illinois: Scott, Foresman and Company, 1984.

Poole, Marshall Scott. "Decision Making in Small Groups I: A Comparison of Two Models." *Communication Monographs* 48 (1981): 1–24.

——. "Decision Development in Small Groups II: A Study of Multiple Sequences in Decision Making." *Communication Monographs* 50 (1983): 206–32.

Poole, Marshall Scott, David R. Seibold, and Robert D. McPhee. "Group Decision-Making as a Structurational Process." *The Quarterly Journal of Speech* 71 (1985): 74–102.

Putnam, Linda L. and Tricia S. Jones. "The Role of Communication in Bargaining." *Human Communication Research* 8 (1982): 262–80.

Putnam, Linda L. and Cynthia Stohl. "Bona Fide Groups: A Reconceptualization of Groups in Context." *Communication Studies* 41 (1990): 248–65.

Name _____ Section _____ Date _____

The Nature of Small Groups

1. From a communication study perspective, what is a small group?

   _____

   _____

2. Why do small groups form?

   _____

   _____

3. How does a therapy group differ from a problem-solving group?

   _____

   _____

4. In what way is the bargaining group distinguished from other small groups?

   _____

   _____

5. What constitutes success in the negotiating process?

   _____

   _____

6. What is a zero history group?

   _____

   _____

7. What is an ongoing small group?

   _____

   _____

8. How are norms affected by zero history versus ongoing groups?

   _____

   _____

9. How does the context in which a group exists affect its functioning?

   _____

   _____

10. What is climate in the small group context?

   _____

   _____

11. What is the relational side in the small group process?

   _____

   _____

12. What is the task side in the small group process?

   _____

   _____

13. How do boundary maintenance, inclusion and exclusion function in a small group?

   _____

   _____

14. How is support accomplished in a small group?

   _____

   _____

15. How do group members establish identities for themselves?

   _____

   _____

16. What is the role of self-regulation in contributing to a small group's success?

   _____

   _____

17. Define a hidden agenda.

   _____

   _____

18. Describe the pattern of concentration and relaxation that research has shown small groups exhibit.

_____

_____

19. What events take place during the orientation step of small group development?

_____

_____

20. How does the sorting out stage work in small group development?

_____

21. In what way is the emphasis of the group in the settling down to work step significantly different from the orientation step?

_____

_____

Name _____ Section _____ Date _____

Introduction to Small Group Communication Assignments

Not all decisions made in our society are the result of individual effort. Frequently it is a group of individuals who collectively reach a decision. Some groups are informal, with little structure and temporary in nature. Others are more formal and have on-going responsibilities.

This unit explains the small group presentation and written assignment which will help you understand the components of the small group process. You will also practice applying the skills necessary to:

1. Effectively communicate with others in a group
2. Be a contributor in a group
3. Enable your group to present an interesting, educational presentation

Suggested Topics for Small Group Presentation

The list below represents suggestions only. If your group thinks of an area of communication that could be presented to your class which isn't on the list, ask your instructor for approval before proceeding with research.

conversation
comforting communication
conflict in interpersonal relationships
communication in friendships
communication in families
cross-cultural communication
classroom communication
gender and communication
a field of communication: public communication, interpersonal communication, organizational
    communication, mass communication, issue management, performance studies
language and communication
conflict and negotiation
perception's role in communication
communication in organizations
symbolism in communication
visual communication
persuasion through communication (advertising)
mass communication shaping our world view
self concept and communication
censorship in the news
listening
feedback and communication
agenda setting function of media
freedom of speech
nonverbal communication

Small Group Presentation Guidelines

Purpose

The small group assignment has a three-fold purpose:

1. Your group will experience working in a small group decision making process which will be good practice for future use in classroom projects as well as in business applications.
2. You will gain in-depth knowledge about one area of communication which will then be shared with the rest of the class to augment instructor presented material.
3. You will gain experience speaking in front of an audience.

Basic Requirements

Your group of 4 to 5 students will prepare and present a creative and informative presentation in which you explain in DEPTH an area of communication. The goal is to present information not already covered by the textbook and to expand the class's knowledge of your chosen topic. A suggested list of subject areas is shown opposite.

Each presentation must be a minimum of _____ minutes in length. Films, slides, etc. may take up no more than _____ minutes of your presentation time.

The group as a whole must develop and submit a typed outline of the presentation format at least _____ days prior to the presentation.

A list of a minimum of _____ sources must be included with the outline; _____ sources must be no more than 5 years old so that the class is presented with up-to-date information from your area.

Each group is expected to work as a unit outside of class in addition to the in-class periods set aside for that purpose.

A dress rehearsal is necessary for timing your presentation.

Evaluation sheets must be handed in by each individual prior to the presentation. Your group will be evaluated according to grading criteria style _____, p. _____.

During the presentation sources must be cited so the class is aware of where information was found.

Each member of the group is expected to participate in the actual presentation as equally as possible. In the event a member of the group is sick, etc., on presentation day and does not show up, other members are expected to cover the missing student's information since this is a GROUP presentation, not a collection of five individual presentations on one day. The group as a whole is responsible for the final product and individual members should be knowledgeable about the entire subject area.

A post-presentation analysis paper (see page 127) is required.

You will offer comments about the other presentations using the observation sheets on pages 129–137.

Additional instructor requirements:

Preparation Timetable

Our Group Topic Is _____ Due Date _____

A systematic approach to preparing your small group presentation is the best way to ensure success. Below is a suggested schedule for developing your presentation. The steps should be followed in chronological order with varying amounts of time possible between meetings. Keep a journal of what takes place at your meetings, who is the leader, what the atmosphere is, etc., in order to facilitate writing the post-presentation paper.

▶ *Step 1* Exchange names and phone numbers with other group members to simplify arranging outside meetings. Compare schedules to find time blocks convenient for all participants. Begin gathering outside information. See bibliographies in this text for a start as well as traditional library sources including books, journals and abstracts. "Library Research in Communication", p. 401 of this workbook, should be helpful in guiding you to pertinent sources.

▶ *Step 2* Narrow your topic. The suggested topics listed are broad, and must be narrowed to focus on more manageable areas of information for the time limit involved. For example, mass media communication might be narrowed to how television newscasts shape our perception of the world around us. As a group divide the topic for additional research. Meet again to review the information and monitor progress. FOLLOW THE PROBLEM SOLVING STEPS outlined in Chapter 8 of this textbook.

▶ *Step 3* Develop an outline. After preliminary research has been conducted to get a general idea of what your area includes, meet to develop a tentative outline for the presentation. Don't fit the outline to the material found to date; decide on what you want, then go out and find the material necessary to fill in the gaps.

▶ *Step 4* Prepare a format. Develop your presentation format as a group. Decide the most interesting way to present your material. Combine a straight-forward presentation of information with role playing, getting the class involved in exercises, questions and answers, discussion, etc. On presentation day talk through with the class the reason for the activities and exercises you've chosen. Don't assume the class will see the relationship between the exercise and the communication concept it illustrates. Work for a presentation which holds the audience's attention through a mixture of ways of presenting material. Use "skits" only when they really prove a point, not merely provide entertainment.

▶ *Step 5* Evaluate the presentation. When you think the development of your presentation is finished, review "Basic Requirements", p. 118 and check off to make sure each requirement has been met. In addition, consider the following areas:

  ▶ If AV equipment is needed, have arrangements been made to have it on hand? Read your text, Chapter 12, for help in using audio/visual aids.

  ▶ Is the material being presented informative about an area of communication as well as interesting?

  ▶ Does all the material support the central theme/topic? Are sources cited by participants to add credibility to the presentation? Is the information presented a supplement to text material, not a rephrasing of it?

  ▶ Can the class follow the presentation just from hearing it? Is it organized? Is there an introduction of group members, an attention getting device in the opening, development of rapport with the audience, and a preview of the content of the presentation? Are there transitions, explanations, internal summaries? Is there a conclusion which summarizes the presentation and leaves the audience with a sense of completion?

  ▶ Are unfamiliar terms defined?

  ▶ Are enough supporting examples given to make the material meaningful?

▶ Has the group practiced the whole presentation to check timing, physical set-up, etc.? This is best done in a classroom similar to the one in which the presentation will be delivered.

Notes:

Evaluation Rationale

All members of the group will receive the same grade since this presentation is a group effort. TURKEY CLAUSE: Occasionally an individual group member will choose, for whatever reasons, not to contribute to the group's efforts at developing a worthwhile presentation. The member may not do research in preparation for the project, miss the majority of out-of-class planning sessions, or withdraw during the work sessions. Each group should attempt to draw such an individual into the group process. Sometimes adjustments need to be made to accommodate work schedules, etc. If in spite of a good faith effort on the part of a group one of its members refuses to be an active participant, the group as a whole may choose to enact the turkey clause, in effect firing the person from the group. If such an action is regarded as necessary, the group must contact the instructor and document the wayward member's action. Upon approval of the instructor the turkey clause will be enacted. A student who is fired by the group will receive an *F* for the assignment.

Sample Bibliographic Entries

Periodicals

An article in a journal with continuous pagination:
Ayres, Joe and Tim Hopf. "Coping With Writing Apprehension." *Journal of Applied Communication Research* 19 (1991): 186-96.
An article in a general publication:
Burka, Paul. "Honesty is the Best Politics." *Texas Monthly* Nov. 1992. 122+

Books

A book by a single author:
Willard, Charles Arthur. *A Theory of Argumentation*. Tuscaloosa: Univ. of Alabama Press, 1989.

An edition of a book:
Cooper, Pamela J. *Speech Communication for the Classroom Teacher*. 3rd ed. Scottsdale, Arizona: Gorsuch Scarisbrick, 1988.

A book chapter:
Nelson, John S. "Political Foundations for the Rhetoric of Inquiry." *The Rhetorical Turn: Invention and Persuasion in the Conduct of Inquiry*. Ed. Herbert W. Simons. Chicago: Univ. of Chicago Press, 1990. 258-59.

A book with multiple authors:
Stewart, Charles J., Craig Allen Smith, and Robert E. Denton, Jr. *Persuasion and Social Movements*. 2nd ed. Prospect Heights, Illinois: Waveland Press, 1989.

Newspapers

Cullen, Kevin. "Canal Dig Yields Key Find." *Journal and Courier* [Lafayette, IN] 12 June 1997: B1

Internet

Basic format:
Author's Last Name, First Name. [author's internet address, if available]. "Title of Work" of "title of line message." In "Title of Complete Work" or title of line/site as appropriate. [internet address]. Date, if available.
Martin, Ralph. [rmartin@recst.monst.edu]. "Where the Deer and the Antelope Play." In "Western Recreational Opportunities." [rec@monst.edu]. 13 June 1997.

An Interview

Doe, John. Professor of Animal Science, Purdue Unviersity. Personal interview, 13 May 1997.

Name(s) _____ Date _____
Group Topic_____ Group Score _____

Small Group Grading Criteria—Style A

For a *C*, the presentation meets the following criteria:

> All members participate in the presentation
> The topic relates to communication
> Introduction introduces group members and previews the presentation
> Presentation has required number of main points
> Transitions are present
> Conclusion summarizes main points
> Speakers are understandable
> Required number of references are used and cited
> Presentation fits the time guidelines

For a *B*, the presentation meets the criteria for a *C* plus the following:

> Involves interaction within the group
> Uses references from highly credible sources, appropriate to the topic, and from recent publications
> Employs supporting materials (visual aids, performances, illustrations) appropriate to the topic
> Speakers do nothing that detracts from their presentations
> Introduction captures the attention of the audience
> Transitions links main points
> Conclusion highlights implications of the material
> Visual aids (posters, pictures, videotape, etc.) supplement the presentation rather than being the presentation

For an *A*, the presentation meets the criteria for a *C* and a *B* plus the following:

> Presentation utilizes an interesting format
> Presentation flows smoothly
> Points strongly supported from credible sources
> Supporting materials are neat, artistic, and clear
> Program is interesting to the audience
> Speakers are energetic
> Presentation evidences maturity of thought
> Program utilizes audience participation

For a *D*, one of the *C* criteria exhibits a major problem.

For an *F*, the presentation is not given, one of the *C* criteria is not done, or several areas exhibit major problems.

Name _____ Date _____

Group Topic_____ Group Score _____

Small Group Presentation Grading Criteria—Style B

Organization 30%

Introduction

       group members introduced

       attention getting opening employed

       rapport developed with the audience

       presentation previewed

Body

       main points obvious

       transitions used between main points

       easily followed

Conclusion

       main points summarized

       implications of material highlighted

       a feeling of completion developed

Content 40%

       unified and related to group assignment

       supported with examples

       clearly presented

       interestingly developed

       appropriate vocabulary chosen

       jargon and unfamiliar terms defined

       expanded beyond the scope of text material

       sources credible

       sources cited

Delivery 30%

       presented within the required time limits

       participation equally divided

       moved smoothly from one speaker to the next

       showed evidence of preparation for conducting exercises, role playing situations, activities, etc.

       visual aid used with confidence

(Individual Student Notes)

       rate appropriate

       eye contact frequent

       volume appropriate

       tone pleasing

       vocal variety exhibited

       absence of fillers

       enunciation/pronunciation correct

gestures meaningful
posture comfortable
communication with audience established

*suggested values only—may be changed by your instructor

Comments:

Name _____ Section _____ Date _____

Written Assignment Small Group Process

You are to analyze your group's interactions in light of the five areas listed below. Your analysis should reflect an understanding of the research and theory presented in the text through your use of appropriate **terminology** for small group processes. Failure to use such terminology will reduce your grade accordingly. Your paper should demonstrate an understanding of the group process. Be sure to give **specific examples** of events and behavior in the group to document the conclusions you draw in your analysis. A **journal** makes writing the paper easier—you will have the specific examples needed to support your claims. It is highly suggested that you take notes after each group meeting to facilitate writing your paper.

Explain what accounted for group strengths. What could have been done differently to minimize any weakness? The questions listed below should start you thinking about possible ways to approach each area to be analyzed.

The material included in your paper will be considered confidential.

THIS PAPER IS DUE _____.

Specific format instructions required by the instructor are:

▶ *Area 1 What decision-making processes were used in your group?* How did your group use the problem-solving agenda given in your text? (Chapter 8) How were decisions reached by the group as you proceeded through the analysis? (majority rule, consensus, compromise) Were they successful? Why? It they were unsuccessful, how could they have been improved? How long did it take for your group to decide what it was that it wanted to do in front of the class? Was it too long? Why? What could have made it better? Were you satisfied with the topic that your group chose? Why or why not?

▶ *Area 2 Describe the leadership process that functioned in your group.* Who REALLY was the leader of the group? Did the leader emerge? If yes, at what point? Why? Was the leader appointed or elected? What was the basis of electing that person? Did several leaders function? If so, how did this affect the group? If you felt your group was leaderless, what are some problems with leaderless groups? What style(s) of leadership was used in your group?

▶ *Area 3 Identify and describe the various roles each member of your group, including you, played during your work sessions.* Give specific examples for each person's role(s). Who did the most talking? Why do you think they did? Did this style continue throughout the group's development? If there was a change, was it a change for the better or worse in your opinion? Why? Did your position or role within the group change from meeting to meeting? How? Why? Were you respected (in terms of your role) within the group? Who did the least amount of talking? What steps were taken to get this person to open up more? Were the steps successful?

▶ *Area 4 How did your group handle interpersonal and analytic conflict, if there was any?* Who was most instrumental in creating conflict? What impact did this conflict have on the group? What steps were taken to resolve the conflict? If no conflict existed, did your group suffer from "group think"? Why was there no conflict?

▶ *Area 5 What kind of climate did your group establish?* What factors in the group process were responsible for the climate which developed? How did you feel about being a member of this group? Did your attitude change about your group from beginning to end? How did the environment in which your group functioned affect its success? Where did the meetings take place for your group? Did you feel comfortable meeting there? Could a better choice have been made? Was the time conducive to accomplishing your tasks?

Include a brief summary of your reactions to working in a small group situation.
Include the evaluation sheet with your paper.

Name _____ Section _____ Date _____

Written Assignment Evaluation Sheet

The paper reflects a knowledge of research and theory from the text based on the use of proper terminology. (10 points)

The paper provides specific examples of events and behaviors to document conclusions. (10 points)

The paper sufficiently analyzes the decision making process employed. (15 points)

The paper sufficiently analyzes the leadership characteristics in the group. (15 points)

The paper sufficiently analyzes the roles members played. (15 points)

The paper sufficiently analyzes the conflict in the group. (15 points)

The paper sufficiently analyzes the climate of the group. (15 points)

The paper is presented in a neat and technically well written manner. (5 points)

Name _____ Group Observed _____

Student Evaluation of Small Group Presentation

Constructive feedback should be

1. Solicited
2. Well timed
3. Descriptive of how you feel, not evaluative
4. Specific rather than general
5. Practical, related to something that can be controlled and changed

In light of these guidelines, offer feedback about the small group presentation you have just watched. Focus on how interesting, informative and organized the presentation was to you. What was the strongest single aspect of the presentation? What one thing would you have done differently?

Name _____Group Observed _____

Student Evaluation of Small Group Presentation

Constructive feedback should be

1. Solicited
2. Well timed
3. Descriptive of how you feel, not evaluative
4. Specific rather than general
5. Practical, related to something that can be controlled and changed

In light of these guidelines, offer feedback about the small group presentation you have just watched. Focus on how interesting, informative and organized the presentation was to you. What was the strongest single aspect of the presentation? What one thing would you have done differently?

Name _____Group Observed_____

Student Evaluation of Small Group Presentation

Constructive feedback should be

1. Solicited
2. Well timed
3. Descriptive of how you feel, not evaluative
4. Specific rather than general
5. Practical, related to something that can be controlled and changed

In light of these guidelines, offer feedback about the small group presentation you have just watched. Focus on how interesting, informative and organized the presentation was to you. What was the strongest single aspect of the presentation? What one thing would you have done differently?

Name _____ Group Observed _____

Student Evaluation of Small Group Presentation

Constructive feedback should be

1. Solicited
2. Well timed
3. Descriptive of how you feel, not evaluative
4. Specific rather than general
5. Practical, related to something that can be controlled and changed

In light of these guidelines, offer feedback about the small group presentation you have just watched. Focus on how interesting, informative and organized the presentation was to you. What was the strongest single aspect of the presentation? What one thing would you have done differently?

Working in Small Groups: Roles and Leadership

Key Concepts

• • • • • • • • • • • •

As we have seen, small groups are a feature of our lives and to function in them requires a balanced handling of a number of factors. Groups do not accomplish their goals without efforts by their members, both individually and collectively, and the quality of work done by the members has a direct impact on the quality of the group's production. A badly functioning research and design committee will not produce high quality suggestions for new products. A badly functioning social group will soon find little reason to continue. Good group communication skills contribute to achieving high quality results.

One of the most common type of groups is the problem solving group. These groups address situations that need changing and attempt to find the best possible way to alter those situations. The problems addressed may be widely varied. A search committee looking for the best person to hire for a position is solving a problem. The decoration committee for a banquet is solving a problem. Social workers meeting to decide on a course of action for child are solving a problem. Even other types of groups—study, social, therapy—will have to function to some degree as problem solving groups. Where will the study group meet? How will the social group provide refreshments? What will the therapy group do about a member who is chronically late to meetings? Even families will meet as a problem solving small group when important questions come up, such as where to go for vacation or how to handle conflicting transportation problems.

As problem solving in some form is fundamental to small groups, we will look closely now at how we can best participate in this process. This chapter will examine the different ways in which members can participate in the group process and the different styles of leadership that can be used in small groups. This chapter will also provide guidelines for planning group meetings. The next chapter will examine the procedure that problem solving groups use to reach a successful solution.

Participating as a Group Member
Recognizing the Nature of Group Work
The Strengths of Small Group Work

To work effectively in groups, we need to recognize the nature of small groups in both its positive and negative aspects. Group work has a number of advantages to offer. For one thing, small groups can bring to bear on a given problem a number of differing views and a range of talents. No one person can have a totally comprehensive view, and by sharing their viewpoints, group members can arrive at a better perspective of a situation. One member might be a thoughtful, slow decision maker while another person reacts incisively and rapidly. Between the two, they can create and judge a wider range of possible solutions than either member could acting alone.

When they work well, small groups also provide a sense of *esprit de corps*, high group morale that is one of the pleasures of working with others. In addition, solutions reached through small groups can often generate more support from those affected than can solutions handed down with little attention paid to those affected. When those affected by a decision or their representatives have a hand in making that decision, they are more likely to support the final effort than if they were left out of the process.

The Weaknesses of Small Group Work

While small groups have much to offer, they are not the answer to all situations. For one thing, *small group decisions often take more time than individual decisions.* Individuals have only to consult themselves; small groups must consult and accommodate all members. Another reason that small groups may take a long time in reaching decisions is that small groups must maintain a web of relationships more complex than that of an individual. A dyad consists of only one interpersonal relationship. A triad contains seven possible interpersonal relationships. Add another member, and a four person small group has twenty-five different relationships to deal with. As the group continues to increase in size, the relationships become greater and even more complex.

Small groups are also *not very good devices for making routine decisions.* As long as matters are proceeding smoothly or problems are minor, little need exists for small group decision making. The person in charge of an activity can simply follow a given pattern. It is only when a significant problem exists within a routine that small groups are called for. For example, purchasing office supplies for a business usually follows accepted patterns. As long as the office staff has sufficient paper, ribbons, pens, and forms, the purchasing can be handled by one person. It would be ridiculous for four people to fill out purchase orders together. When, however, shortages become acute and interfere significantly with the office work and routines, it is likely a group will address the problem. A group is needed because it would be very difficult, if not impossible, for one person to reflect the views of all parties involved in the problem: the buyers, the vendors, the delivery service, the financial accountants, and the users.

In addition to recognizing the strengths and weakness of small groups, group members must also realize the demands that small group work will place on them.

Members' Responsibilities

Members Should Give Their Time

Because small group work is often time consuming, patience will be necessary to work through the issues faced by a group. At some points, members may wonder if the group is making any progress at all as members make

suggestions, propose ideas, and then discuss and debate them all.

Members Should Be Prepared

To save time, members need to do individual work outside the meeting, then bring the results of that work to the meeting. Some of the activities members may do outside include gathering information through research or interviews, preparing documents, reading materials, preparing reports, even supplying refreshments. If members arrive without having done the necessary preparation work for the meeting, the group's progress will be significantly slowed and relationships strained.

Members Should Take Active Roles

In addition to being prepared to interact and contribute, group members should also take the next step and actively participate in the group's activities. Members should carry their parts of the load. Being active in group discussion is one aspect of participation. Groups exist and function through the interaction of their members, and for people to remain forever silent in meetings is to hamper the group's progress. While a good discussion leader will attempt to bring out the reluctant, a better approach is for members to put themselves forward.

▲ **Figure 7.1.** Group members should take active roles to help the group accomplish its purpose. (Coyle)

Group Members Should Be Constructive

Members' contributions should aid the group in its work. Group members will inevitably disagree with each other. Despite the disagreement, members should still work to be respectful of those with differing opinions and be sensitive to their feelings and ideas. What one is tempted to say in the heat of a conflict and what one should say for the good of the group may be two different things. For the sake of the group, the member should choose the latter. Another part of respect for others is allowing them to express themselves. Long winded orations have little place in small groups.

Positive Group Member Activities

Small group work can be a rewarding process that leads to the accomplishment of significant goals. It can also be a time consuming exercise in frustration. The difference between the two possibilities is decided by the way in which group members play their roles. For a group to succeed, it will need to accomplish a number of tasks. Who accomplishes the tasks is not as important as that the tasks be done. Sometimes the group leader displays the necessary skills for many of the activities. At other times, the tasks will be distributed evenly throughout the group. One person may possess only one of the skills yet contribute an enormous amount to the group by the use of that talent.

▲ **Figure 7.2.** Providing information is a valuable service performed by group members.

Providing and Evaluating Information

The best decisions are informed decisions. A group must have accurate information in sufficient quantity if it is to make the best possible decisions. The group must also decide what kind of information is valuable and what kind of information is acceptable. A student government committee investigating parking problems on campus would need to gather information on the number of spaces on campus, the number using the spaces, and university plans for expansion of parking. If that information were not recent, however, it would be of little use.

Creating Ideas

For a group to act, it must have some idea of its possibilities. The person coming up with new ideas for solutions, criteria, and information sources helps the group widen its horizon. To be inventive in group problem solving is to further the process.

Elaborating Ideas

A group member may be creative with ideas but may not be able to see the possibilities in those ideas. An elaborator is a person who takes an idea and expands it to show its potential. The elaborator may not be the person who came up with the original idea, but the elaborator is the person who can envision the idea's potential. One might suggest polling student commuters to see what their perceptions of the problem are. An elaborator would pick up on the idea and see the possibilities in it by suggesting polling by interviews or by surveys and how the interviews or surveys could be carried out.

Clarifying/Explaining

Clarification and explanation are necessary in groups because all members do not possess the same kind of knowledge and background and abilities. A group member in computer science or computer technology might suggest a computer model of campus parking as a way to understand the problem and search for solutions. Some members might be unfamiliar with a computer model, and those understanding the concept might not understand how one is constructed. To put their ideas across, the computer advocates would have to be adept at explaining—in essence, teaching—other groups members so they could properly evaluate the merits of the suggestion.

Testing Ideas

One of the most important jobs in a group is that of testing ideas. Here a person sets up objections to an idea so the group can be sure it has considered all the possibilities and all the ramifications of its ideas. These are the people who play the role of "devil's advocate"[1] and are also know as the "negative other." While staying in tune with the purpose of the group, they take stances against ideas and point out their flaws and shortcomings. They may even make counterproposals. The point is not to turn the group into a debating society, but to make sure that the group has considered all the possibilities in an idea or course of action.

Encouraging

Group members may have good ideas or suggestions but be reluctant to express them. Sometimes, they are reticent communicators. At other times, they may be intimidated by the climate in the group. They may lack self confidence. Whatever the cause, their ideas may not be expressed if someone does not provide motivation. Encouragement can come in many forms. It may be done through the creation of a positive group climate. It can be done by an individual who coaxes a person into talking. It can be done by following the statement with positive reactions. Even if the idea is of marginal value, the member can still be praised or thanked for contributing.

Empathizing

Much of what transpires in a problem solving situation is rational, but that does not mean that emotions do not play a part in the process. It is frustrating to feel that our ides are not appreciated or that nobody understands our situation. The expression of empathy in a group can aid understanding. It adds to the relational aspect of the group and shows respect for the feelings of group members.

In the investigation of campus parking, an empathic member could foster the work of the group in many ways. If the chair of the university parking committee feels that the member interviewing him understands the difficult nature of the committee's decisions, the chair is more likely to provide information. If a frustrated commuting student on the committee feels that group members have some feeling for her difficulties in getting to class, she will be more likely to contribute to the group's work.

Mediating

Not all group members will agree on all issues. Some conflicts are readily solved. The two parties arrive at a mutually acceptable viewpoint. At other times, however, a group may find itself fracturing into two sides or two members may take opposing positions and refuse to budge. In these cases, a mediator is of immense help to the group.

A mediator will work back and forth between the opposing sides, trying to understand the positions, empathizing, and offering suggestions to resolve the impasse. By taking an active role and seeking solutions, the mediator allows the group to progress in its work rather than come to a halt over the difference of opinion.

Relieving Tension

Groups may need to find ways to relax for several reasons. Tension relief is commonly needed when the group first meets. Members arrive but may not know the others in the group. They may be uncertain about where to sit. They may be nervous at the prospect of meeting strangers or working on the problem. Here tension can be relieved by someone who greets them in a friendly manner, introduces them to other members, finds them a place to sit, or supplies them with refreshments.

Another way tension relief is useful to the group is in the progress of its work. We have already noted that groups work by alternating between concentration on the task and relaxation. Relieving tensions provides the group with a way of releasing its emotional involvement in the task and then returning to its work with a new perspective. Here the tension relief may come through a brief statement, a joke, or a short recess.

▲ **Figure 7.3.** Negative roles such as withdrawing hamper the group. (Coyle)

Groups have numerous needs, and members providing skills in both the problem solving process and the relational aspects of the group aid the group in its work.

Negative Group Member Activities

As group members can all make positive contributions to the problem solving process, group members can also make negative contributions to the group process. These negative activities can arise from personality problems, distractions, or pressures from inside or outside of the group.

Withdrawing

One of the simplest ways in which group members may contribute to the group's difficulties is to remove themselves from the group. A member quits showing up for meetings, or if the person shows up, the person is unprepared to participate in the meeting. Instead of being involved at the center of the group's activities, the person stays on the edges of the activities or removes himself totally from the group.

The problem can sometimes be solved by the group's consenting to letting the person go, then regrouping and continuing the work. At other times, a confrontation is necessary to make the individual aware of the group's feelings and to deliver an ultimatum to the person.

Fighting

Groups, by their nature, will have disagreements. Fighting is an unproductive way of dealing with the disagreements. Group members engage in fighting when the point of their actions is not to help the group solve its problem but to score points in an argument with other group members. Instead of remaining focused on the group's work, fighters focus on themselves and the rewards they get from vocal combat with other group members.

Dominating

Groups should be a melding of members' viewpoints and contributions. When one member takes over the group and forces her will on the group, that person becomes a dominator. As the dominator plays a dictatorial role, the person subverts the entire group process by stifling group interaction. When group members are not free to participate, they will feel frustrated and are likely to make few contributions or to withdraw from the group.

Manipulating

Group members manipulate the group process when they work to accomplish goals which they cannot accomplish in group meetings. Outside of the meeting, promises may be made, private compromises offered, or bargains struck. The results of these are then brought into the group process. Since they do not involve the entire group or allow for full discussion, the group is hindered in its work.

Manipulation also occurs when group members attain their personal goals through unethical means. Those manipulating the group provide incomplete or false information to lead the group toward the desired goal.

Excessive Socializing

One of the pleasures of group work is the relationship one enjoys with other group members. When one is in a social group, that is the main purpose for the group's existence. While socializing may be a pleasant part of a problem solving group, too much socializing can distract the group from the task.

The student parking committee might find itself in the position that on a given evening the members feel more like talking about upcoming midterm exams than discussing statistics on parking. At the end of the meeting time, they may find that they had a good time airing their views but little work was done on the parking problem. That makes the work load double for the next meeting and increases the time pressures as the group tries to meet a deadline.

Group members control the direction of their group's development. Positive contributions such as supplying information and testing ideas will speed the group process. Negative activities such as withdrawing and dominating will hamper and perhaps destroy the group process.

Participating as a Group Leader

What Is Group Leadership?

In addition to the work of the group members, another key factor in the success or failure of a group is the way leadership is handled. Like other aspects of group work, leadership grows out of the interactions of the group members.

We often think of the group leader as the person assigned to that post by rank, election, or authority. Military groups have officers; committees have chairs appointed by officials; boards elect one of their own as presidents. These types of leaders are generally known as *"appointed leaders."* Appointment is not, though, the only way groups acquire leaders. Zero history leaderless groups begin with no designated roles whatsoever, yet leaders emerge in those groups. When leaders come to the fore from the body of the group, they are known as *"emergent leaders"* because they come into being as the group places more and more confidence in them.

Whether appointed or emergent, effective group leaders accomplish the same basic task: they help the group in accomplishing its goals. As one has put the matter, leaders are the group members who aid "groups in constructing a collective structure which facilitates achieving desirable goals and removing obstacles from their goal paths" (Barge 237–38).

Leadership is not a matter of the actions of the leader in and of themselves, but rather leadership is a cooperative effort in which leaders take their cues from their groups and groups take their cues from their leaders.

Leadership Responsibilities

Group Leaders Should Be Prepared

The advice, *be prepared*, for group members applies even more strongly to group leaders. Leaders not only need to do the appropriate share of homework and research as other group members, but group leaders must also devote time to thinking about the group and its work. Group leaders will need to assess how well the group is accomplishing its goals and then plan what approach is best for aiding or correcting the group's direction.

Group Leaders Should Be Sensitive to Group Needs

One of the prime characteristics of effective group leadership is awareness of what is transpiring in the group. If a person cannot determine the feelings and ideas of the group, it will be difficult to guide the group in appropriate directions. No one technique is the best for leadership. Sometimes, the best way to encourage discussion is for the leader to say nothing. If the group is interested in the topic, making lively contributions, and respecting each other's right to speak, the leader has little to do. At other times, the leader may have to supply a series of provocative questions to encourage group responses or may have to act as a referee in the midst of heated argument.

Leaders will need to balance a number of factors. One factor is when to *encourage* and when to *discourage* discussion. If the leader knows a group member has thought about the problem at hand but is reluctant to speak, the leader needs to draw that person out. If someone is dominating the discussion and discouraging other viewpoints, then the leader must dampen that member's enthusiasm so that others can talk. In a larger sense, the leader must also make sure that ideas have been sufficiently considered and agreements reached that reflect the true sentiments of the group.

Leaders must also help the group *balance the tensions between task activities and relational activities*. A social group that spends all its time planning will not be very enjoyable for its members. Neither will a problem solving committee accomplish its goal if it spends all its time in conversation.

A leader should also help the group *maintain its focus*. As with conversation, one topic may lead to another in group discussion until the group finds itself a long way from its starting point. While digressions may help the group relieve tensions, a group leader needs to make sure that the group does not stray too far from its path.

Another important function of group leadership may be *motivating the group to perform its task*. Even the most dedicated of groups find themselves in flat spots where the potential rewards of the work appear to be outweighed by the discouragement of the present.

One of the major reasons for discouragement with a task is that people fail to see how the work at hand will benefit them. It helps, too, to remember that "benefits" can come in a variety of ways. Some benefits are easily measured. Salary, bonuses, work load, time off, size and decor of offices, and improved working conditions can be tangible benefits people seek on the job. Other benefits may be equally important but less obvious. Among these would be such things as a pleasant group to work with, a sense of personal satisfaction with the work, a sense of respect, and accommodations of one's feelings.

A good group leader will *realize the needs and desires of the group* and attempt to reinforce those in the group process. In a work environment, the group's efforts may result in increased status for its members, status which may result eventually in professional advancement. Other professional advantages one may discover in working with a small group are increased contacts, a widening social circle, and acquisition of knowledge.

In other settings, the group may be reminded of how its efforts will aid causes valued by the members. Paul Janacek, for example, is a thirty-three year old executive in the loan department of Second National Bank. His work involves dealing with commercial property and thousands of dollars. He works at home at night either on bank matters or reading financial articles and books. He sees himself as an informed, experienced financial officer whose time would be wasted were he asked to work as a teller, counting change, or doing janitorial work. Yet, one evening a week, he spends three hours opening boxes and stacking canned goods, simple labor. The work contrasts vividly with his professional job, but he does it because the work is at the local food finders. The organization collects surplus food and distributes it to low income families. He does the menial work because he sees it as valuable to others. Here the need and reward are not monetary but altruistic. He receives a reward knowing that he is helping others.

Another major motivational factor is the *respect* group members experience in the group process. By respect, we mean a consideration of the feelings, ideas, and contributions of group members. When group members feel they are treated with integrity, they are more likely to invest themselves in the group process than when they are treated badly.

Respect does not mean that all contributions of all members are treated as if they were wonderful. Rather, it means that members share equally in the right to express opinions, that their contributions will be given serious attention, and that their feelings will be considered

Lack of respect can lead to needless tensions in a group. The Manchester County School Board is conducting contract negotiations with the teachers' association. At their first planning meeting, the new board member, Harold Watkins, makes a suggestion that they change the site of the negotiations from the school cafeteria to the conference room. The conference room, he thinks, would be more intimate, comfortable, and more conducive to discussion.

"That's the stupidest thing I've ever heard," responds Michael Ralston, board member for twenty-three years. "It's easy to see you've never had any experience with this."

Watkins asks a few more questions and then is silent until the latter part of the meeting when he speaks against a suggestion by Ralston about where to park at the negotiation meeting. The group spends fifteen minutes listening to them argue about the parking.

Group leadership is a talent that allows the leader to balance a number of factors in the group process. A good group leader will help the group attain its goal while maintaining good relationships within the group.

Leadership Styles

Authoritarian

Leaders may work in a number of fashions. Leadership styles are characterized by the amount of direct control the leader exerts over the group. A structured, centralized style would be the *authoritarian* style. Here the leader exercises tight control over the group's activities, often telling the group what will be done. An authoritarian group leader will decide on the course of action for the group and then make assignments for the group to carry out. Authoritarian leadership is often appropriate when time is limited, group members are disoriented, and the group leader possesses the power to enforce decisions. Some roles that would call for an authoritarian style would be those in military or semi-military units, teachers of small children, tour guides, and crew chiefs.

Paula Myrivelos has been hired as an office manager for the Kelsey Clinic, a six doctor medical business specializing in pediatric medicine. The office has numerous problems with staffing, procedures, record keeping, and patient satisfaction. Myrivelos has been hired to correct the situation.

From her experience and training, Myrivelos can see immediately what is causing some of the problems. As the office is in disarray, she takes steps necessary to change the situation.

Myrivelos lets the part-time accountant go and hires a full-time bookkeeper. She revises the routing system for the files. In private, she talks with the appointments secretary who is noted for her brusqueness. Myrivelos provides her with guidelines for dealing with the staff and patients and tells her that if changes are not made, she will be let go. She stresses to the doctors that all laboratory requests must be accompanied by a request form. She buys more play equipment for the waiting room and subscribes to parenting and family magazines. After several weeks, the office routine becomes easier and people

start using the new procedures. In this correction of problems, Myrivelos has used an authoritarian style of leadership. She has made decisions on her own and put them into effect.

Democratic

A second form of leadership is the *democratic* style. In this style, the leader consults with the group and after hearing its views, makes a decision. A democratic leader is not one who submits every issue to a vote of the group but rather is one who allows the group to express opinions about the problems to be solved. Final responsibility for the decision, however, rests with the leader. Members will contribute ideas and efforts. The democratic leader weighs the group's input and then responds. Often, the democratic leader will go along with the group's decisions, but if the group's suggestion is out of keeping with the leader's conclusions, the leader's opinion will be the one that prevails. A democratic style of leaderships is most appropriate when members are involved with each other in their task, when the leader is trusted to reach a fair and responsible decision, and when enough time exists to solicit opinions from all concerned.

Having made the necessary immediate changes, Myrivelos changes her leadership style. She still faces problems, however. One problem is handling vacation times. At present, the staff simply informs the office manager when they will be taking vacations and then leaves. The policy often creates critical shortages on the staff.

To attack the problem, Myrivelos schedules a series of meetings with the clerical staff, the laboratory technicians, the nurses, and the doctors. She listens carefully to all their opinions and viewpoints.

After listening to the opinions, Myrivelos issues a policy statement on vacation leave. Vacation times must be requested at least a month in advance. After circulating the tentative policy and receiving reactions, Myrivelos issues a final policy on vacations and begins to make decisions based on it.

By listening and including a great deal of group comments, Myrivelos has initiated a policy through the democratic process of leadership.

Laissez-faire

A third method of leadership is *laissez-faire*. Roughly translated, "laissez-faire" means "let people do as they please" (Webster's *Seventh New Collegiate Dictionary*, 1967). When using this style of leadership, the leader does little or nothing to influence the group's decision or actions. The laissez-faire leader is one who sits back and lets what happens, happen. When a group is functioning well, has created a supportive climate, and the members are capable and self-motivated, a laissez-faire system may be best for the group. When all members are doing what they are supposed to, the best policy is to leave them alone to do their work. On the other hand, if the group is disoriented and members are incapable of dealing with a situation, laissez-faire leadership may be disastrous.

Myrivelos uses a laissez-faire approach when two workers come to her after the vacation policy is in place. The two tell her that they have been talking and are wondering if it would be possible for them to trade vacation times. Myrivelos checks and sees that their absences would not interfere unduly with the fairness of the policy or office procedures. She tells them, "Work it out between yourselves and let me know what you decide." By turning the decision over to the two workers, Myrivelos exemplifies the laissez-faire approach.

No one style of leadership is right for all groups nor is one style of leadership likely to be best for one group all the time. A skilled leader will shift styles as necessary to keep the group functioning at its best.

Planning Meetings

One of the factors contributing to efficient group work is proper planning of meetings. Giving forethought to what should transpire in a meeting will help the group to use its time most efficiently and contribute positively to both problem solving and group climate.

Set Meeting Times

Simple as it sounds, *setting meeting times* and making sure that all members have the information is an important part of successful small group work. Meeting times should allow for optimum attendance, preferably for all members, and should be at a time when the group can do its best work.

Choose Appropriate Settings

The place where a group does its work is also important. The *setting* should be comfortable so that the environment does not interfere with the group's efforts. The setting should also provide what the group needs to do its work such as privacy for discussion or room to spread out materials. The setting should be free from distractions such as noise, interruptions, inadequate space, or inadequate furniture that will divert the group from its task.

The awards committee for the United Fund drive needs to meet. The chair of the committee, Mike Jinnah, reasons that all members have to eat lunch, so he calls for a meeting in the restaurant just down the block from his law office. The restaurant turns out to be packed with other diners. The group has difficulty hearing each other. Worse yet, one of the potential recipients of an award is seated only two tables away. The group accomplishes very little of its work. Having learned his lesson, Jinnah schedules the next luncheon meeting for the conference room in his law firm and has the meal catered.

Create an Agenda

An *agenda* is a *schedule of what the group plans to do in a meeting*. It is a guide for the group that paces its work and keeps it focused on its task. The agenda, be it written or oral, should tell what is to happen at the meeting or series of meetings, what is expected of group members, and what they should expect to accomplish.

In setting agendas, keep in mind the rate at which small groups function. A wise leader does not plan too much for a single meeting. It is better to overestimate the amount of time a task will take rather than face frustrating time pressures. Groups also work better in a series of short meetings rather than in long marathon sessions, as people find it difficult to pour their energies into meetings for prolonged periods of time.

Here, for example, is what the agenda of Mike Jinnah's awards committee should look like:

12:00–12:05	Settling in, hanging up coats, etc.
12:05–12:15	Serving lunch
12:15–12:20	Opening remarks, committee's goal, meeting's agenda
12:20–12:35	Reports on nominations, candidate's credentials, and selection criteria
12:35–1:00	Discussion of candidates, selection of finalists
1:00–1:15	Closing remarks, setting time and place of next meeting

Gather Materials

Another important aspect of meetings is making sure that the group has all that it needs to perform its work. The needs may be varied. Decision making groups may need reports, statistics, and other information. The United Way awards committee, for example, should have readily available its guidelines, a list of nominees, and appropriate information about them. A decorating committee will need a sufficient supply of materials with which to work. A group preparing to present a report may need audio visual equipment with which to rehearse. Steps should be taken to supply whatever is necessary for the group to do its work well.

Conclusion

For group work to be successful, members must accomplish a number of tasks. They must recognize the nature of small group work. They must invest themselves in the process and play roles that contribute positively to the group's progress. Group leadership may manifest itself in several styles. The most appropriate style will be the one that best matches the group's purpose, membership, and circumstances. Well planned meetings are another aspect contributing to effective small group work.

• • • Notes

[1] "Devils advocate" is the popular name for the "promoter of the faith" in the Roman Catholic Church. In the procedures which decide whether or not to designate a person a saint, the promoter of the faith or "devil's advocate" raises objections and argues against the case for sainthood. ("Devil's Advocate." *New Catholic Encyclopedia.* 1967.)

• • • Discussion Questions

1. For what kinds of decisions would a small group be best? Why?

2. What kinds of decisions would best be handled by an individual? Why?

3. Why is it important that group members assume responsibilities for the performance of the group?

4. What are some of the positive activities in which group members can engage? Why are these activities regarded as positive?

5. What are some of the negative activities in which group members can engage? How do these subvert the group process?

6. What is "group leadership"?

7. What are the responsibilities of a group leader? Why are these important?

8. What are the different styles of group leadership? In which situations is each style best?

9. What examples of differing leadership styles have you observed?

10. What considerations should be given to planning group meetings?

11. Why is an agenda important to group meetings?

• • • Sources and References

(The references here are to those works cited specifically in this chapter. A fuller bibliography of small group material influencing this chapter can be found at the end of Chapter Eight.)

Barge, J. Kevin. "Leadership as Medium: A Leaderless Group Discussion Model." *Communication Quarterly* 37 (1989): 237–49.

Name _____ Section _____ Date _____

Working in Small Groups: Rules and Leadership

1. List the advantages of working in a small group versus working individually.

   _____

   _____

   _____

2. What disadvantages are there in working in a small group versus working individually?

   _____

   _____

   _____

3. Group success is the culmination of a number of factors. What responsibilities must an individual member of a group assume to contribute to group success?

   _____

   _____

   _____

4. What are the positive contributions to the problem-solving process that group members can make?

   _____

   _____

   _____

5. What role does empathy play in a small group's success?

   _____

   _____

   _____

6. When can a mediator be useful in a small group?

   _____

   _____

   _____

7. What part does tension relief play in the work of a small group?

_____

_____

_____

8. What negative behaviors should be avoided by members in small group deliberations?

_____

_____

_____

9. How can a small group solve the problem of a member withdrawing from participation?

_____

_____

_____

10. Explain the distinction between an appointed leader and an emergent leader.

_____

_____

_____

11. What is the primary function of a group leader?

_____

_____

_____

12. A leader can take a number of steps to encourage positive group functioning. What are these steps?

_____

_____

_____

_____

13. Define an authoritarian leader.

_____

_____

14. When is it appropriate to use the authoritarian style of leadership?

_____

_____

_____

15. How does a democratic leader function in a small group?

_____

_____

_____

16. If there is a difference of opinion in a democratic group, how is the matter settled? Which opinion prevails?

_____

_____

_____

17. When is the democratic style of leadership most appropriate?

_____

_____

_____

18. Define *laissez-faire* leadership.

_____

_____

_____

19. Describe the circumstances when *laissez-faire* leadership is best used.

_____

_____

_____

20. An effective leader makes certain that details are arranged in connection with small group meetings. What would be included in a checklist of things to arrange prior to a small group meeting?

_____

_____

_____

_____

_____

21. What is an agenda and what should it include?

_____

_____

_____

_____

8

Working in Small Groups: Problem Solving Procedures

Key Concepts

We have now examined a number of aspects of small group communication. We have seen how groups work and the contributions members may make in their various roles. All of these factors come together and contribute to the success or failure of the group to discover a workable solution to the problem it addresses.

Effective Problem Solving

When a problem solving group sets to work, it has several courses of action available to it. Solutions to the problem at hand may be pursued in a number of ways, both ineffective and effective.

Ineffective Problem Solving

Effective problem solving depends on a full consideration of information and possibilities offered to the group. Ineffective problem solving uses decision making processes that fail to consider available information and that thwart the group process.

Autocratic decision making is one approach to problem solving. In this style, group leaders decide which solution best benefits them and then announce the decision to the group. In these cases, the group members have no option but to go along with the decision or to resign.

Another inferior method of decision making is *rushing to judgment.* Here the group disregards or severely limits investigation and discussion and picks the first solution offered. Groups may make these kinds of decisions because of limited time or fatigue. Because it fails to investigate possibilities, the group's solution often fails to remedy the problem situation.

Mob rule is another method of group decision making but a poor one. It is a rush to judgment coupled with strong emotions. Caught up in its feelings and seeking a way to vent its anger, the group picks a solution which appears to offer a quick fix while providing a way for the group to express its anger. Usually, these decisions create more problems than they solve.

The Rational Model of Problem Solving

A better way to solve problems is for the group to adopt procedures that encourage in-

vestigation and definition of the problem, generation of possible solutions, and sound judgment in reaching decisions. Such a method was outlined in the early part of this century by John Dewey and further refined in the thirties by James H. McBurney and Kenneth G. Hance. The method is widely used and taught and has undergone continual refining. The method describes the steps that groups should go through to reach the best possible solution.

Define the Problem

The first task sounds simple enough but is not always used. The group must first decide what <u>is</u> its task: it must *define the problem.* The decision is an important one as it will shape much of the group's subsequent activity. Discussing solutions and courses of action is pointless unless the group knows for what it is searching. Failure to articulate the problem to be attacked will result in lost time and duplicated efforts.

Sometimes, the decision is a simple one: the group is given an assignment. The Undergraduate Committee is told to pick the "Outstanding Senior;" the design committee is charged with the creation of a logo; the entertainment committee of a club has the responsibility to plan the spring banquet.

At other times, the task is not so easy. Group members may have a general sense of uneasiness about a situation, but that sense does not articulate the problem to be approached. In their search for the problem, groups may light on a symptom of the problem rather than the problem itself. Different group members may define the problem in different ways. The group must find agreement on what is the goal of the group.

For example, in response to complaints, the student senate may create a committee on tuition charges at the school. Designating the committee does not, however, create a purpose for the group. Is the group to investigate and report information to the senate? Is the group to lobby legislators during the debate on the state's educational budget? Is the committee to seek student opinions? Is the group to propose ways to avoid tuition hikes? Without a clear statement of purpose, the group will be without direction.

▲ **Figure 8.1.** Research or investigating the problem is a major task for problem solving groups. (Dawe)

Investigate the Problem

Once the group has articulated the problem to be solved, the next step is to *investigate the problem situation*. The goal in this stage is to find out as much as possible about the problem to be solved and what surrounds the problem. This allows the group to work from knowledge rather than ignorance. At this stage, a number of questions need to be asked and answered:

▶ What is the origin of the problem?
▶ Why did this problem develop?
  • What circumstances led to the creation of this problem?
  • What people led to the creation of this problem?
▶ What perpetuates this problem?
▶ What solutions to this problem have already been tried?
▶ What resources do we have available to solve this problem?
  • How much money do we have available?
  • How much time do we have available?
  • What people and talents are available?
  • What materials are available?
▶ To whom do we report our conclusions?
▶ Who puts the solution into effect?

At this point in the problem solving sequence, the group needs to be as open as possible. The research step should utilize as many types of information as necessary. Relevant information may be found in print sources, in electronic media, and in people. In short, wherever the group needs to look, it should look.

Some of the sources a group might find helpful are:

▶ Newspapers: local, other cities, foreign, national dailies,
▶ Periodicals: general audience periodicals (*Esquire, Redbook, Working Woman, Psychology Today*), special audience magazines (*Motor Trend, Outdoor Photography, Computer World*), academic journals (*Quarterly Journal of Speech, Management Quarterly, Metallurgy Journal*) trade publications (*Heating and Air Conditioning Bulletin, Auto Mechanic, Pipe Trades*),
▶ Books
▶ People resources: interviews, expert testimony
▶ Electronic media: news reports, documentaries, special topic programs (*Western Civilization, The Civil War, Creativity*)

The job of information gathering is well suited to small group work. Members can divide up the research work, pool their resources, and accomplish the task much more quickly than could an individual.

Set Criteria for a Solution

Once the group has gathered information and provided itself with the basis for informed judgments, it moves on to the next step in the process, *setting criteria for the solution*. Here the group creates and agrees on a set of "goals" for the solution with the best solution accomplishing the greatest number of goals. Considerations in creating the criteria would be such aspects as available time, money, space, resources, and feasibility.

The criteria act as a measuring stick for all proposed solutions. Formulating the criteria provides the group with an accepted basis for evaluating and making decisions. The final standard is not one group member's idiosyncratic preference for a given solution. The final standard is the set of criteria accepted by all group members.

A family trying to decide where to go on vacation might list as criteria: a beach, nice campground, good shopping, pretty scenery, and within one day's drive from home. The undergraduate committee selecting the outstanding senior might generate criteria such as: senior standing, high grade point average, rigorous plan of study, service activities, and professional plans. The entertainment committee looking for a banquet site would probably have criteria such as: good food, comfortable banquet room, reasonable price, availability on desired date, and easily reached from campus.

Formulate Possible Solutions

With a solid base of knowledge from which to work and with consensus reached on the criteria for judging possible solutions, the group should next *formulate possible solutions.* Decisions will usually be better if groups debate the strengths and weaknesses of several possibilities rather than immediately settling on one solution.

The family will propose several sites that might meet the criteria. The undergraduate committee will select a group of finalists. The entertainment committee will discuss the three restaurants or catering services available.

Select the Best Alternative

Once a list of possible solutions is on the table for discussion, the group then moves forward to *select the solution it deems best.* The decisive factor should be which solution comes closest to meeting the criteria created earlier. Sometimes, one solution will emerge clearly as superior to the others. In other cases, the group may agonize over the relative merits of two solutions, each with strengths and weaknesses that balance the other.

In choosing a solution, the group must remember that "best" does not mean "perfect" and that "consensus" does not mean "everyone thinks it is perfect." Most solutions will have both positive and negative aspects. In some situations, the key question will be which option offers the fewest negatives, and the group will be forced to decide which of two bad alternatives it wants. This kind of decision will be a difficult one, but the final choice would be the option that offers the best combination of characteristics.

Put the Chosen Solution into Effect

After selecting the best possible solution, the group needs to change its focus yet again and take up the task of *putting the chosen solution into effect.* In some cases, the group will report its findings to an administrative officer, a client, or to yet another group such as the board of trustees or the city commissioners. In other cases, the group will itself be the unit enacting its decisions. The scheduling committee for a social group, for example, after deciding on the best course of action, would issue the schedule of meetings to the members and possibly start looking for speakers or entertainment.

Decide What Happens to the Group

Once the solution is put into effect, the major work of the group is over, but it still has one task left to accomplish. That task is to *decide what happens to the group once the solution has been put into effect.* The group may disband, refine the solution, find another solution, or take up another problem.

Many groups break up once their work is done. Once a recipient is found and the award made, an award committee has little else to do. An *ad hoc* committee, commissioned to study a particular problem, disbands once its work is through. No more *hoc,* no more committee.

Other groups stay in touch with the problem and monitor how well the solution is working. A curriculum committee in a university may create a new core of class. Following that work, the committee would watch the core to see how well it was working and to make necessary changes if it were discovered that classes were not available, students' degree progress was unduly hampered, or classes were not accomplishing their intended purpose in the core.

The last possibility is that the group continues functioning but leaves behind the problem just completed and takes up a new problem. This is the course of action followed by standing committees. Once an issue is decided, the committee moves on to another issue and another issue after that and another after that, *ad infinitum.*

Case Study of Group Decision Making

The Midway Agency, a twenty-two member real estate company is outgrowing its quarters. Office space is cramped. Parking is difficult. Agents find it increasingly difficult to talk to clients in private.

The director and owner of the company creates a committee to make recommendations about finding a better facility. The committee consists of the director, three agents, the business manager, and the office manager.

Define the Problem

At their first meeting, they discuss whether they are looking for a temporary or a permanent solution. They decide on a permanent solution as the most efficient way to approach the problem. The problem then becomes: We want to find the best facility for the business that will meet present needs and projected needs for the next ten years.

Investigate the Problem

The committee turns its attention to deciding what are the present shortcomings of their facility and what will be their future needs. Some of the information they consider are equipment needs (telephones, computers, fax machines, copy machines, etc.), client preferences, optimum office space, traffic patterns in the office, routing of information, parking facilities, access to major streets, traffic patterns, census figures, city growth patterns, and company revenues.

Set Criteria for a Solution

After gathering as much relevant information as they can, the committee members then create the set of criteria against which to measure suggested plans. Many of the criteria grow out of the information they have collected. The list of criteria includes:

► Convenient location for customers to reach
► Pleasant neighborhood
► Sufficient parking for employees and customers
► Sufficient office space for all employees
► A conference room

► Storage space for supplies
► Expansion space to handle growth in next ten years
► Adaptable floor space
► Room for equipment (copiers, computers, etc.)
► Kitchen
► Attractive building
► Attractive decor
► Economically profitable.

Formulate Possible Solutions

After creating the criteria, the committee then turns its attention to the options available to it. Knowing the real estate market makes this step easier for it than it would be for other businesses. The main options available are to rent space in an existing building, buy an existing building, rent in a facility to be built, or build their own building. The committee investigates all the possibilities. The three best options are: (A) to rent space in a new office complex being built a half mile from their present site, (B) rent larger quarters in an existing office complex, or (C) buy and renovate a former sporting goods store in the downtown area.

Each site has its advantages and disadvantages. Options A and B offer almost unlimited parking. Option C offers less parking than they have now. In terms of cost, buying and renovating the building would be more expensive, but little guarantee can be given that rents in Options A and B will not rise. Option A provides some room for expansion of the business, Option B more room, and Option C almost unlimited room. The discussion continues on each point of the criteria for each option.

Select the Best Alternative

After long discussion, the group ranks their options and endorses Option C as its choice. While it is not without drawbacks, its advantages outweigh those of the other options and its problems are not large enough to cancel out its advantage.

Decide What To Do With the Group

Once the decision is made, the group disbands. The problem of selecting a site for the business will not occur for at least ten years. If a problem arises with the preferred option, the group may be reconstituted to begin again, but if the group has done its work well, its task is at an end.

Successful small group work involves an awareness of the nature of small group processes and the willingness of group members to participate in the process. By following the steps of small group decision making, groups can discover the best solutions to the problems which they address.

Methods of Decision Making

The major work of a problem solving group is the decision of which solution to adopt. Along the way to that major decision will be a history of other decisions, small and large, ranging from setting meeting times to how to handle issues to who pays for refreshments. Groups may make their decisions in a variety of ways. The appropriate method of decision making will depend on the nature of the decision and the nature of the group. An understanding of the different ways in which groups may make decisions will help us function better in groups.

Decision Making by the Group Leader

In authoritarian groups, often the decision is made by the leader, with or without discussion with group members. When the leader is knowledgeable or time is short, this method may be the best method. With only thirty seconds for a huddle, the quarterback on a football team will simply announce the next play. He will not stop the game for a thirty minute group meeting. In a business meeting, the leader may have a series of cases to be investigated, and she simply tells the committee members who is to take which case.

Leaders may also consult with group members, then make decisions. In the assignment of cases, one member may say why he would be particularly good at working with a given case or may give reasons why he would prefer not to have a case. After listening to the comments, the leader would then make the final decision.

Majority Rule

A simple way of making decisions is to take a vote and the option receiving the largest number of votes becomes the committee's course of action. This method works best if the issue is one that can be decided by a "yes" or "no" reaction. The majority rule method of decision making is the one employed by appeals courts and supreme courts. A decision must be made and total agreement may be impossible. Majority rule is a quick and efficient way to settle the matter.

Majority rule may also have its drawbacks. Majority rule works best when group members are on an equal footing as in the Supreme Court. When members are divided by various means—economic, ethnically, status, age, etc. —majority rule can be a way of shutting off the influence of the minority group.

A committee investigating parking problems on campus might be made up of students, faculty, and administrators. If the parking committee consists of four faculty members, four administrators and two students, one would expect the group's solutions to reflect strongly the point of view of the older members. Similarly, if the ratio were switched and the committee composed of eight students, one administrator, and one faculty member, students would hold the power in the group and decisions would likely reflect their views.

Parliamentary Procedure

Similar to majority rule but bound by more regulations is parliamentary procedure. Here the group adopts a set of rules which spell out exactly how proposals are to be made, how they are to be amended, and what kind of votes are necessary for the proposals to pass. The final decision is made by the group voting.

At first glance, parliamentary procedure may seem like a complicated and fussy way to do business, but it offers a number of advantages to a group. When it is impossible for the entire group to agree on a measure, some way has to be found to make the final decision. Parliamentary decision sets the guidelines for an orderly discussion and disposition of measures. One of its foremost virtues is that it keeps the attention of the group focused on the matter at hand. Once a motion is made, discussion must be pertinent to that motion. Parliamentary procedure is also useful in that it ensures that all members of a group are subject to the same set of uniform rules. Disputes about procedures can be solved by referring to the rules of order.

Consensus

Perhaps the best way for small groups to reach decisions is by consensus. Consensus is achieved when all agree on the decision. Consensus does not mean that all have the same level of positive feelings about the decision, but it means that all concur in the decision. Consensus is sometimes difficult to achieve because contested issues demand a great deal of mediation, negotiation, and discussion. If accomplished, however, consensus unifies the group both in the decision and in support of the decision. When all have a hand in the decision, the members will be more supportive of the decision than if it were made by another method.

In the process of their work, groups make a number of decisions. The best method of making these decisions will depend on the group and its circumstances.

Dealing with Difficulties

Group work can be highly rewarding, but it can also be highly frustrating. Learning how to handle difficult situations can, however, make the process more productive and more enjoyable.

Conflict

As noted earlier, conflict arises from incompatibilities between people. The incompatibilities may be in viewpoints, ideas, or behavior. As with interpersonal relationships, conflict is not in itself the sign of a faulty relationship and may instead be the sign of a very healthy relationship. As some have observed, "conflict is productive to the extent that it helps a group discover and examine its options as completely as possible" (Wall and Galanes 63). In group work, we can expect conflicts to arise. The im-

portant thing is not whether or not conflict exists in a group but rather how productively the group handles the conflict.

Minimizing Conflict

One way to handle conflict is to *cultivate the best possible group climate.* When group members respect each other and the group has a positive climate, members are less likely to create conflict and more likely to settle conflict productively than when a negative group climate exists.

As part of the climate, the group can *create norms that discourage unnecessary conflicts.* The group can set limits on what kind of language is acceptable in the group, for example. If some members find a particular phrase offensive, the group can find another way of referring to the subject. By being sensitive to each other's feelings and viewpoints, the group can avoid a great deal of problems.

When group members *contribute positively,* conflict will be minimized. The fault finder's role is an easy one to assume, but constant negative reactions from a member or members become in themselves an impetus to conflict. Members may disagree, but comments and ideas should be phrased in a way that attempts to help the group in its work, not simply to point out its problems.

The group can also establish norms relating to how it will handle conflict. Group members can decide how disagreements are to be stated, how the parties in a conflict are to address each other, and when mediation is to be introduced. With consensus reached on the ways in which conflict will be handled, the group can feel more secure about conflict when it arises.

Dealing with Conflict

Once conflict becomes open, the group members can use a number of approaches and techniques to deal with the problem. One of the first things a group member should do in the presence of conflict is to *gauge the importance of the conflict.* Conflicts range from small nuisances to major upheavals. Not all require strenuous effort or even recognition on the part of the group. Some of the seriousness of a conflict will be decided by the group and the

▲ **Figure 8.2.** Conflict must often be faced in small groups. (Coyle)

norms it sets. In one group, gum chewing or snuff dipping may get on members' nerves so much that the matter becomes of concern to the whole group. In other groups, these practices would be accepted without question.

To gauge the importance of a conflict, we can ask ourselves several questions. One of these is, "How much does this conflict impair our ability to function as a group?" If the matter is extraneous to the group's work, we should probably leave the matter alone. For instance, people may work for different political parties and oppose each other in local elections while at the same time cooperating as members of the board of the local symphony orchestra. The political issues are extraneous to the function of the symphony board and are ignored in that context.

Another question is, "How much does this conflict interfere with my ability to function as a group member?" If we find ourselves increasingly reluctant to participate because of the actions of another, we should probably address the conflict.

We can also ask, "How long will I have to work under these conditions?" We may find ourselves having to deal with an obnoxious person, but if we have only one meeting with the group and it lasts only an hour, we would do better to put up with the person instead of trying to eliminate the boor's grating habits.

Another important question is, "Is the conflict whether or not I like this person?" (Bormann and Bormann 152). Working relationships in groups do not necessarily mean warm personal relationships between the members.

If one decides that a conflict is impairing the group process and needs to be faced, the way in which the conflict is addressed can have positive or negative results for the group. The best way to talk about conflicts in a group is to *speak to the issue, not the person*. Again, this principle echoes earlier advice about dealing with interpersonal conflict.

If a person objects to the statement of another, the response should focus on the statement and not the person who made it. To say, "How stupid can you be to make a statement like that?" is to put the other person on the defensive on a personal level. To say, " I think the solution you suggest will cause other problems" is to focus discussion on the issue at hand. The second approach is the more productive of the two because it downplays personalities yet still addresses the difference of opinion.

Coupled with the idea of speaking to the issue and not the person is the need to *respect the feelings of others*. People invest themselves in their ideas and their work, and do not like to see their efforts fail. Group members can disagree over issues but still compliment each other on the amount of time and effort and thought they have invested in the project.

Similarly, group members can *focus on the group* and do much to solve conflicts. To function well in a group, the individual members must be willing to make sacrifices, to some degree, of their personal preferences. Keeping in mind the advancement of the group will help members maintain a helpful perspective on matters.

One approach to conflict is to flee from it. Another is to announce positions and dig in to defend them. If a conflict is a major, these techniques will only hamper the group in accomplishing its goals. Group members should be willing to *explore the conflict*. Acknowledging differences is one way to start. The next step is trying to determine what the reasons are for the disagreement. A battle over meeting times may, in truth, not be a problem of meeting times but a problem in finding child care, finding transportation to meetings, or a one time conflict with an exam. By probing what is the interest of the parties in the conflict, the group will resolve conflicts effectively.

Members should also *be willing to negotiate.* One does not have to give up all one's preferences to function in a group, but flexibility is necessary to perform well as a group member. If the proposed solution does not satisfy several members, the most troublesome aspect might be eliminated while keeping the bulk of the idea intact. The answer to conflicts over meeting times may be to vary the times so that no one member is inconvenienced more than the others. If a group wishes to solve a conflict rather than suppress it, negotiation is the way to resolution.

Conflict may be a part of group procedures, but by building a positive group climate and following productive communication patterns, conflict can be minimized in a group and its resolution speeded.

Dealing with Difficult Group Members

All groups will need to deal with conflict in some way. In addition to expected patterns of conflict, groups may find themselves faced with an additional source of conflict. One or more members may act in ways that put them at odds with the rest of the group and may display some of the negative characteristics noted above such as withdrawing, fighting, or dominating. While these individuals can make life difficult for their groups, some methods may be useful in resolving the problems they create.

Groups will need to *recognize the problem.* For a short time, it may be useful to overlook the problems caused by one member. Again, the question is, "What is best for the group?" If the problem becomes long term and is hampering the work of the group, group members should recognize the person's behavior as one of the problems to be dealt with on the group's way to finding a solution for its stated problem.

One way to address the problem is simply to ask the person or persons why they are acting as they are. The offensive or obnoxious behavior may have its base in a larger problem, and addressing the larger problem may make the person more cooperative.

The planning committee for the Civic Theatre annual fundraiser traditionally meets at Kelly's Bar and Grill for a late lunch and discussion. One of the new members, Paul Johnson, arrives late and makes few contributions. When the group finally confronts him, it discovers that his work takes him out of town. It is an inconvenience for him to break off his appointments to make it to the meetings. The group decides to shift the meetings to breakfast meetings. Johnson can meet with the group, then have the rest of the day undisturbed.

In dealing with difficult people, group members should also *look for problem areas and sensitivities.* These are areas where group members are likely to take strong stands. Discussion in these areas may turn into what one calls "battles of the will" in which the only way to resolution is for one party to back down (Fisher and Ury 85). A simple way around these difficulties is to avoid the inflammatory issues if they are peripheral to the functioning of the group. Two group members may have equally strong but opposing feelings about a local environmental situation. If the situation has nothing to do with the work of the committee, then the topic should be left out of the group discussions.

Another way to deal with "battles of the will" is to hold the group to objective standards in making decisions (Fisher and Ury 84–86). As noted, an important step in group problem solving is the creation of criteria for selecting a solution. All relevant factors should be discussed and all members participate in the creation of the criteria. The criteria then become the measuring standard which determines the acceptability of all possible solutions. A group member may feel strongly about a pet solution, but if that solution does not meet the criteria, the group can reject it, not from a personal whim but from a reasoned standard.

Because of dwindling enrollments, a school board must revamp its use of buildings. A committee is created. One of the standards the committee decides upon is that school buildings may be closed if they are operating below seventy per–cent capacity, require extensive repairs, or both. In the discussion, it becomes clear that Earhart Elementary is operating below the recommended capacity and is in need of extensive and expensive repairs.

One of the committee members attended the school and has fond memories of it. He argues strongly against its closing because of the sentimental value it has to its neighborhood. He threatens to resign from the committee if Earhart Elementary is marked for closing. The committee chair reminds him that while the group can empathize with his feelings about the school, the final decision is to be based on the objective criteria generated by the committee. The committee moves ahead with its business.

Another way to deal with difficult people in small groups is to *look for common ground between the person and the group*. Here the group would try to find a way in which its desires and the desires of the troublesome group member might be perceived as one. In the case of the school closing, the committee might remind the reluctant member that they all share the common goal of doing what is best for the education of the town's children. The sentiments about the school might be echoed by other members. Members might reflect upon the difficulty of the decisions that they all face. The more group members feel akin to other group members, the easier it will be for them to deal with each other.

Finally, a group may be able to deal with difficult members by finding ways to *provide difficult members with a safety valve*. By "safety valve," we mean some means by which the member's feelings may be expressed or recognition given to the person's views. Sometimes, this may be accomplished by letting people talk freely about their views. At other times, a more formal outlet may be provided. If the group members do not all concur in a decision, the dissenting parties may submit a "minority report" along with the report of the committee.

Creative ways may be found to recognize the feelings of the dissenting minority. In the case of the school closing, part of the proposed plan might be to put an historical display of the closed school in the library of an existing, nearby school. Sale of the building might be limited to those who would continue to use it as an educational facility, thus retaining its image and function. Sometimes, small concessions to dissenters can result in major gains for the group.

Avoiding Groupthink

We have dealt at length with conflict and resolving conflicts in small groups and stressed that unresolved conflicts may be detrimental to a group. One might think, then, that the ideal small group would be the one that exhibited the maximum amount of group harmony. That is not necessarily the case. Too much solidarity in a group can be as disastrous as too much discord. When a group becomes so unified and cohesive that it entertains no conflict, no real disagreements, the usual result is a bad decision. When a group develops in this manner, it is exhibiting "groupthink" which is defined as "a deterioration of mental efficiency, reality testing, and moral judgments that results from ingroup pressures" (Janis, *Groupthink* 9).

The term "groupthink" was coined by Irving L. Janis and is based on his examination of major foreign policy decisions both good and bad. The Kennedy administration, for example, made a disastrous decision to support the ill-planned and ill-fated Bay of Pigs invasion of Cuba. The invading forces were poorly prepared. The landing site offered no "fall back" position. The invading forces were easily defeated, and the project was a total fiasco. Later, though, the same administration responded well to the Cuban Missile Crisis and gained world wide respect for its actions. In this incident, Kennedy and his advisors faced the threat of war with Russia and made decisions that averted armed conflict and defused the situation. Janis' main question was, "How could intelligent, well-meaning people make decisions so different in outcomes?"

The answer was that the good decisions arose from groups following the guidelines of openness and give-and-take that we have discussed. The bad decisions resulted from groups that put such a high premium on their unity that they ignored information they did not like, failed to examine ideas critically, and in short, spelled the doom of their own plans.

Groupthink is a kind of negative consensus. The group agrees to agree so strongly that the problem solving process is thwarted before a good solution is found. Rather than examining all possibilities, the group may discuss only one or two courses of action. In-group criticism of plans is discouraged and dissenters are ostracized. Little attempt is made to obtain relevant information. Outside criticism is regarded as the work of fools or scoundrels attempting to sabotage the group. Therefore, the group fails to consider carefully information and alternatives by employing effective decision making practices.

When groupthink prevails, the situation is similar to a preventable auto accident. Everyone in the car is pleased with how the trip is progressing and the good spirit in the car, but nobody pays attention to where they are going, and they drive happily over a cliff.

If a group seems closed to outside opinion and keeps internal criticism to a minimum, the group may be developing groupthink. If the group is congenial within itself and hostile to outsiders, again the group may be displaying groupthink. If the group seizes rapidly on a solution to a problem but has not investigated or discussed the problem fully, it is again showing signs of groupthink.

To avoid groupthink, the group should make provisions for full discussion of ideas and policies. Issues should be thoroughly researched. The group should discuss proposals from all sides. One member may even be designated the idea tester to see how well the group's proposals stand up against criticism. A climate of openness and honesty will also do much to prevent groupthink.

Vigilance in Problem Solving

The preceding chapters have outlined how groups can function best. If we lived in an ideal world, all small groups would approach problem solving with an open mind, sufficient time to effect the optimum solution, and would follow fully the guidelines provided here. As more than one person has observed, however, we do not live in an ideal world.

In the multitude of our activities—both professional and personal—we must deal with problems, pressures, and limitations on our abilities to deal with them. A person may be appointed to a committee at work only to discover that the committee cannot find the time, re-

sources, or people necessary for the committee to do its job fully. In addition, not all decisions merit the time and expense of group meetings. Deciding how to staff an office will probably require the efforts of a group whereas the number of small daily decisions—ordering supplies, sorting mail, forwarding calls—will not.

Faced with the limitations we often find in our decision making situations, we should still practice *vigilance in problem solving* (Janis, *Decisions*). In the hurly-burly of life, it is often impossible to carry out the step-by-step problem solving procedures that we have described. The fact that not all problems can be approached in a textbook manner does not mean, though, that the process should be abandoned if conditions are less than perfect. Instead, the process should be preserved as completely as possible. Whenever possible, the step-by-step method should be followed because it allows for the best possible solutions and the best consequences arise from the best decisions. "The quality of procedures used to arrive at a fundamental policy decision is one of the major determinants of a successful outcome" (Janis, *Decisions* 20.) If it is impossible to work through the recommended procedures, they should still be approximated as closely as possible.

Practicing vigilant problem solving means that people follow two principles, both of which require awareness and sensitivity. The first is deciding how important an issue is and how much attention it demands. Routine matters are handled in routine ways. Ordering paperclips is probably an insignificant decision in most offices. Not all small decisions, though, are created equal. If the paper clip order is seen by a staff member as usurping his authority or questioning his abilities, then the issue involves more than simple judgment. Sensitivity to the ramifications of decisions will lead to better analyses of problems and better decisions about solutions.

The second main point of vigilant problem solving is that we must do the best we can in the circumstances in which we find ourselves. The procedures of people who make good decisions "involve working to the best of their limited abilities, within the confines of available . . . resources, to exercise all the caution they can to avoid mistakes in the essential tasks of information search, deliberation, and planning" (Janis 29).

In short, vigilant problem solving is doing the best we can with what we have. One may not have the time necessary to assemble all the available information on a problem. One response would be to say, "Since we cannot obtain all the necessary information, we will not gather any." Though the group may have to rely on brief summaries by knowledgeable people or may be able to look at only a fraction of relevant material, the group should still gather as much information as it can. Some information in the problem solving process is better than none.

A group may have to deal with members whose personalities clash and who have difficulty discussing what course of action to take. The group's leader may be tempted to duck the issue and make the decision unilaterally. If the leader were practicing vigilant problem solving, the leader would try to foster as much creative discussion as possible even though the discussion might be limited by the clashing personalities.

Vigilant problem solving is an approach to decision making that takes into account the limitations we face as a part of life. Exercising vigilance in our problem solving procedures—doing the best we can in our circumstances—will help us find good solutions. While vigilant problem solving will not eliminate all the pitfalls of making decisions, vigilance will ensure that the pitfalls are kept to a minimum.

Conclusion

Functioning in a small group is not an easy matter. It demands effort from leaders and members alike. Effective problem solving groups will move through stages in their searches for solutions. Beginning with the task of defining the problem, they will search for possible solution, evaluate them, and finally choose the best alternative. Each of these steps requires discussion, give-and-take, and decision making. Decisions may be made by several means: by the leader, by majority vote, by parliamentary procedure, and by consensus. Conflicts may arise in the group process, but by appropriate measures, conflict can be handled productively. Alertness and diligence will avoid the problem of groupthink and contribute to the best decision making possible. Good small group work allows us to address problems we encounter, discover solutions, and create positive relationships.

• • • Discussion Questions

1. Why are autocratic decision making, rushing to judgment, and mob rule ineffective approaches to problem solving?

2. What examples can you think of that would illustrate ineffective approaches to problem solving?

3. Why is it important to follow the steps of the rational model of problem solving? What advantages does this approach to problem solving have over other methods?

4. When would decision making by the group leader, majority rule, parliamentary procedure, or consensus be the most effective way of making decisions? When would each be the least effective means of making decisions?

5. What would introduce conflict into a small group?

6. Why is it important for small groups to handle conflict productively?

7. How can small groups keep conflict to a minimum?

8. What would make group members "difficult"?

9. How could personal goals become mixed with group goals?

10. Why is it important to practice vigilance in problem solving? How does one foster vigilance in problem solving?

• • • Sources and References

Andrews, Patricia Hayes. "Performance-Self-Esteem and Perception of Leadership Emergence: A Comparative Study of Men and Women." *Western Journal of Speech Communication* 48 (1984): 1–13.

Barge, J. Kevin. "Leadership as Medium: A Leaderless Group Discussion Model." *Communication Quarterly* 37 (1989): 237–49.

Benne, Kenneth D. and Paul Sheets. "Functional Role of Group Members." *Journal of Social Issues* 4 (Spring 12948): 41–49.

Bormann, Ernest G. "Symbolic Convergence Theory and Communication in Group Decision-Making." *Communication and Group Decision-Making*. Eds. Randy Y. Hirokawa and Marshall Scott Poole. Beverly Hills: Sage Publications, 1986. 219–36.

Bormann, Ernest G. and Nancy C. Bormann. *Effective Small Group Communication*. Edina, Minnesota: Burgess Publishing Company, 1988.

Broome, Benjamin J. and David B. Keever. "Next Generation Group Facilitation: Proposed Principles." *Management Communication Quarterly* 3 (1989): 107–127.

Bunyi, Judith M. and Patricia Hayes Andrews. "Gender and Leadership Emergence: An Experimental Study: *The Southern Speech Communication Journal* 50 (1985): 246–60.

Chilberg, Joseph C. "A Review of Group Process Designs for Facilitating Communication in Problem-Solving Groups." *Management Communication Quarterly* 3 (1989): 51–70.

Cline, Rebecca J. Welch. "Detecting Groupthink: Methods for Observing the Illusion of Unanimity." *Communication Quarterly* 38 (1990): 112–126.

Cragan, John F. and David W. Wright. "Small Group Communication Research of the 1980s: A Synthesis and a Critique." *Communication Studies* 41 (1990): 212–36.

Dewey, John. *How We Think*. Boston: D. C. Heath and Co., Publishers, 1910.

Fairhurst, Gail T. and Teresa A. Chandler. "Social Structure in Leader-Member Interaction." *Communication Monographs* 56 (1989): 215–39.

Folger, Joseph P. and Marshall Scott Poole. *Working Through Conflict: A Communication Perspective*. Glenview, Illinois: Scott, Foresman and Company, 1984.

Friedman, Paul G. "Upstream Facilitation: A Productive Approach to Problem-Solving Groups." *Management Communication Quarterly* 3 (1989): 33–50.

Gouran, Dennis S. "Inferential Errors, Interaction, and Group Decision-Making." *Communication and Group Decision-Making*. Eds. Randy Y. Hirokawa and Marshall Scott Poole. Beverly Hills: Sage Publications, 1986. 93–111.

Gouran, Dennis S. and Randy Y. Hirokawa. "Counteractive Functions of Communication in Effective Group Decision-Making." Eds. Randy Y. Hirokawa and Marshall Scott Poole. *Communication and Group Decision-Making*. Beverly Hills: Sage Publications, 1986. 81–90.

Hewes, Dean E. "A Socio-Egocentric Model of Group Decision-Making." *Communication and Group Decision-Making*. Eds. Randy Y. Hirokawa and Marshall Scott Poole. Beverly Hills: Sage Publications, 1986. 265–91.

Hirokawa, Randy Y. and Dirk R. Scheerhorn. "Communication in Faulty Decision-Making." *Communication and Group Decision-Making*. Eds. Randy Y. Hirokawa and Marshall Scott Poole. Beverly Hills: Sage Publications, 1986. 63–80.

Hirokawa, Randy Y. and Dennis S. Gouran. "Facilitation of Group Communication: A Critique of Prior Research and an Agenda for Future Research." *Management Communication Quarterly* 3 (1989): 71–92.

Janis, Irving L. *Crucial Decisions: Leadership in Policymaking and Crisis Management*. New York: The Free Press, 1989.

———. *Groupthink: Psychological Studies of Policy Decisions and Fiascoes*. 2nd ed. Boston: Houghton Mifflin Company, 1982.

Keltner, John. "Facilitation: Catalyst for Group Problem Solving." *Management Communication Quarterly* 3 (1989): 8–32.

McBurney. James H. and Kenneth G. Hance. *The Principles and Methods of Discussion*. New York: Harper and Brothers, 1939.

Monroe, Crain, Mark G. Borzi, and Vincent S. DiSalvo. "Conflict Behaviors of Difficult Subordinates." *The Southern Communication Journal* 54 (1989): 311–29.

Poole, Marshall Scott. "Decision Development in Small Groups I: A Comparison of Two Models." *Communication Monographs* 48 (1981): 1–24.

———. "Decision Development in Small Groups II: A Study of Multiple Sequences in Decision Making." *Communication Monographs* 50 (1983): 206–32.

———. "Decision Development in Small Groups III: A Multiple Sequence Model of Group Decision Making." *Communication Monographs* 50 (1983): 321–41.

———. "Do We Have Any Theories of Group Communication." *Communication Quarterly* 41 (1990): 237–47.

Poole, Marshall Scott and Joel A. Doelger. "Developmental Processes in Group Decision-Making." *Communication and Group Decision-Making*. Eds. Randy Y. Hirokawa and Marshall Scott Poole. Beverly Hills: Sage Publications, 1986. 35–62.

Poole, Marshall Scott, David R. Seibold, and Robert D. McPhee. "A Structurational Approach to Theory-Building on Group Decision-Making Research." *Communication and Group Decision-Making*. Eds. Randy Y. Hirokawa and Marshall Scott Poole. Beverly Hills: Sage Publications, 1986. 237–64.

———. "Group Decision-Making as a Structurational Process." *The Quarterly Journal of Speech* 71 (1985): 74–102.

Putnam, Linda L. and Tricia S. Jones. "The Role of Communication in Bargaining." *Human Communication Research* 8 (1982): 262–80.

Putnam, Linda L. and Cynthia Stohl. "Bona Fide Groups: A Reconceptualizations of Groups in Context." *Communication Studies* 41 (1990): 248–65.

Putnam, Linda L. and Charmaine E. Wilson. "Communicative Strategies in Organizational Conflicts: Reliability and Validity of a Measurement Scale." *Communication Yearbook* 6. Ed. Michael Burgoon. Beverly Hills: Sage Publications, 1982. 629–52.

Serafini, Denise M. and Judy C. Pearson. "Leadership Behavior and Sex Role Socialization: Two Sides of the Coin." *The Southern Speech Communication Journal* 49 (1984): 396–405.

Sykes, Richard E. "Imagining What We Really Might Study If We Really Studied Small Groups from a Speech Perspective." *Communication Studies* 41 (1990): 200–11.

Smith, Christie McGuffie and Larry Powell. "The Use of Disparaging Humor by Group Leaders." *The Southern Speech Communication Journal* 53 (1988): 279–92.

Wall, Victor D. and Gloria J. Galanes. "The SYMLOG Dimension and Small Group Conflict." *The Central States Speech Journal* 37 (1986): 61–78.

Wheeless, Lawrence and Lisa S. Reichel. "A Reinforcement Model of the Relationship of Supervisor's General Communication Styles and Conflict Management Styles to Task Attraction." *Communication Quarterly* 38 (1990): 372–87.

Zorn, Theodore E. and Lawrence B. Rosenfield. "Between a Rock and a Hard Place: Ethical Dilemmas in Problem-Solving Group Facilitation." *Management Communication Quarterly* 3 (1989): 93–106.

Name _____ Section _____ Date _____

Working in Small Groups: Problem Solving Procedures

1. How does an autocratic leader approach decision making?

   _____

   _____

   _____

2. What is rushing to judgment?

   _____

   _____

   _____

3. What is the difference between rushing to judgment and mob rule?

   _____

   _____

   _____

4. Describe the seven-step process for effective decision making.

   _____

   _____

   _____

   _____

   _____

   _____

   _____

5. Describe authoritarian decision making.

   _____

   _____

   _____

6. What are the characteristics of majority rule?

    _____

    _____

    _____

7. What is parliamentary procedure?

    _____

    _____

    _____

8. How would a small group make a decision by consensus?

    _____

    _____

    _____

9. What is a drawback to majority rule?

    _____

    _____

    _____

10. How can conflict benefit a small group?

    _____

    _____

    _____

11. What is the best way to handle conflict that is impairing group progress?

    _____

    _____

    _____

12. Define "groupthink".

    _____

    _____

13. How can groupthink be avoided?

_____

_____

_____

14. What is meant by vigilance in problem solving?

_____

_____

_____

Decision Making Exercise

The "John J. Watson Outstanding Senior Award" was created by its namesake, a successful and wealthy alumnus of State University. Watson feels that his experiences at State U. prepared him well and led to his success in business. He wished to recognize present students who have done well at the school and has instituted this award which is given annually and carries a one thousand dollar prize. In addition, the winner's name is placed on a plaque in the Student Services Building.

You are a member of the selection committee charged with designating the outstanding senior, "that person who best exemplifies the qualities of academic success, leadership, service, achievement, and contribution to the school." Five finalists have been chosen. You and your colleagues are to choose the final winner.

John Porter—GPA 3.75/4.00; computer science major; State PC Club; research assistant in computer science; co-author, "Disk Changing Strategy for Elimination of Write-through," *ACM Transactions on Computer Systems*; volunteer tutor, Learning Center; works thirty-five hours a week at K-Mart to pay for schooling; intended profession: computer science professor.

Mary Jeffrey—GPA 3.8/4.0; electrical engineering major; business manager, *Debris* yearbook; vice-president, president, YYY sorority; president, Panhellenic; Student Union Junior Board; Student Union Senior Board; summer intern, IBM; intended profession: electrical engineer.

Susan Holland—GPA 4.0/4.0; physical education and recreational studies major; equestrian club; Special Olympics assistant; Director, student volunteers for Special Olympics; Student Body Vice-President; Young Republicans; Golden Key Honorary; modern dance troupe; intended profession: physical therapist.

William Huang—GPA 4.0/4.0; English major; team captain, School of Liberal Arts telethon; photography club; First Place Team, Midwest Mock Trial Competition; English Department literary awards: freshman, "Best Descriptive Essay," junior, "Best Analytic Essay," senior, "Best Poem"; student representative, University Board of Trustees; president, Young Democrats; intended profession: attorney.

Nancy Flores—GPA 3.9/4.0; creative arts major; campus director, Big Sisters program; docent, State Galleries; teacher, Super Saturday Arts Program; vice-president, Whittier Housing Cooperative; departmental recipient, three years, Delta Phi Delta scholarship; winner, Outstanding Senior in Creative Arts; president, two years, Fine Arts Club; winner, Sudler Commencement Prize for Outstanding Achievement in the Arts; summer intern, Indianapolis Museum of Contemporary Art; intended profession: art museum director.

Sample Group Outline I
"Group Roles and Group Leadership"

Introduction (Margaret)

    A. The purpose of our presentation is to describe and depict group roles and styles of leadership.

    B. Definition: "A group is two or more interacting persons who share common goals and who perceive themselves as a group" (Baron and Byrne, *Social Psychology*).

    C. Groups exhibit four different aspects.

        1. Group members play roles.

        2. Groups create status relationships among members.

        3. Groups create norms.

        4. Groups create cohesiveness.

  I. Groups create three different kind of roles (Baron and Greenburg, *Behavior in Organization*).

    A. Task-oriented roles help the group achieve its goals.

    B. Relational roles are concerned with relations within the group.

    C. Self-oriented roles hamper the group in its work.

        1. With self-oriented roles, group members place their own desires first.

        2. Blockers are resistant to taking part.

        3. Recognition seekers direct attention to themselves.

        4. Dominators assert their authority.

        5. Avoiders isolate themselves from the group.

Skit One: The scene is a kindergarten class. Matt, Dale, Mandi, and Keely play the parts of students in the class. Each group member is labelled with one of the self-oriented roles. Their task as a problem solving group is to assemble a puzzle. The "dominator" tries to make the others assemble the puzzle the way he thinks it should be done. The "avoider" refuses to take part. The "blocker" keeps interfering with the process. The "recognition seeker" wants everyone to pay attention to her.

  II. A group leader is defined as "a person's ability to influence others to work toward achieving personal and organizational goals" (Megginson, Mosley, and Pietri, *Management: Concepts and Applications*). (Corinna)

  III. Group leaders may be classified according to their styles. (Corinna)

    A. Leaders may be classified according to their approaches to people.

        1. Autocratic leaders make decisions unilaterally.

Skit Two: Margaret plays the role of the teacher. She steps into the classroom and assigns each student a part of the puzzle to assemble.

        2. Participative-democratic leaders involve all in the decision making process.

Skit Three: Margaret again plays the teacher. She asks the students which part of the puzzle each would like to assemble. She assigns tasks according to what each would most like to do.

    B. Leaders may be classified according to their orientation towards the job.

        1. People-oriented leaders show concern for the welfare and feelings of group members.

Skit Four: Margaret talks with each student and learns what task each likes to do. She encourages them to work together and enjoy finishing the job. They appear to be having a good time.

        2. Product-oriented leaders focus on getting the job done.

Skit Five: Margaret directs the students to concentrate on finishing their work. She guides them individually and reminds them of a penalty if they are not finished.

  IV. Which style of leadership is best depends on the nature of a given group. (Corrina)

    A. Hersey and Blanchard's Life-Cycle Theory states that a group leader's style should be appropriate to the group situation (Megginson, Mosley, and Pietri, *Management: Concepts and Applications*).

    B. The graph explains how factors interact.

        1. The x-axis indicates task behavior.

        2. The y-axis indicates relationship behavior.

        3. Maturity of the group plays a role.

        4. Choices for leadership can be indicated by which quadrant best describes the group.

           a. A group highly oriented to task and with good relations should work best with a leader who uses a "selling or coaching" style.

           b. A group low in task orientation but with good relationships should work best with a leader who uses a "participating and supporting" style.

           c. A group highly oriented to task and low in relationships should work best with a leader who uses a "structuring and telling" style.

           d. A group low in task orientation and low in relationships should work best with a leader who uses a "delegating" style.

Conclusion: (Corinna)

We have attempted to demonstrate to you the types of roles found in small groups and the importance of leadership in small groups. We have simplified the setting and the task for our group, but you can readily see the effects of different leadership techniques on the self-oriented roles in the group. The key thing to remember is that no one form of leadership is best under all conditions and in all situations. The best style of leadership is the one that is best adapted to the roles and tasks of a given group.

Matt Boatman
Dale Brier
Margaret Farrell
Keely Fountain
Mandi Hepler
Corinna Mikesell

Bibliography

Bacon, Robert A. and Donn E. Byrne. *Social Psychology*. 6th ed. Boston: Allyn and Bacon, 1991.

Bacon, R. A. and Jerald Greenburg. *Behavior in Organizations*. 3rd ed. Boston: Allyn and Bacon, 1990.

Cartwright, Dorwin and Alvin Zander. *Group Dynamics: Research and Theory*. 3rd. ed. New York: Harper and Row Publishers, 1968.

Cherrington, David J. *Management of Human Resources*. 3rd ed. Boston: Allyn and Bacon, 1991.

Dobson, James. *Love Must Be Tough*. New York: New York Press, 1989.

Farley, J. E. *Sociology*. 2nd ed. Englewood Cliffs, New Jersey: Prentice-Hall 1992.

Hare, Paul A. *Handbook of Small Group Research*. 2nd ed. New York: The Free Press, 1976.

McGoldensen, Robert. *The Encyclopedia of Human Behavior, Psychology, Psychiatry, and Mental Health*. New York: Doubleday and Company, 1970.

Megginson, Leon, Donald Mosley, and Paul Pietri, Jr. *Management: Concepts and Applications*. 4th ed. New York: Harper Collins, Publishers, 1992.

Muchinsky, P. M. *Psychology Applied to Work*. 3rd ed. Pacific Grove, California: Brooks/Cole Publishing Company, 1990.

Phillips, Gerald M. and Eugene Erickson. *Interpersonal Dynamics in the Small Group*. New York: Random House: 1990.

Schikendantz, Judith. *Understanding Children*. 3rd ed. New York: The New York Press, 1991.

Shaw, Marvin E. *Group Dynamics: The Psychology of Small Groups*. New York: McGraw-Hill, Inc., 1976.

Sher, Barbara and Anne Gottlieb. *Teamwork: Building Support Groups that Guarantee Success*. New York: Warner Bros., 1989.

Smith, Robert E., Jr. *Principles of Human Communication*. 3rd ed. Dubuque, Iowa: Kendall/Hunt Publishing company, 1992.

Sample Group Outline II
Effective Communication in Job Interviewing

Introduction (Jo)

I.   The job interview is a topic with which we can all relate.

II. We invite you as an audience to interact with the presentation.

   A.   Score the mock interviews.

   B.   Decide which person is playing which role.

III. I will talk with the interviewer (Ed) to ask about the type of questions he will ask.

IV. I talk to each of the interviewees.

   A.   "How nervous are you?"

   B.   "Remember that your ability to communicate effectively in a stressful situation is of critical importantance" (Ryan and Cooper, *Those who Can, Teach*).

II. Each group member illustrates a different kind of interviewer.

   A.   Scott—Mr. Unprepared

   B.   Teresa—Ms. Shy

   C.   Kristine—Ms. Ingratiator

   D.   Mike—Mr. Slob

   E.   Jamie—Mr. Perfect

III. Positive communication is highly important in a successful interview. (Jamie)

   A.   Positive nonverbal communication helps you as an interviewee (Dick Fox, "Learn to Sell Yourself in an Interview," *AgriMarketing*).

   B.   Answering questions in a clear, positive fashion is helpful (Kehoe Group, "Interviewing Success").

IV. Being too casual contributes to an ineffective interview. (Mike)

   A.   Mr. Slob's clothing, t-shirt and jeans, were too informal for the interview.

   B.   Mr. Slob's manner communicated disinterest in the position.

      1. He did not pay attention to the questions.

2. "Good communication always is the essence of a successful interview" (Jennifer Laabs, "You Don't Say," *Personnel Journal*).

V.   Do not dominate the interview. (Kristine)

    A. quotation: "You will occasionally run into an interviewee who tries to dominate the interview" (Diane Arthur, *Interviewing . . .Orienting New Employees*).

    B. Be careful not to talk too much. That can lead to babbling.

    C. Let the interviewer ask questions of you.

    D. Nonverbal communication is important.

        1. Maintain appropriate distance.

        2. Don't dominate nonverbally.

    E. "There is a fine line between persistence and being a pain in the neck" (Lois Smith Brady, "Ambitious? Just go fot It," *Working Woman*).

VI. Assertive communication is important to a successful interview. (Teresa)

    A. ". . . the recipient of nonverbal behavior is usually the superior" (Martin Remland, "The Effects of Nonverbal Involvement and Communication Apprehension . . .", *Communication Quarterly*).

        1. Ms. Shy communicated her lack of confidence by a number of nonverbal cues.

            a. She sat a long distance from the interviewer.

            b. She avoided eye contact.

            c. She looked ill at ease.

        2. Others make assumptions about us based on our nonverbal cues.

    B. The question, "What salary do you expect?" was answered with a noncommittal response.

        1. "Job seekers asking for an equal to greater amount than their last position get hired within the first three months of looking" ("Asking for Less . . . *HR Focus*).

        2. Employers regard "bargain rate" candidates as people easily lured away.

VII. Good preparation is essential for a successful interview. (Scott)

    A. Mr. Unprepared was just that.

        1. He was unsure of himself.

2. He did not know what to expect.

3. He was ignorant of the company's product.

B. The extent of your preparation can reflect your desire, maturity, and organizational skills.

C. Plan ahead for the interview.

   1. Know yourself and your goals.

   2. Research commonly asked interview questions.

   3. Prepare concise and informative answers.

   4. Research the company.

      a. Learn the products and services.

      b. Learn the company structure.

      c. Review recent performance.

      d. Use your research as the basis for your own questions.

Conclusion (Jo)

A. These interviews were changed to make points.

   1. They were shorter than real interviews.

   2. The characters were exaggerated.

B. Our purpose was to highlight behaviors.

   1. We provided insight into interview questions.

   2. We showed how people should and should not respond.

C. We showed the importance of nonverbal communication in eye-contact, dress, gestures, and proxemics.

D. We showed the importance of verbal communication.

   1. Be assertive but not overbearing.

   2. Be prepared to answer tough questions.

   3. Be alert and attentive.

Teresa Hurrle
Kristina Kitts
Jamie Moore
Scott Nelson
Mike Sellers
Ed Weakley
Johanna White

Bibliography

Arthur, Diane. *Recruiting, Interviewing, Selecting, an Orienting New Employees.* New York: ANACOM, 1991.

"Asking for Less Often Means More Time to Find Jobs." *HR Focus* Jan. 1992: 16.

Brady, Lois Smith. "Ambitious? Just Go For It." *Working Woman* July 1991: 71–73.

Dettore, Albert A. "The Art of the Interview." *Small Business Reports* Feb. 1992: 11–15.

Fox, Dick. "Learn to Sell Yourself in an Interview." *Agri-Marketing* May 1992: 22–24.

Freeman, Robert D. "Back to the Basics of Interviewing." *HR Focus* Jan. 1992: 10.

Grossman, Jack. "How to Sell Yourself: A Guide for Interviewing Effectively." *Advanced Management Journal* 56 Spring 1991: 33–36.

Kacmar, Michelle. "Look Who's Talking." *HR Focus* Feb. 1993: 56–58.

Kehoe Group, The. "Interviewing Success." *Business Communication Activities.* 1988.

Kituse, Alicia. "Manager's Tool Kit." *Across the Board* Jan.–Feb. 1992: 62–63.

Laabs, Jennifer. "You Don't Say." *Personnel Journal* Sept. 1991: 125.

Remland, Martin S. "The Effects of Nonverbal Involvement and Communication Apprehension on State Anxiety, Interpersonal Attraction, and Speech Duration." *Communication Quarterly* 37 (1989): 170–83.

Ryan, Kevin, and James M. Cooper. *Those Who Can, Teach.* Boston: Houghton Mifflin Company, 1992.

Skopp, Jennifer. "Dress for Success Becoming More Casual in Today's Workplace." *HR Focus* Jan. 1992: 18.

9

Public Speaking: Beginning

Key Concepts

At Macalester Industries, the Director of Human Services is presenting to the staff of the Human Services Office the recently issued Federal guidelines on hiring.

At the City Council meeting of a university town, citizens are walking to the microphone to voice their opinions about a new regulation limiting the number of unrelated people who may share a residence.

As the shift changes at St. Elizabeth Hospital, the floor nurse in the surgical ward reports on the conditions of the patients to the incoming shift.

At Stevenson Elementary School, the chair of the booster committee explains to the parent teacher organization how funds from the winter carnival will be spent.

At noon, in a room in the local cafeteria, the Lions Club meets and hears a report on its sponsorship of a summer softball league.

At the Forbes Group Home building, a facility for juvenile wards of the court, a contractor outlines for the board a plan to replace the windows in the building.

In the Lassiter Co-op House, one of the members is explaining to the assembled group how they will undertake this year's service project, painting houses for several elderly people.

Public Speaking

All of the above have in common that they are participating in public speaking. Though we often think of public speaking as the activity of professionals, such as politicians and ministers, public speaking is an activity that may engage us all. The skills to present material clearly to a group of people may be a requirement in a number of the roles we play: parent, citizen, organizational member, professional, coach, teacher, or club member. By *public speaking*, we mean simply that *a person addresses an audience of several or more people to accomplish some communication goal.* The communication goal may be one of many. Typical reasons for giving a speech are to inform, to persuade, to entertain, to honor, or to mark an occasion. For reasons of time and length, our discussion of public speaking will limit itself to informational speaking and persuasive speaking.

The Creative Process

Public speaking is like any of the other skills we have acquired. It is a blend of our natural abilities and our learned behaviors, both of which can be enhanced by study and practice. Public speaking is not so much "giving a speech" as it is entering into a creative process that leads from the seeming disorder and chaos of its early stages to the ordered and crafted final product. As one has pointed out, the question in making a speech is not whether or not we will be creative. "Creativity is a matter of degree," and thus the true question is, "How creative will we be?" (Kim 84).

Entering into the process of creating a speech may be intimidating. Some of the trepidation people feel may be relieved by recognizing the nature of creativity, whether it the creation of a speech, a painting, a dance, a novel, a research project, or a way of solving problems. It also helps to realize that once past the trepidation, the creative process can also be exhilarating.

While the final product is expected to be orderly, planned, and neatly arranged, *the creation process itself tends to be sloppy, particularly in the early stages.* Occasionally, some genius conceives an idea and carries it through from first to last with little modification and little doubt, but these cases are extremely rare. Even when they occur, they are the result of long and regular practice. Brilliance and inspiration come to those who already know what they are doing, not to the totally unpracticed.

The creative process is characterized by false starts, mistakes, problems, revisions, changes, starting over, and trying out far more things that do not work than those that do. Even in biological terms, creation is characterized by excess and by far more failures than successes. Out of a brood of one hundred baby sea turtles, only about twenty will survive to adulthood. Of the thousands of seeds produced by a single tree, only a few will germinate.

The engineer looking for a solution to a building problem may investigate a number of possibilities before finding the one that works. A painter may make a number of sketches before putting brush to canvas. Playing a musical instrument makes the process clear to many of us. The first rendition of a piece is marked by bad timing, missed notes, and repetitions. We achieve a polished playing of the piece by producing a number of renditions that do not sound very good. The stereotype of writers, including those writing communication texts, filling their wastebaskets with crumpled paper as they try to find the rights words is not far from the truth, except in these days the writer uses "delete" instead of the wastebasket. The finished novels we buy have gone through a number of drafts before they reach the bookstore shelves.

The same pattern of repetition and refinement is at work in the process of composing speeches. We may create a list of thirty topics to find the one we want to talk about. We may have to look at a number of periodicals before locating the key articles for our speech. Certainly, we will need to rehearse the speech many times before giving it, just as athletic teams practice plays over and over before using them in a game.

At times the creative process will be difficult and seem to drag along. At other times, the process will go so smoothly we may wonder from where all our wonderful ideas came. When one is working well, one has the impression that some outside source is assisting in the process. If we find things going smoothly, we should sit back and enjoy the ride, and it can be

▲ **Figure 9.1.** The process of creating a speech can be an uneven one.

an exhilarating one. If things are not going smoothly, the important thing is to keep trying. Persistence is a major ingredient of creative accomplishment. Eventually, ideas will fall into place; the right wording will appear; the organization will become clear.

In the early stages of creating a speech, *the key word is "freedom."* The time will come soon enough to be critical of the work, but the critical stage should be one of the later stages of work on the speech. In fact, we can create problems for ourselves if we become too critical too early and shut off the flow of ideas necessary to the work. In the early stages, we need to give our minds and imaginations free rein.

Another good guideline for creativity is to *begin the creative process early.* Creativity is both conscious and unconscious. We put some ideas together by actively thinking about them. Others come together when we are *not* actively thinking about them. Somehow, in the dark of our minds, connections are made, and when brought into the light, the new ideas make sense in ways we had not yet imagined. For the process to take place, we need to have time for ideas to germinate.

Generally, the earlier we discover a topic for a speech, the better the speech will be. Even if we cannot do a great deal with the topic for a while, just knowing the general subject will be helpful. One way to severely hamper the creative process is to put off working on a speech until the last minute, then in a whirlwind of energy and exasperation try to fashion a speech without sufficient time for development.

Sizing up the Situation

One of the first tasks of giving a speech is to analyze our audience, our situation, and ourselves. No one element of the triad constitutes the communication event, but through the interplay of the three, an environment is created and lived in. Change any one of the three elements, and the situation is altered. The wording of the speech, for example, may be brilliant, but if spoken by a lifeless, mumbling speaker, the speech will not live up to its potential.

The process of analyzing the three is not a matter of attending to each one in order. We are more likely to find ourselves jumping from one to another as an insight into the nature of the audience leads to a change of wording which leads us to seek more knowledge which leads us to reinterpret the audience, and so on. Working back and forth simply means that we are creating a well-rounded presentation.

The Speaker

The first part of the triad is relatively easy since, presuming we are the speakers, we should already be something of authorities on ourselves. In an earlier chapter, we discussed the various elements that contribute to our capabilities as communicators. We may still, though, make discoveries about ourselves as we work toward the speaking situation.

Some of the questions we want to ask ourselves as we analyze a speaking situation are:

▶ How much do I already know about the topic?
▶ Where can I find information about the topic?
▶ What information resources are available to me?
▶ What kinds of visual aids are available to me?
▶ How much time do I have to prepare?
▶ How do I feel about this presentation?
▶ What personal stake do I have in making this speech?
▶ What is my motivation for making this speech?
▶ What are my strengths as a speaker?
▶ What are my weak points as a speaker?
▶ What can I do to minimize my weaknesses?
▶ What can I learn from this experience?

As we answer these questions, we come to a better understanding of ourselves and our role in the speaking situation. The understanding will guide in the choices we make in creating the speech.

The Audience

The better a speaker analyzes an audience, the more likely the speaker is to be effective. Speeches are, after all, situations in which hu-

▲ **Figure 9.2.** In analyzing your speaking situation, you need to consider yourself, your audience, and your message.

man beings connect with other human beings. Knowing the nature of the people on the other side of the relational equation will help us react most appropriately.

In some cases, the job of audience analysis is fairly easy. Giving a classroom speech, for example, usually involves students talking to people who are very much like themselves. Even if the ages are dissimilar, the audience will still have a number of traits in common. All are interested in a college level class. All are, or should be, concentrating on the goal of finishing the class in good order. All are at roughly the same level of ability. A classroom speech also gives people the opportunity to observe the audience over a long period of time and adjust to its interests and abilities.

In other cases, insight, rapport, and empathy with the audience may be harder to achieve. We may be called upon to give a speech to a civic group or club that we have never heard of before. Here we would have to analyze carefully the characteristics of the people to whom we would be speaking. A number of factors may determine the nature of the audience and guide the speaker in crafting the presentation. Some of the characteristics which should be examined are:

▶ The age or ages of audience members
▶ The gender of the audience
▶ The educational level of the audience
▶ The political beliefs of the audience
▶ The religious beliefs of the audience
▶ The values held by the audience
▶ The reason the audience has assembled

► The audience's knowledge of the speaker
► The audience's knowledge of the topic
► The social class(es) of the audience
► The race of the audience
► The profession(s) of the audience
► The expectations of the audience
► The circumstances under which the audience is meeting
► The place and time of the meeting.

All these elements will shape the consciousness of an audience, the consciousness to which speakers must relate if they are to be effective. Knowledge of the audience allows speakers to shape their messages so that they will be the most effective with a given group. A variation in one or two of the audience's characteristics may be enough to change the speaking situation drastically. A farm co-op may have the same members attending two meetings yet be two very different audiences as when discussing drought relief and when gathering for its annual banquet. In the first instance, it will be a group of people concerned with emergency aid and economic survival. In the second, the audience will be a group of people ready to be entertained and to celebrate their accomplishments. The audience attending a national political convention—either Democratic or Republican—will be a different audience after the candidates are chosen than it was before. Before the candidate is chosen, speakers focus on the merits of their favorite nominees. After the candidates are chosen, the emphasis is on unifying the party for the upcoming election.

Audience analysis is a combination of research and imagination. We will seldom be asked to speak to an audience about which we know absolutely nothing. Drawing upon what we know, we can begin to sketch an idea of what will be important in adapting to the audience and then complete the picture by study and integration of what we discover.

If, for example, someone were called upon to speak at the Westminster Retirement Village, one would know quickly that age would be an important factor. Most audience members will be in their sixties or older. If the speaker were not acquainted with people in this age bracket, the speaker would need to discover the charac-

▲ **Figure 9.3.** Different audiences demand different approaches to communication. (Dawe)

teristics of those over sixty. To find the information, the speaker could talk with someone well acquainted with the Village to determine the economic, political, social, and educational standings of the audience as well as other factors. The speaker could also read materials by or about retirees and interview people.

Without investigation, one might make some major errors in evaluating the audience. Some young people think that retirees spend their time wrapped in shawls and sitting in rocking chairs or doddering about while mumbling over pictures of their grandchildren. Many retirees are very active and involved with travel, the arts, politics, and numerous service activities.

The Message

While we are discovering as much as possible about the audience, we should also be giving thought about what is to be said and how to say it. At this point, we are beginning to think rhetorically, giving thought how to best adapt ideas to the audience and the audience to the ideas. The working out of this task is the composition of the speech.

Composing the Speech
Finding a Speech Topic
When the Topic Finds the Speaker

Interestingly enough, for a large amount of the public speaking we are called upon to do, the topic finds us rather than us finding the topic. That is, the circumstances dictate the topic of a speech. For various reasons, we find ourselves in situations in which we rise to the occasion of addressing a topic. Let us look again at some of the speech situations we sketched at the beginning of this chapter.

The Director of Human Services at a manufacturing plant speaks about hiring guidelines because the company is under some compulsion to adhere to those guidelines and the Director is the person charged with the responsibility to see that the guidelines are followed.

At a city council meeting, citizens speak out because they feel the topic affects them and their living situation. They feel impelled to express themselves on the subject.

The student providing information about the service project and the parent in charge of the school's booster club do so because speaking is necessary to the successful completion of their tasks.

In all these examples, the speeches rise out of people's responses to their circumstances. The speeches are also fueled by the desires of the audience. The employees of Macalester Industries find the topic of hiring guidelines necessary to their work. The city council has invited people to express opinions on the given topic. The members of the co-op house want to participate effectively in the service project and need the speaker's information to do so. Instead of expending creative energy trying to discover a topic, the speakers go directly to work on the topic thrust upon them. They begin to examine the topic, analyze the audience, and bring the two together.

When the Speaker Has to Search

In some instances, however, the topic of the speech may be elusive, and our initial task will be to find a subject or topic that will fit speaker, audience, and occasion. One of the most intimidating of speaking assignments can be to "talk about whatever you want to talk about." When topic selection is the speaker's first step, some free ranging imaginative work may be helpful.

Talk About Things You Love. Speeches are usually best when the speaker and topic coincide. What is a sparkling presentation for one speaker may be dreary for the next. The differ-

Figure 9.4. One way to find a speech topic is to consider the things you like to do. (Dawe)

ence is often due to the relationship between speaker and topic. One way to find a topic for a speech is for us to consider the things about which we feel strongly. Thus, what we find personally rewarding is a good source for speech topics[1].

Let us say that someone has a pet, a cat. Simply settling on "cats" as a topic area provides the person with a long list of possible topics. The person could talk about the history of cats, cats in literature, cat diseases, breeding cats, showing cats, cat diet, training cats, songs about cats, the psychology of cats and more. If a person had an interest in cartoons, the person could talk about famous cartoonists, the history of cartoons, political cartoons, comic strips, animated cartoons, styles of cartoons, drawing cartoons, the syndication of cartoons, and the printing of cartoons. Any area can yield a number of possible speech topics.

Think About Things You Hate. Besides feeling good about things in our life, we probably also have some things that we abominate. These, too, can offer possibilities for speech.

A person may be bothered, for example, by people who drive around with their windows down and their stereos punching out music at high volume, a rude imposition on the unrequesting public. A subject like this could lead to a range of topics: the rise of car stereos, problems in designing car audio systems, how to select a car stereo system, damaging effects of loud noise, municipal noise ordinances, etiquette of the nineties, even personal liberty versus public good.

Another person may strongly dislike professional wrestling. Here the subject would also yield some interesting speech topic: the history of professional wrestling, why is professional wrestling popular, the marketing of professional wrestling, the typical wrestling fan, recruitment of wrestlers, the training of wrestlers, and wrestling publications. One need not be a fan of a cultural phenomenon to explore it and its ramifications.

Try Clustering to Find a Topic. Clustering is a technique originally designed to foster writing skills (Rico). An important part of understanding clustering is to realize the different functions performed by the two hemispheres of the brain. The left hemisphere operates in a sequential, rational, logical manner while the right hemisphere operates in a nonsequential, subjective, holistic fashion. The right hemisphere is primarily the source of concepts and creativity while the left hemisphere is primarily the source of order and critical analysis. Clustering works by giving the creative, noncritical portion of the brain free rein.

Clustering is similar to brainstorming in that the main principle is to bring out as many ideas as possible without critiquing them. Clustering

differs from brainstorming in that it is a personal activity rather than a group activity and that ideas are recorded in a nonlinear fashion.

One begins clustering with a word or concept. We draw a circle around that . From that center, we radiate out other ideas inspired by the original word. We link each new idea to the original idea or to ideas growing out of the original. Gradually, we create a web of associations.

As one goes through this process, it is vitally important to avoid evaluating the ideas. The procedure should be one of simple creation, not creation and judgment. No idea is too wacky, too stupid, or too ridiculous not to be considered. We simply go where our imaginations lead us. Following this process, even the simplest of words can lead to a wealth of topics.

Let us think of a familiar building, say, one made of red bricks, a humble enough building material but not one thought of as inspiring. To begin we put "red brick" in the middle of a sheet of paper.

The next step is to put down whatever concepts pops into our head that is linked to "red brick." If we think of "red brick building," we would put "building" close to "red brick," circle "building" and draw a line linking it to "red

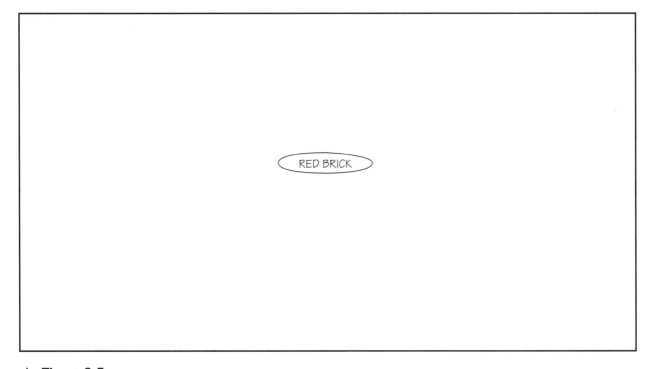

▲ **Figure 9.5a.**

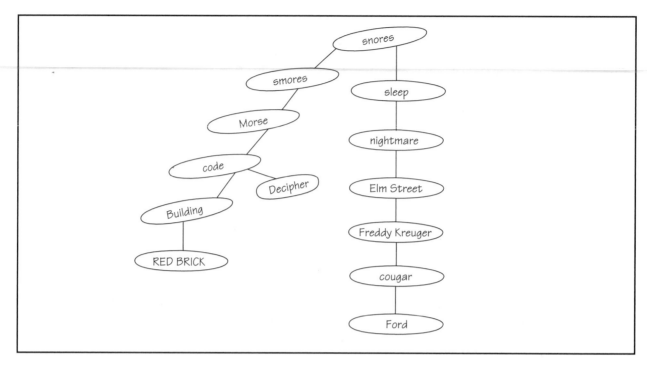

▲ **Figure 9.5b.**

brick.," Each new idea that comes to us will be circled and linked to its appropriate neighbor. "Building" might make us think of "code" which could lead us to think of "Morse" which could lead to "smores" (a treat of marshmallows, chocolate, and graham crackers) which might make us think of "snores" which could lead to "sleep" which brings "nightmare" to mind which leads to "Elm Street" which makes us think of "Freddy Kreuger" which leads to "cougar" which we link to "Ford" and so on and on.

As we work along, we just let the words and connections come out. We should not try to force the associations. We let the links arise naturally. Some ideas will chain off the original direction; others will chain off into new directions. If we find ourselves stumped, we can ask, "what do I feel about this?" or "what strikes me here?"

After clustering for a while, we may begin to see ideas come together. We should resist the urge to stop and continue until something leaps out at us, until the light bulb comes on in our heads and inspiration strikes us. This kind of "aha!" experience is a strong indication that we have found a profitable direction to pursue. We may need to begin the clustering process again with our "aha!" idea at the center. This

will lead us to other considerations of the topic, but by this point we have already passed the stage of finding a topic and are working on narrowing the topic.

Other Considerations. Besides ourselves, we need also to look at other resources in the discovery process. One major consideration will, of course, be the audience. A good guideline for topic selection is to ask, "What will my audience find interesting?" Analyzing the intended audience can suggest topics and help narrow a general topic area.

A group of college bound, high school seniors would probably be interested in a topic such as "How to Select the Right College for You" while seniors in college would be more interested in "How to do Well in Job Interviews." Credit cards usage is widespread, but that does not mean all talks about credit cards are well suited to all audiences. In college, a person might be interested in a topic such as "Tuition and Credit Cards." Someone working and travelling would find more interesting a talk on "Using Your Credit Card for Expense Accounts."

Research can also lead us to topics. The more informed we are, the greater our range of subjects and the possibilities for speeches.

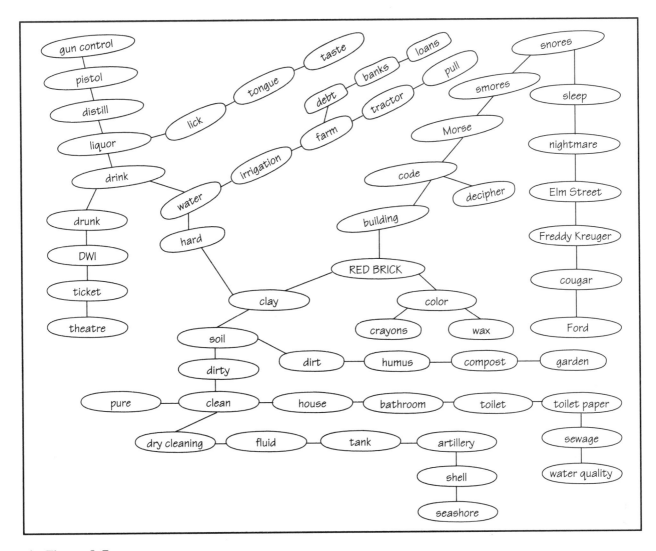

▲ **Figure 9.5c.**

Reading widely gives us the scope necessary to find topics to fit various occasions and provides us with supporting information.

Narrowing the Topic: The Thesis Statement

Once we are over the hurdle of finding a topic, the next jump to be cleared is deciding what it is we want to say about that topic. If a topic has any breadth to it, we will not be able to say everything about it, even in a lengthy speech. Whether we want to talk about "pigs," "kitchen knives," "word processing," or "population control," we will need to concentrate on a small portion of the topic that can be covered in the allotted time.

Shrinking the Subject Area

One way to narrow a topic is to break it down into major areas or divisions. Then we pick the most interesting or relevant division as the subject of the speech. For example, the four topics above can be subdivided into the following areas:

Pigs: evolution of pigs, characteristics of pigs, breeds of pigs, raising pigs, marketing pigs, showing pigs

Kitchen Knives: types of kitchen knives, manufacture of kitchen knives, selecting kitchen knives, using kitchen knives, care of kitchen knives

Word Processing: history of word processing, word processing programs, learning word processing, economics of word processing, impact of word processing on office work, impact of word processing on writing styles

Population Control: world populations, populations of countries, rate of population growth, educational programs, sterilization programs, effect of population on food sources, effect of population on ecology, effect of population on economics, effect of population on politics

If the first efforts at dividing the topic into areas do not sufficiently narrow the topic, then a good course of action is to choose the most interesting division and subdivide it. For example, our original topic may have been "Pigs" of which one of the subdivisions was "Characteristics of Pigs." That subdivision can be divided even further: Characteristics of pigs: eating habits, temperament, likeable characteristics of pigs, unlikeable characteristics of pigs, reproductive systems of pigs, behavior of pigs, intelligence of pigs, etc.

Creating a Thesis Statement

We can further refine a topic by creating an appropriate thesis statement.[2] This statement will unite the elements of the speech in a sensible, coherent way. In fact, if we can compose a comprehensive thesis statement for a speech, a major portion of the compositional work has been accomplished.

The thesis statement should include three key elements. The first is, naturally enough, the *topic*. In addition to the topic, the thesis statement should also include the speaker's *position*

on the subject. By "position," we mean a judgmental statement that indicates how the speaker views the topic. The view may be "good" or "bad," but it may also be phrased in words that indicate the topic's usefulness, effect, or characteristics. In most thesis statements, the topic will be the subject of the sentence and the position portion of the sentence will follow the verb "is" or "are."

Topic		Position
Pigs	are	likeable
Kitchen knives	are	good
Word processing	is	comfortable
World population growth	is	threatening

The last part of the thesis statement, the *amplification*, is the support or illustration the speaker offers to back up the judgment made in the first part of the sentence. In the amplification, we specify why the topic is what we say it is. We offer reasons for our viewpoint. We show why our announcement of the topic and our phrasing of our position is valid.

Finally, we should make sure our thesis statement meets a fourth criterion; it should be stated in a declarative sentence. "World population growth, a threat to environment and world economy" would not be an acceptable thesis statement as it contains no verb. Thus, it is not a full sentence. "Is world population growth a threat to the environment and economy" is not an acceptable thesis statement either. It contains a subject and verb but is phrased as a question, an interrogative sentence, instead of making a statement.

Topic		Position	Amplification
Pigs	are	likeable	because they are clean, intelligent, and amusing.
Kitchen knives	are	good	when they fit the job, are made of proper steel, and are sharp.
Word processing	is	comfortable	to learn because it uses skills you know and is learned in stages.
World population growth	is	threatening	because of the pressures it exerts on the environment and the world economy.

Variations in Thesis Statements

While an effective thesis statement should contain the three elements of topic, position, and amplification, the three elements do not have to appear in the same order in every statement. One of the simplest variations is to place the position before the topic. The "kitchen knives" statement above could be rephrased and perhaps improved by changing it to "Good kitchen knives fit the job, are made of good steel, and are sharp." Here the position word "good" is used as an adjective describing "knife" rather than being placed after the verb. Whatever the word order, a thesis statement should still meet the four criteria: it should contain a topic, a position, amplification, and be a declarative sentence.

The Major Divisions of the Speech

Selecting Major Points

If we have done a good job of formulating a thesis statement, we already have a general outline of the speech. The main points of the speech will be what is included in the amplification part of the thesis statement. Each piece of amplification becomes a major point.

If we are using the "pigs" sentence as the basis for a speech, the three main points become: (1) pigs are clean, (2) pigs are intelligent, and (3) pigs are amusing. Similarly, if the "population control" statement is the basis for a speech, the speech would have two main points: (1) population growth has a negative effect on the environment, and (2) population growth has a negative effect on the world economy.

Arranging the Major Points

Effective communication has organization to it, some pattern that makes sense to both the communicator and the audience. We use a number of organizing strategies in our communication, often without being aware of them. When we tell a joke, we know the punch line should come at the end of the joke. Somewhere in introductions, names need to be disclosed. When we tell stories, we put the parts of the story into an order that makes the story easier to tell. Similarly, we organize our speeches in patterns and have several available to us.

A student goes home for a weekend after the first month at the university and runs into an old friend who asks, "What's it like at ____ University?" The person starts to answer but stops, not quite sure where to begin. The manner in which the student finally frames the description of university life will influence the nature of the response.

The student could tell the story in a *chronological* pattern. Here the main points of the story would be arranged in a sequence based on time relationships. The story would be told in a manner which goes, "When I first arrived, I thought . . . Then after a week, I felt . . . "Now, after a month, I think. . . ."

Another way the student could organize the story is in a *spatial* pattern, a pattern based on the geographic location of important aspects. Here, the story would move from place to place: "I enjoy living in the dorm . . . I go to classes in the Liberal Arts and Education Building . . . For recreation, I go to the student gym. . . ." Some of the organizing terms useful with a spatial pattern of organizing are "north, east, south, west," "up and down," and "inside and outside."

Still another approach is the *problem-solution* method of organization. The essentials of this pattern are first a difficulty and second a method of overcoming the difficulty. "The biggest problem I had was getting all my things into our small room . . . Then my roommate and I decided to build a loft."

Yet another way of organizing material is to use a *structure-function* pattern. With this pattern, one first describes an object then shows its application. Here the student's story might include, "One of the most important things you need on campus is your student identification card. This card is about the size of a credit card and . . . This cards allows you to do a lot of things . . . ."

If the main points do not fall easily into one of the major patterns, the student may relate the story with a *topical* pattern. Here the main points are simply arranged in a sensible or at least workable pattern. Often with a topical approach, one can change the order of the main points without damaging its sense: "The three things that impress me most about the university are the food, the dorms, and the high grading standards."

The above patterns of organization are the ones that recommend themselves for the organization of speeches. As speakers, we can adjust our thesis statements and the arrangements of our points so that we reach the best form for a speech. Some topics can be accommodated by only one approach while others lend themselves to all approaches. The "kitchen knives" speech could be organized in any of the five methods.

Chronological: "The first knife you should buy is . . . The second knife you should buy is. . . ."

Spatial: "When working at a cutting board . . . When working at the stove. . . ."

Problem-Solution: "For paring and peeling, use . . . For carving, use . . . For heavy chopping, use. . . ."

Structure-Function: "A well made kitchen knife is constructed of good steel with a properly shaped blade and a comfortable handle . . . These qualities allow you to use the knife in the most efficient way. . . ."

Topical: "My favorite kitchen knives are. . . ."

No one pattern of organization is superior to another. The question to be answered is: "Which pattern best fits this speaking situation?" The goal is to find a method of arranging the speech that makes the topic as clear as possible for the audience and allows the speaker to perform at optimum levels.

Conclusion

With the major points arranged in an appropriate fashion, a major portion of the speech will be composed. At this stage, we will have moved through several important steps. We will have either been assigned a topic or discovered a topic that fits the speaker and audience. We will have analyzed the audience as completely as possible to effect an harmonious fit between it and the speaker's ideas. We will have composed a thesis statement that provides a foundation for the speech. What remains to be done is to consider the finer details of the speech which will provide it with the polish needed to put it at its highest level.

• • • Discussion Questions

1. What kinds of activities do we think of as creative?

2. How does creativity manifest itself in areas other than speechmaking? In sports? In business? In relationships? In other forms of communication?

3. What does a speaker bring as a person to the speaking situation?

4. How do the variables between audiences (age, gender, education, professions, etc.) affect how a speech is composed, delivered, or perceived?

5. Why would strong feelings (love/hate) about a topic be an asset to the speech composition process? How might such feelings be a detriment?

6. How could you narrow a topic (horses, university life, space travel, etc.) to a size appropriate for an five to seven minute speech?

7. Why are the four characteristics of a thesis statement necessary for the statement to be effective?

8. Give an example of how a topic could be arranged in a chronological pattern.

9. Give an example of how a topic could be arranged in a spatial pattern.

10. Give an example of how a topic could be arranged in a problem-solution pattern.

11. Give an example of how a topic could be arranged in a structure-function pattern.

12. Give an example of how a topic could be arranged in a topical pattern.

• • • Notes

[1] For the "love/hate" idea, the author is indebted to Maureen Jungblut.

[2] The basic idea for this discussion was provided by Brenda Avadian, Speech Mapping Short Course, Central States Communication Association Convention, 14 April 1988, Schaumberg, Illinois.

• • • Sources and References

Avadian, Brenda. Speech Mapping Short Course. Central States Communication Association Convention. 14 April 1988, Schaumberg, Illinois.

Jungblut, Maureen, Conversation with the author.

Kim, Steven H. *Essence of Creativity: A Guide to Tackling Difficult Problems.* New York: Oxford University Press, 1990.

Rico, Gabrielle Lusser. *Writing the Natural Way: Using Right-Brain Techniques to Release Your Expressive Powers.* Los Angeles: J. P. Tarcher, Inc., 1983.

Name _____ Section _____ Date _____

Public Speaking: Beginning

1. What is public speaking?

   _____

   _____

   _____

2. Name three guidelines for encouraging creativity in thinking.

   1. _____

   2. _____

   3. _____

3. Analysis is important prior to a speech. What three things should a well prepared speaker analyze?

   1. _____

   2. _____

   3. _____

4. Why does it benefit speakers to choose topics about which they feel strongly?

   _____

   _____

   _____

5. What is clustering?

   _____

   _____

   _____

6. What three key elements should be included in a thesis statement?

   1. _____

   2. _____

   3. _____

7. What grammatical form should the thesis sentence take?

   _____

8. Which key element of the thesis statement contains the main points of a speech?

   _____

9. Explain each of the following patterns of speech organization:

   chronological _____

   _____

   spatial _____

   _____

   problem-solution _____

   _____

   structure-function _____

   _____

   topical _____

   _____

10. Give an example of a speech topic that could be arranged for each pattern of organization.

    chronological _____

    spatial _____

    problem-solution _____

    structure-function _____

    topical _____

Name _____ Section _____ Date _____

Narrowing a Topic Exercise

Subdivide each of the following topics into at least three areas. Compare your answers with other classmates to see the variety of ways a single topic can be divided.

1. The environment

    a.

    b.

    c.

2. Politics

    a.

    b.

    c.

3. Student rights

    a.

    b.

    c.

Choose one of your subdivisions from "the environment" and subdivide it further.

answer from above:

further subdivision:

1.

2.

3.

Discuss as a class the further narrowing of the topic.

Name _____ Section _____ Date _____

Thesis Statement Development Exercise

Develop a completed thesis statement in the examples below by adding your amplification of the topic.

	Topic	**Position**	**Amplification**
1.	Aerobics	are beneficial	
2.	Stress	is damaging	
3.	Hobbies	are desirable	
4.	Physics	is difficult	
5.	Jazz	is enjoyable	

Provide a position and amplification for the topics below to form a completed thesis statement.

	Topic	**Position**	**Amplification**
1.	Dancing		
2.	Computers		
3.	Russia		
4.	Football		
5.	The President		

Write five thesis statements below on topics of your choice

   1.

   2.

   3.

   4.

   5.

Name _____ Section _____ Date _____

Topic Organization Exercise

Identify which organizational pattern you would use for the following topics. Explain the reason for your selection. Possible organizational patterns: chronological, spatial, problem-solution, structure-function, topical.

Topic   **Organizational Pattern**

1. "Getting Through Chemistry 101"

2. "My Vacation at Padre Island"

3. Why My Favorite Novel Is . . ."

4. "Changing Population Centers in the U.S."

5. "Using the Library"

6. "How to Prepare for an Exam"

7. "Overcoming Stagefright"

8. "Developing Good Study Habits"

9. "Interest Assessment Tests"

10. "The Fastest Way to Get to State U. from Chicago"

Introduction to Public Speaking Assignments

While few of you will be professional public speakers, most of you will be called upon from time to time to speak before an audience, even while still a student. Sometimes the purpose of a speech is informative: explaining a project in a class; introducing a visiting alumnus to a housing unit; detailing a vacation for the travel club. Other times the purpose is persuasive: arguing against a tuition hike before the board of trustees; convincing the dorm' committee to change visitation rules; recruiting donors for a campus blood drive.

After college there will be business presentations, community service activities, and opportunities to direct the forces that impact your daily living routine and will require good public speaking skills.

Suggested Topics for Informative Speech

Choose a topic you are knowledgeable about or one which interests you enough to investigate. Below are suggestions to get you started. Your topic does not have to come from the list below but must be approved by your instructor.

what something is	fishing lures
how something works	thimbles
how something is done	puppeteering
how something is viewed	Special Olympics
unusual place I've visited	Toastmasters
hobby	square dancing
organization I belong to	clogging
special interest group	jewelry crafting
noteworthy person I've met	Cajun food
book worth reading	basket weaving
food's origin	photography
frightening experience	vegetarianism
embarrassing moment	anorexia
person worth imitating	training horses
favorite screen character	dolphin intelligence
least favorite job	teen alcoholism
favorite job	EMTs
Hall of Fame I'd most like to be elected to	Administering CPR
place I'd like to visit	agribusiness
favorite author	food irradiation
history of a modern invention	the Shakers
course I've taken	bocci ball
animal husbandry	volunteering
tombstone rubbings	gourmet cooking
Civil War history	organized crime
restoring old cars	being a nerd
herb gardening	world dictator
reforestation	collective negotiations
rappelling	robotics
orienteering	enterprise networking
arrowheads	genetic engineering
spelunking	What is a cooper?

cricket
Halloween
television
rugby
Japan
oil painting
Indy 500 Motor Speedway
sky diving
trout fishing
violins
Middle East
coffee
waste disposal
bicycles
elephants
dictionaries

fountain pens
book selling
kayaking
race horses
great leaders
big brothers
micro computers
learning methods
philosophers
silver screen
theater
blacksmithing
herbal medicines
hang gliding
hot air ballooning

Speaking Options

As part of this course, you will make three presentations, public speeches. Of these, two are informative speeches while the third is a persuasive speech. To meet this requirement, your instructor will select one or both of the following options. Each option allows you to choose, research, and present topics in a different way. Previous to selecting the topic for your first speech, you will need to indicate your choice to your instructor. The two options are free choice or thematic. Both options include research as part of the preparation process. In addition to the typical library research, you may also use sources such as interviews, trade journals, and technical manuals, if they are appropriate.

▶ Option 1—Free Choice
   With this option, you have a free choice of topics. You may use whatever topic you choose as long as it meets the requirements of the assignment, informative or persuasive. The first two speeches will be informative speeches on *different* topics. The speech will include appropriate research as indicated by your instructor. Your instructor will specify the type and format of the persuasive speech.

▶ Option 2—Thematic
   With this option, you will select a topic of concern or issue on the local, state, or national level (safety lighting at the university, legalized gambling, organ donation, health care, etc.). The more specific the issue, the more likely you will be able to address the issue significantly within the time limits of the class. "Pesticide Residue in Soil" is a more workable choice, for example, than "Saving the Environment." You will thoroughly research the topic. Your instructor will specify the number of sources needed. These sources should inform all three of your speeches. The first informative speech will introduce your audience to the topic, its impact, and how it affects us. The second informative speech will address a major area of the topic. The persuasive speech will build on the two preceding presentations and persuade the audience to take some action relevant to the issue.

Good luck with your speeches!

Name _____ Section _____ Date _____

Public Speaking Assignment I
Informative Speech

Purpose

The first public speaking assignment has a three-fold purpose:

1. You will learn the techniques to successfully compose a speech
2. You will learn how speaking style differs from written style
3. You will gain experience speaking in front of an audience.

Basic Requirements

▶ You will develop and present to the class an original, informative speech on a topic approved by your instructor.

▶ You should choose a topic you feel comfortable talking about, one which is of particular interest to you.

▶ Each speech must be _____ minutes in length.

▶ _____ sources should be used in preparing the speech.

▶ An outline of the speech must be submitted (due date) _____ to the instructor.

▶ Speeches will be graded according to the criteria on p. _____, which must be handed in prior to the speech.

▶ You will complete the observation sheets pages 219–227 for designated fellow speakers.

▶ Additional instructor requirements:

Informative Speech I Worksheet   **Speech Due Date** _____

   1. possible topics:

   2. selected topic:

   3. possible narrowed topic areas:

   4. narrowed focus of speech:

   5. thesis statement:

   6. main points:

       1.

       2.

       3.

   7. support for main points: source:

       support for 1. a.

                       b.

       support for 2. a.

                       b.

       support for 3. a.

                       b.

   8. transitions to connect main points:

       transition between 1 and 2:

       transition between 2 and 3:

   9. possible attention getting devices to open the speech:

  10. selected attention getting device:

  11. conclusion that can be drawn from speech:

Notes:

Name _____ Date _____

Topic _____ Score _____

Informative Speech I Grading Criteria—Style A

For a *C*, the speech will meet the basic requirements of the assignment:

> Introduction announces the topic and previews the main points
> Speech has appropriate number of main points
> Main points are clear
> Transitions are present
> Sequence of ideas is easy to follow
> Conclusion summarizes the main points
> Physical communication does not distract (no swaying, bobbing, etc.)
> Vocal communication is understandable
> Speech is free of disfluencies ("uh," "um," "you know," etc.)
> Speaker maintains eye contact with audience 50% of the time
> Speech fits the time limits
> Speech fulfills requirements of assignment (informative or persuasive, appropriate number of visual aids, appropriate notes, etc.)
> Visual aids are clear, neat, and legible.

for a *B*, the speech will meet the requirements for a *C* plus the following:

> Introduction has attention step, establishes credibility, establishes relevance, and previews main points
> Each major point is fully developed
> Transitions establish links between major points
> Conclusion highlights applications of material
> Sources are credible
> Assertions are supported with evidence
> Speaker maintains eye contact with audience 75% of the time
> Speech topic is significant to the audience
> Physical communication emphasizes points of the speech
> Vocal communication is energetic and clear
> Language is fully appropriate to the material
> Visual aids strongly support the main points
> Visual aids are handled smoothly.

For an *A*, the speech meets the requirements for *C* and *B* plus the following:
> Introduction shows creativity
> Transitions show flow of ideas
> Speech evidences maturity of thought
> Conclusion creates a sense of completion
> Speaker is poised (in control of notes, visual aids, delivery)
> Speaker maintains eye contact 90% of the time
> Speaker develops rapport with the audience.

For a *D*, one of the areas for a *C* shows major problems.
For an *F*, the speech is not given or several areas show major problems.

Name _____ Date _____

Topic _____ Score _____

Informative Speech I Grading Criteria—Style B

Topic 10%*
- subject of speech appropriate to audience, assignment
- topic appropriately narrowed to fit time guidelines

Organization 30%*
Introduction
- attention getting opening employed
- speaker credibility developed
- rapport developed with the audience
- speech previewed
- thesis made clear

Body
- main points obvious
- transition used between main points
- easily followed

Conclusion
- implications of material highlighted
- a feeling of completion developed

Content 30%*
- significant material developed in speech
- related to thesis
- supported with example
- clearly presented
- interestingly developed
- vocabulary appropriate
- jargon and unfamiliar terms defined
- sources credible
- sources cited
- visual aid(s) well constructed, enhanced speech

Delivery 30%*
Physical
- eye contact frequent
- gestures meaningful
- posture comfortable
- notecards properly used
- sense of communication with audience established
- visual aid(s) used properly, with confidence

Vocal
- energetic

---

*Suggested values only—may be changed by your instructor.

- rate appropriate
- volume appropriate
- tone pleasing
- vocal variety exhibited
- enunciation/pronunciation correct
- absence of fillers

Comments

Providing Positive Feedback

Goal
To compliment a person on a positive aspect of that person's performance

Procedure
1. Attend carefully to the person's presentation.

2. Select some aspect of the performance that communicated well to you. Some aspects you might want to regard would be dress, posture, voice, visual aids, clarity of organization, humor, language, speaking style, or tone of the speech. Feel free to pick any other aspect that you wish.

3. Phrase your reaction using an "I" statement, for example, "I really liked your introduction. It caught my attention." The statement should tell what you like ("your introduction") and why you liked it ("It caught my attention.")

4. During the feedback session following the performance, make your statement to the performer. The performance goals are:
    ▶ To attract the instructor's attention by raising your hand,
    ▶ To look at the person you are addressing,
    ▶ To tell the person what you like,
    ▶ To speak so the person can hear you.

Providing Corrective Feedback

Goal

To provide a person with advice for improvement

Procedure

1. Attend carefully to the person's presentation.

2. Select an aspect of the performance that could be improved, something that interfered with the clear communication of the material. Some aspects you could consider would be dress, posture, voice, visual aids, clarity of organization, humor, language, speaking style, tone of the speech, or any other area which made for some difficulty in communication.

3. Keep in mind that effective feedback should be specific and within the performer's power to change.

4. Phrase your reaction using an "I" statement, for example, "I had difficulty seeing your visual aids. I think they would be clearer if they were larger."

5. During the feedback session following the performance, make your statement to the performer. The performance goals are:
   ▶ to attract the instructor's attention by raising your hand,
   ▶ to look at the person you are addressing,
   ▶ to tell the person your reaction,
   ▶ to speak so the person can hear you.

Name _____ Section _____ Date _____

Student Evaluation of Informative Speech I

In light of the guidelines for constructive feedback, offer observations about the speech you have just watched.

What were the main points?

What new information did you hear?

What was the speaker's strength?

What one thing would you suggest the speaker work on to improve?

Name _____ Section _____ Date _____

Student Evaluation of Informative Speech I

In light of the guidelines for constructive feedback, offer observations about the speech you have just watched.

What were the main points?

What new information did you hear?

What was the speaker's strength?

What one thing would you suggest the speaker work on to improve?

222 Principles of Human Communication

Name _____ Section _____ Date _____

Student Evaluation of Informative Speech I

In light of the guidelines for constructive feedback, offer observations about the speech you have just watched.

What were the main points?

What new information did you hear?

What was the speaker's strength?

What one thing would you suggest the speaker work on to improve?

Name _____ Section _____ Date _____

Student Evaluation of Informative Speech I

In light of the guidelines for constructive feedback, offer observations about the speech you have just watched.

What were the main points?

What new information did you hear?

What was the speaker's strength?

What one thing would you suggest the speaker work on to improve?

Name _____ Section _____ Date _____

Student Evaluation of Informative Speech I

In light of the guidelines for constructive feedback, offer observations about the speech you have just watched.

What were the main points?

What new information did you hear?

What was the speaker's strength?

What one thing would you suggest the speaker work on to improve?

10

Public Speaking: Tending to the Details

Key Concepts

• • • • • • • • • • • •

Successful craftsmanship demands that we pay attention to the finer points of the process. The amount and type of spices give foods their distinctive tastes. What makes a house into someone's home is, among other things, the type of furniture and decorations that are added to the basic structure. The annual report of a business could be typed on plain paper, but most businesses enhance their reports with graphics, special paper, four-color layouts, and other details that suggest a vibrant and successful image. To be at their best, speeches also require attention to details beyond creating the thesis and major points.

Introductions, Transitions, and Conclusions

Introductions

While the introduction is the first thing the audience hears, most speakers will probably find it easiest to compose an introduction if it is saved until the last steps of the composition process. The conclusion is also best left for the latter stages of composition. The reason for the seeming delay is simple: one cannot introduce a topic until one knows what one is going to say about it. Similarly, we cannot wrap up our main points until we know what those main points are and how we feel about them. The first step is to have the body of the speech in place, then go to work introducing it and concluding it.

Functions of an Introduction

The introduction should function as a warm-up and preparation for both the speaker and the audience. It allows the speaker to begin talking and ease into the major points. It allows the audience to tune in on the topic and prepare to process the speaker's remarks. Keep in mind that throughout the speech, the audience has a formidable job of processing information. It must attend to the speaker's ideas, understand them, and react to them, all on the basis of one hearing. If printed material is difficult, the reader can re-read the material any number of times until it is clear. A speaker's audience usually does not re-hear the speech. Hence, the more aid speakers give audiences to process the speech, the more likelihood that the speeches will be successful

In some cases, such as presidential addresses, the text of the speech may be known in advance of the speech. In most cases, however, the audience will have little foreknowledge of what the speaker is to say. If the speaker were to start immediately with the first point of the speech, the audience would have trouble keeping up with the speech.

The basic task of an introduction is to take the audience from where it is—usually ignorant of the speaker's ideas—to the point where it can attend to the topic and put the ideas into the proper perspective. The speaker needs to help the audience move intellectually and emotionally to this point.

Goals of an Introduction

How a speaker chooses to introduce the speech will vary according to the audience, topic, and other factors in the speech situation. An informative speech will be introduced in a different fashion than a persuasive speech or a ceremonial speech. Whatever kind of speech one is giving, the introduction should accomplish several goals.

Gain Attention. First of all, an introduction should *gain the attention* of the audience or strengthen its attention if it is already focused on the speaker. We want to create an interest in the topic and in ourselves as speakers, and a curiosity for what will follow. Here we are answering an unspoken question of the audience, "*Should* we listen to you?" Of course, the steps a speaker takes to gain the audience's attention should fit with the topic and tenor of the speech. As speakers, we have a number of ways in which we can gain the attention of the audience.

A speaker can make a *startling statement.* "Each of us is worth one hundred thousand dollars. That is the amount it is estimated it takes to raise a child from birth to age eighteen."

A *rhetorical question* can work well. A rhetorical question is one that is asked for the sake of making a point, not for the sake of receiving and answer. If one were speaking on the rising costs of a university education, one could begin with, "Do you want to pay another thousand dollars for your schooling next year?"

Humor serves as an attention getter even though it is probably the most stereotypical way of beginning a speech. If one resorts to the familiar, "A funny thing happened to me on the way to speak today. . . .," it will probably send the audience into a serious case of the ho-hums. On the other hand, wit, well applied, can work effectively.

Keep in mind that humor varies from one person to another and from one audience to another. What one audience finds hilariously funny may fall flat with a different group. For example, some may find the following story an amusing beginning for a speech on the perceptions of children; others may not find it amusing at all:

> A kindergarten teacher was working with her class one day when the principal entered the room. Instead of leaving teachers' paychecks in their mailboxes, it was his custom to hand them to the teachers personally. He gave the kindergarten teacher her paycheck and left.
>
> One of the children was curious as to what he had seen, so he asked the teacher, "Why did the principal give you an envelope?"
>
> The teacher explained that the principal liked to hand the teachers their paychecks and the envelope contained her pay for working.
>
> "Oh," the student responded, "where do you work?"

In using humor, we should keep in mind also that what is acceptable terminology to one group may be offensive to another. One theory of humor is that it is a way of expressing in socially acceptable ways that which would otherwise be unacceptable. Humor is a way of venting aggression, cynicism, obscenity, and skepticism (Freud 203–04). Thus, humor has a built-in potential for offending. Wise speakers are careful to use humor in ways that are in tune with the sensitivities of their audiences.

▲ **Figure 10.1.** One way to gain attention in your introduction is to wear special clothing or to bring in an interesting object or both.

A *quotation* that capitalizes on the speaker's idea or reflects the theme of the speech can also provide a good beginning. For a speech on phobias, one could begin with Franklin Roosevelt's well-known remark, "We have nothing to fear but fear itself." For a speech on public service, John F. Kennedy's invitation would be fitting: "Ask not what your country can do for you, ask rather what you can do for your country."

Tell a story and tell it well, and the audience will probably respond positively. As part of an introduction, a story will have to be short, but an anecdote, serious or light, can set the mood for the speech. A speech about one's work experience could begin with a story: "My first day on the ranch, the foreman came to me and said they had just the right horse for me. As I had never been on a horse before, he thought I ought to have a horse that had never been ridden."

If one wears *special clothing*, one can be a walking advertisement for the speech. For a speech on judo, a student wore his judo *gi*, the uniform for that sport. Another student, talking about training procedures at McDonald's, wore her McDonald's uniform.

Another way is to *display an interesting object.* Wheeling in oxy-acetylene welding equipment for a speech on welding should gain the audience's attention as would bringing in a saddle, an assortment of knives, or a bunch of balloons.

A speaker may choose to *give a short demonstration.* Here one does a little bit of what one is going to talk about. A speech on juggling could begin with the speaker giving a short sample of his abilities.

Show Relevance. If gaining the attention of the audience supplies an answer to the question, "*Should* we listen to you?", then the relevance portion of the introduction answers the question, "*Why* should we listen to you?" Here the speaker makes the speech interesting by showing how the topic relates to the audience. A speaker can refer to the needs of the audience members, their backgrounds, their interests, or their wish for entertainment or knowledge.

At first glance, a speech about the Coast Guard would seem to have little relevance for an audience in the landlocked Midwest. One way the topic could be made relevant would be to link it to the feelings of the audience: "When we take a trip in our cars, it is reassuring to know that emergency aid is available should we need it. We know that the highway patrol, sheriffs' departments, ambulances, and wreckers are standing by. The same need for service and protection is felt by people at sea. That is where the Coast Guard comes in."

Establish Credibility. The introduction should tell why the speaker is worthy of the audience's attention. Here, the question to be answered is, "Why should we listen to *you?*" That is, the introduction should establish the speaker as a trustworthy source of information.

One way to establish credibility is to *show experience* with the topic. For example, one student began a speech on harness racing by pointing out that she had worked at a harness racing track for three summers.

One can establish credibility by *citing research.* Here the speaker demonstrates an above average knowledge of the topic. If one were speaking about crime rates, references to the sources examined could establish the speaker as a knowledgeable source of information: "In comparing the crime rate for our university and a similar school in an urban area, I examined the police reports of both universities for the past five years." Background research can also include people as well as print resources: "To find out about athletics and academics at our university, I talked with the athletic director, the basketball coach, the associate dean of students, and three varsity athletes."

Speakers can gain credibility if they *show long-term interest in the topic.* Here the experience is proof of the speaker's interest and genuine involvement. A speech about horses could begin with, "I began showing horses when I was twelve, and I continue to participate even though I am a full-time student living on campus."

Provide an Overview. The introduction should also give the audience an idea of what to expect in the body of the speech. The question to be answered in this portion of the introduction is, "What are we going to hear?" Providing the audience with an overview or preview gives it a framework to use while attending to the rest of the speech. When the audience knows the topic and general ideas the speaker will deal with, it is easier for it to follow the specifics of the speech. The simplest way to provide an overview is to use the thesis statement as part of the introduction. Having gained the audience's attention, shown ourselves to be credible sources, and demonstrated the relevance of our topics, we then tell the audience what it is about to hear.

Transitions

In addition to moving smoothly into the speech and out of it, a speaker should also move smoothly between the main points. Stopping at the end of one main point and jumping to the next makes for a choppy speech. Without knowing the speaker has finished one point and is starting another, the audience may have trouble following what is being said.

One can effect transitions in several ways. The most primitive way is to *announce the finish of one point and the start of the next*: "That finishes my first point. Here is my second point." Even a primitive transition is usually better than none.

A more sophisticated approach to transitions is to compose a *mini-conclusion* to the first point and a *mini-introduction* to the second. Thus, a good transition is like a hand-off in a relay race. The momentum of the first runner is finishing while that of the second is beginning, yet for a moment, the two separate runners are linked together as they pass the baton.

To create a smooth transition, a speaker can compose two *parallel statements*. The first summarizes the first point while the second introduces the second point. If the topic were "word processing" or "child training," the transitions might be phrased like this:

"Learning how to use a word processor involves basic skills that you already have (first point). For those skills that you do not have, your learning can take place in easy steps. (second point)"

"Children can understand the limits of behavior when those limits are clear (first point). Since children cannot process complicated information, no matter how clear it is to adults, your guidelines should also be simple (second point)."

Another useful way to create transitions is to signal the audience with transition phrases.

These are parallel constructions in which the first phrase or word indicates a summation of the first point and the second phrase or word indicates the next set of ideas. Some examples would be:

- ▶ "We have looked at . . . Let us now look at . . . ;"
- ▶ "So much for . . . But what about . . .;"
- ▶ "Now that we understand . . . Let us examine . . .;"
- ▶ "On the one hand . . . On the other hand . . .";
- ▶ "One of the most important ideas is . . . Another important idea is . . .;
- ▶ "We have examined . . . We will examine next . . .;"
- ▶ "Now that we have seen . . . Let us turn to . . .;"
- ▶ "As we have observed . . . Another important aspect is . . .;"

By creating smooth transitions, we move ourselves and our audiences from point to point and make the speaking situation easier for both parties.

Transitions can also serve as a check on the effectiveness of main points and their arrangements. If a speaker is having difficulty linking the main points with transitions, the problem may not be with the transitions but with the main points. They may not be developed fully or they may be arranged in a confusing or ineffectual order.

Conclusions

In finishing a speech, speakers need to make a smooth shift from motion to rest. Concluding is different from just stopping. When a speaker merely stops—abruptly quits speaking—the audience is left hanging without any sense of completion. When one concludes, one brings together the ideas of the speech, signals the audience the speech is ending, and eases out of the subject. A good conclusion reinforces the body of the speech and leaves the audience with a feeling of completion and finality.

Several approaches are available for ending speeches smoothly. Interestingly enough, many of the techniques for concluding a speech mirror the techniques for introducing one. A standard method of concluding is to *summarize the main points* and finish with a wrap-up sentence. If one were speaking on "pigs" and using the thesis statement we formulated in the previous chapter, the conclusion might sound like this: "Despite their reputation as being filthy, sloppy, and smelly, pigs are really likeable animals. They are clean; they are intelligent; and they are amusing. Instead of just being bacon on the hoof, they can be animals to like and to enjoy."

A *quotation* can provide the final touch for a speech. Here the speaker chooses a memorable statement that capitalizes on the ideas and moods of the speech. The quotation may be serous or humorous, but it should reinforce what has already been presented. The climax and conclusion of Martin Luther King, Jr.'s stirring "I Have a Dream" speech was a quotation from a spiritual: "Free at last! Free at last! Thank God Almighty, we are free at last!"

Another way to end a speech is to finish with a touch of *humor*. To finish a speech on early education, one might summarize the main points and conclude with, "Perhaps it was Sherlock Holmes who best summarizes my position. When Doctor Watson asked Holmes which part of a person's education was most important, Holmes replied, 'Elementary, my dear Watson'."

A *rhetorical question* can also serve to close a speech. Such a question brings together the main points and asks the audience for a silent response that reinforces the theme of the speech. In a speech on "Use of Credit Cards," the speaker could end with a rhetorical question such as, "We have seen how students can incur a large amount of debt with cards, and we have seen how we can avoid that debt. All it takes is some planning and a little self-discipline. Are you going to let your financial life be controlled by a piece of plastic?"

For a more powerful ending, the final sentence can be a *powerful statement*. Here one ends with a vivid image, a declaration of intent, or a statement of strong conviction. The best known example in American oratory is probably Patrick Henry's conclusion to his speech urging independence for the American colonies: "I know not what course others may take, but as for me, give me liberty or give me death!"

Sometimes, one can conclude with a *story*. The tale or anecdote or fable should capture the theme of the speech and provide a memorable illustration of the point or points the speaker wants to make. Often, a concluding story will illustrate the consequences if the audience uses or fails to use the information provided in the speech. A speech about safety in the workplace could conclude with a story about someone who wore (or did not wear) appropriate safety garb. If the speech were on, "Consulting Your Interests to Pick the Right Job," the speaker could conclude with a story such as this one:

> A friend of mine grew up on the seacoast. His father was a naval engineer, and my friend and his brothers spent a lot on time on the water. He really liked ships, but he thought he ought to try other possibilities. So one summer, he got a job on a dairy farm.
>
> One of his first jobs was to go to the pasture in the afternoon, open the gate, and start the cows back to the barn for milking. One day he went to the pasture, opened the gate, and all the cows started for the barn. All but one, that is.
>
> He urged the cow to go. She wouldn't. He tried chasing her. She still avoided the gate. All the time he was getting madder and madder. Still the cow would not cooperate.
>
> After a while, the farmer drove up in his truck, got out, and watched my friend chasing the cow. The farmer watched for a few minutes, then said, "It looks like you have a little problem."
>
> "They all went," my friend said, "except for this stupid cow!'
>
> "Well, son," the farmer said, "I think there's a reason for the problem."
>
> "What's that?" my friend asked.
>
> "That cow," the farmer said, "is a bull."
>
> That was when my friend decided that where he belonged was where his interests were already—on a ship.

The conclusion should incorporate what is needed to summarize and wrap-up. Conclusions should avoid including other elements. The conclusion is not the place to introduce a new main point. The conclusion should reinforce what the speaker has already said, not start in a new direction when the speaker has no time to develop the point.

Language Choice

When we talk about composing a speech, we are talking about how we use words to construct a message. The speech composition process is one of trying to find the right words and the right arrangements of words that will allow an audience to translate what we are saying so as to arrive at a viewpoint similar to ours. As language is the vehicle that will carry our intentions and meanings, choosing language is an important part of constructing a speech.

Language Should Fit the Topic— Of RAMS and Ewes

To be effective as speakers, our language must *fit the topic* even to the pronunciation of words. To illustrate, let us look at two topics, one electronic, the other agricultural.

If a person were going to talk about personal computers, the person would need to be familiar with the terms used in describing personal computers and their components. Similarly, if a person were going to talk about sheep, the person would need to be at ease with the breeds of sheep, characteristics of sheep, and how to pronounce words associated with sheep. If the speaker pronounced "ewes" as if it were "ee-wees," anyone with a rudimentary knowledge of sheep would know immediately that the speaker had little acquaintance with the animals. If the speaker on computers referred to RAM (random access memory) as if it were an object—"This computer needs more power. I want to put more rams in it."—the audience would know the person had little experience with the chosen topic.

Language Should Fit the Audience

Besides fitting the speaker comfortably, the language of a speech should also *fit the audience.* People vary widely in their backgrounds, and thus the same topic may have to be expressed in different terms for different audiences. Ex-plaining sheep to urban children would require different language than a speech on sheep raising for 4-H members, and still different language would be appropriate for the Wool Growers of America. Terminology for computers should differ when one is talking to a group of novices on "How to Get Started in Personal Computing" as opposed to talking to the local Mac Users Club or Hackers Anonymous.

Language Should Fit the Speaker

Another criterion that language should meet is that it should *fit the speaker.* Each of us has a different speaking style, and language use is an important part of that style. We want to pick words that fit us, but at the same time, we should be open to expanding our vocabularies. When using new terminology, we should become fluent enough that the new words and phrasing emerge naturally instead of sounding forced.

Language Should Fit the Mood

Language should also *fit the mood* of the speech. Besides creating understanding, speakers also work to create emotional states in their audiences. Wording will differ from speech to speech depending on the emotional tone a speaker wishes to set. For a speech on "waterbeds," for example, the language would vary according to what the speaker wanted to say about the subject. If the person were speaking to the staff of a nursing home about the therapeutic value of waterbeds, the language should show that the speaker understands the serious work of running a nursing home and recognizes the important of patient welfare. On the other hand, if the person were giving a humorous, after dinner speech about waterbeds, the speaker would point out the frivolous problems—leaks, squishes, seasickness, and weight—while making jokes and puns about the subject.

Lining up the Speech

In the process of composing a speech, we reach a point fairly quickly when we feel the need to commit our ideas to writing. As we progress, the arrangements of points and sub-

▲ **Figure 10.2.** Developing your outline is a major part of creating a good speech. (Coyle)

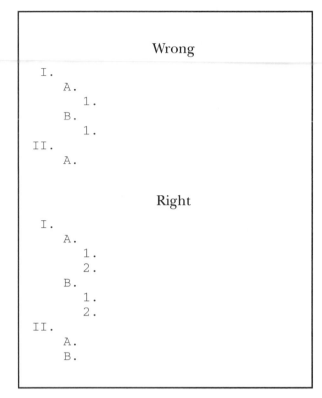

▲ **Figure 10.3.**

```
Thesis Statement
Introduction:
  I. Main Point
     A. Subpoint
        1. sub-subpoint
        2. sub-subpoint
     B. Subpoint
        1. sub-subpoint
        2. sub-subpoint
 II. Main Point
     A. Subpoint
        1. sub-subpoint
        2. sub-subpoint
     B. Subpoint
        1. sub-subpoint
        2. sub-subpoint
III. Main Point
     A. Subpoint
        1. sub-subpoint
        2. sub-subpoint
     B. Subpoint
        1. sub-subpoint
        2. sub-subpoint
Conclusion
```

▲ **Figure 10.4.**

points becomes increasingly complex. In between the notion and the act, our notes act as a rough draft of the speech. Notes put ideas into visible form and allow us to alter what we want to say. Eventually, some form of notes accompany us to the lecture and serve as a guide while we speak. While notes are not an end in themselves, good notes are a valuable tool in the process of creating a speech.

Outlining

In the early stages of composing a speech, we may find ourselves jumping from one point to another, forward and backwards. That is fine for that stage of composition. The final outline, however, should arrange its items in the correct order for speaking.

Composition Notes

We can outline in a number of different ways—sentence, phrase, word—and we can vary the amount of details. The method we will describe involves sentence outlines which are later reduced to speaking notes. This approach allows us to develop the speech in detail and provides flexibility in the speaking situation.

To create an outline, we start with the thesis statement. So that it will be a constant reminder of what we are speaking about, we place it at the top of the outline. The next item is the intro-

Thesis Statement: Dogs are good pets because of their social characteristics, their habits, and their hygiene.

Introduction: Some of them may have celebrity names. Some may have fancy names. Some may have plain names. The celebrity names are those like Lassie, Rin-Tin-Tin, and Benji. Fancy names often come with pedigrees, names like "Sir Wellington's Knight of King's Ridge." The plain names are Spot or Blackie or Old Blue or Squeaker. Whether the names be fancy or plain, dogs have been our friends and protectors for thousands of years, ever since some wolf, separated from its pack, attached itself to a human being. I have had dogs all my life. Most of you have probably had a dog as a pet. I have sometimes wondered why we have such close ties with dogs but not with other animals such as racoons, possums, and other wildlife that may live close to us but not with us. In looking at a number of books on pets, I have found several reasons why we have such long and close ties with the canine world. Dogs are good pets because of their social characteristics, their habits, and their hygiene.

I. Dogs are good pets because of their social characteristics.

    A. Dogs are descended from wolves, animals which have strong social instincts.

        1. Wolves are pack oriented.

           a. Wolves bond themselves to groups.

           b. Wolves enjoy associating with other wolves.

        2. Wolves are responsive to a pack leader.

           a. The "Alpha leader" is at the head of the wolf pack's hierarchy.

           b. The "Alpha leader" establishes his position by dominating the others.

    B. The dog's inherited characteristics make it a good pet.

        1. Instead of bonding with other animals, dogs bond with human beings.

        2. Dogs recognize their owners as "leaders of the pack."

           a. As our dogs' "Alpha leader," we can discipline them and control them.

           b. Recognizing us as their "Alpha leaders," dogs respond to our wishes.

▲ **Figure 10.5.** Sample outline: "Why Dogs Make Good Pets"

3. "Unlike man's other favorite domesticate, the cat, a dog adjusts with

difficulty . . . to an independent and wild existence and draws heavily

on the mutual exchange of pack members and the guidance of a pack

leader, or a human master, who is in fact a surrogate pack leader

("Dogs" *Encyclopedia Britannica:* Macropedia, 929)."

II. Dogs are good pets because of their habits.

    A. Dogs' schedules fit well with human schedules.

        1. Many animals such as racoons, flying squirrels, and skunks are nocturnal

and keep their owners up at night.

        2. Dogs follow human sleeping patterns with ease.

    B. Dogs' natural behavior is not destructive to humans.

        1. Some animals' "playfulness" can be hazardous to your health.

           a. An adult racoon can rip your ear off or bite you to the bone.

           b. A "playful" cougar can disembowel you with one swipe.

        2. Dogs can learn easily how to behave with humans.

        3. Some animals tear up your house.

           a. Racoons, for example, will clear a closet shelf for their sleeping

quarters.

           b. Dogs can learn to live and respect your property.

        4. Some animal's feeding habits make their life incompatible with humans.

           a. Some are such voracious eaters that you would spend most of your time

providing them food.

             1. The common mole must eat constantly.

             2. The field mouse must eat its own weight in food every day.

           b. Some animals such as weasels and skunks, prosper on a diet of live

animals such as mice.

           c. Dogs eating habits are easy.

             1. They eat at regular intervals.

             2. They eat food that is easy to obtain commercially.

▲ **Figure 10.5.** *continued*

III. Dogs are good pets because of their hygiene.

    A. A dog's smell is more compatible with humans than other animals.

        1. Woodchucks and possums, for example, smell bad.

        2. A dog's odor is easily remedied.

            a. Some breeds, such as poodles, have little odor.

            b. "Doggy odor" can be controlled by grooming and bathing.

    B. Dog's elimination habits make them compatible with humans.

        1. Nobody wants to live with urine and fecal matter.

        2. Wild animals are difficult to housebreak.

        3. Dogs are housebroken easily.

            a. Dogs do not like to foul their own quarters.

            b. Dogs respond well to training.

            c. Combining these two characteristics, it is easy for dogs to develop control of their elimination.

            d. Dogs can be trusted on valuable furniture and rugs.

Conclusion: We can see that we live with dogs for good reasons. Their characteristics match up well with our own, and dogs provide us companionship and loyalty at a minimum of effort to ourselves. When you go home at break and see Spot or Blackie or Old Blue, those friendly tail wags and warm welcomes are not accidental. They come from years of close association. You and your dog, My and I dogs, do well together because the dog's social characteristics, the dog's habits, and the dog's hygiene are so well suited to life with humans.

Bibliography

"Dogs." *Encyclopedia Britannica: Macropedia.* 1982.

Fox, Michael. *Superdog.* New York: Howell Book House-Macmillan Publishing Co., 1990.

Milani, Myrna M. *The Body Language and Emotion of Dogs: a Practical Guide to the Physical and Behavioral Displays Owners and Dogs Exchange and How to Use them to Create a Lasting Bond.* New York: William Morris-Quill, 1986.

▲ **Figure 10.5.** *continued*

Monks of New Skeet. *The Art of Raising a Puppy*. Boston: Little, Brown and Company, 1991.

___. *How to Be Your Dog's Best Friend: A Training Manual for Dog Owners*. Boston-Toronto:

Little, Brown and Company, 1978.

New Dog Encyclopedia. 1970.

Rood, Ronald. *May I Keep This Clam, Mother? It Followed Me Home: The Care and Feeding of*

Wild Pets. New York: Simon and Schuster, 1973.

Villiard, Paul. *Wild Mammals as Pets*. Garden City, New York: Doubleday and Company, Inc.,

1972.

Woodhouse, Barbara. *No Bad Dogs: The Woodhouse Way*. New York: Summit Books, 1982.

▲ **Figure 10.5.** *continued*

duction. Here we would do well to write it out in full to make sure it contains all the necessary ingredients: attention, relevance, credibility, and an overview.

Following the introduction comes the main point and below it, the supporting material and expansion of the point. The second (and third and fourth, etc.) point follows in like manner. It is also a good idea to write out the transition between the main points. The conclusion comes last, again written in full so we can be sure to include everything necessary.

In making an outline, we should make sure that points come in the proper order. Main points are the most important ideas. Under them, in descending order of importance, will be the various subdivisions. If a point is to be divided, it needs to be divided into two subpoints. Subdivisions are just that, divisions, and it is difficult to divide something into one part. Instead of a sequence of I-A-1-a, we need a sequence of I-A-1-2-B-1-2.

These sample outlines show how material can be arranged.

Speaking Notes

The closer we come to the speaking situation, the more the purpose of the outline changes from organizing the speech to serving as a memory aid for our remarks. When we move to actually giving the speech, we should be familiar enough with the material that we do not need to rely on a complete sentence outline. At this point, we can reduce the sentence to phrases or words and condense much of the outline. Speaking notes for our speech would look much like (Figure 10.6).

Speech Mapping

Besides the standard outline described above, we can also use speech mapping to organize a speech (Avadian). The difference between the two approaches is that speech mapping employs a fan-shaped format instead of a block format. The core of the speech map is the thesis statement which is written out in full at the left side of the page, halfway down. Branching off from the thesis statement are the major points. Branching off from them are the subpoints. The transitions are written on the strands connecting the thesis statement and the main points. The introduction is written out in the upper left of the page, the conclusion in the lower left of the page.

When we speak from a speech map, we begin by delivering the introduction. The thesis state-

```
Speaking notes: "Why Dogs Make Good Pets"
Intro:
Celebrity names: Lassie, Rin-Tin-Tin, Benji
Fancy names:  Sir Wellington's Knight of King's Ridge
Plain names:  Spot, Blackie, Old Blue
Dogs are our friend and protectors
I have had dogs all my life.
Most of you have had dogs.
I have wondered why we have such close ties with dogs and not other animals.
I found several reasons for long and close ties with canine world.
Dogs are good pets because of their social characteristics, their habits, and their hy-
giene.
    I. Social characteristics
        A. descended from wolves—strong social instincts
            1. pack oriented—bond and enjoy association
            2. responsive to pack leader, "Alpha leader"
        B. inherited characteristics
            1. bond with humans
            2. recognize owners as "alpha leader"
Quotation:  "Unlike man's other favorite domesticate, the cat. a dog adjusts with diffi-
culty . . . to an independent and wild existence and draws heavily on the mutual exchange
of pack members and the guidance of a pack leader, or a human master, who is in fact a
surrogate pack leader ("Dogs," Encyclopedia Britannica: Macropedia, 929.
   II. Habits
        A. schedules fit well with humans'
            1. raccoons, flying squirrels, skunks nocturnal
            2. dogs follow human sleeping patterns
        B. natural behavior not destructive
            1. "playfulness" of some hazardous to your health—raccoons, cougars
            2. dogs learn to behave with humans
            3. some tear up your house—raccoons vs. dogs
            4. feeding habits
                a. voracious eaters
                b. live food for weasels and skunks
            5. dogs eating habits easy—regular times commercially available
  III. Hygiene
        A. smell compatible with humans
            1. animals stink—woodchucks and possums
            2. dog's odor easily controlled—breeds, grooming
        B. elimination habits
            1. living with urine and fecal matter disgusting
            2. wild animals difficult to housebreak
            3. dogs easily housebroken
                a. don't foul own quarters
                b. respond to training
                c. combine the two for good results
                d. can trust trained dog in the house
Conclusion:
live with dogs for good reason
characteristics match ours
provide companionship and loyalty
when you go home and see Spot or Blackie, tail wags not accidental
result from years of close association
You and your dog, My and I dogs go well together because the dog's social characteristics,
the dog's habits, and the dog's hygiene are so well suited to life with humans.
```

▲ **Figure 10.6.** Sample speaking notes: "Why Dogs Make Good Pets"

Introduction: Some of them have celebrity names. Some may have fancy names. Some may have plain names. The celebrity names are those like Lassie, Rin-Tin-Tin, and Benji. Fancy names often come with pedigrees, names like "Sir Wellington's Knight of King's Ridge." The plain names are Spot or Blackie or Old Blue or Squeaker. Whether the name be plain or fancy, dogs have been our friends and protectors for thousands of years, ever since some wolf separated from its pack and attached itself to a human being. I have had dogs all my life. Most of you have probably had a dog as a pet. I have sometimes wondered why we have such close ties with dogs but not with other animals such as racoons, possums, and other wildlife that may live close to us but not with us. In looking at a number of books on pets, I have found several reasons why we have such long and close ties with the canine world.

Thesis Statement: Dogs are good pets because of their social characteristics, their habits, and their hygiene.

Conclusion: We can see that we live with dogs for good reasons. Their characteristics match up well with our own, and dogs provide us with companionship and loyalty at a minimum of effort to ourselves. When you go home at break and see Spot or Blackie or Old Blue, those friendly tail wags and warm welcomes are not accidental. They come from years of close association. You and your dog, I and my dogs, do well together because of the dog's social characteristics, the dog's habits, and the dog's hygiene are so well suited to life with human beings.

▲ **Figure 10.7.** Sample Speechmap: "Why Dogs Make Good Pets"

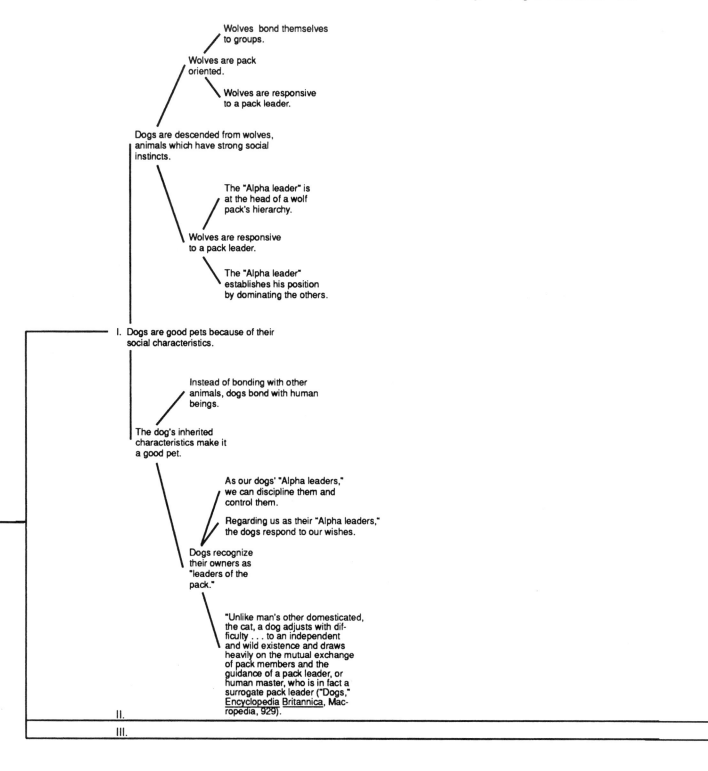

▲ **Figure 10.7.** *continued*

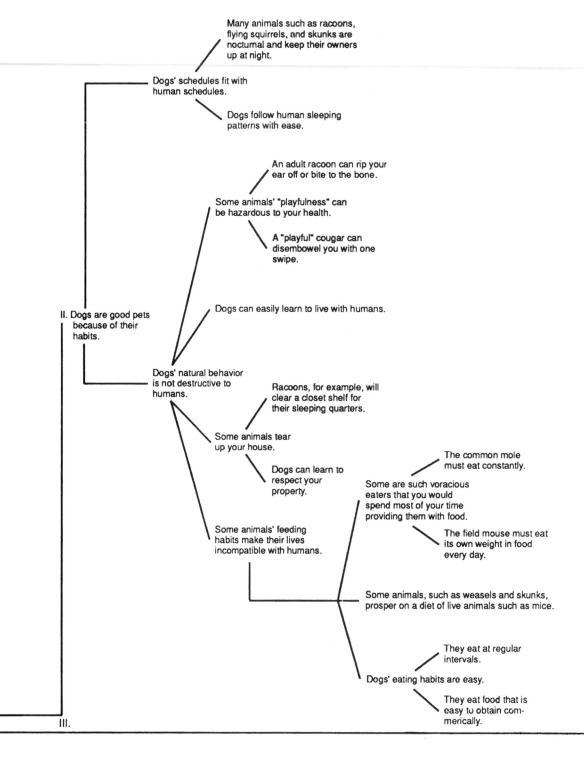

▲ **Figure 10.7.** *continued*

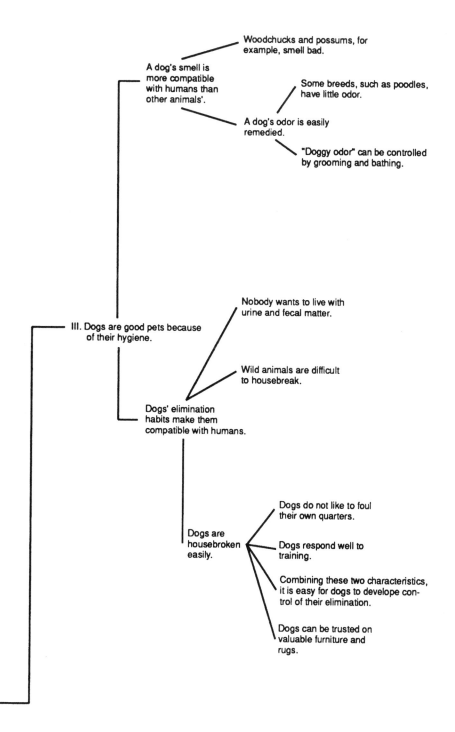

▲ Figure 10.7. *continued*

ment provides an overview of the topic. We follow the transition to the first main point, then follow the lines until we reach the end of a section. We backtrack to the next point until we have exhausted a division. We then return to the thesis statement and follow the transition to the next point. When we have finished all the divisions, we move to the conclusion and deliver it to finish off the speech.

Which form of outline one uses—the standard form or speech mapping—will depend on which form the person finds most comfortable. Each has its advantages and disadvantages. The standard outline frames the speech in the order that the points will be addressed. The speech map allows a speaker to place all the ideas on one page and clearly shows the connections between the points. Speech maps may become cluttered when used for longer presentations, whereas outlines can be expanded to accommodate any length of presentation.

Rehearsing the Speech

The Nature of Rehearsal

Composing a speech involves a great deal of work with ideas and words. Creating an outline goes a long way towards helping create a speech, but if one stops with the words on paper, one still does not have a speech. The *sine qua non* of a speech is not putting words on paper but, rather, putting words into the air. Until a speaker gives the ideas voice, we do not have a speech.

The creation of a speech is not a matter of making an outline, then practicing that outline with no changes. The rehearsal period is as much a time for revisions and changes as any other. After trying to speak our ideas, we may even decide to scrap the entire speech and start over. If necessary, that is fine. What happens in rehearsal should inform the creation of a speech as much as the research, the imaginative work, and the writing. If our rehearsal periods make us revise and rethink earlier work, we should not worry. That is just part of the process.

How to Rehearse

The appropriate way to rehearse a speech is fairly simple: we need to rehearse aloud and in

conditions as close to the speaking conditions as possible. Running over a speech in our minds is helpful, but it does not begin to supply us with the knowledge that full rehearsal brings. We need to try out the actual behaviors—speech and movement—that we will perform when we speak. Only in this way can we have a true idea of what we will sound and look like to the audience and to ourselves.

Placing ourselves in the speaking environment can make the task of giving a speech much easier to accomplish. The more familiar we are with the setting for a speech, the more comfortable we will be. Rather than having to deal with the distraction of an unfamiliar situation, we can be at ease with the familiar. If we are to give the speech in a classroom, we should try to find a time when the room is empty and rehearse the speech in the actual room where we will deliver the speech. If the actual room is closed, we should try to find a similar place. If that does not work, we can at least use our imaginations to visualize what the room will be like.

If possible, we should also rehearse before a trial audience. The audience may be a roommate, a few friends, or family members. We should give the speech, then listen to their comments, particularly the ones we find ourselves affirming. Perhaps we are unsure about the effectiveness of our visual aids. If our roommate makes a comment that they are difficult to decipher, we have a good indication that the visual aids indeed need reworking. If our family says that they think our strongest point is our first one, we can adapt accordingly.

Speakers can also critique themselves. If as we rehearse a speech, we feel bothered by how a particular portion is going, chances are the audience will be bothered as well. We need then to rework and revise that portion until we are comfortable with it.

It helps, too, to keep in mind that each speech we give is itself a rehearsal for the next one. Finishing a given speech does not signal the end of one's speaking career. What we do in a given speech, be it good or bad, will have some influence on subsequent speeches. After giving a speech, we should give ourselves a little time to develop some objectivity about what happened,

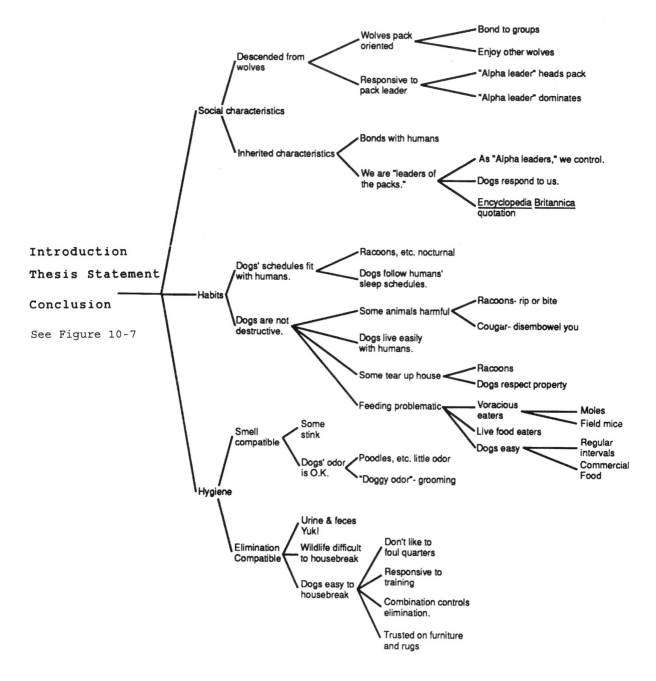

▲ **Figure 10.8.** Speechmap as Speaking Notes: "Why Dogs Make Good Pets"

▲ **Figure 10.9.** Rehearse your speech in conditions as close as possible to those in which you will speak. If possible, have someone listen to your speech and give your feedback. (Coyle)

then assess how the experience went. Here we weigh the comments received and add them to our feelings about the speech. If some things went well, we polish the successes and use them in our next speech; if some things went badly, we work to eliminate the problems.

A Word about Plagiarism

The speech composition process will take us far afield as we assemble ideas and put them into our speeches. Few of us are so well versed in a subject that we know all about it from our own resources and do not have to consult others. Research, either formal or informal, is often an integral part of preparing a speech. The ideas of others add richness to our own. Borrowing ideas from other is perfectly legitimate—unless in doing so we commit plagiarism.

Plagiarism is a form of thievery. Instead of taking a person's money, car, or jewelry, we steal a person's words or ideas. Using ideas and wording from somebody else does not constitute plagiarism, but borrowing and not

giving credit to our sources does. When we pass off borrowed ideas as our own, we commit plagiarism.

The most obvious kind of plagiarism is acquiring a speech from somebody else and giving it as our own. A more subtle form is to copy a small portion of the speech from another and not to acknowledge that source. For example, a person may be speaking on "gun control" and discover an article that says what he wants to say. In the speech, the person uses ideas from the article and some of the wording but does not cite the source. That is plagiarism.

To avoid plagiarism, we need to acknowledge the source of our ideas or borrowed wording. We can acknowledge these sources in several ways. One is in the introduction. Here we simply insert a sentence that tells where we found the material: "In my research I found an article by John Doe which, I think, goes to the heart of the matter." We can also cite sources in the body of the speech. As we introduce the idea, we tell where we found it: "An article in the April 1994 issue of *Public Policy* points out the shortcomings of the proposed gun control law."

If we borrow wording, we can indicate that as well. Here we mention the author, then follow that with the words we are borrowing: "As John Doe has said in the April 1994 issue of *Public Policy*, 'The constitution provides ammunition to both sides of the gun control controversy'."

Besides being ethical, avoiding plagiarism is relatively easy and is the mark of a good speaker.

Conclusion

In addition to the major steps of creating a thesis statement and major points, speech making demands attention to the details that polish a speech. The introduction, conclusion, and transitions add important elements to the speech. Appropriate language choices increase communication and understanding. Outlining gives form to the speech while rehearsal provides a simulation of the actual speech. Material discovered in research needs to be included into the speech with credit given to the sources.

• • • Discussion Questions

1. What are the goals of a good introduction? Why are they important?

2. How are introductions used in other forms of communication such as newscasts and standup comedy routines?

3. Why have transitions in a speech?

4. What examples of conclusions can you think of that occur in communication situations other than speeches? How do these conclusions function in comparison with the conclusions in speeches?

5. How do language choices affect communication? How do language choices particularly affect public speeches?

6. What is the point of outlining a speech?

7. What is the difference between plagiarism and research?

• • • Sources and References

Avadian, Brenda. Speech Mapping Short Course. Central States Communication Association Convention. 14 April 1988. Schaumberg, Illinois.

Name _____ Section _____ Date _____

Public Speaking: Tending to the Details

1. What is the basic task of a speech's introduction?

   _____

   _____

   _____

2. What four areas should be included in the introduction?

   1. _____

   2. _____

   3. _____

   4. _____

3. Give an example of three of the eight different ways to gain an audience's attention.

   1. _____

   2. _____

   3. _____

4. What question does the relevance portion of the introduction answer?

   _____

   _____

5. The answer to the question, "Why should we listen to you?" establishes what in the introduction?

   _____

6. How can a speaker demonstrate credibility?

   _____

   _____

7. Why is providing the audience an overview or preview important?

   _____

   _____

8. A smooth transition can be created in several ways. Describe four of them.

   1. _____

   2. _____

   3. _____

   4. _____

9. What purpose(s) does a transition serve in a speech?

   _____

   _____

10. What should be included in a good conclusion?

    _____

    _____

11. What should be the effect of a good conclusion?

    _____

    _____

12. List six different ways to conclude a speech.

    1. _____   4. _____

    2. _____   5. _____

    3. _____   6. _____

13. What should be avoided in a conclusion?

    _____

    _____

14. Several guidelines are given for choosing the language used in a speech. What are those guidelines?

    1. _____

    2. _____

    3. _____

    4. _____

15. What should go at the top of the outline used for developing speaking notes?

   _____

   Why? _____

   _____

16. Describe the process of converting an outline to speaking notes.

   _____

   _____

   _____

17. What is speechmapping?

   _____

   _____

18. How does speechmapping differ from traditional outline format?

   _____

   _____

   _____

19. How would you use a traditional outline format in a speech?

   _____

   _____

20. How would you use the speechmapping format of organization in a speech?

   _____

   _____

21. What are the benefits of speechmapping?

   _____

   _____

   What are its drawbacks?

   _____

   _____

22. What would be the ideal way to rehearse a speech?

_____

_____

23. What is plagiarism?

_____

_____

24. How can a charge of plagiarism be avoided?

_____

_____

25. If you use an article as the source of information for a speech, but put it into your own words, do you still need to credit the source in your speech to avoid plagiarism?

_____

Why? _____

Making an Announcement

Goal: To announce an event of interest to the class

1. Select an event. It can be a sports event, social event, meeting, day to be commemorated, lecture, play, movie, or anything else you think interesting.

2. Create a brief introduction that creatively captures our interest.

3. Organize the announcement making sure that you tell us:
   WHAT the event is
   WHEN the event will take place
   WHERE the event will take place
   WHO will be involved
   HOW one may attend the event.

4. Create a brief conclusion that summarizes the event, urges us to attend, emphasizes what the event has to offer, or some other final statement.

5. Deliver the announcement. The performance goals are:
   To stand up
   To face the audience
   To introduce the announcement
   To make the announcement
   To conclude the announcement
   To speak so the audience can hear you
   To use only one note card
   To sit down.

Adapted from: Auer, J. Jeffrey. "Creating an Extra 'Real Life' Public Speaking Assignment." *The Speech Communication Teacher* V, iii (Spring 1991): 3. Used by permission of Speech Communication Association.

Announcement Speaking Notes

Introduction

If you have ever wanted a chance to travel back in time, you have an opportunity to do that this weekend.

Announcement

I.   The Feast of the Hunter's Moon: what it is

II.   Features
    A. re-enactors
    B. musical groups
    C. craft workers
    D. foods
    E. costumes

III. Where—Fort Ouiatenon on South River Road

IV.   When
    A. Saturday and Sunday, September 26 and 27
    B. 10:00 to 5:00

V.   How
    A. eight dollar admission
    B. take the shuttle bus from the amphitheater on N. River Road

VI.   Why
    A. See how other people lived.
    B. Have fun.

Conclusion

So, if you want to experience life in a different time period, go to the Feast of the Hunter's Moon this weekend.

Sample Announcement

Introduction

If you have ever wanted a chance to travel back in time, you have that opportunity this weekend.

Announcement

The Feast of the Hunter's Moon is a restaging of the annual meeting of French traders and trappers and Indians during the eighteenth century (what). The event will feature re-enactors, musical groups, craft workers, and foods from the era (who). Those participating will be in authentic costumes.

The Feast will be held at Fort Ouiatenon on South River Road (where) this Saturday and Sunday, September 26 and 27, from 10:00 until 5:00 (when). Admission is eight dollars. The best way to get there is to take the shuttle bus from the the amphitheater on N. River Road (how).

The Feast is an opportunity to see how people lived in a different historical period and to have fun seeing a variety of activities (why).

Conclusion

So, if you want to experience life in a different time period, go to the Feast of the Hunter's Moon this weekend at Fort Ouiatenon.

Brush with Greatness Speech

Goal

To tell an incident in your life when you encountered someone or something well known

Procedures

1. Pick an incident in your life during which you had a "brush with greatness." This incident could be seeing or meeting a famous person, attending a well known event, or visiting a famous place.

2. Compose a story that tells about the incident. You will want to tell:
   WHAT happened
   WHERE it happened
   WHEN it happened
   HOW it happened
   WHO was involved
   what EFFECT it had on you.

3. Tell the story to your audience. The performance goals are:
   ▶ To face your audience
   ▶ To tell your story
   ▶ To speak so your audience can hear you
   ▶ To use positive nonverbal communication
   ▶ To speak extemporaneously.

Adapted from: Raftis, Sean. "Brush With Greatness." *The Speech Communication Teacher* V, ii (Winter 1991): 5. Used by permission of Speech Communication Association.

Favorite Object Speech

Goal

To explain to your audience the importance an item has for you.

Procedures

1. Pick an object that is important or significant in your life in some way. The item could be, for example, a souvenir from a trip, a gift from someone close to you, an important tool, or something in which you have invested a large amount of time and effort.

   The object must meet two criteria. It must be in some form that you can bring it to class. (We will not go out to the parking lot to look at your car.) It may not be a live subject. (Leave Waldo the Wonder Guinea Pig at home.) You may, however, use a photograph or picture of objects not meeting these criteria.

2. Create an introduction to your presentation about the object.

3. Create a short (2–3 minute) presentation. At a minimum, you will need to tell your audience:
   WHAT the object is
   HOW you came to have it
   WHY it is important to you.

4. Create a conclusion to your presentation.

5. Deliver your presentation to your audience. The performance goals are:
   ▶ To face your audience
   ▶ To introduce your presentation
   ▶ To make your presentation
   ▶ To conclude your presentation
   ▶ To speak so your audience can hear you
   ▶ To use positive nonverbal communication
   ▶ To speak extemporaneously.

Adapted from: Gill, Mary. "Successful Self-Disclosure." *The Speech Communication Teacher* II, iii (Spring 1988): 7, 16. Used by permission of Speech Communication Association.

Favorite Outfit Speech

Goal

To explain to your audience the significance of your favorite outfit.

Procedure

1. Select an outfit that is indicative of how you like to dress. Wear something to class that "is you."

2. Create an introduction to your presentation.

3. Create a short (1 1/2–3 minute) presentation about your outfit. At a minimum, you will need to tell your audience:
    WHAT the outfit is
    HOW you obtained it
    WHY you like to wear it
    WHAT you think it communicates to other people.

4. Create a conclusion to your presentation.

5. Deliver your presentation to your audience. The performance goals are:
    ▶ To face your audience
    ▶ To present your introduction
    ▶ To make your presentation
    ▶ To conclude your presentation
    ▶ To speak so your audience can hear you
    ▶ To use positive nonverbal communication
    ▶ To speak extemporaneously.

Adapted from Rollman, Stephen A. "Classroom Exercises for Teaching Nonverbal Communication." II, iii *The Speech Communication Teacher* (Spring 1988): 13. Used by permission of Speech Communication Association.

"Bragging" Speech

Goal

To tell something about yourself of which you are proud.

Procedures

1. Select three things which you have done which you feel good about having accomplished. These could be things such as scoring points in a game, reading a difficult book, achieving a particular grade, taking a trip, meeting a person, learning a skill, completing a craft project, or helping somebody in trouble.

2. Create an introduction to your presentation.

3. Create a short (2–3 minute) presentation telling about your accomplishments. At a minimum, you will need to tell your audience:
    WHAT you accomplished
    WHEN you accomplished it
    WHERE you accomplished it
    HOW you accomplished it
    WHY you accomplished it
    WHY you feel good about the event.

4. Create a conclusion to your presentation.

Recommend/Warn Speech

Goal

To recommend a positive course of action to your audience or to advise your audience as to an action to avoid.

Procedure

1. Select a positive or negative experience that you have had locally. The experience might be a delicious/awful meal in a restaurant, an exciting/boring movie or play, a helpful/hindering service, or a friendly/cold business.

2. Create an introduction to your presentation.

3. Create a short (1 1/2–3 minute) speech in which you inform your audience of something it might want to try or want to avoid. At a minimum, you will need to tell your audience:

   WHAT the entity (business, play, etc.) is
   WHAT your experience with the entity has been
   whether you RECOMMEND or WARN about the entity
   WHY you take the stance you do.

4. Create a conclusion to your presentation.

5. Deliver your presentation to your audience. The performance goals are:
   ▶ to face your audience
   ▶ to present your introduction
   ▶ to make your presentation
   ▶ to face your audience
   ▶ to introduce your presentation
   ▶ to make your presentation
   ▶ to conclude your presentation
   ▶ to speak so your audience can hear you
   ▶ to use positive nonverbal communication
   ▶ to speak extemporaneously.

Adapted from suggestions by Kathy Rowan, Purdue University.

11

Public Speaking: Informational Speaking

Key Concepts

Murry Kaplan, a retired bank executive, is walking his dog through his suburban neighborhood. A car pulls to the curb beside him. The driver rolls down the window and asks, "How do I get to Oak Street?

In the meeting room at the corporate headquarters of Monroe Life Insurance, Becky Li, chief financial officer for the company, addresses the board of trustees about the company's standing. They are contemplating acquiring a Canadian insurance company and need to know their financial position.

On the production line at Linn Gear, the foreman, Sam Jackson, is reminding the shift of the new safety procedures to be adopted that day.

In the third grade classroom at Walton Elementary, Oskar Runeberg, is giving his students instructions about what to bring, what to wear, and how to behave on their field trip to the Children's Museum.

At the lunch meeting of the Rotary Club at the BLD Cafeteria, Sandra Spaak, an attorney, is telling the group about living wills.

In millions of conversations and talks, information passes between people. We inform each other and on the basis of that information, act. Organizations run poorly or well depending on how well they obtain, disseminate, and use information. In corporations, planning officers need sales and production figures. In unions, leaders need to know the problems and desires of the membership. In families, information is continually exchanged as members coordinate eating times, transportation, activities, and chores.

Information passes between people in myriad ways. We talk to each other on the phone. We leaves note on electronic mail and under magnets on the refrigerator. We write letters; we compose memos. In areas of high noise (factories) and in areas of low noise (underwater), we use hand signals to communicate.

One common way of disseminating information is through speeches. The speech may be as short as five minutes, such as the presentation of material at the start of a work shift. The speech may be so elaborate that is a series of presentations as people are taught a new procedure or learn about a new product. The audi-

ence may be as small as three or four people, such as, an office staff. The audience may number in the thousands and be linked by satellite transmission. Whether the message is simple or complex, the audience large or small, informational speaking is an important method of disseminating information.

The Purpose of Informational Speaking

Informational speaking has as its aim the communication of facts, figures, procedures, and ideas. The *goal* of informational speaking is the *transmission of knowledge.* Informational speakers want to make their audience aware of the existence of something about which they are unaware. The speakers want to move their audiences from ignorance to knowledge. An informational speech is a "what is" speech as it aims at making an audience aware of what exists and how it exists.

Approaches to Informational Speaking

Because everything we can think of involves knowledge of some kind, virtually anything is a potential topic for an informational speech. Presuming we have a topic, the problem then becomes how to make the topic comprehensible to our audience. In adapting an informational topic, we have at least four avenues we can take in composing the speech.

▲ **Figure 11.1.** Audiences for informational speeches may be only a few people. (Dawe)

Talk About What Something Is

This approach to informational speaking aims at making the audience aware of the characteristics of an object or entity, person, or event. When the speech is finished, the audience should understand the nature of the subject. What would be important in this approach would be the materials, the components and the classifications of our topic.

Here are some possible topics for an informational speech:

- ▶ Abraham Lincoln
- ▶ Golf clubs
- ▶ The space shuttle
- ▶ Automotive fuel injection systems
- ▶ Personal computers
- ▶ The Battle of Tippecanoe
- ▶ Yellowstone National Park
- ▶ Cameras
- ▶ Dogs
- ▶ Cooking.

Were we to approach these topics from the standpoint of talking about what they are, the speeches would be organized along these lines:

"Three Stages of Abraham Lincoln's Life: Frontier Boyhood, Lawyer, President"

"Major Types of Golf Clubs: Woods, Irons, and Putters"

"Three Parts of the Space Shuttle: Lift-off Rocket, Booster Rockets, and Shuttle"

"The Components of Automotive Fuel Injection Systems: Control Computer, Sensors, Injectors, and Injector Controls"

"The Components of a Personal Computer System: Computer, Keyboard, Monitor, Mouse, and Printer"

"The Two Sides at the Battle of Tippecanoe: Harrison and Soldiers, and the Prophet and Indians"

"Attractions of Yellowstone National Park: Geysers, Mudpots, Wildlife, and Scenery"

"The Three Camera Formats: Large, Medium, and Small"

"Major Types of Dogs: Hunting, Working, and Companion"

"Basic Cooking Skills: Baking, Broiling, and Boiling."

Talk About How Something Works

Another approach to informational speaking is to explain the way in which something functions or functioned. This approach features steps in a process and the product of the process. The process could be mechanical, something performed by humans or animals, or something created by natural causes.

If a speaker approached the list of topics from this viewpoint, the speeches would likely be along these lines:

Abraham Lincoln—"Moving Toward Gettysburg: Composing the Famous Speech"

Golf clubs—"How a Good Driver is Made"

Space shuttle—"How a Space Shuttle Booster Rocket Works"

Automotive fuel injection—"From the Gas Tank to the Combustion Chamber: How Fuel Injection Works"

Personal computers—"How a Hard Disk Functions"

Battle of Tippecanoe—"From Attack to Victory: The Course of the Battle of Tippecanoe"

Yellowstone National Park—"Why 'Old Faithful' is Faithful"

Cameras—"How Film Captures an Image"

Dogs—"Why Herding Dogs Perform"

Cooking—"Why Puff Pastry Puffs."

Talk About How Something Is Done

Similar to discussing how something works is speaking on how something is done. The heart of the speech is still the description of a process, but instead of describing the process, this type of speech tells how to accomplish a goal. This type of speech is basically a "how to do it" speech.

A speaker using this approach on the list of topics would go in directions such as these:

Abraham Lincoln—"Getting the Most Out of Your Visit to Springfield, Illinois"

Golf clubs—"Lower Your Golf Score With Good Putting"

Space shuttle—"How to Track the Shuttle's Flight"

Automotive fuel injection—"The Care and Feeding of Your Car's Electronic Fuel Injection System"

Personal computers—"How to Use Style Sheets in Word Processing"

Battle of Tippecanoe—"How to Fire a Black Powder Rifle"

Yellowstone National Park—"How to Enjoy Our Most Popular National Park"

Cameras—"How to Take Better Snapshots"

Dogs—"Housebreaking Your New Pet"

Cooking—"Desperation Dinners: How to Put a Good Meal on the Table Quickly."

Talk About How Something Is Viewed

Besides observing and participating, we also consider the relationships between events, people, places, and things. We make judgments about the effectiveness of a process. We discuss ideas and concepts. We probe the motivation behind actions. The world of ideas is another area for informational speeches. In speeches of this kind, we discuss how people see or regard a subject. Important areas would be analyses, theories, feelings, predictions, reflections, and concepts.

Viewing the list of topics from this angle, the speeches would feature ideas connected with the topics:

Abraham Lincoln—"Lincoln's Plans for Reconstruction"

Golf clubs—"The Physics of a Golfball's Flight"

Space shuttle—"Space Exploration Policies of the Clinton Administration"

Automotive fuel injection—"Anti-Pollution Laws: The Drive Toward Cleaner Air"

Personal computers—"Personal Computers: The Blessing/Bane of Our Lives"

Battle of Tippecanoe—"Tecumseh's Dream of an Indian Confederacy"

Yellowstone National Park— "The National Park System's Philosophy of Wildlife Management"

Cameras—"Photographs as Art"

Dogs—"Americans and Their Pets"

Cooking—"Attitudes Toward Food."

Combining Approaches

The four approaches we have discussed can provide us with ways to explore and develop speech topics. Besides being used alone, the ap-

Figure 11.2. In an informational speech you may approach your topic from several directions.

proaches can also be combined. If someone were explaining a new piece of equipment, the person would probably want to tell the audience what the equipment is, how it works, and how they can use it. The speaker may even want to talk about the idea behind it, why it was created, or why it was obtained. If the speaker is discussing an idea, the speaker may also want to show how people can put that idea to work in their lives.

Principles of Effective Informational Speaking

Whichever approach to a topic we take, we want to keep in mind the two major goals of good informational speaking: (1) the speech should be easy to understand, and (2) the information should be as easy as possible to retain. We can accomplish these goals by following the principles of effective informational speaking: clarity, repetition, relevance, significance, and memorability.

Clarity

Just as it is hard to see through a dirty window, it is hard to understand a muddled speech. A clear speech is one which the audience finds easy to follow and understand. Attention to several details will increase the clarity of a speech.

In making *language choices*, the speaker should choose words which the audience will readily understand. If unfamiliar words or concepts are used, they should be explained or defined. In some instances, one could appropriately say, "We should not obfuscate the issue" or "The quickest method of egress is the window" or "He is a superannuated faculty member." With other audiences, these sentences could be more confusing than enlightening. In those cases, the speaker might do better to say, "We should not confuse the issue," "The fastest way to exit is through the window," and "He is a faculty member who has been here a long time."

The *organization* of a speech can aid the clarity of the presentation. Using the methods discussed in the previous chapter, a speaker could provide an introduction which would create a sense of expectation. Providing an overview with a thesis statement would give the audience an idea of how it is to respond. Further, the order of ideas can be helpful. The listener should be able to go from point to point smoothly. A speech on how to prepare an income tax return would probably be organized along these lines:

▶ Reading the Instructions
▶ Summarizing Your Records
▶ Filling out the Proper Forms
▶ Submitting Your Return
▶ How to Respond If You Are Audited.

If the audience had to jump from point to point without seeing an apparent order, the speech would be more difficult to follow:

▶ Submitting Your Return
▶ Summarizing Your Records
▶ How to Respond If You Are Audited
▶ Filling out the Forms
▶ Reading the Instructions.

A speaker's *delivery* can contribute to the clarity of a speech as well. If the speaker articulates poorly or has low volume, the audience will have difficulty following the speech. If the speaker's visual aids are hard to see or difficult to manage, the audience's attention will shift from the information to the problems with the visual aids. While we will discuss voice and visual aids in the next chapter, let us acknowledge here their importance.

Repetition

A student, on a number of occasions in his college career, wondered why professors repeated class assignments so many times. The student would have the information about the requirements in his notebook, and he found

the repetition of the assignment and its details monotonous, if not insulting. Then that student became a professor and discovered why his instructors repeated assignments. If he did not repeat the assignments, some students would not get the information.

Like cheap paint, a one time application of information will not cover the subject very well. To do well on exams, we have to look at class materials a number of times. To publicize an event well, we put posters on every available bulletin board, pass out fliers, run ads in the paper, and make announcements in classes. Similarly, in public speaking, speakers need to expose their audiences to information more than once.

The repetition of information should be integrated into the smooth flow of the speech. A typical speech format provides a number of places where material may be repeated. The title of the speech can provide the first view. The introduction gives the topic and main points. As they summarize material and point to the next main point, transitions are another opportunity to emphasize information. The main points, of course, elaborate on the information. As the speech closes, the conclusion provides one last opportunity to reiterate important information.

Visual aids can also reinforce information. Two channels are better than one when it comes to making an impact with information. In addition to the speaker's words, the visual aids provide ways to illustrate, emphasize, and clarify points.

Relevance

We pay attention to those subjects which affect us most closely. A talk on "Tuition Raises at the University of Moscow" would not be as interesting as a talk on tuition raises at our own university. "How to Thaw Water Pipes" is a good topic for an informational speech, but the speech will probably elicit more attention in January with sub-zero temperatures than it will in July.

People will understand information best when they see it as having importance for them. To be relevant, the speech should address the needs, concerns, and interests of the audience. Careful audience analysis can indicate the direction a speaker should take in composing a speech. The object is to make the topic one the audience sees as having an impact on their lives.

The speaker may show how the topic will be useful to the audience. Here the speaker demonstrates how the topic will make the lives of the audience members easier. For example, a speech on "How to Take Good Snapshots" informs people how they can save money and increase their enjoyment. They save money by not having to pay for bad pictures. Their enjoyment increases because their pictures come closer to capturing the mood they wished to preserve. A speech on the university budget may promise to be a dry subject, but the topic becomes livelier when it is shown to have an impact on every student's pocketbook.

A speech topic may also be relevant because it appeals to people's curiosity and offers to satisfy that curiosity. Few of us will be astronauts, but many of may still wonder how the space shuttle gets into space and back again. An informational speech can broaden our knowledge even if we are not directly connected with the subject.

The language of the speech will have bearing on how relevant the speech appears to the audience. If the topic is addressed in clear and familiar terms, it is more likely to appear to be a part of the world of the audience. A speaker using an unfamiliar and difficult vocabulary may make the topic appear distant and removed.

Significance

Closely related to the relevance is the consideration of significance (Pearson and Nelson). As speakers, we should relate the information to our audiences, but we should also make sure the topic is one of significance to the audience.

Insignificant topics would be those considered by the audience as too simple or trivial or peripheral. An audience of college students, for example, would find relevant a topic that addressed the need to do well in school, provided them with a useful skill, and involved something they use daily. A speech on "How To Sharpen a Pencil" would meet these three criteria. The speech topic, though, concerns a skill they all mastered a long time ago.

A significant topic would better address the educational level of the audience. It would be one that promised a significant impact on the lives of the audience members.In this context, a significant speech would more likely be one on "How to Improve Memory Skills," "Creative Thinking," or "Avoiding Math Anxiety."

Memorability

If information can be put into some striking format, it is easier to remember than if it is presented flatly. Hence, the profusion of jingles, rhymes, and slogans that stick in our minds and serve as handy tools for retaining information. We could say, "Beginning with January, the longer months alternate with the shorter months until we reach August when the pattern reverses itself." Instead, we put the idea in rhyme which makes it catchier, "Thirty days hath September, April, June, and November."

Informational speakers need to look for ways to make the information vivid. As mentioned above, catchy wording can reinforce an idea. Students in water safety classes remember the proper sequence of rescue techniques by recalling "reach, throw, row, go." We can decide the proper direction to turn screws, nuts, and jar lids if we can remember the alliterative description, "Right is tight; left is loose." Port and starboard, directions on a ship, can be remembered when we associate the known with the unknown. "Port" has the same number of letters as "left." That leaves "starboard" to be "right."

Visual images can reinforce information. A speaker can say that using safety harnesses in cars is good protection in case of an accident. The point is more vividly made if we watch a slow motion film of unharnessed crash dummies breaking apart and flying through the windshield as a car hits a barrier in a crash test. The words of a speech on child abuse can make an audience aware of the problem, but the picture of one battered, innocent victim can be galvanizing.

Skills for Informational Speaking

The principles of good informational speaking can be accomplished in several ways. By developing skills in defining, describing, story telling, and demonstrating, we can aid our audiences in assimilating the information we present.

Defining

As we noted in our discussion of language, the meaning of words depends on the thoughts or perceptions of people, not on meanings inherent in the words themselves. The principle is one to keep in mind when composing informational speeches. If speakers presume that they and their audiences automatically share meanings, they may be in trouble. If audience members have one meaning for a word while the speaker has a second, misunderstanding rather than understanding may be the result.

A speaker was presenting information on negotiation between teachers' organizations and school boards. One of the points to which the speaker kept returning was that negotiations centered on two areas of disagreement, salaries and language. Neither term was defined. One audience member thought "negotiation about language" meant that the teachers were concerned about the language arts program (reading, literature, and writing) and wanted to negotiate changes in the teaching program. The speaker's meaning of the term was "contract language." By her definition, "negotiation about language" meant that the two parties negotiated about the terms of the contract such as class size, sick day policy, pay dates, and personal leave days. With the difference in understanding of the term "language," the speech was confusing to the audience member.

This kind of misunderstanding can be avoided if the speaker tells the audience the intended meaning of a word or concept. An audience may also be so unfamiliar with a word or concept that it has no meaning for it until the speaker provides one.

One way of defining is to refer to an authoritative source, as in "By 'meditation,' I have in mind the definition found in *Webster's New Collegiate Dictionary*. Or, "In the auto industry, 'captive import' means a car built by a foreign manufacturer but imported and marketed by an American company."

Speakers can also supply their own definitions of terms: "When I speak of 'house pets,' I am referring only to cats and dogs, those pets that may be given free run of the house."

A speaker can also define terms by referring to information common to the audience. Here the speaker utilizes the experience of the audience: "When I say 'long lines,' I am not thinking about five or six people in front of you. I'm talking about the lines we saw at registration that stretched from the bursar's windows, out of the building, and halfway up the mall."

Describing

Describing is using words to create images in the mind of an audience. Good description can help audience members to see how parts of a whole are linked together, to make audience members part of an experience, or to create empathy with the subject. Good description can make the abstract ideas of a speech concrete for the audience.

One way to describe is by making a series of statements that provide mental pictures for the audience. If feasible, the mental pictures can be reinforced by the actual objects. In a speech on making a salad, the speaker would describe the steps of the process: "To make a Caesar salad, the first thing you do is assemble the ingredients: Romaine lettuce, coddled eggs, lemons, garlic, anchovies, and oil. Next you take a large wooden bowl and coat the inside with oil . . .".

Another way of describing is to provide examples of a concept or process. Here again, the speaker is trying to make an abstract idea concrete by providing specific instances that illustrate the main idea. For a speech on dog training, the speaker might use examples to describe in this way: "Despite what entertainment would like for us to believe, dogs cannot reason at the levels displayed by Lassie, Rin-Tin-Tin, or Benji. Dogs see things in broad classifications. Your dog cannot tell the difference between the old shoe he may chew on and your new, hundred and twenty-five dollar high-tops which he may not chew on. Your dog cannot understand why it is all right to jump on the vinyl couch in the den but not all right to jump on the polished cotton couch in the living room."

A third method of description is by contrast. An idea or concept is made vivid by measuring it against another idea or concept. The comparison brings out the qualities of both items described. In discussing the ferocity of a blizzard, a speaker might describe the situation thusly: "A normal snow will mean freezing temperatures and some wind. A blizzard brings temperatures that threaten human life and gale force winds. In a blizzard, snow does not just fall. It blows, whips, whirls, stings, and drifts."

Analogies provide a fourth way of describing. Rather than telling what something is directly, we tell what it is like. An honor student could describe maintaining a scholastic record in terms that compare it to a difficult task: "High grades are great to have, but they are not without their drawbacks. Picture yourself trying to carry a cup filled to the brim with hot coffee as you walk across a pure white oriental rug. That's how I felt carrying a straight *A* average into the last semester of my senior year with a schedule that included two of my toughest courses."

Storytelling

Stories have a strong impact on us. As children, we learn how to behave by listening to stories that show the consequences of good and bad actions. "The Little Engine that Could" makes a point about persistence. "Winnie the Pooh" tells us of the value of friendship. "Where the Wild Things Are" helps us come to grips with our chaotic urges. Fables and parables comment on life and religion. Some points are best made when they are illustrated by a story, rather than defined and discussed.

Stories can enliven our informational speeches by providing examples and applications of our points. Stories can be collected from newspapers and magazines. We can find stories in literature. We can use personal experiences as stories. We can pay attention to the stories that others tell us.

Good stories have form to them. They are not just a rambling collection of facts and events. To tell a story well, we need to know who the characters are, what they do, and how the events tie together. A well-told story establishes a sense of expectation in the audience as events move to a high point or climax, as in this story:

When you are hooking up jumper cables to start a car, make sure that the cables are properly connected. The red

ones go to the positive terminal. The black ones go to ground, some metal connection in the car. If you hook them up improperly, you can be in big trouble. I know. I did it one time.

I was helping a friend start his car at night. The light was bad, and he hooked up the cables backward in his car. Instead of positive to positive, we were going negative to positive. When I tried to clamp the cable to the battery terminal, sparks flew in all directions. I heard loud popping sounds. I jerked back and banged my head on the hood of the car.

We figured out the problem and managed to start his car. The next morning when I looked at my car, I found that we had melted two holes in my battery connector.

Remember to hook up jumper cables positive to positive, red to red. Then clamp the black ones onto the frame or engine.

Showing

We learn many things by listening and reading, but some things, activities primarily, are usually best learned by doing or watching someone else do them. Dancing, cooking, horseback riding, dog grooming, pool shooting, tightrope walking, and giving medical injections are skills that are usually learned by first watching someone else do them. In informational speaking, the speaker often becomes the "someone else" doing the activity, while the audience becomes the learning observer.

When speakers are showing or demonstrating, they become a kind of living visual aid. Besides speaking the words of their speeches, they carry out the actions they are describing. For a speech on golf, they demonstrate the proper grip and stance. For a speech on medical injections, they fill the syringe, eliminate the air, then inject it. Some of the best examples of the value of showing to communicate information are the televised cooking shows such as, "The French Chef" and "The Frugal Gourmet." In these presentations, the cooks mix, chop, blend, saute, and broil in time with their words.

Then, finally, they show the finished product to cap the speech.

Adopting a "show and tell" approach to informational speaking places extra demands on speakers. They not only have to give the speech clearly, they have to be able to talk while they are involved in an activity. Coordinating the words and actions requires extra practice and preparation. For example, a cooking show may prepare three or four versions of the featured dish to show what it looks like at various stages. The ready-to-cook dish is popped into the oven, and immediately thereafter, the cook pulls out the finished product. The payoff of the extra work is that the speech has added impact and interest for the audience.

Developing the skills of defining, describing, story telling, and showing will help a speaker develop a well-rounded approach. With these skills, a speaker should be well equipped to adapt to the demands of information and audience.

Conclusion

Informational speaking is "what is" speaking. Its aim is to help the audience to understand, to help it acquire knowledge. In approaching topics, speakers can frame their speeches in many ways. They can talk about what something is, how something works, how something is done, or how something is viewed. Principles of effective informational speaking include clarity, repetition, relevance, significance, and memorability. To reach one's potential as an informational speaker, one needs to develop skills in defining, describing, story telling, and showing. By combining these principles and skills, informational speaking can be effective, enlightening, and enjoyable.

• • • Discussion Questions

1. What examples can you think of that involve the communication of information?

2. Select a topic for an informational speech. How could that topic be approached by talking about how something works? How could the topic be approached by talking about what it is? How could the topic be approached by talking about how it is done? How could the topic be approached by talking about how it is viewed?

3. What is meant by "clarity" in informational speaking?

4. What examples can you think of where repetition plays a part in the communication of information?

5. What makes a speech topic relevant to an audience?

6. What makes the difference between a speech topic that is trivial and one that is significant for an audience?

7. In what ways can we make information memorable?

8. Select a word or concept. How can you define that word so that others understand your meaning?

9. Select an object or a process. How can you describe it so that your audience can understand it?

10. How do stories convey information?

11. Why is showing or demonstrating an effective means of communicating information?

• • • Sources and References

Pearson, Judy and Paul Edward Nelson. *Understanding and Sharing: An Introduction to Speech Communication.* 5th edition. Dubuque, Iowa: William C. Brown Publishers, 1994.

Name _____ Section _____ Date _____

Informational Speaking

1. What is the aim of informational speaking?

   _____

2. List four potential topic areas for an informational speech.

   1. _____

   2. _____

   3. _____

   4. _____

3. What are the two major goals of informational speaking?

   1. _____

   2. _____

4. How can these goals be accomplished?

   _____

   _____

5. What is clarity in speech writing?

   _____

   _____

6. How can you increase the clarity of a speech?

   _____

   _____

7. How should repetition be effectively used in a speech?

   _____

   _____

8. What must a speech incorporate in order to be considered relevant by the audience?

   _____

   _____

9. How can you make a speech memorable?

    _____

    _____

10. In what way can a speaker's use of good descriptive language be helpful for audience members?

    _____

    _____

11. List four types of describing.

    1. _____

    2. _____

    3. _____

    4. _____

12. In what way can storytelling be beneficial when speaking?

    _____

    _____

13. How may showing or demonstrating be useful in conveying information?

    _____

    _____

12

Public Speaking:
Performance Consideratations

Key Concepts

• • • • • • • • • • •

After the speech is composed, speakers still lack one thing. They have to take what they have created through imagination, research, and rehearsal and place it in public view. Public speaking differs from expression through writing. With writing, the author creates a manuscript that can be regarded independently of its creator by audiences far removed from its creation. With a speech, the author embodies the ideas and feelings, and creates the message in time and in the presence of its audience. That process allows public speaking an immediacy and impact missing from other forms of presentation. It also places an extra responsibility on speakers as they must make performance decisions in addition to the other decisions of composition. This chapter will present some guidelines to assist speakers in making effective choices.

Handling Speaking Notes

In extemporaneous speaking, most speakers rely on some kind of memory device such as: notecards, a speechmap, a teleprompter, or cue cards. The choice of what to use will depend on one's speaking style and the circumstances in which one finds oneself. Whatever the format, good notes can inspire confidence and contribute considerably to the speech.

The basis for one's speaking notes is the outline prepared in the process of composing the speech. The outline contains the introduction, main points, transitions, and conclusion. The speaking notes condense the outline into a form that is informative and easy to handle.

A typical method is to put the notes on 4x6 or 3x5 cards. Five cards should be sufficient for a three point speech. The first card carries the introduction, the next three each carry a major point, and the last one carries the conclusion.

◀ **Figure 12.1.** Handling notes smoothly can aid your speech.

The notes should be in outline form and contain only notes, not the entire speech. The function of notes is to jog the speaker's memory when needed, not to supply the speaker with a manuscript.

Good notes should be *highly legible*. The less time a speaker spends looking at notes, the more effective the speech will be. A speaker should be able to glance at the notes, pick up the next point, and smoothly incorporate it into the speech. If the notes are jumbled or squeezed onto the cards in miniscule printing, the speaker may have a hard time finding the appropriate point in the confusion of entries.

It is also important to *rehearse with the actual speaking notes*. Using the same notes for rehearsal and speaking follows the principle of rehearsal we discussed earlier: a speaker should rehearse in conditions that are as close as possible to the conditions of the speech.

Speakers need to work with their notes until they can move easily from one point to the next, one card to the next. Part of the rehearsal process is learning how to handle the notes so that they attract as little attention as possible. For example, when moving from one notecard to the next, it is a good policy for a speaker to maintain eye contact with the audience while changing the cards.

If a speaker elects to use a speechmap, the speechmap should be fitted onto one page. This way the speaker will not have to worry about shuffling notes and can easily follow the flow of the speech from point to point. As with notecards, a speaker using a speechmap should rehearse with the same speechmap that will be used in the actual speech.

Visual Aids

In earlier chapters, we have alluded to the importance visual aids can play in clarifying information and making points memorable. The words speakers compose and encapsulate in their notes can create a variety of images for their audiences. Words, though are not always sufficient to create the fullest of understanding. Visual aids can provide additional emphasis, clarity, and interest to a speech.

Two basic principles stand out in the effective use of visual aids. First, good visual aids are *visual*, and second, good visual aids are *aids*. The concept is more than a tautology.

Visibility

If an audience cannot readily see or interpret the speaker's visual aids, then the speaker has created a visual hindrance instead of a visual aid. Instead of smoothly synthesizing the speaker's ideas with the visual materials, the audience is forced to choose between trying to listen to the speaker, and trying to decipher the small print or fuzzy pictures on the visual aids. Instead of the two media complementing each other, they are in conflict.

The test for visual clarity is an easy one. We set up our visual aid. Then we step back from the visual aid as far as the last row of the audience. If we can still see all the details of the visual aid clearly, the visual aid is a good one. If we cannot see the details clearly and immediately, we need to revise the visual aid.

Here are the keys to high visibility.

Size

A visual aid may be a perfect illustration of the speaker's idea, but it will be ineffective if it is not large enough to be seen in detail. If one were making a speech on counted cross-stitch,

beetles, or computer chips, the actual samples would be so tiny that few in the audience, if any, could see them. A photograph can provide a vivid illustration, but the standard photographic print is so small that details are lost at the distance of a few feet. The answer to the problem is to make the object larger and more visible by such devices as drawing diagrams and using photo enlargements.

Detail

A good visual aid will include only as much detail as can be easily seen and comprehended by the audience. It is also a good idea to include one idea or concept per visual aid. For example, an epidemiologist, someone who studies the spread and control of diseases, could be talking about the frequency of six different diseases in a state. Here the visual aids would probably be clearest if the speaker used a different visual aid for each disease. Trying to put all six on the same visual aid would result in considerable overlap. Sorting out the areas affected by each disease would be a difficult task for the audience.

Color

Some colors show up better than others at a distance. One would think that red and yellow would be good colors for visual aids because they are bright. Contrary to popular opinion, they are not. At a distance, red and yellow lettering tends to fade out. Blues, greens, and browns will work better.

Aiding the Speech

The "aids" in visual aids means that the visual elements in a speech should assist the speaker in making ideas clear. The visual aids should support the speaker's points instead of becoming the primary channel of communication.

A speech on animated cartoons, for example, could certainly include film or video clips that illustrate the speaker's points about action, continuity, or the use of backgrounds. If, however, the clips were so long that the audience became caught up in the plot or antics of the characters, the visual portion of the speech would cease aiding the speaker's ideas and take on a life of its own.

▲ **Figure 12.2.** Often you can use the actual object as a visual aid. (Coyle)

▲ **Figure 12.3.** If the actual object is too large or too small for use as a visual aid, you can use a model such as this model of a silk worm larva.

Types of Visual Aids

Keeping in mind the guidelines for effective visual aids, speakers have available a wide range of materials to enhance their speeches.[1]

Actual Objects

The first approach to visual aids is to illustrate the speech with the actual items about which one is speaking. This approach works well if the items are large enough to be seen and small enough to be handled easily. Speeches on geodes, track shoes, or violins, for instance, could easily be illustrated by the speakers displaying actual geodes, track shoes, or violins.

Models

While actual objects can provide a sense of authenticity to a speech, they are not always the best visual aids. The story is told at Purdue, a university with noted programs in agriculture, that an instructor heard some unusual sounds in the hallway just prior to class. Investigating, he found four students trying to herd a Holstein cow up the stairs and into the classroom. The cow was to have been the visual aid for one of the student's speech on dairy production. While indeed authentic, the novelty of the cow, not to mention the possibility of the cow's byproducts, would be so distracting that the point of the speech would probably be lost. One

hopes the instructor had the presence of mind to tell the students that their choice of a visual aid was udderly wrong.

When the actual object is too large, too small, or too impractical to function as an effective visual aid, a model can be used. A speech on the harmful effects of music at high volume would probably need to show the workings of the middle and inner ear. Besides being difficult to obtain, these components of the body are so tiny that few could see them. One way to solve the problem would be to use a large model of the ear that would make the parts evident to the audience. A speech on volcanoes, for example, could use a paper mache or fiberglass model to show how volcanoes are formed and how they behave.

Pictures

Pictures are another way of handling items which are of difficult size or difficult to obtain. A poster, drawing, or enlarged photo of the item can be used instead. A speech on diamond cutting would want to show the differences between rough stones and finished stones. Using actual diamonds would be ineffective as the audience would not be able to see them. Much better would be large pictures of the rough stone, the planned cuts, and the finished product. At the other end of the scale, a speech on

▲ **Figure 12.4.** Pictures offer many possibilities for visual aids.

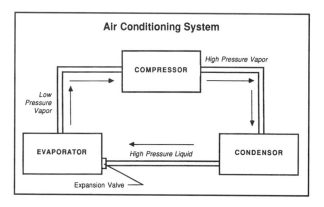

▲ **Figure 12.5.** Processes and systems may be illustrated with diagrams.

intercontinental ballistic missiles would also require pictures as visual aids.

Diagrams

Diagrams are akin to pictures, but diagrams are less realistic and more symbolic. Diagrams can be used to show spatial relationships and patterns not readily observable in actual objects or pictures. Diagrams can also exclude unnecessary details and can emphasize a portion of a system or object. A speech on an automobile air conditioning system could use a diagram that showed the components and their relationship. The diagram would be clearer than trying to point out the components in a picture of an engine compartment.

Charts and Graphs

Actual objects, pictures, and diagrams are ways to illustrate concrete objects. When speakers need to demonstrate relationships, particularly numerical relationships, they turn to graphs and charts. These help audiences to understand the nature of a situation and help the audience compare the effects of different variables in a situation.

The three main types of charts and graphs are pie charts, bar graphs, and axis or line graphs. The first, the *pie chart*, is so named because it indicates the quantity of an item by showing how big a "slice" it takes of the "pie," a

circle representing one hundred percent of a population. One draws a circle, then indicates the proportions of its divisions, and labels them appropriately.

A *bar graph* uses different lengths of bars or columns which are measured against a scale. The side-by-side illustration makes it easy for the audience to compare the different elements against the scale and against each other. For comparing two makes of cars, the speaker could use several bar graphs to show the differences between the two in cost, performance, mileage, and wind resistance.

An *axis* or *line graph* shows the relationship between two related sets of numbers. The horizontal and vertical axes represent two variables that interact with each other. Typical sets of figures would be such things as age and income, income and health care protection, time and economic growth, city size and pollution levels,

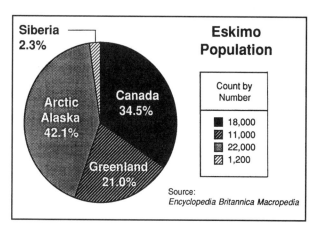

▲ **Figure 12.6.** Pie charts show how quantities are divided.

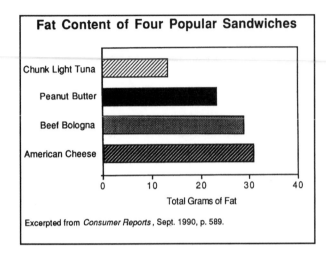

▲ **Figure 12.7.** Bar graphs can compare quantities.

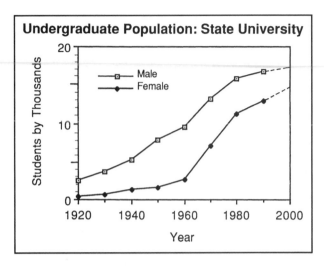

▲ **Figure 12.8.** Axis or line graphs show the relationship between two factors such as time and growth.

classroom space and school enrollments, and rehearsal time and speech success. With an axis or line graph, one can obtain specific information, such as school enrollment in a given year, and one can also see the progression of a situation or condition such as enrollment trends.

Displaying Visual Aids

Once the visual aids have been made, the speaker should work to make them an integral part of the speech. Much of the success of visual aids depends on how well they are incorporated into the overall presentation. The format of visual aids will depend on such considerations as, the topic of the speech, the speaker's abilities, the audience, and available equipment.

Handling Objects

If the speaker is using actual objects or models, the items should be readily available when they are needed. At the same time, they should not be so prominent that they call attention away from the speech. A good practice is for speakers to place the objects of models on a table to the side of themselves. The items should be arranged in the order in which they will be needed for the speech. When an object is needed to illustrate a point, the speaker picks up the item, uses it, then replaces it on the table when it is no longer needed. The process can be mastered by the speaker working with the objects during the rehearsal period.

One also needs to make sure that besides being at hand, the items are ready to use. For example, if the speaker needs to unscrew a jar lid while speaking, the lid should be loosened sufficiently before the speech. If the speaker wants to use a battery powered device, the batteries should be fresh.

Posters

One of the most common methods of displaying pictures, graphs, and diagrams is to put them on posterboard. Particularly for classroom speeches, posterboard is an easy and economical approach. Lettering can be done with stencils, lettering kits, or templates.

During the speech, the posters should be displayed on a sturdy stand. When they are placed in the chalk tray, they usually do a nose dive onto the floor.

A standard principle of the use of visual aids is "Use it, then lose it." Visual aids need to be shown only while they are relevant to the point being made. Until it is needed, the first poster should be covered. When the speaker is finished with a poster, it should be removed or covered.

Flip Charts

Flip charts are large tablets that allow the speaker to place information on succeeding sheets. This format allows a speaker to remove quickly a display when it is no longer needed. One simply flips the sheet from the front of the tablet over the top and lets it hang down the back. The first display is out of sight and the next one is showing.

As with posters, the graphic work on a flip chart needs to be clearly and neatly done. The flip chart should be placed on a sturdy support. Speakers must practice with the flip chart so they can move easily from one display to the next.

Transparencies

Many places will have an overhead projector available for speakers. These are valuable because the visual aid can be created on regular sized paper then enlarged to a much bigger format. Displays for an overhead projector are made on transparent sheets of plastic, either clear or tinted.

Speakers can create transparencies in three ways. One is the "draw while you talk" approach. While the speech is being delivered, the speaker sketches the visual aid directly onto the roll of transparency material stretched over the base of the projector. Special pens designed for overhead transparencies will need to be used.

The advantage of the approach is that it helps keep the attention of the audience. One drawback is that the speaker must be sufficiently artistic to create a clear and useful illustration while attending to several other matters at the same time. This approach also allows little margin for error. It the speaker makes a mistake in creating the visual aid, it is immediately apparent to all.

The second way to create transparencies is to draw the transparencies in advance. Here the speaker draws each display on a single sheet of transparency material.

The third way is to do the work on paper, then take the paper to a photocopy shop that can turn it into a transparency. Using a photocopy machine to create transparencies allows speakers to use a wide variety of materials from print sources: headlines, line drawings, cartoons, etc.

The proliferation of personal computers, particularly computers with the potential for desktop publishing, has made creating visual aids an easy process for many. One creates a graph, chart, or picture using the computer, prints out the result, then has that made into a transparency.

Besides print materials, photographs can also be used as the basis for transparencies. Again, the work will need to be done by a photocopy shop, but many of them have the ability to convert snapshots into transparencies.

Like all visual aids, transparencies should be highly legible. A handy test for visibility is to put the transparency on the floor, then try to read it. If we cannot read it at that distance, our audience will have difficulty reading it when it is projected onto the screen.

To use transparencies as visual aids, they should be placed in the proper order. The projector should be turned off until it is needed. Before the speech, if possible, the speaker should check the overhead projector to make sure where the off-on switch is located and to ensure that the projector is properly focused.

When it is time for a transparency, the projector is turned on and the transparency slid onto the base of the projector. If while facing the audience, the speaker can read the transparency, it is on the projector properly. If the speaker needs to point out details of the display, these can be indicated on the transparency with a pencil, pen, or some other kind of small pointer. It is usually not a good idea to point out details on the image on the screen. The speaker has to stand in the glare of the projector and usually blocks some of the material

If a second transparency is needed immediately following the first, the speaker simply removes the first one and brings on the next. If the next transparency is not needed immediately, the projector should be turned off so that the audience is not staring at a blinding, white screen. If turning the projector off and on is distracting, one could cover the base of the projector with some kind of opaque material such as a sheet of cardboard.

Transparencies can also be used in overlays to create a sense of the relationship between elements of an illustration. Instead of showing each item in succession, the items are added to each other until a composite picture is formed. For example, if one wanted to illustrate the main stages in constructing a tire, one could use three transparencies. The first would show the body of the tire. Laid atop that would be a second transparency showing the belts of the tire. The third transparency would show the tread. This technique can be used to show steps in a process, special locations or structural elements.

Slide Projectors

Slides offer the possibility of dramatic illustrations that may not be available otherwise. As photographs are primarily of things that truly exist, they can have a stronger impact than other media. The horror of a car wreck or the poignancy of a parent and child can be captured and communicated by a vivid photograph. The problem of using slides is that they require a room that is at least semi-dark if they are to show up. The darkness makes it difficult for speakers to see notes and for the audience to observe nonverbal behavior.

A remote control for the slide projector is a major help. Without one, the speaker has to speak from the back of the room. The slides should be in the proper order and right side up. Again, rehearsing with the slide projector will help eliminate any problems in the presentation.

Speakers using slide projectors should make sure they have a spare projector bulb on hand. Using a slide projector without a backup bulb is like taking a car trip without a spare tire. We run the risk of being stranded in the middle of the speech with no way to show our visual aids.

If the speech has stretches in which no slides are being used, the speaker should insert a blank slide between sections of slides. Blanks are made by placing a piece of opaque material such as aluminum foil or thin cardboard into a slide frame. The empty slide frames are available at photography stores.

Videotape

Videotape and video cassette players are seemingly ubiquitous now. Besides that, one finds them everywhere. Videotape can be a powerful way to reinforce or illustrate points whether the tapes are professionally prepared or homemade. Because of its power, videotape is best used sparingly. As it combines both sound and sight, it is a strong medium unto itself and will compete for attention with the speaker.

Speakers using videotape should have the tape cued to the starting point before they begin speaking. Speakers lose valuable time and may lose credibility as well if they have to fast-forward and rewind the tape to hunt for the appropriate section. If a speaker is using parts of several tapes, the speech will look more polished if the parts are edited onto one tape in the correct order. Using only one tape eliminates the distracting shuffle of loading and unloading a series of tapes.

Visual Aids and Speaker Credibility

We should keep in mind that visual aids communicate more than just the information they carry. If the visual aids are well done, easily seen, and smoothly integrated into the presentation, the speaker will be perceived as a person who has spent time preparing and hence as a person knowledgeable about the subject. Good visual aids will also likely increase the audience's willingness to attend to the speech. On the other hand, if the visual aids are sloppy, hard to see, and done in a slapdash manner, the speaker's credibility will suffer. The audience may well feel that if the speaker does not care enough about the occasion to spend time making good visual aids, then it does not care to listen to what the speaker has to say.

Visual Hindrances

While visual aids can enhance a speech, they can also detract from a speech. When the visual elements begin to call attention to themselves and away from the speech, we have created not a visual aid but a visual hindrance.

Pass Arounds

One major hindrance is "pass around" visuals. These are usually small items introduced with, "I'm going to pass around these (pictures, rocks, stamps, insects, etc.), and you can look at them while I speak."

This approach is problematic for several reasons. Audience members are more likely to be paying attention to what they have in their hands instead of what the speaker is saying. Interested listeners will be distracted by people passing the items. The speaker has little control over when the audience pays attention to the words of the speech and when it pays attention to the visual support. Also, only a fraction of the audience will be able to see an item at the appropriate time in the speech.

Unmanageable Items

Another hindrance is items that cannot be handled easily. If the visual aids do not fit smoothly into the speech, the speaker should probably look elsewhere for supporting materials. Some items may be too large and heavy such as a tractor tire or a tombstone. Some, such as an engine part, may be too dirty to use in the speaking situation. Other items may be too messy or too dangerous.

Unmanageable items also include animals. The patient, well-behaved animals seen on television are the result of long training periods by professional handlers. These animals are accustomed to performing in the welter of lights, cameras, and strangers. Unless one's dog is obedience trained, the animal may panic at the strange collection of smells and sounds he encounters. When cats are frightened, they climb. A speech on the pleasures of cat ownership will be severely undermined if the speaker has to keep tearing the cat off her head.

Weakly supported items can imperil the best speech. One's posters may be beautiful, but if they keep falling to the floor, the effectiveness of the speech may fall with them.

Visual aids can be a major component in the success of a speech. If well done, they can reinforce major points and add clarity to concepts. They can also add to the overall atmosphere of the speech and increase or decrease audience attention. Thoughtful use of the various media distinguishes good speakers.

The Speaking Voice

The speech composition and visual aids are important ingredients of a speech. So, too is the way in which speakers use their voices to deliver their work. Knowledge of how one's voice works will aid in making better presentations.

Breathing for Performance

The process of voice begins not with sound but with breathing. Voices are created by the passage of air over the vocal folds, two membranes of skin located in the windpipe just behind the thyroid cartilage. The thyroid cartilage is in the front of the neck and is commonly know as the "Adam's apple." The group of muscles and cartilages making up the vocal mechanism is called the larynx. If we put tension on the vocal folds, the air passing over them will cause them to vibrate and produce sound, our voices. That basic sound is then given resonance and finally shaped by the articulators (tongue, teeth, and lips) to form words.

When we breathe for survival, as a baby does, breathing is an automatic process of moving air in and out of the lungs in orderly fashion. When we breathe for speech, the process is more complicated because we have to time inhalation, control exhalation, and guard against muscular tension. The basic idea is to bring air into the body as efficiently as possible, then control the exhalation for maximum efficiency.

To breathe for speech, we need to take in as much air as we can comfortably. With good breath support for the voice, we can talk with sufficient volume and for sufficient time. Quick, shallow breathing is not only uncomfortable, it decreases volume and creates a sense of choppiness in the delivery. Note that when we breathe for sustained vocalization, we inhale through our mouthes instead of our noses. Breathing through the nose is simply too slow.

We want also to keep tension out of the neck area as it affects the voice production mechanism adversely. Breathing should be controlled from the shoulders down with the muscles of the chest and abdomen doing the major effort. If we are breathing properly, the rib cage and abdominal area will move noticeably, but the shoulders will move very little.

Characteristics of Voice

Proper breathing relaxes the speaker and makes the speech more intelligible to the audience. In addition to producing voice, we can do things vocally to make the communication clear and understandable. We can utilize the various characteristics of voice-paralinguistics to emphasize points, build emotions, and create moods.

Pitch

Pitch is the highness or lowness of our voices on a musical scale and is a function of the number of vibrations per second produced by the vocal folds. The higher the number of vibrations, the higher the voice. An *A*, the note to which symphony orchestras tune their instruments, is 440 vibrations per second. Simply listening to the voices of others makes it obvious that people employ a variety of pitches in speaking. Further awareness of pitch also shows us that pitch may indicate things about the speaker. Generally, men's voices are lower than women's voices. Children's voices are higher than those of adults. A person speaking at the top of the pitch range often sounds tense and strained. A low pitch may sound relaxed.

No ideal pitch exists except in the terms of each individual's vocal range. The best pitch for a person is called the *optimum pitch* and is located one-fourth to one-third from the *bottom* of the pitch range. At this point, a person can speak most comfortably and efficiently.

The best way to find one's optimum pitch is to first find out what one's vocal range is. We can do this by singing scales or matching tones on a piano. We count the number of steps it takes to go from the bottom of our range to the top of our range. We then count up one-fourth to one-third from the bottom of the range, and that is our optimum pitch.

Besides finding a comfortable basic pitch, we should also learn to use rising and falling pitches to communicate. Upward and downward inflections in English communicate ideas beyond the words themselves. An upward inflection connotes questioning, a lack of finality, or indecisiveness. Contrastingly, a downward inflection connotes finality, decision, or command. If we say a statement such as "You are going to dinner" with a rising inflection, our audience will hear the statement as, "You are going to dinner?" If we say the same words with a downward inflection, the audience will hear "You are going to dinner" as a command.

Stated in a level pitch, the words would probably be interpreted as a statement of fact.

Loudness

We use varying volumes in our speaking as well as varying pitches. At a basketball game where the score is 87-86 with fifteen seconds left to play, we cheer at a different volume than we speak across the table in a candlelit restaurant. The ability to vary volume is one we can use productively in our presentations.

Reaching the Audience. For starters, speakers must speak loudly enough that the audience—all of the audience—can hear them. Speaking more loudly than conversational levels requires increased effort and energy. Speakers unprepared for the physical demand may find it difficult to respond. Increased volume does not mean shouting, that is, simply making more noise. We need to maintain control over the voice so that intelligibility is not lost as the volume goes up.

Good volume is a matter of good breath support for the voice, hence the importance of good breathing practice for speaking. Increased volume will demand more air, so we will need to breathe more deeply or more frequently, or both.

One way to make sure we are speaking at an appropriate volume is to think of ourselves as speaking not to the audience in the front rows but to the audience in the last row. If we imagine our auditors as being in the front row, we will probably reduce our volume to fit the close distance. If we imagine reaching those in back, we are more likely to use the right volume for the entire audience. If the farthermost reaches of our audience are not hearing us, we are failing as speakers.

Stress. One of the most important vocal tools we can develop is the proper use of stress. *Stress is added volume to a word or phrase.* Stress is the vocal equivalent of underlining or italicizing. When we wish to call attention to a particular word, we pronounce it more loudly than the rest of the sentence. The effect is to make that word stand out and to call attention to it. Stress makes the difference between a statement like, "This matter is important" and a statement like "This matter *is* important."

Besides emphasizing a word, stress can also be used to show the relationship between ideas. By giving words varying amounts of stress, we can indicate which is important, more important, and most important.

Modulating the volume with which we pronounce words can make distinctions between them:

▶ "For our grandparents, the environment was a *problem.*
▶ For our parents, the environment was a *greater* problem.
▶ For us, the environment is our *greatest* problem.

Finally stress can offer differing interpretations of the same words. Even a simple sentence takes on a variety of meanings depending on which words are stressed.

▶ "*Now* is the time for us to do something." (We must act immediately.)
▶ "Now is the time for *us* to do something. (We have the responsibility to act, not someone else.)
▶ "Now is the time for us to *do* something." (We should act instead of idly sitting by.)
▶ "Now is the time for us to do *something.*" (However futile our effort, we must make an attempt.)

Much of our concern for sufficient loudness has been solved by the advent of electronic amplification, but even the use of a microphone requires practice. If we can, we should rehearse with the microphone to be used with the speech, even if the rehearsal is nothing more than a few minutes spent at the podium before the audience arrives. If we need to find out if the microphone is on, we should tap it rather than blowing into it. Blowing into the microphone produces a crazy collection of high frequency sounds that can damage an amplification system.

We should try out some of our speech until the sound is adjusted appropriately. Microphones can vary widely in sensitivity. We should move about while rehearsing so that we can develop a sense of how close we must remain to the microphone to be heard clearly. We can then adapt our movements to be most effective.

If we can manage without a microphone, we may want to forego its use. The unamplified human voice can be more pleasant to listen to than the same voice boosted through a tinny amplification system.

Time

As we have noted, speech is an activity that takes place in time. As we speak, our words come out in a temporal order, each occupying a different place in time. We can rearrange the words of a sentence, but we cannot say all the words at the same time nor can we run the sentence in reverse to make the words disappear. Timing can add effectiveness to our speeches in addition to the other qualities of voice.

As with pitch and loudness, a base level exists for clear speaking: we must speak at a rate comfortable for the audience. If we speak rapidly, they may have trouble understanding us. If we speak too slowly, we may sound so apathetic as to make it difficult for the audience to attend to what we say.

No one rate of speaking is best for all materials. The most effective rate is one which best matches the speaker, the situation, and the material. Even with broadcast speakers, we may notice a shift in rate as the evening news program moves from news to weather to sports. To inject a note of importance and excitement into their material, sportscasters often adopt a rate faster than that used by the newscaster. Even newscasters will vary the rate depending on the story. The report of thousands killed in an earthquake will be read more slowly than will the account of the joyous meeting of two brothers reunited after twenty-five years.

Similarly, speakers need to adapt their rates to the subject matter and audiences. The general rule is that serious, tragic, and thoughtful material is delivered at a slower rate than light, comic, easy-to-understand material. If we are giving an entertaining speech at the conclusion of a luncheon meeting, our rate will likely be a little faster, a little more upbeat than will the rate for a speech on the environmental crisis.

An important part of timing in speeches is the use of *pauses.* A pause is nothing more than a moment in which we stop speaking. Beginning speakers are usually afraid of pauses and seem to feel that a moment without sound is a detriment to their speeches. Consequently, they fill the time with "uh" and "um" and "you know" and other disfluencies that signal nervousness and an absence of thought.

A pause can be used in several ways. A pause can build expectation, particularly when the pause is linked with an upward inflection. "And then it ended" has a different effect when spoken without a pause and when spoken, "and then . . . it ended." Pauses can also signal transitions. A pause between points serves to indicate to an audience that the speaker is finished with one idea and is about to pick up another. A pause at the end of a speech signals that the speakers are, indeed, finished and provides time for them to collect themselves and their notes before moving off the podium.

Quality

The final characteristic of voice is quality, the characteristic which is the most difficult to understand and control. Quality is the product of resonance, the way the basic sound is reverberated in the body before it is released.

Quality is the overall effect of our voice and may, for example, be harsh, nasal, breathy, denasal (no nasal resonance), or distinguished in other ways. In terms of the physics of sound, quality is the particular combination of tones and overtones that we produce with our voices.

The effect of resonance is evidenced in the way sounds are produced in musical instruments. A guitar string of a given diameter and stretched to a given tension will produce a note, say a *D*, when strummed. The basic note will be the same whether the guitar string is stretched between two nails in the wall or between the anchor plate and keys of a fine guitar. The two strings, however, will vary greatly in the richness of the notes they produce. The string on the guitar will have its note resonated in the body of the guitar and the result will be a fuller, richer sound.

The human vocal mechanism works in much the same way. After the sound is produced in the larynx and before it emerges, it is resonated in the throat, the mouth, and the nasal cavities. When the sound emerges, it is a complex com-

bination of the basic pitch and overtones that give it its characteristic sound.

As quality is the most complex of the vocal characteristics, it is also the most difficult to correct and control. By listening to a recording of our voices, we can determine how pleasant or unpleasant they are for listeners. If we find that our voice is grating or sounds nasal, then we should work to eliminate those unpleasant characteristics. Experimenting with a trial and error process can help us obtain a more pleasant sound. If we have a large problem with vocal quality, we may have to seek the services of a speech clinician to correct the problem.

As voice is one of the main media we use in our communication, particularly in speeches, attention to voice and its characteristics will help us become effective speakers. Along with proper breathing, learning how to use pitch, loudness, time, and quality will give us increased capabilities for communication.

Physical Communication

Besides communicating with our voices, we also communicate physically. We occupy space, and how we handle ourselves in space can send messages to our audiences.

Good physical communication is not a matter of inserting appropriate gestures at the right times. Good physical communication is a combination of poise and movement that takes into consideration the speaker, audience, and occasion.

Like other aspects of a speech, good physical communication begins in rehearsal, not at the moment when the speech begins. The better speakers know their material and the more they have rehearsed, the better prepared they will be in all aspects.

In the rehearsal period, speakers should have several goals. One is achieving a comfortable *stance* which will serve as the basis for gestures and movement. Speakers should avoid slouching, leaning on the podium, swaying, bouncing around, and other distracting actions. A good speaking stance is one that is comfortable, balanced, and relaxed. A good starting point is to stand with the feet about shoulder width apart and placed so that the ball of one foot lines up with the arch of the other. Standing in this position, we can easily gesture or move in any direction.

As to *gestures*, the best gestures are usually those that grow naturally out of the situation. Observing people in conversation, we can see them spontaneously punctuate their remarks with a number of different gestures. That same sense of spontaneity should characterize gestures made while speaking.

As our speeches progress through the rehearsal period, we may find ourselves making hand and arm movements to punctuate our points. Some may be made to indicate size or direction. Others may be made to emphasize a point. Still others may express our feelings. These should be allowed to develop. Generally, the better acquainted we are with the material of our speeches, the more likely we are to communicate effectively with gestures.

We need to keep in mind that the audiences of speeches are usually located beyond conversational distances. Gestures will thus need to be adapted to the larger setting. A general principle is to make gestures above the waist and broad enough so that the audience can see them.

We should also keep in mind that *clothing* communicates. Appropriate dress is, like other

◀ **Figure 12.9.** A comfortable stance helps you feel in control of your speaking situation.

factors, determined by the speaking situation. An attorney would be out of place addressing a court while wearing jeans, boots, a flannel shirt, and a cap advertising a grain elevator. In another set of circumstances, talking to a group of farmers in the field, that dress might be most appropriate.

Discovering appropriate dress is part of the job of audience analysis. We can talk with someone acquainted with the audience and the audience's expectations to discover what would be best to wear. If unsure or unable to find that information, it is better to err on the side of formality rather than informality. If one arrives dressed in a suit only to find the audience in casual clothes, one can always remove the jacket, take off the tie or scarf, and roll up the sleeves. If one arrives in a sweatshirt and jeans to find the audience dressed in suits and dresses, one has little recourse but to brave out the situation as best one can.

Once arrived at the speaking situation, we should keep in mind that we begin to communicate before we ever open our mouths. We are "on" as soon as the audience focuses its attention on us, and we are not "off" until it turns its attention elsewhere. The audience receives messages from the way we dress, how prepared we appear to be, and how we approach the lectern. By plodding forward reluctantly, we tell them, "I really don't want to be here doing this." By being too nonchalant, we may communicate, "My speech is really unimportant" or "You people are not worth talking to." The message we want our audiences to receive is, "I am prepared, and I want to talk to you about an interesting topic." We need to approach the front of the room in a manner that shows we are prepared and ready to speak. We can do this by having all our materials assembled and ready, and by moving forward in a confident manner.

Once at the podium or lectern. we need to take time to arrange our notes. When they are in place, we can take a relaxing deep breath and begin speaking.

When referring to notes, all we should do is drop our eyes to the cards or speechmap, pick up the next idea, and continue speaking. The less time spent looking at notes, the better.

When finished, we should not leave before our notes do. We can finish our last sentence, pause a moment to give impact to the conclusion, then gather our materials and move back to our place.

Flexibility

A well planned, well practiced speech can provide us with reassurance and confidence when we face an audience. A well delivered speech, though, is not necessarily one in which we do exactly and precisely everything we practiced in rehearsal. We need to be prepared for variations in the speech even as we give it to an audience.

As one experienced speech teacher has pointed out, "Become reconciled to the fact that you will never give a talk exactly as your planned it" (Nadeau 83). In a well prepared speech, the differences between the rehearsed version and the delivered version will not be major such as dropping a main point and composing another on the spot. The differences will more likely be in timing, wording, gestures, and other details.

Perhaps, in rehearsal we always used the same words to express the first main point. Then, in the actual speech we find a variation of these words coming out of our mouth. Changes like these are no cause for concern. To speak well extemporaneously, we must be flexible enough to accept variations and not be disturbed when changes pop up in the midst of delivery.

As speakers gain more confidence, they find that the variations can make the difference between a good speech and a great speech. If the speech is already well composed, these moments of inspiration make it even better. We should welcome these moments, incorporate them into future presentations, and be ready for more pleasant surprises.

Communication Apprehension

Being called upon to perform may elicit feelings of nervousness as may times when we are called upon to act in unfamiliar ways. Playing in an athletic event, driving a car on ice, taking an exam, or asking someone for a date may all make us feel apprehensive. So, too, may the prospect of giving a speech.

Recognition

One of the first steps in dealing with feelings of trepidation before a speech is to realize that we are not unique. Nervousness before speaking appears to be an almost universal phenomenon.

Sitting in class on a speaking day, we find our mouths are dry, our palms sweaty, our heartbeat is elevated, our breathing is becoming rapid, and we feel a strong urge to go to the bathroom. We have a gnawing fear that somehow we are going to make a fool of ourselves in public.

Everyone else in the room looks calm. The others scheduled to speak are reviewing their notes, even chatting with other. We know we are the only ones about to dissolve into a puddle of anxiety.

We are wrong.

If we talk to those other people, we will discover that they, too, have the same symptoms, the same feelings. They may have been looking at us and wondering how we could be so cool.

Another thing to consider is that what we are experiencing may not be so much fright as it is anticipation. Let us consider a time when we really wanted to do something: go sking, have a date with X, acquire our driver's license, or attend a concert. In all likelihood, the same symptoms we associate with apprehension about speaking are the same symptoms we experienced before the big event, sweaty palms, elevated heart rate, etc. The only difference is that in one case, we label the symptoms "fright" and in the other we label them "anticipation" (Burleson). Much of our apprehension may lie in the way we define the situation.

Concentration

One approach that is not very useful in dealing with apprehension is to try to master our fears by overpowering them. Trying to discipline ourselves out of nervousness is an exercise in futility. By concentrating on the behaviors we want to eliminate, we usually make them worse. The better approach is to *concentrate on what we want to accomplish*. We will be in a better position if we direct our energies to the positive aspects of the situation rather than the negative ones. Instead of thinking about physical symptoms we are experiencing, we should think about the main points we want to make. Concentrating on those will channel our energies toward their proper goal, the delivery of the speech.

Visualization

Another way to make the speaking experience easier is to visualize ourselves giving the speech before we actually give it. Here we use our imaginations to walk ourselves through the speaking experience and see ourselves doing well in the process. We need to find a quiet time and a comfortable place. We close our eyes and relax. If the speech is to be given in a class, we begin by seeing ourselves sitting at the desk in the classroom.

We see that our notes are in good order. We see ourselves as confident and ready to speak. If that image makes us nervous, we stop with it. We keep the image in our minds until we feel comfortable seeing ourselves in the classroom. When we are at ease with that image, we move ahead. We see ourselves as our name is called. When we are comfortable with that step, we move on to the next. We see ourselves standing up and walking alertly to the front of the room. Again, if that image is problematic, we stop or retreat to an earlier, more comfortable image and work there until ready to advance.

We go through the entire speech this way, all the way to the point where we move back to our seat hearing the applause of our audience.

Practice

The first few times we try any new enterprise, we probably feel awkward and uncomfortable. We have so many things to remember. We feel uncertain about our ability to perform all the tasks we have to do. The more we practice the activity, however, and the more we receive helpful criticism, the easier the activity becomes.

Learning to ride a bicycle involves some spills and scrapes, but once we learn, the process becomes as easy as walking. People learning to swim want to stay in the safety of shallow water. Being in water over their heads is scary. After they learn to swim, they seek the deep water because it provides more room to maneuver.

The same principle applies to speaking. The more we do it, the more comfortable we become. The details begin to fall into place, and we feel increasingly comfortable with our roles as speakers. If we want to become less nervous in speaking situations, we need to seek them out instead of avoiding them.

Preparation

Knowing that we have done all we can in preparation can be a major calming factor. If we have researched the topic, if we have composed the speech in a clear manner, if we have rehearsed the speech, then we can look back confidently on what we have done and know we can reproduce it for an audience.

Keeping these concepts and practices in mind will help us feel less anxious when facing speaking situations.

Conclusion

In preparing to speak, we need to deal with many factors. The mechanical aspects of the speech need attention. Well done notes—either cards or speechmaps—will aid in presenting the speech. Visual aids can be a great help to a speech. Creating effective visual aids involves following the principles of high visibility and using visual aids as support for ideas.

Proper use of the voice can provide ways to make speaking vivid and interesting. Good physical communication can underscore the message we want our audience to receive.

Anxiety may be a part of the speaking situation. Recognizing that such feelings are common can help alleviate them. We can further reduce anxiety by preparing well, using visualization, and concentrating on the idea of the speech rather than on our feelings of inadequacy.

Finally, having assembled all the elements of the speech, we must be ready for variations in its presentation. We need to accept the variations and use them to our advantage.

• • • Discussion Questions

1. What kind of concepts can be clarified with the use of visual aids?

2. What is the difference between radio news which cannot provide visual images and television which can?

3. For what topics would a speaker use an actual object as a visual aid? A model? A picture? A diagram? A chart or graph?

4. How does a good speaking voice enhance communication in a speech?

5. In what ways can physical communication enhance a speech?

6. In what ways can physical communication detract from a speech?

7. In what situations, other than giving a speech, have you been made to feel nervous or anxious? Why do you think you felt this way? What remedies did you find that helped?

8. What is the difference between fear and anticipation?

• • • Notes

[1] This taxonomy of visual aids is from Ray E. Nadeau, *A Basic Rhetoric of Speech-Communication*. Reading, Massachusetts: Addison-Wesley Publishing Company, 1969. 103–12.

• • • Sources and References

Avoiding Communication: Shyness, Reticence, and Communication Apprehension. Eds. John A. Daly, and James C, McCroskey. Beverly Hills: Sage Publications, 1984.

Burleson, Brant. "Remarks for Teaching Assistant Orientation." Purdue University, West Lafayette, Indiana. 29 August 1989.

Crannell, Kenneth. *Voice and Articulation*. 2nd ed. Belmont, California: Wadsworth Publishing Co., 1991.

Eisenson, Jon. *Voice and Diction: A Program for Improvement*. 5th ed. New York: Macmillan Publishing Company, 1985.

Glen, Ethel c., Phillip J. Glen, and Sandra H. Foreman. *Your Voice and Articulation*. 3rd ed. Englewood Cliffs, New Jersey: Prentice Hall, 1993.

Nadeau, Ray E. *A Basic Rhetoric of Speech-Commmnication*. Reading, Massachusetts: Addison-Wesley Publishing Company, 1969.

Richmond, Virginia and James C. McCroskey. *Communication Apprehension, Avoidance, and Effectiveness*. Scottsdale, Arizona: Gorsuch Scarisbrick, Publishers, 1989.

.

Name _____ Section _____ Date _____

Public Speaking: Performance Considerations

1. For a three point speech, how should note cards be arranged?

   _____

   _____

2. List two guidelines for effectively using notecards in a speech.

   1. _____

   2. _____

3. How does using speechmapping differ from using notecards?

   _____

   _____

4. How can you test for the clarity of a visual aid?

   _____

   _____

5. How much detail should be included in a visual aid?

   _____

   _____

6. What colors should you avoid in a visual aid?

   _____

   _____

   What colors are desirable in a visual aid?

   _____

   _____

7. When is it inadvisable to use actual objects as visual aids for a speech?

   _____

   _____

8. How can models serve to augment a speech?

_____

_____

9. What can graphs and charts represent that actual objects, models or pictures can't?

_____

_____

10. How long should visual aids such as posters be prominently displayed during a speech?

_____

_____

11. Describe three ways to use transparencies as visual aids.

1. _____

2. _____

3. _____

_____

12. How can the use of visual aids increase a speaker's credibility?

_____

_____

13. When can visual aids become a hinderance?

_____

_____

14. Why is it undesirable to pass visual aids around during a speech?

_____

_____

15. What is pitch?

_____

_____

_____

16. What is optimum pitch?

_____

_____

17. Why is it advisable to vary the pitch and volume of your voice during a speech?

_____

_____

18. How can you determine the proper volume to use for an audience?

_____

_____

19. What is stress in the context of the voice?

_____

_____

20. What is the most effective rate for speaking?

_____

_____

_____

_____

21. How can pauses be used effectively in speaking?

_____

_____

22. What is vocal quality?

_____

_____

23. What are the characteristics of good physical communication?

_____

_____

_____

24. Describe a good speaking stance.

_____

_____

_____

_____

25. What is the general principle for making gestures during a speech?

_____

_____

26. How should you properly use notes during a speech?

_____

_____

27. If you suffer from speech apprehension, what four steps can you take to overcome it?

1. _____

2. _____

3. _____

4. _____

Name _____ Section _____ Date _____

Public Speaking Assignment II
Informative Speech

Purpose

The second public speaking assignment has a three-fold purpose:
1. You will gain additional experience speaking before an audience;
2. You will refine your public speaking skills by concentrating to improving areas pinpointed in; the small group presentation and first public speaking assignment;
3. You will learn how to effectively choose and use a visual aid to enhance your speech.

Basic Requirements

- You will develop and present to the class an original informative speech on a topic approved by your instructor. See suggested topics pages 213–216.
- Each speech must be _____ minutes in length.
- _____ sources must be used in preparing the speech.
- At least two visual aids are required.
- An outline of the speech must be submitted by _____.
- Speeches will be graded according to criteria on p. _____, which must be handed in prior to the speech.
- You will complete the observation sheets on pages 305–313 for designated fellow speakers.
- Additional instructor requirements:

Informative Speech II Worksheet

1. possible topics:

2. selected topic:

3. possible narrowed topic areas:

4. narrowed focus of speech:

5. thesis statement:

6. main points:

   1.

   2.

   3.

7. support for main points: source:

   support for 1. a.

              b.

   support for 2. a.

              b.

   support for 3. a.

              b.

8. visual aid(s) to augment speech (chart, graph, photo/drawing, three-dimensional object):

9. transitions to connect main points:

   transition between 1 & 2:

   transition between 2 & 3:

10. possible attention getting devices to open the speech:

11. selected attention getting device:

12. conclusion that can be drawn from speech:

Notes:

Name _____ Date _____

Topic _____ Score _____

Informative Speech II Grading Criteria—Style A

For a *C*, the speech will meet the basic requirements of the assignment

> Introduction announces the topic and previews the main points
> Speech has appropriate number of main points
> Main points are clear
> Transitions are present
> Sequence of ideas is easy to follow
> Conclusion summarizes the main points
> Physical communication does not distract (no swaying, bobbing, etc.)
> Vocal communication is understandable
> Speech is free of disfluencies ("uh," "um," "you know," etc.)
> Speaker maintains eye contact with audience 50% of the time
> Speech fits the time limits
> Speech fulfills requirements of assignment (informative or persuasive, appropriate number of visual aids, appropriate notes, etc.)
> Visual aids are clear, neat, and legible

For a *B*, the speech will meet the requirements for a *C* plus the following:

> Introduction has attention step, establishes credibility, establishes relevance, and previews main points
> Each major point is fully developed
> Transitions establish links between major points
> Conclusion highlights applications of material
> Sources are credible
> Assertions are supported with evidence
> Speaker maintains eye contact with audience 75% of the time
> Speech topic is significant to the audience
> Physical communication emphasizes points of the speech
> Vocal communication is energetic and clear
> Language is fully appropriate to the material
> Visual aids strongly support the main points
> Visual aids are handled smoothly

For an *A*, the speech meets the requirements for *C* and *B* plus the following:

> Introduction shows creativity
> Transitions show flow of ideas
> Speech evidences maturity of thought
> Conclusion creates a sense of completion
> Speaker is poised (in control of notes, visual aids, delivery)
> Speaker maintains eye contact 90% of the time
> Speaker develops rapport with the audience

For a *D*, one of the areas for a *C* shows major problems.
For an *F*, the speech is not given or several areas show major problems.

Name _____ Date _____

Topic _____ Score _____

Informative Speech II Grading Criteria—Style B

Topic 10%*
- subject of speech appropriate to occasion/audience
- topic appropriately narrowed to fit time guidelines

Organization 30%*
Introduction
- attention getting opening employed
- speaker credibility developed
- rapport developed with the audience
- speech previewed
- thesis made clear

Body
- main points obvious
- transitions used between main points
- easily followed

Conclusion
- implications of material highlighted
- a feeling of completion developed

Content 30%*
- significant material developed in speech
- related to thesis
- supported with examples
- clearly presented
- interestingly developed
- vocabulary appropriate
- jargon and unfamiliar terms defined
- sources credible
- sources cited
- visual aid(s) enhanced speech

Delivery 30%*
Physical
- eye contact frequent
- gestures meaningful
- posture comfortable
- notecards properly used
- sense of communication with audience established
- visual aid(s) used properly, with confidence

Verbal
- rate appropriate
- volume appropriate

---

*suggested values only—may be changed by your instructor

- tone pleasing
- vocal variety exhibited
- enunciation/pronunciation correct
- absence of fillers

Comments:

Name _____ Section _____ Date _____

Student Evaluation of Informative Speech II

In light of the guidelines for constructive feedback, offer observations about the speech you have just watched.

What was the thesis of the speech?

What were the main points?

What new information did you hear?

What was the speaker's strength?

What one thing would you suggest that the speaker work on to improve?

Name _____ Section _____ Date _____

Student Evaluation of Informative Speech II

In light of the guidelines for constructive feedback, offer observations about the speech you have just watched.

What was the thesis of the speech?

What were the main points?

What new information did you hear?

What was the speaker's strength?

What one thing would you suggest that the speaker work on to improve?

Name _____ Section _____ Date _____

Student Evaluation of Informative Speech II

In light of the guidelines for constructive feedback, offer observations about the speech you have just watched.

What was the thesis of the speech?

What were the main points?

What new information did you hear?

What was the speaker's strength?

What one thing would you suggest the speaker work on to improve?

Name _____ Section _____ Date _____

Student Evaluation of Informative Speech II

In light of the guidelines for constructive feedback, offer observations about the speech you have just watched.

What was the thesis of the speech?

What were the main points?

What new information did you hear?

What was the speaker's strength?

What one thing would you suggest the speaker work on to improve?

Name _____ Section _____ Date _____

Student Evaluation of Informative Speech II

   In light of the guidelines for constructive feedback, offer observations about the speech you have just watched.

What was the thesis of the speech?

What were the main points?

What new information did you hear?

What was the speaker's strength?

What one thing would you suggest the speaker work on to improve?

To Read, To Memorize, or To Speak

This is an exercise designed to make you aware of the effect of different styles of delivery.

On one sheet of paper write five steps which you think a person should follow to find a job. On the second and third sheets of paper write a paragraph about each step describing how someone might actually carry out that step. This information should be practical, common sense advice. No outside research is required for this assignment.

Bring the papers you have written to class where they will serve as the basis of the exercise.

Adaped from: Gauland, Joan M. "To Read, To Memorize, or To Speak": *The Speech Communication Teacher* V, iii (Spring 1991): p. 11. Used by permission of Speech Communication Association.

13

Persuasive Speaking:
Influencing Decisions

Key Concepts

The phone rings at the Crisis Center Hotline. The counselor picks it up and says, "Crisis Center Hotline. How may I help you?" The person on the phone says, "I feel so bad I want to kill myself."

It is Thursday before spring break. One student says to another, "Cut your four-thirty class tomorrow, and we can leave two hours earlier." "I don't know," the other replies, "The instructor is going to take attendance and give a quiz. I've missed a lot already, and my quiz scores aren't very good."

A person in her early twenties enters an automobile dealership. A sales representative approaches. "I'm graduating in May," the student says, "and I'm looking for a car."

At the state headquarters of the Teachers' Association, the legislative committee is meeting. "We need to send a strong signal to the legislature," one says.

On the grounds of the state capitol building, two groups are carrying signs and chanting. Television crews move from one group to another, taping the crowds and interviewing designated speakers, asking opinions of people entering and leaving the building and people passing on the street. One group chants, "Two, four, six, eight, you can't make us procreate!" The other group chants, "Abortion is murder!

Human beings are not automatons. While we are to some degree programmed by our genetic heritage and our society, we still possess the ability to choose, to make decisions, and then live out our lives with the results of those decisions. Some of our decisions are of little significance: "Which pair of socks shall I wear today?" Other decisions have greater significance: "Shall I marry X?" Some decision are made on a personal scale while others are made on a national scale and have far-reaching implications. The Supreme Court decision in Roe v. Wade created the legal right to abortion, a decision that has given birth to massive movements both for and against its consequences. The case of Brown v. Topeka set aside the idea of "separate but equal" education for different races and launched school integration. The implications of that decision are still being debated and worked out today.

Decisions are not made in vacuums. They are made in the light of experience, information, emotions, and the counsel of others. When decisions are to be made, people influence each other in a variety of ways. Decisions about which college to attend are made after consulting with friends, family, counselors, schools, brochures, recruiters, and sometimes, banks. Decisions about business are made after considering knowledgeable opinions and information. Court decisions are based on arguments presented by opposing attorneys, the law, and the precedents set by earlier cases.

In the decision making process, we often see one solution as superior to others, but that opinion may not be shared by other people involved in the decision. Families split over a decision of where to go on vacation, Disney World or the Rockies. Businesses split on decisions of whether or not to bring out a new product and whether to expand, cut back, or maintain production levels. Schools split on decisions of what courses should constitute a required core, when courses should be offered, and who will teach them. In situations like these, people work to convince others of the rightness of their viewpoints. When people work to convince others to change their minds or their behavior, persuasion is at work.

Persuasion

Persuasion is a complex phenomenon and thus difficult to define. One scholar has created a list of six features shared by most persuasive situations (O'Keefe 15–16).

Persuasion is an attempt to influence others. The aspect of influence is so inherent in the idea of persuasion that we think of persuasion as a *successful* attempt to influence. We may say, "I tried to persuade him, but I failed," but we would never say "I persuaded him but failed." Thus, when we are involved in persuasion, we are trying to affect or alter another person or party.

Persuasion involves a criterion or goal. With conversation, we join with others for the pleasure of communication. In informational speaking we attempt to create understanding. When we try to persuade someone, we have something in mind we would like to see that person do.

▲ **Figure 13.1.** We are bombarded daily by persuasive messages. (Coyle)

Persuasion implies an attempt to reach that goal. Not only do we have a goal in mind, we put try to move the other party toward that goal. Persuasion implies effort.

Persuasion involves some measure of freedom and choice on the part of the persuadee. If someone knocks us unconscious and takes our wallet, that would most definitely not be persuasion. On the other hand, we may receive a call soliciting a donation for a group such as the Citizens' Action Coalition, the National Association for Historical Preservation, or the Fraternal Order of Police. The group wants our money, but we have the option of agreement or refusal.

Persuasion is achieved through communication. The use of communication is a direct outgrowth of the concept of free choice. Rather than resorting to physical coercion, we try to effect a change through interaction with the other person or party. Police departments, particularly large city police departments, may be called upon to deal with someone on a high building who is threatening to commit suicide. Specially trained units are dispatched to "persuade" the person not to jump. Part of their tactics involves communication, talking to the person to lower the sense of desperation. At some point in the proceedings, however, the team may simply physically overpower the person— "have to jump him"—and drag him to safety (Dass and Gorman 105–07). When the team moves from talking to overpowering the per-

son, persuasion is at an end and coercion has taken over.

Persuasion "involves a change in the mental state of the persuadee" (O'Keefe 116). Through persuasion, we attempt to change the way another person views the world or at least a small part of it. We may also change the way someone else behaves, but the change in behavior will need to be proceeded by a change of mind. We may wish a person to sign a petition asking for more safety lighting on campus, for the cessation of logging in a state forest, or the rezoning of a neighborhood. People will not sign the petition unless they see some good reason for doing so. If they do not want to sign the petition, we must find some way of changing the way they regard it. Without the change of mind, we will not achieve the desired behavior.

With these concepts in mind, we will offer a definition of persuasion that attempts to incorporate them: *Persuasion is the attempt through communication to change the way people think, act, or feel.*

Misconceptions of Persuasion

Despite its complexity and its universality, persuasion is still seen by some in a limited sense. Some, for example, think that persuasion is only involved with selling a product. While it is true that selling involves persuasion, sales are only a small area of persuasive activity.

Another mistaken concept is that persuasion is a formula or a set of steps one goes through to talk people into a course of action. As to persuasion being a handy-dandy procedure guaranteed to work on anyone, anywhere, the idea is sheer nonsense. Sales representatives often learn a pattern of exchanges, but those exchanges are by no means universal in their application. A procedure that works well in one setting may be a fiasco in another.

Some people, too, adhere to the "hypodermic needle" theory of persuasion "which suggests that the advocate 'injects' the audience with a persuasive message that makes them change their attitudes . . . " (Benoit 183). Like all communication, persuasion involves both parties as active participants in the event. Persuadees are involved parties in the persuasive process.

Ethics of Persuasion

As we have seen in an earlier chapter, ethics is the study of what is proper and improper, what is good and bad, and what standards of conduct we should meet. Ethics arise from the fact that we impinge on others and, as human beings, we can measure or evaluate our effects on others. The ethics of persuasion recognizes the interactive nature of communication. Through persuasion we may influence others in beneficial or non-beneficial ways. While the ethics of persuasion can involve an extended discussion, we would like to make two points which should be considered before launching a persuasive effort.

Ourselves as Persuaders

The first consideration of ethical persuasion is to put our own ethical houses in order. We should realize that the final goal of any persuasive effort is to change the way someone else sees the world. When engaged in persuasion, we are attempting to alter another's life in some way, be that way large of small. Realizing this intrusion upon others, we should be convinced in our own minds that the course of action we are promoting is worthwhile. The product we are selling should live up to the claims made about it. The petition we are carrying should promote some course of action we see as having positive benefits.

The Persuadee

Secondly, we need to consider the effect of our persuasive efforts on the persuadee. We should be able to say, "I stand behind this as having good personal consequences for the individual whom it will affect" (Tead 46). What we want the other person to do should benefit the other person as much as possible. In sales, we would not persuade someone to buy a product that is faulty or ill-suited to the customer's needs. As a realtor, we would not knowingly sell a house with termite damage. As a termite exterminator, we would not urge a method of treatment that would endanger the resident's health or damage the building. As an attorney suing the exterminator, we would not persuade our client to accept a low settlement when a higher one is available, nor would we pursue a groundless case.

▲ **Figure 13.2.** You should be able to say of any persuasive effort, "This course of action will have positive consequences for the persuadee." (*Purdue Exponent*)

If we cannot affirm that the course of action we are advocating would have the highest positive effects for the person we are attempting to persuade, then we should refrain from the effort or recast our thinking.

Having an ethical stance in persuasion does not mean, however, that everyone will agree with what we propose. People can ethically hold diametrically opposed positions.

A town, for example, may have a large tract of land and is debating what to do with it. One person may want to preserve the land in a wild condition as a nature preserve. Another may want to turn the area into a park to be enjoyed by all the population. A third may want to convert the area into an industrial park to provide jobs needed to keep the community prosperous. All three may have highly ethical intentions, but they will be far from agreement on the issue.

Ethics in persuasion also applies to the content, arguments, and tactics we use in the persuasion process. An ethical persuader is not one who believes the end justifies the means. Falsifying data, for example, would violate standards of honesty as would withholding important information from the audience. Misrepresenting ourselves or our proposal would be un-ethical as would arguments based on racial prejudice. In persuasion, as in our other communication, we should act with integrity and respect for the other party.

How People Make Decisions

Belief Systems

In making decisions, people show their individuality. Each of us, as we grow, collects and assembles a group of ideas about who we are, what is our purpose in life, how we should treat other people, how society should arrange itself, what is good and bad, and numerous other such views. These beliefs are the result of our culture, our families, our societies, and our individual selves. By *"belief"*, we mean *"the conviction that something—an object or an idea—exists or does not exist or that a set of conditions should or should not exist."* The belief may be a simple assertion about the presence or absence of an object: "I believe I own a car." The belief may assert the existence of a concept and even the worth of that concept: "I believe I should drive safely for my sake and the sake of others."

The person who says, "I do not believe in anything" is self-deceiving. Without some structure of beliefs, one cannot live. We seek order in our lives and structure our views of the world in such a way that we can function as individuals and as members of society. Whether we are religious or agnostic; whether we are royalist, democratic, fascist, or communist; whether we are North Americans, Cambodians, or Nigerians; we create orders of beliefs and then base our conduct and decisions on those beliefs.

The most basic beliefs we have are, in essence, faith assumptions. We may assume the existence of God, the eternal nature of matter, the primacy of our own survival in the universe, the ultimacy of reason, or some other basis. On that basic assumption, we make other assumptions, and hold other beliefs about the nature of the world and our place in it. Depending on our most basic assumptions, we will view in different ways our relationships to family, work, income, and moral conduct. These views will, in turn, influence other decisions and actions.

▲ **Figure 13.3.** Our actions and our decisions, such as attending college, are based on our belief systems. (Coyle)

Beliefs and Values

When *beliefs imply a strongly held judgment of worth,* we call that particular class of beliefs, *"values."* Values are often central to our view of the world and influence our actions and our decisions in numerous ways.

People may hold the belief that "families are a major division of society." This viewpoint expresses a judgment about the existence or non-existence of an entity. Going beyond this belief, people may hold convictions about the nature and worth of families. One person may hold the belief that "strong families are positive forces in the development of individuals and society." A second person may believe that "families are of minor importance." A third may hold that "families are the expression of a repressive capitalistic system." These latter three beliefs we would call "values."

None of us simply holds one belief or value. We have a number of these expressions of our convictions about the worth of people, races, genders, relationships, work, recreation, housing, religion, and other items. Grouped together, they form our "value system." This system is a collection of beliefs that are an important force in shaping our responses to our world and our communication because we base our decisions and actions on these values.

We can graphically represent a person's belief system with a pyramid. At the bottom of the pyramid, creating its base, are the basic beliefs we hold, beliefs which influence other, less important beliefs. As we ascend the pyramid, our

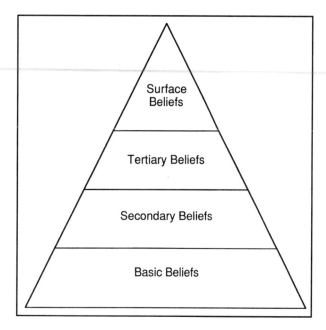

▲ **Figure 13.4.** One way of viewing belief systems is to picture them as a pyramid with the most important beliefs at the bottom, the least important at the top.

beliefs become less and less important, yet more specific (Hart, Friedrich, and Brooks, 240–41).

A person might, for example, hold a very basic belief that the United States should be preserved and defended. Arising from that belief would be a secondary belief that American industry should be kept strong. From that view would come another view that the American automobile industry should be supported. From that belief would come the belief that one should not buy an imported car. The final result would be that the person buys an American-made car rather than an import. Another person, starting from the same basic belief, might decide to support a Japanese auto plant in the United States because it would provide jobs for Americans.

A person might have a a very basic belief/ value that "Good health is important." That assumption would lead to a more concrete belief that "Good diet is a major factor in achieving good health." In turn, that would lead to the assumption that some foods are to be avoided such as those high in fat, cholesterol, or sugar. The final belief would be, "I should have a salad and frozen yogurt for lunch instead of a hamburger and a hot fudge sundae."

Attitudes

Our belief systems give rise to our *attitudes,* our *general dispositions to act and react in certain ways.* If a person believes that American industry should be kept strong by avoiding foreign made products, then that person's attitude toward a Japanese car, Mexican roofing materials, or Argentinian beef would be a negative one. Even if the person did not know of a specific foreign made product, the attitude would lead the person to oppose it were it known.

Belief Systems and Persuasion

Belief systems are not static. Faced with a changing environment and a bombardment of daily decisions, we alter and adjust as necessary. A firm supporter of American industry might be talked into buying a Japanese or German car. A health-conscious person might decide to have a hot fudge sundae with all the trimmings. When approaching a persuasive situation, we need to keep in mind several of the subtleties of how we arrange our beliefs and decide our actions.

Importance of Beliefs

For one thing, it is usually the less important beliefs that are most open to change. People are more likely to change their minds when the change does not require a major restructuring of beliefs. A farmer may be convinced to switch from a "high till" method to a "low till" method of farming or even to a "no till" method. It would be far more difficult to convince the farmer to abandon farming, let the land go wild, and turn it into a nature preserve. In the first instance, the decision is over the means of tillage, not the elemental belief, "I want what is best for the farm." The second instance would demand a decision at a much deeper level, "How shall the land be used?"

Similarly, a health-conscious person could be persuaded to "just this once, just for fun" eat something ordinarily considered forbidden. The same person would be very resistant to persuasion that exercise programs should be abandoned, high fat diets should be followed, and the person should start smoking. A small variation in habits does not demand a change in the basic assumptions as does a major change.

Strength of Beliefs

The strength with which one holds beliefs is a factor in persuasion as well. How committed we are to beliefs will affect how open we are to persuasion on a matter. People are more willing to give up ideas that they hold lightly than ideas they hold tenaciously. People may label themselves "Democrat" or "Republican," thus announcing their belief in the political philosophy of a given party. The success of persuading people to do "cross-over voting"—voting for a member of the opposing party—will depend on how strongly a person holds to the belief, "I should support the Democratic/Republican ticket."

If people are "knee-jerk Republicans" or "yellow dog Democrats," it will be extremely difficult to persuade them to cross party lines. A "knee jerk Republican" is someone who votes for a Republican candidate as unconsciously as a person's leg jerks when the physician hits the knee with a rubber hammer. A "yellow dog Democrat" is a person who will vote for any Democratic candidate, even if the candidate is "an old yellow dog." To other voters, declaring party allegiance is a minor point. While they are generally in favor of a party's stance, they have few misgivings about "crossing over" to vote for a candidate of the opposite party.

The strength of a belief depends on several factors. One of the most important is how strongly a given belief is linked to other beliefs, particularly basic beliefs (Hart, Friedrich, and Brooks 223–26). If a "minor" belief is linked to a "major" belief, it will be more difficult to persuade a person to give up the minor belief than it will if the minor belief is independent of any deeper belief or value. Conversely, it will also be easier to persuade someone to act on a minor belief if that belief is tied to a deeper belief or value than when the minor belief is held independent of a deeper belief or value.

Most people would say, "Yes," when asked, "Do you believe that we should help other people?" How much they are actually willing to

help others will depend on how strongly that belief is linked to more basic beliefs. Let us say that someone is collecting for a charitable cause or relief fund. One person approached may have as a basic belief, "I need to make my life as comfortable as possible." Prying that person loose from money will be difficult because any contribution to others diminishes the person's potential for enjoyment. Another person approached may have as a basic belief, "God tells me to be charitable to others." Still another may believe deeply that, "I should alleviate suffering if I can." The last two are more likely to be convinced to give generously than is the first.

When two beliefs come into conflict, the one tied most deeply into a person's belief system will usually win out. We often say, "What people wear is unimportant. We should judge them by their character." Yet, if we look at any group of friends, particularly teenagers, we will probably find them all dressing in the same manner and dubious of someone who dresses differently. Here the belief that clothes are unimportant runs afoul of a deeper belief, perhaps unstated, that "I want to fit with my group."

Ego Involvement

Often what affects a person's openness to persuasion on an issue is the person's degree of ego involvement with the issue. The more a belief touches on what we feel is the essence of our nature, the more reluctant we are to give up that belief. Let us say that we have a person who is president of the XXX Fraternity, whose grandfather, father, and brothers were members of the XXX Fraternity, and whose best friends are in the XXX Fraternity. It would be difficult to persuade that person to the belief that "fraternities are useless and should be abandoned."

Changing Belief Systems

When a person changes deeply held beliefs, it causes a readjustment of the entire belief system, often in dramatic ways. "Conversion" aptly names the situation, for in a change of basic beliefs, a person's entire belief system is rearranged in accord with the new basic belief or beliefs. A person's belief system is changed or converted from one thing into another. The biblical story of St. Paul is a vivid example. After his conversion, instead of being a persecutor of Christians, he became a major force in the spread of Christianity. Malcolm X, the Black leader, was, at one time, a petty thief, a pimp, and a convict. After his conversion to the Black Muslim Faith, he behaved in ways radically different from his earlier life.

Major changes do not need to be tied to religious conversion. Numerous stories exist of people who went into war as frivolous or callow youths and emerged with a serious and changed outlook on life. After surviving a life threatening illness, people often find their beliefs and values altered in large scale ways.

Belief systems can also be changed from the top down, but the process is gradual rather than dramatic. "*Erosion*" is the characterizing terms in this case. Small change follows small change until the small changes add up to a major change. A person may be dedicated to the belief, "I should exercise to stay healthy." The person regularly jogs, swims, or does aerobics. Then job pressures build up, and an exercise period or two are missed. A change in schedule makes it more difficult to find the time to exercise. A move puts the exercise facility farther away and harder to reach. A stretch of bad weather sets in. More and more exercise periods are missed until the person may have quit exercising all together and reached a new belief, "Exercise is not necessary for good health" or "Exercise is necessary, but I just don't have time."

Individuality of Beliefs

Another important consideration for persuasion grows out of the nature of belief systems; people will be persuaded on the basis of what *they* believe. The important aspect of a successful persuasion effort is not what the persuader thinks is important but rather what the *persuadee* thinks is important. People make decisions based on their belief systems, not upon the belief systems of others. One observer has put the matter this way: ". . . we do not change people through the things in them that we would wish to change, but through the things that they themselves wish to change" (O'Con-

nor 441). If a persuasive effort does not speak to the beliefs of the persuadee, the effort is highly likely to fail.

If someone is carrying a petition through a neighborhood opposing a factory to be built nearby, the concerns of the various property owners should be addressed. To one person, property values may be the most important concern in the matter. To another, increased taxes may be the most important factor. To a third, the safety problems caused by increased traffic to the factory may be the chief objection. To succeed in persuading each person to sign the petition, the petition carrier must address the specifics concerns of each.

Consistency of Beliefs

As people act and make decisions based upon their belief systems, they attempt to maintain a harmony of balance among the various ideas that they hold. We strive for consistency in our beliefs. We are uncomfortable when we feel our beliefs contradict each other and comfortable when our beliefs appear to be in agreement. We tend to act in accordance with our beliefs rather than in contradiction to them. When we act in contradiction to our beliefs, we usually feel some distress and begin to seek a balance between belief and action.

The consistency of beliefs and actions can be seen in very simple ways and very complex ways. People who think football is exciting watch games either in person or on television. People who do not find football interesting do not pay much attention to football games. On a more complex level, a number of beliefs and actions may cluster together. If one of our major beliefs is "Education is important," then we will spend time on school work, support educational institutions, and, eventually, encourage our children to study hard and do well in school. In addition, that belief may also influence what job we accept, where we live, what car we drive, the person whom we marry, and the kind of birthday presents we buy our grandchildren.

When we speak of "consistency," we must realize that the term is something of a misnomer. We are not necessarily totally balanced in our views. In fact, we may feel very comfortable holding views that are totally contradictory. The consistency comes not from the rational arrangement that we give our beliefs but rather from our ability to fit our view into a pattern comfortable to us. While we often see our selves as rational beings acting out of a tightly organized system of beliefs and values, most of us are walking sets of contradictions. The limits of our consistency do not extend beyond three or four major views.

The "Letters to the Editor" page of a newspaper can provide us with numerous examples of our contradictory nature. One may praise free speech, then several lines later specify which groups should be barred from demonstrating on the courthouse grounds. Another may complain of high taxes and bad roads, never acknowledging that the shortage of tax funds may be a major contributing factor to the sorry shape of the roads.

One woman wrote a letter praising a national chain store for being closed on Easter Sunday. She told how pleased she was to go to church, then out to eat, then to drive by the closed store and think how nice it was that the store's employees did not have to work. Her conclusion was that people should not be required to work on Sundays. Several days later, another letter appeared in reaction. It asked why she was eating in a restaurant on Sunday if she thought people should not work on that day. The first writer saw "not working on Sunday" as including store workers but not including the cooks, waiters, and others in restaurants.

People may be inconsistent on even large issues. Often the difference in views occurs when an issue directly touches us personally. Most believe, for example, that municipalities should dispose of trash and garbage. Yet, few would favor the construction of a landfill or trash transfer station next to their own property. The people who are in favor of a project until it adversely affects them have been labeled "Nimbys," an acronym for "Not In My Back Yard."

Contradictions may appear in a number of ways. A personal belief may contradict a political belief. People may be very charitable to people they know but oppose any kind of foreign aid, even famine relief. Even a strongly held view may not be probed to its furthest manifestation. People who oppose abortion on the basis of a belief in the sanctity of life may also argue in favor of capital punishment. On the other side of the question, people who support abortion may also argue against capital punishment, again on the basis of protecting the sanctity of life.

How truly consistent people are or how consistent they are from our point of view is of less interest in persuasion than in how consistent they feel themselves to be. If they are satisfied with their views of the world, they will be less open to persuasion than if they are dissatisfied with their views. Realizing what beliefs a person holds and how those beliefs fit together allows us to be effective in our persuasive efforts.

The Status Quo: "If It Ain't Broke, Don't Fix It"

If people are comfortable with the *status quo, the way things are*, then they will see little reason to change. Once we reach a level of comfort and balance, we are disinclined to move (Festinger 1). Change raises possibilities of discomfort. If a business is profitable, why should it change its procedures? If a family's schedule is working well in balancing meals, games, and activities, why change it? If we are happy attending a given school, why would we want to transfer? If we like the food we eat, be it healthy or unhealthy, why change? If we feel that we can consume liquor and still drive safely, why not drink and drive?

▲ **Figure 13.5.** Unless people perceive a compelling reason to change viewpoints or action, persuasion will not be successful.

We are likely to change beliefs when we feel discomfort in our situation. Unless we perceive some kind of problem with our world, we see no reason to change it. Dissatisfaction, not satisfaction, leads to change.

Sometimes, we discover our own reasons for needing a change and go looking for the solution to our problems. If we are short of funds, we may find a job and change leisure time into work time. If we are having roommate problems, we start trying to find ways to move the roommate or ourselves. If we know that our car has a leaky radiator, a balky transmission, and burns lots of oil, we will start looking into other solutions for our transportation problems: repairs, a new car, a bicycle, or public transportation.

At other times, the perception of a problem comes from an outside source. We are satisfied with present conditions until someone points out enough bad features of the situation that we begin to question how truly satisfactory it is. Knowing a problem exists, we are then open to persuasion, to being convinced to change our way of thinking, action, or feeling so that we can alleviate the distress we feel.

We may be happy with our reliable car. Then, one day, a friend remarks that the squealing noise we hear when we stop means that the brakes are going bad. We check with three mechanics, all of whom say the same thing. The car, which seemed perfectly fine a short time ago, now seems a threat to our safety. Realizing that something must be done, we are quite open to being persuaded to spend a large sum of money to fix the brakes.

We may find our major in college very fulfilling and rewarding, and we look forward to spending our life in our chosen profession. The thought of changing majors is an idea we have never entertained. Then we discover that few jobs are available in our area and that the jobs pay poorly. Our chosen profession does not look as promising as it did at first. While we would not have been very open to persuasion earlier, we may now be a prime candidate. The solution may be to change majors, add a minor that looks promising, or become more aware of the intangible rewards of our chosen field. Whatever our decision, we will find our world altered in some way. From being satisfied, we have moved to dissatisfaction. After finding a solution, we are again satisfied but our situation has changed from its original character.

Dissatisfactions arise not only from *needs* but also from *desires*. Our car may be economical and run well but not be a very prestigious model. It does not satisfy our longings for a car that projects the image we want. Our dissatisfaction with the car increases until we find ourselves at a car dealership purchasing a newer/sleeker/faster/richer looking model. We leave with a lighter heart and heavier debt. What impelled us to our choice of a new car was not the need for transportation as much as our personal desire for a different car.

Perceiving a difficulty motivates us to seek a way to remove the difficulty and to reestablish our sense of balance, to rearrange our network of beliefs and actions so that we can again feel comfortable. Persuasion is at work when someone, or even ourselves, tries to convince us that a problem exists in our world and then suggests a way to solve that problems. The problem may be personal, professional, social, or global. The changes sought may be our view of the matter, our attitudes, or our actions. As most of us are never totally satisfied with our lives, we are constantly open to persuasion on one topic or another.

Conclusion

Persuasion is the attempt through communication to change the way people think, act, or feel. Good persuasion takes into account ethical considerations. Persuasion depends on what beliefs people hold and how they order those beliefs. Factors which may influence a persuasive effort are the import of a belief, the strength with which a person holds a belief, one's ego involvement with a belief, and how strongly a belief is tied to one's basic beliefs. In ordering their belief systems, people strive for what they perceive to be balance and harmony. Persuasion works when disharmony is introduced and a person seeks a way to re-establish a sense of balance and comfort. Realizing the nature of persuasion allows us to be more effective in our communication as both persuader and persuadee.

• • • Discussion Questions

1. What examples can you give of persuasion as an attempt to change the way people think? Of the way people act? Of the way people feel?

2. Look at an issue of the campus newspaper. What persuasive efforts can you find in it?

3. In what situations in your own life have you wished that you could be more persuasive?

4. In what instances in your life have you been persuaded to do something you did not want to do or wished you had not? How did someone persuade you to act against your own wishes?

5. What, to you, constitutes an ethical approach to persuasion?

6. What examples can you give of people's actions that stem from their basic beliefs?

7. What examples can you give of people's secondary beliefs that stem from their basic beliefs?

8. "I should go to college" is a belief that leads to a great expenditure of time, money, and effort. What basic beliefs could prompt a person to make the decision to attend college?

9. What examples can you think of where people hold inconsistent views yet feel that their belief system is harmonious?

10. What examples can you give of the status quo as a factor in decision making?

• • • Sources and References

Benoit, William L. "Argument and Credibility Appeals in Persuasion." *The Southern Communication Journal* 52 (1987): 181–97.

Brembeck, Winston L. and William S. Howell. *Persuasion: A Means of Social Influence.* 2nd ed. Englewood Cliffs, New Jersey: Prentice-Hall, Inc, 1976.

Dass, Ram and Paul Gorman. *How Can I Help?: Stories and Reflections on Service.* New York: Alfred A. Knopf, 1986.

Festinger, Leon. *A Theory of Cognitive Dissonance.* Stanford, California: Stanford University Press, 1957.

Hart, Roderick P., Gustav Friedrich, and William D. Brooks. *Public Communication.* New York: Harper and Row, Publishers, 1975.

Larson, Charles U. *Persuasion: Reception and Responsibility.* Belmont, California: Wadsworth, Inc., 1989.

Littlejohn, Stephen W. and David M. Jabusch. *Persuasive Transactions.* Glenview, Illinois: Scott, Foresman and Company, 1987.

Nadeau, Ray E. *A Basic Rhetoric of Speech-Communication.* Reading, Massachusetts: Addison-Wesley Publishing Company, 1969.

O'Connor, Frank. "Expectation of Life." *Collected Stories.* New York: Alfred A. Knopf, 1981. 431–43.

O'Keefe, Daniel J. *Persuasion: Theory and Research.* Newbury Park, California: Sage Publications, Inc., 1990.

Simons, Herbert W. *Persuasion: Understanding, Practice, and Analysis.* 2nd ed. New York: Random House, 1986.

Stewart, Charles J., Craig Smith, and Robert E. Denton, Jr. *Persuasion and Social Movements.* 2nd ed. Prospects Heights, Illinois: Waveland Press, 1989.

Tead, Ordway. *Administration: Its Purpose and Purpose.* New York: Harper, 1959.

Name _____ Section _____ Date _____

Persuasive Speaking: Influencing Decisions

1. What are the six features shared by most persuasive situations?

   1. _____ 3. _____ 5._____

   2. _____ 4. _____ 6._____

2. Define persuasion.

   _____

   _____

3. List three situations involving the use of persuasion other than selling a product.

   1. _____ 2._____ 3._____

4. Why is it a misconception that persuasion is a formula or set of steps one goes through to talk people into a course of action?

   _____

   _____

5. What is the hypodermic needle theory of persuasion?

   _____

   _____

   How valid is the theory?

   _____

   _____

6. What are the two main principles of the ethics of persuasion?

   _____

   _____

7. What two points, especially, should be considered before beginning a persuasive effort?

   1. _____ 2. _____

8. What is a belief?

_____

_____

9. How are our belief systems developed?

_____

_____

10. What is a value?

_____

_____

11. What is a value system?

_____

_____

12. What is the relationship between beliefs and values?

_____

_____

13. What is an attitude?

_____

_____

14. Are belief systems static or permanent?

_____

Explain your response.

_____

_____

15. When trying to persuade someone, is it the more important belief or less important belief which is easier to change?

_____

Why? _____

_____

16. What determines the strength of a person's belief?

_____

_____

17. When two beliefs come into conflict, which one will usually win out?

_____

_____

18. How does ego involvement interact with a person's openness to persuasion?

_____

_____

19. What happens when a person changes deeply held beliefs?

_____

_____

20. What is the difference when belief systems are changed from the top down (least important to most important) rather than from the bottom up?

_____

_____

21. How consistent is a person's belief system?

_____

_____

22. What is the primary factor that makes people susceptible to making a change?

_____

_____

Public Speaking Assignment III
Persuasive Speech

Purpose

The presentational speaking assignment has a four-fold purpose:

1. You will gain further experience speaking before an audience;
2. You will continue to improve your public speaking skills;
3. You will learn how to construct a persuasive message;
4. You will learn how to adapt a persuasive message to a particular audience.

Basic Requirements

- You will develop and present to the class an original persuasive speech on a topic approved by your instructor. Suggested topics are listed on page 334.
- The presentational speech must show that a problem currently exists and present a proposal to reduce or eliminate that need.
- The persuasive speech must concentrate on advocacy, persuasion and attitude change.
- Your instructor may require that the speech be a presentational speech oriented toward a specific hypothetical audience and urging a course of action even though it will be delivered to your class. If no audience is assigned, you may select a hypothetical audience of your choice or speak to the real class population. In either case, identify which choice has been made and who your audience is.
- Whether the audience identity is hypothetical or real, the audience should be in a position to act upon the proposal.
- The assignment includes questions and answers with the audience about your proposal either during or after the presentation.
- Each speech must be _____ minutes in length.
- _____ sources must be used in preparing the speech.
- At least two visual aids are required.
- An outline of the speech must be submitted by _____.
- Speeches will be graded according to criteria on p. _____, which must be handed in prior to the speech.
- You will complete the observation sheets on pages 343–351 for designated fellow speakers.
- Additional instructor requirements:

Suggested Topics for Persuasive Speech

You will be most effective in your presentational speech if you select a topic about which you have a genuine interest and have developed a position. Below are suggested areas to start you thinking. You will have to narrow the suggested topic to a manageable aspect appropriate to the time limits. You do not have to select from the list, but topics must be approved by your instructor.

Change a Lifestyle for Better Health

chewing tobacco
eating breakfast
energy through exercise
vegetarianism
reducing stress
responsible alcohol use
alcohol and pregnancy

Contribute to the Common Good of Society

donate blood
join the Peace Corp
organize a Community Watch program
vote
participate in community government
volunteer for a social agency
    tutor non-readers
    crisis center
    women's shelter
    Big Brothers/Big Sisters
    S.A.D.D.

Participate in an Activity for Enjoyment

join a special interest group
support women's athletics
travel to _____

Campaign Regarding an Environmental Issue

nuclear power—America's future
alternate energy sources
cross-state refuse dumping
recycling waste
whale hunting
animal rights vs. scientific experimentation
pet overpopulation
dolphin-safe tuna fishing

Address Student Concerns

sexual harassment
date rape
library resources
education funding
teaching assistants vs. professors in the classroom
dorm policies
student representation in university policy development
managing parking problems on campus

Support/Reject and Issue of Public Policy

conscientious objector status
reactivation of the military draft
women participating in combat during wars
mandatory two-year service to the U.S.
gun regulation
computer information banks/privacy
defining pornography
euthanasia
ownership of the airwaves
defense spending
Strategic Arms Limitation
a national medical insurance plan
socialized medicine
prison reform
criminal rehabilitation programs
fighting the drug problem
legalizing all drugs
funding medical research for uncommon diseases
combating organized crime
addressing inner-city social problems
alternative educational systems
combating unemployment
censorship

Name _____ Section _____Date _____

Persuasive Speech Worksheet

Speech Due Date _____

1. possible topics:

2. selected topic:

3. possible narrowed topic areas:

4. narrowed focus of speech:

5. thesis statement:

6. attention step:

7. development of need: support/evidence:

    1.

    2.

    3.

8. proposal details—how plan would work:

9. future implications if nothing is done to change problem:

    support:

10. how implementing proposal could solve problem:

    support:

11. steps audience should take to implement proposal:

12. visual aid ideas:

13. conclusion that can be drawn from speech:

Notes:

Name _____ Date _____

Topic _____ Score _____

PERSUASIVE SPEECH GRADING CRITERIA—STYLE A

For a *C*, the speech will meet these requirements:

>Introduction previews main points of problem
>Transitions are present
>Speech establishes need, has specific proposal, urges action
>Main points are clear
>Sequence of ideas is easy to follow
>Conclusion reviews the need and solution
>Physical communication does not distract (no swaying, bobbing, etc.)
>Vocal communication is understandable
>Speech is free of disfluencies ("uh," "um," "you know," etc.)
>Speaker maintains eye contact with audience 50% of the time
>Speech fulfills requirements of assignment (persuasive, appropriate number of visual aids, appropriate notes, time limit, etc.)
>Visual aids are clear, neat, and legible.

For a *B*, the speech meets the requirements for a *C* plus the following:

>Introduction has attention step, establishes credibility, shows relevance, and previews main points
>Transitions link main points
>Each major point is fully developed
>Conclusion summarizes argument and calls for acceptance
>(optional) speech uses five steps of the Monroe Motivated Sequence: attention, need, satisfaction, visualization, and action
>Assertions supported with evidence
>Sources cited
>Speaker maintains eye contact with audience 75% of the time
>Speech is adapted to its audience
>Physical communication emphasizes points of the speech
>Vocal communication is energetic and clear
>Language is appropriate to topic and audience
>Visual aids strongly support the main points
>Visual aids are handled smoothly.

For an *A*, the speech meets the requirements for *C* and *B* plus the following:

>Introduction shows creativity
>Transitions show the flow of ideas
>Arguments are logical and fitting
>Speech cites highly credible sources
>Speaker is poised (in control of notes, visual aids, delivery)
>Speaker maintains eye contact 90% of the time
>Speaker develops rapport with audience.
>(optional) steps of the Monroe Motivated Sequence well developed

For a *D*, one of the areas for a *C* shows major problems.
For an *F*, the speech is not given or several areas show major problems.

Name _____ Date _____

Topic _____ Score _____

Persuasive Speech Grading Criteria—Style B

Topic 10%*
- subject of speech appropriate—proposal centered
- topic appropriately narrowed to fit time guidelines

Organization 30%*
Introduction
- attention getting opening employed
- rapport developed with the audience
- speaker credibility developed
- speech previewed
- thesis made clear

Body
- main points obvious
- transitions used between main points
- easily followed

Conclusion
- implications of material highlighted
- a feeling of completion developed

Content 30%*
- audience identified
- significant material developed in speech
- related to thesis
- need:
-   well developed
-   supported with evidence
- proposal:
-   clearly explained
-   specific
-   supported with evidence
- implications of action/non-action detailed
- action steps for audience outlined
- persuasive techniques employed
- adapted to specific audience
- positive interaction with audience
- visual aids enhanced speech
- vocabulary appropriate
- jargon and unfamiliar terms defined
- sources credible
- sources cited

---

*suggested values only—may be changed by your instructor

Delivery 30%*

Physical
- eye contact frequent
- gestures meaningful
- posture comfortable
- notecards properly used
- sense of communication with audience established
- visual aids used with confidence

Verbal
- rate appropriate
- volume appropriate
- tone pleasing
- vocal variety exhibited
- enunciation/pronunciation correct
- absence of fillers

Comments:

Name _____ Section _____ Date _____

Student Evaluation of Persuasive Speech

In light of the guidelines for constructive feedback, comment on the speech you have just watched.

What was the thesis of the speech?

What was the need outlined by the speaker?

How complete was the proposal?

Would you enact the recommendations of the speaker? Why or why not?

What was the speaker's strength?

What one thing would you suggest the speaker work on to improve?

Name _____ Section _____ Date _____

Student Evaluation of Persuasive Speech

In light of the guidelines for constructive feedback, comment on the speech you have just watched.

What was the thesis of the speech?

What was the need outlined by the speaker?

How complete was the proposal?

Would you enact the recommendations of the speaker? Why or why not?

What was the speaker's strength?

What one thing would you suggest the speaker work on to improve?

Name _____ Section _____ Date_____

Student Evaluation of Persuasive Speech

In light of the guidelines for constructive feedback, comment on the speech you have just watched.

What was the thesis of the speech?

What was the need outlined by the speaker?

How complete was the proposal?

Would you enact the recommendations of the speaker? Why or why not?

What was the speaker's strength?

What one thing would you suggest the speaker work on to improve?

Name _____Section _____Date _____

Student Evaluation of Persuasive Speech

In light of the guidelines for constructive feedback, comment on the speech you have just watched.

What was the thesis of the speech?

What was the need outlined by the speaker?

How complete was the proposal?

Would you enact the recommendations of the speaker? Why or why not?

What was the speaker's strength?

What one thing would you suggest the speaker work on to improve?

Name _____ Section _____ Date _____

Student Evaluation of Persuasive Speech

In light of the guidelines for constructive feedback, comment on the speech you have just watched.

What was the thesis of the speech?

What was the need outlined by the speaker?

How complete was the proposal?

Would you enact the recommendations of the speaker? Why or why not?

What was the speaker's strength?

What one thing would you suggest the speaker work on to improve?

14

Composing a Persuasive Speech

Key Concepts

As we have seen, as long as we are satisfied with our situation, we see no need to change it. When we begin to sense that something is wrong, then we are open to possibilities for change. At the heart of the persuasive process is the interplay between a perceived difficulty and the search for relief from that difficulty.

The difficulty may be financial, moral, emotional, political, spiritual, or involve any facet of ourselves. The solution may be for us to act differently, think differently, or feel differently. We may change our habits; we may change our views; we may change our emotions.

Persuasion may be attempted in any manner of ways. Advertising bombards us daily with persuasive messages aimed at making us admire, then want, then buy. It is impossible to pick up a magazine or a newspaper, to turn on a radio or television set without subjecting ourselves to a host of persuasive efforts. Dealing with family and friends, we try to influence each other. In business institutions, persuasions goes on in dyads, in small groups, in bulletins, newsletters, and meetings.

Narrowing the field of persuasive communication to speeches still leaves us with an array of possibilities. We can make speeches to convince people to change either as a group or as individuals. We can try to persuade people to support an activity with their good will or with their arguments or with their money or with their labor.

Analyzing Your Audience

One of the most important aspects of persuasive speaking is audience analysis. A strong awareness of our audience should guide us throughout the composition process, because persuasion is effective only when the proposed changes match with the sensibilities of the audience. To be effective persuaders, we need to understand such audience characteristics as educational level, socioeconomic level, age, family status, professions, gender, political affiliation, religious affiliation, and nationality. Most importantly, we need to know our audience in terms of its beliefs and values. If the course of action we advocate does not mesh with the values and beliefs of our prospective persuadees, our efforts will be for naught.

▲ **Figure 14.1.** Analyzing and adapting to your audience is a critical part of persuasive speaking.

The analysis of beliefs and values needs to be as specific and detailed as possible. While an audience may agree on major concepts, minor areas may still show a divergence of viewpoints. A presentation made to a business, for example, would focus on the main concern of any business: what is in the best interest of the company? Yet, within that overarching concern, audience members may have other concerns. One person may demand that any course of action preserve the company's traditions. Another may want to encourage family relations within the company. Another may be sensitive to environmental issues. One may place a high value on innovation. One may rank quarterly returns as an important goal while another sees long term growth as the most important goal. The most acceptable course of action to this group would be the one that could come closest to addressing the concerns of all.

We also need to see what other factors such as timing, morale, and public knowledge may influence an audience. Advising a business on how to improve personnel relations or sales will require one kind of approach in a time of economic strength and another in a time of economic hardship. On a personal level, a group may be influenced by the loss of a member or may be buoyed by a recent success. A school board under fire in the local press will function differently than it will when praised publicly or when working in relative obscurity.

One expert, a management consultant, was called in by a company whose plant was operating badly. The consultant's job was doubly hard in that another consultant had been working with the company for three years with little success. The first consultant's approach was to persuade the workers to better efforts with the threatening argument, "If this factory is not profitable, you will lose your jobs and the town will lose the factory."

As the second consultant drove into town, he noticed another factory that had closed. The people in the town, he decided, were not concerned whether businesses stayed open or not. He would have to find some other approach to the problem. After talking with people, he discovered that while they were unconcerned about the larger economic picture, they saw hard work as a matter of pride. He also noticed that they had little understanding of what they were trying to accomplish in the factory.

Instead of using "you will lose your job" as an approach, he used a different tack, one adapted to the audience's beliefs and values. His approach was, "To do a good job, you need to know what you are doing." A clarification of goals together with the workers' desire to show effort brought the factory back up to production as well as raising morale.

As persuasion is a matter of influencing the beliefs of an audience, the better acquainted a speaker is with those beliefs, the greater the chances of successful persuasion.

Composing a Persuasive Speech

Composing a persuasive speech is much like composing other speeches in that the process demands imagination and organization. Due to its nature, however, a persuasive speech will demand particular patterns of organization.

Styles of Persuasive Speeches

Approaches to Persuasive Speaking

One of the first tasks in composing a persuasive speech is to determine the goal of the speech. Do we wish the audience to change the way it thinks about an issue, the way it feels about an issue, or the way it acts? Or do we wish to touch on all the possibilities?

For example, a community may be involved in a controversy about a proposed dress code at the local high school. One question would be, "Is the proposed dress code legal?" Here, the main issue would be a critical one to be decided by reviewing laws and legal precedents. Persuaders for or against the code would seek to influence the way audiences considered the issue.

Another question might be, "Is the code fair?" The feelings of the audience would be of high importance here. Another issue would be, "Should we enact the dress code?" The main point of persuasion here would be some kind of action, a vote from the authoritative group to support, modify, or reject the proposed code.

Another important aspect of persuasive speeches is the way in which decisions will be made. In some cases, the persuadees make their decisions individually; in other cases the decisions are made by a group. In terms of the dress code issue, the student body may be urged to attend the school board meeting where the decision is to be made. In response, each student would make an individual decision whether or not to attend. When faced with the final decision, the school board would act as a group. Whatever decision was reached, it would be binding on all members.

Presentational Speech— A Special Case

The presentational speech is a special type of persuasive speech in that it involves a particular kind of decision making and seeks a particular outcome. *A presentational speech is a persuasive speech given to a decision making body urging a course of action.* Or, as another has put it, "presentational speaking is interactive advocacy of a specific proposal before a decision making group" (Vibbert).

The presentational speech has three important characteristics. The first is that it is *given to a decision making body*. The "body" can range in number from a small group of several people to an audience of hundreds. Examples of such "decision making bodies" would be school boards, county commissioners, city councils, grade appeals committees, families, church officers, club officers or administrative committees, councils, and a host of committees in business and society. All of these groups are charged with the oversight of activities or facilities and must make decisions about how best to carry out their responsibilities. The decisions they make are made by the members acting as a group and not as individuals. The responsibility for the consequences of the decision will be borne by all.

Another major characteristic of a presentational speech is that it urges a *course of action*. While ways of thinking and feeling may be influential in a presentational speech, the aim of the speech is to persuade the decision making body to do something. The speaker wants the audience to respond in a certain way, to adopt the action the speaker recommends: the school board is asked to raise teachers' salaries; the county commissioners are asked to approve or disapprove a noise ordinance; the grade appeals committee is asked to raise a student's grade; or the budget committee of a corporation is asked to allocate additional funds to a department. Other decisions would include courses of action such as voting a certain way, endorsing a candidate, committing resources, or beginning planning. Whatever the speaker's goal, it will call for tangible results.

The final characteristic of a presentational speech is that it is *interactive*. In a presentational speech, the speaker does more than present a viewpoint and sit down. In a presentational speech, the audience may stop the speaker and ask for clarification of points or illustrations. When the speech is finished, the speaker may face questions that probe ideas advanced in the speech. A good speaker will be prepared for what may happen during the course of the speech and after the speech is given.

The Persuasive Thesis Statement

The thesis statement of a persuasive speech should include the three main elements of any thesis statement: topic, position, and amplification. The persuasive thesis statement, however, will formulate these elements in a way that expresses a strong sense of "ought." While a thesis statement for an informative speech concentrates on making people aware of knowledge they do not have, the persuasive thesis statement concentrates on what the audience should do.

Let us say the topic is the recycling of newspapers, glass, and cans and that the audience is the town's, West Lafayette, city council. The thesis for an informative speech on the topic might be, "Recycling is a good way to dispose of trash because recycling is economical, easy, and protects the environment." Such a speech would describe recycling and its benefits. If the same topic were used in a persuasive speech, in addition to providing information, the speech would urge a course of action. A persuasive thesis statement might be, "The city of West Lafayette should initiate a recycling program because such a program is economical, easy to run, and beneficial to the environment." Here the thesis statement proposes that something be done: "initiate a recycling program." Further, the word, "should," implies a directive to action.

An even better thesis statement would be one that incorporates not only the course of action—the solution—but one that includes both the problem and the solution. *The problem-solution equation is at the heart of persuasion*, and a good persuasive thesis statement will include both major elements.

Reworking our thesis statement about recycling, we would add the problem to the statement: "To alleviate the problems of the present landfill program, the city of West Lafayette should initiate a recycling program." The statement contains the three elements of a topic sentence arranged to urge a course of action. The topic is "recycling program." The position is "should initiate." The amplification is "to alleviate the problems."

The elements of the basic thesis statement can be arranged in different ways and can be simple or elaborate. However the thesis statement is constructed, the main thrust should still express the existence of a problem and the possibility of a solution.

For example, the main points of the problem and solution could be included: "To alleviate the cost, difficulty, and environmental harm of the present landfill program, the city of West Lafayette should initiate a recycling program that is cheaper, easier to operate, and environmentally sound."

Variations in wording can also be used: "Because the present landfill program is costly, difficult to operate, and environmentally dangerous, the city of West Lafayette should initiate a recycling program which will be cheaper, simpler, and safer environmentally."

In some cases, the problems may be implied in the thesis statement rather than being expressed directly. Let us say that the Parking Committee at a major university is urging the conversion of a newly acquired piece of property into a parking lot for commuting students. The committee might put forth a statement such as, "The property bounded by North, Apple, South, and Walnut Streets should be made into a commuters' parking lot to make parking easier for commuting students." Here the problem is suggested by the fact that the new parking lot would make life easier for commuting students. The implication is that without the new parking lot, life will continue to be difficult for a certain group of students.

The best persuasive thesis statement would still incorporate all three elements: "The property bounded by North, Apple, South, and Walnut Streets should be made into a commuters' parking lot to alleviate the congestion and inconvenience in the present commuter parking lots and provide the commuting students with parking close to classrooms on the west side of campus." The sentence is longer, but it recognizes more clearly the situation being addressed. The topic is clear: "The property bounded by North, Apple, South, and Walnut Streets . . . ." The position is clear: "should be made into a commuters' parking lot . . . ." The amplification is clear: "to alleviate the congestion and inconvenience of the present commuter lots and provide commuting students with parking close to classrooms on the west side of campus."

Organizational Patterns

As one might suspect by now, one organizational pattern is the preferred one for persuasive speeches: the *problem-solution pattern*. Other patterns may be useful in certain parts of the speech. In describing the problem, one might use a chronological sequence to show how the problem developed. To explain how the solution works, one might use a structure and function pattern. A spatial pattern might be employed to show the impact of the problem in different neighborhoods or areas. The main pattern, though, should be what we have already stressed: show "that a problem is serious enough to require doing something about it" and then suggest "a plan to solve it" (Nadeau 181).

The Thesis Statement as an Organizational Tool

As we observed earlier, when we are making an informational speech, a good technique is to place the thesis statement near the end of the introduction. Here the thesis statement provided an overview of the speech and cues the audience about what it can expect.

Using the entire persuasive thesis statement in the same way may not be such a good idea. The reason is simple: if we announce our solution before convincing the audience of the existence of a problem, we may needlessly antagonize the audience and hamper our efforts. After all, we give persuasive speeches because our audience does not yet accept our position. In our example of recycling, some council members may be dubious about the need or feasibility of a recycling program. Announcing at the start that we are promoting a recycling program may elicit a hostile reaction and strengthen their opposition. Introducing the solution after they have agreed that a problem exists will make our job easier.

Instead of inserting the thesis statement into the introduction, we will probably be more successful if we divide the thesis statement into two major parts. We use the "problem" part of the statement as the organizing concept for the first part of the speech and the "solution" portion as the organizing concept for the second part of the speech.

Adding the other necessary ingredients of a speech to the basic problem-solution framework, a simple outline of a persuasive speech would be:

▶ Introduction
▶ Problem
▶ Solution
▶ Conclusion

As we researched and developed the speech, the outline would expand to include appropriate headings under the main divisions:

Introduction

I. Problem
  A. Source of the problem
  B. Nature of the problem
  C. Future effects of the problem

II. Solution
  A. Description of the solution
  B. How the solution solves the problem
  C. Why the solution is the best course of action

Conclusion

The subheadings would not, of course, have to exactly match those above but, would be chosen according to the dictates of the given subject.

The problem-solution patterns serves as a kind of action-reaction scheme. What we introduce in the first half is matched by what we introduce in the second half. The problem and the ramifications that we outline in the first part are answered by the solution offered in the second part.

With this format, the two halves tend to mirror or parallel each other. If we deal with "extent of the problem" in the first half, we will need to deal with "extent of the problem" in the second half and show how the problem would be contained. If we deal with "source of the problem" in the first half, we will need to show in the second half how the source can be stopped, slowed, or circumvented.

To return to our topic of recycling, an outline of the speech would look like this:

Thesis statement: "The city of West Lafayette should begin a recycling program to alleviate the economic, logistical, and environmental problems of the present landfill system."

Introduction: The recent announcement of the closing of the landfill by state authorities has made us all aware of the problem we face in disposing of our trash. Our task force has studied the problem for several months. We have done extensive research. We have consulted with the city engineer, the street department, the landfill operators, and environmental experts. We are convinced that our present system is inadequate and that a better course of action is available to us. Let us look first at our present situation.

I. The current landfill program presents us with economic, logistical, and environmental problems.
  A. The current landfill program is expensive.
    1. Specialized equipment is needed to collect and compress garbage.
    2. Landfill rates are high.
      a. The cost per individual load is _____.
      b. The monthly cost of the landfill program to the city is _____.
    3. Our total cost of pickup and disposal is _____.
  B. Trash and garbage collection is difficult.
    1. Routes must be run twice weekly.
    2. Trucks must be driven a long way to the landfill.
  C. The landfill program has negative environmental effects.
    1. The landfill collects dangerous materials.
    2. With the landfill close to capacity, more land will soon be needed.
    3. The use of the landfill makes many items usable only once.
      a. New trees must be cut to provide more paper.
      b. New mining operations must be done to provide more metals.

II. A recycling program for newspapers, glass, and cans would be superior to the landfill program.
  A. Recycling would be cheaper than the landfill program.
    1. Recyclable materials are valuable and can be sold.
    2. Recycling would require fewer trips to the landfill.
    3. Recycling would require little specialized equipment.
    4. Our total savings from instituting this program would be _____.
  B. A recycling program would be easier to run than the landfill program.
    1. Recycling would cut garbage runs to once a week.

2. Recycling pickups are quicker than regular trash pickups.
3. Garbage trucks would be used less and last longer.

C. Instituting a recycling program would have a positive effect on the environment.
1. With less going to the landfill, less land will need to be devoted to trash disposal.
2. Recycling materials puts less strain on our resources.
   a. Fewer trees will be cut for paper.
   b. Less mining will be needed for steel and aluminum.

Conclusion: As we have seen, the present landfill program creates a number of problems for the city. A recycling program offers a method of disposing of trash and garbage that is cheaper, easier to run, and more protective of the environment than what we are doing now. For these reasons, we should initiate a recycling program as soon as possible.

Refinements in the Pattern. Not every persuasion situation is such that all we need to do to be successful is to present the problem and then present the solution. Most major decisions in life are made by weighing the pros and cons, the goods and bads of various options. In making our decisions, we try to strike a balance between all the factors that we see as important: our beliefs, our values, our attitudes, our needs, our desires, and our possibilities.

The final course of action is often one which has notable drawbacks but is still the one in which the advantages most outweigh the disadvantages. We may place a high value on saving money, but faced with the need for transportation, we buy a car and take on a large debt. We may value our close ties to our families but elect to attend college at some distance because the school offers the program we want, more financial aid, or what we consider the best education. Similarly, our persuadees must choose a course of action, and the choice is often made from several possibilities, each of which has advantages and disadvantages.

As few solutions are perfect, we may need to acknowledge the strengths and weaknesses of the course of action we are promoting. Failure to do so may indicate a limited understanding of the situation and undercut our persuasive effort and lower our credibility. In this case, we would acknowledge the shortcomings of our plan but also point out how the positive aspects of our plan outweigh the disadvantages. If we cannot find a solution with more advantages than disadvantages, then we need to rethink our approach to the problem.

Presenting both the pros and cons of a solution, that portion of the outline would look like this:

II. Description of the solution
    A. Disadvantages of the solution
    B. Advantages of the solution

Here we would have a "speech within a speech." Our major persuasive effort would be to show that our solution would relieve the problem. In this portion, we would try to persuade our audience that the positives of our solution so outweigh the negatives that our solution is worth accepting. We may also need to show how, compared with other possible solutions, our solution offers the best ratio of advantages to disadvantages.

A variation of the advantages-disadvantages approach is to present the most likely solutions and show the problems and advantages in each. Our preferred solution would need to show the greatest ration of advantages over disadvantages.

An outline of this procedure would look like this:

II. Possible solutions
    A. Solution one
       1. Disadvantages
       2. Advantages
    B. Solution two
       1. Disadvantages
       2. Advantages
    C. Solution three
       1. Disadvantages
       2. Advantages

Conclusion: Solution _____ is the best for the following reasons.

The Monroe Motivated Sequence. Another variation on the problem-solution sequence was developed by Alan H. Monroe, a professor at Purdue University. Called the "Monroe Motivated Sequence," Monroe's approach leads an audience through a natural sequence of problem solving thought. For persuasive speaking, the Monroe Motivated Sequence moves through five steps as it progresses from introduction to conclusion (Monroe 186-214; Gronbeck, McKerrow, Ehninger, and Monroe 180-205).

The five steps of the Monroe Motivated Sequence are: *attention, need, satisfaction, visualization, and action.*

The *attention* step is the introduction to the speech. Like any other introduction, its aim is to move the audience from ignorance to awareness and to create an interest in the topic. The attention step should make the audience alert to what is about to be said. The attention step should be composed in such a way that the audience's response is, "I want to listen." Whether it is shocking or suave, the attention step should capture the audience's interest.

The *need* step is the presentation of the problem. Here the audience is made aware of a situation that is problematic and serious enough to require action. The speaker's aim in this portion of the speech is to help the audience realize, "Something needs to be done."

The *satisfaction* step is similar to the solution step we have discussed above. Having made the audience aware of a need or desire, the speaker furnishes a means of eliminating the need to satisfying the desire. The goal in this section of the speech is for the audience to feel, "This is the thing to do (believe, or feel) to satisfy the need."

The fourth step is the *visualization* step in which the speaker creates a word picture of what will happen if the proposed satisfaction is adopted or not adopted. The speaker calls on the audience to use its imagination to see the plan in operation and to experience is effects.

A speaker may take several approaches to composing the visualization step. One approach is to be positive and to show the benefits of the proposed plan. Here the speaker creates

▲ **Figure 14.2.** Visualization is an important step in the Monroe Motivated Sequence and an aid to persuasion.

a picture of the good that would result from adopting the proposed satisfaction. A second approach is to use a negative view to show the detrimental effects of rejecting the proposed solution. The picture created here would be one of a bad situation continuing or becoming worse.

The two approaches can also be combined into a compare-and-contrast method which opposes the goods and bads of courses of action. First, the negative consequences of ignoring the situation are vividly described. Then the good resulting from adoption of the solution is presented in striking images.

With the visualization step, the speaker wants the audience to respond with the feeling, "I can see myself enjoying the benefits of such an action."

The last step of the sequence is the *action* step. If no change occurs in the audience's ways of thinking, feeling, or acting, no persuasion has taken place. In the action step, the speaker asks the audience to do something specific, to take the final step of committing to change. The response the speaker seeks in this closing portion is, "I will do (believe, or feel) this," This steps forms the conclusion of the speech.

Here are two brief examples of how topics can be organized according to the motivational sequence.

Example I

Attention: Last year thousands of babies were killed in the United States.

Need: They were not killed by accident or illness. They were not even allowed to enter this world. They were sucked out of their mothers' wombs and ripped to pieces by abortion.

Satisfaction: House Bill 1234 will require a twenty-four hour waiting period after a woman contacts an abortion facility before the abortion can be performed.

Visualization: Instead of rushing capriciously into an abortion, women will be required to give thoughtful attention to the consequences of their actions. As they think about what they are considering, their minds will be changed, and lives will be saved.

Action: Write your legislators and ask them to support House Bill 1234.

Example II

Attention: This may look like a coat hanger, but it is really a murder weapon.

Need: Before Roe v. Wade legalized abortion, this and other gruesome methods were the only way out for pregnant women trapped by rape, poverty, or sexual abuse. Back alley abortions using crude instruments resulted in the agonizing deaths of thousands of women who, because of rape or incest, found themselves pregnant through no fault of their own. House Bill 1234 is another attempt to put abortion back into dirty corners by making a useless waiting period mandatory.

Satisfaction: House Bill 1234 needs to be defeated.

Visualization: Women are already responsible. A woman entering an abortion facility does not do so lightly. This bill would put a policeman at the door saying, "You do not know your own mind."

Action: Writer your legislators and ask them to defeat House Bill 1234.

Evidence—Support for Points

A persuasive speech is, by its nature, a speech about possibilities and interpretations of situations. One person views a matter positively; another views it negatively; a third is undecided on the issue. One person's problem is another person's solution. Many of the statements made in a persuasive speech are debatable. A speaker's claims to the truth of a fact or the pressing need for action may not, by themselves, be enough to change the mind of the audience. For persuasion to take place, the audience needs to see support for the speaker's claims and views.

The material that supports and reinforces the speaker's ideas is *evidence.* Broadly defined, evidence is "anything the audience will believe when presented" (Crable 174). In other words, evidence is matter offered to the audience in support of arguments and accepted by the audience as valid or truthful. We often think of evidence as "facts and figures," but evidence can also be subjective and even made up, as with a story offered to make a point. The primary consideration in choosing evidence is "what will be the most effective with a given audience?"

In matching evidence and audience, we have a wide range of materials from which to choose.

Facts

Facts may well constitute acceptable evidence. By "facts," we mean the specifics of a situation and its circumstances, the observations we make about the attributes of a given case. Most of us look to facts to give us a valid understanding of a situation. We ask, "What happened? What caused it? When and where was it done? How was it done?" A newspaper account of traffic accident would, for example, be a compilation of facts about the incident. Many sources can supply us with factual evidence: newspapers, magazines, surveys, books, specialized publications, and eyewitness accounts, among others.

Figures

Numerical evidence is a type of factual evidence. Instead of reasoning from the physical attributes of a situation, we use the mathematical relationships. These may be as simple as counting: "Last year Tippecanoe County recorded 'X' number of traffic accidents related to alcohol." The mathematical relationships may be complex and the result of complicated statistical calculations: "Given the current rate of property taxes, the limits set on taxing by law, the rate of inflation, and the projected birth rate for the next five years, we will need 'X' dollars for new school construction."

Testimonials and Expert Opinion

Testimonials and expert opinions are evidence offered by individuals. While the two are related, they vary in the amount and scope of experience people bring to a topic. Testimonials are based upon personal knowledge of an area while expert opinions are offered by people who, through extensive study or experience, are thoroughly versed in an area. Both types can be effective when used properly.

A neighborhood, for example, may have what it considers a dangerous intersection, one dangerous enough that members of the neighborhood want to persuade the city council to install a traffic light at the intersection. In making the presentation, both testimonials and expert opinion could be offered as evidence for the need for a traffic light.

Testimonials would include statements from parents who are worried about their children's safety and stories from drivers who have had accidents or near accidents at the intersection. Expert opinion would come from people such as a police officer from the town's traffic division or a civil engineer specializing in vehicular traffic. The police officer could cite the accident rate at the intersection and could offer judgments based on police records. The civil engineer could provide research data. This data could include statistics on the number of vehicles using the intersection as well as the physical features of the intersection, such as the width of the street, bordering shrubs, etc. The engineer could project the amount of traffic expected in the future at the intersection and provide evaluations of the situation based on study and professional practice.

Stories

Narrative or stories can offer powerful evidence to persuasive efforts. With stories, we can offer examples and illustrations of the points we wish to make. In persuasion, a well told story may make the point as nothing else will. If we are urging fire prevention in homes, statistics on the damage caused by fires may be persuasive. More persuasive may be the story of the parents forced to listen to the screams of their children trapped in a burning house because they did not teach the children how to escape a fire.

Emotions

While we think of ourselves as rational beings, we make numerous decisions based upon our feelings. In American society, for instance, it is considered crass to base the major decision of whom to marry upon rational grounds such as the potential spouse's projected health, financial success, and social standing. The decision is to be made by what we feel about the potential spouse. We purchase cars and clothing, to some extent, according to how the items make us feel. Warm clothing is a necessity in wintertime, but the decision of what to buy—a parka, a bomber jacket, a trench coat, or a fur coat—is based in part on whether or not we like the feel and look of the garment.

We are often persuaded by emotional evidence. Humane societies urge us to neuter our pets by showing us lovable puppies and kitties abandoned because pet owners contributed to pet overpopulation. Most restaurants do not appeal to our scientific knowledge of calories, vitamin and mineral content, and percentage of fat in their foods. Rather, they portray the restaurants as attractive places where we can enjoy the experience of satisfying our hunger and find engaging relationships.

Emotional evidence may take many forms. Indeed, any form of evidence may be couched in emotional terms. Facts and figures may be objective, but if the implications of the facts and figures are emotionally charged, the data and statistics become the subject of feelings as well.

Credibility

Properly chosen and used, evidence can bolster a persuasive effort and make it effective. Another important factor in the success or failure of a persuasive speech is the speaker. How we are perceived as persons may greatly help or hinder our persuasion. Whether our audience views us as a novice or an expert, trustworthy or untrustworthy, organized or disorganized may well determine the impact of our speech. The influence of the speaker on the success of a persuasive speech has been discussed ever since the topic of persuasion arose. Twenty-three hundred years ago, Aristotle in his *Rhetoric* spoke of the persuasion that "depends on the personal character of the speaker" (1365b). Aristotle's term for this quality was "ethos." Modern rhetoric broadens the term to call it "credibility."

In a question of sickness or illness, we would more likely take the opinion of a physician over that of a lawyer. Both may be equally intelligent and ethical, but due to the fact that the physician has more experience in the area of medicine, we would be more likely to believe the physician's opinion. In a question of law, we would give the attorney higher credibility.

In a debate over whether or not to initiate a recycling program, whose analysis would we be most likely to believe: the owner of the county landfill, the owner of a recycling company, a professor of environmental science with no financial stake in the matter, or a person living next to the landfill? The answer to the question would depend on who we are and how we see the matter.

The person or party in a dispute most likely to be credible to us is the one who comes closest to our feelings and viewpoints. As college students, we would most likely believe the professor of environmental science because we have little stake in the business of trash disposal and because we place a high premium upon education. If the local landfill were owned by our family and we were dependent on it for our livelihood, we would probably give higher credibility to someone with direct experience in running a landfill. If we had a financial investment in a recycling company, we would be more likely to believe the owner of the recycling company. If our highest values concerned privacy and protection of private property, the testimony of the landfill's neighbor might receive our strongest support.

Kenneth Burke, a modern philosopher, has put the matter well: "You persuade a man only insofar as you can talk his language by speech, gesture, tonality, order, image, attitude, idea, identifying your ways with his" (55). Credibility is not something we possess as speakers as much as it is something that is given or assigned

to us by audiences. The closer we come to the concerns, sympathies, and manners of our audience, the greater the chances that we will be persuasive and the greater the chances that the audience will endow us with credibility. The more we *identify* with our audience and the audience with us, the better our chances of successful persuasion.

To achieve credibility, it is necessary to communicate in ways that place the audience and speaker on common ground. Dress is one way speakers can demonstrate commonality between themselves and their audiences. Consciously or unconsciously, groups develop ways of dressing that become almost uniforms for them. Different companies develop different company cultures that lead to varying ways of dressing. One company may create an atmosphere in which most employees wear casual clothes. Another may have suits as the norm. A third may have company uniforms for the workers. In social groups, people tend to dress alike whether the dress be sweatshirts and jeans or designer wear.

By wearing the same clothing as the audience, a speaker can show an approval of the audience's taste and an identification with its lifestyle. Dress can also allow a speaker to fulfill the audience's expectations of what a person should look like in a given role. If, for example, a pharmacist were speaking to an audience, the expectations would be that the person would be knowledgeable about medications. In addition, because pharmacy involves health and careful dispensing of medication, the audience would also expect the person to be clean and neat and orderly. If the pharmacist showed up wearing old, dirty clothes, needing a haircut, and smelling bad, the audience would probably wonder if the right person had arrived to speak, much less grant the person high credibility.

Speaking style is another way of identifying with the audience. Using language commonly used by the audience can demonstrate a commonality. If the audience believes that an excited speaker is a committed speaker, then the speaker needs to be animated and lively. If an audience believes that an excited speaker is a superficial speaker, then the a lower-keyed approach to the topic will be better.

The kind of evidence deemed most acceptable by an audience is also important in establishing common ground. Audiences deem speakers credible when speakers argue in ways acceptable to the audience. Some audiences place a high premium on numerical evidence, others on subjective evidence. Research viewed as authoritative by one group may be regarded as highly questionable by another. To be convincing, speakers need to find evidence that the audience will see as convincing.

In arguing for a recycling program, a speaker would need to adapt the use of evidence to varying audiences. A city council would probably be most concerned with finances and feasibility. Here the speaker would want to argue from the advantages of the recycling program in dollars and cents. For an environmental group, the pragmatics would be important, but more important would be arguments that demonstrated the benefits of recycling to the quality of air, soil, and water.

An important question to ask in approaching a persuasive speech is, "What does the audience see as important?" Tying the presentation to the concerns of an audience can give added impact. Even if the speaker is arguing against a position held by the audience, the speaker can gain credibility by recognizing and empathizing with the views of the audience.

A recycling program, on the surface, looks like a simple matter for residents. All they have to do is to put out the trash and garbage in a different way. Even that change, though, has ramifications for people, ramifications which would need to be addressed by a speaker arguing for such a program. The cost of city programs is paid by taxes which, in turn, are paid by homeowners. Sorting papers, bottles, and cans takes time. Habits would have to change. Space would need to be found for storing recyclables before they were put at the curb. While these are small issues, enough problems with these considerations could swing opinion against a program. To be convincing, a speaker would need to show that all these matters had been carefully considered.

To convince those unsupportive of the proposed program, a speaker would need to show understanding and empathy for the objections.

Acknowledging the inconvenience and trouble would at least provide the speaker and the audience with a common level of understanding. The audience could feel that, despite the difference in views, the speaker is someone who knows how they feel.

If we find that we already share many of the characteristics of our audience, then we may create identification with the audience by reminding it of our similarities. As a college student speaking to other college students, it would be easy to find a number of similarities. If we were speaking to persuade a group of students to contribute to a scholarship fund, we could bring up the financial difficulties we have experienced, the opportunities we have, and our plans for the future. The audience's contribution, we could argue, would allow others to overcome the same obstacles, to have the same positive experiences, and to look forward to the same opportunities.

If we do not share a great deal of common ground, we will need to search for ways to bridge the gap. As a college student speaking to a group of retirees, we would face an audience that differed widely from us in age, family status, professional status, economic status, social life, and outlook. Calling upon our experience, we could show empathy and understanding by talking about our grandparents or other relatives, family friends, or neighbors who are similar to our audience. If we have worked with retirees, we could mention that and the positive aspects of that experience. If we have little direct experience with retirees, we could allude to books and articles we have read on older citizens. The evidence we offer could show our understanding. Our stories and examples, for instance, would involve people the age of our audience.

To convince this group to contribute to a scholarship fund, we could talk about what they have found important in their lives and careers and how education was influential in these. We could talk about their concerns that their grandchildren do well. Their contributions, we could say, would help others to lead the fulfilling lives that they have enjoyed and help people like those they value highly, their grandchildren.

In establishing common ground through identification, we need to use common sense and good judgment. One value in American society that seems universal is a dislike for hypocrites and phonies. While seeking common ground with our audience, we should not stray so far from our own personality and style that our concerns and behavior no longer appear to be genuine. Identification is regarded as positive by audiences, opportunism as negative.

Handling Interaction

A persuasive speech, and particularly a presentational speech, may present us with a new challenge in public speaking—handling interaction. Even if we are not stopped in the course of a speech and asked to clarify a point, we may face questions and reactions after the formal part of the speech is over. Doing well in interaction demands knowledge, preparation, flexibility, and a speaking style different from the straightforward presentation of an informative speech.

One goal of speaking in interaction is to maintain poise. The same kind of poise and control that is appreciated by an audience during a speech is appreciated in a question and answer session. While reacting to the audience, we want to continue to show ourselves as competent communicators. In some situations, a major part of maintaining poise may be staying cool. If respondents are angry or inflammatory, we should avoid the temptation to respond in kind. Persuasion is not a matter of out-shouting or out-arguing the other party but, rather, bringing the other person to see our point of view. Alienating people unnecessarily makes it difficult for them to find common ground with us.

Maintaining poise is easier to do when we have prepared in advance instead of regarding interaction as an off-the-cuff process. We can prepare for interaction by imagining what kinds of responses the audience is likely to have. We can then compose possible answers or at least establish the most effective ways of responding. Having someone listen to our presentation, then play the role of questioner can prepare us as well.

▲ **Figure 14.3.** Handling interaction is a necessary skill for presentational speaking. (Coyle)

Being informed will also allow us to respond in our best fashion. For this, we will need to have information and evidence beyond what we have incorporated into our speech. The interaction may not call upon us to use all that we have assembled, but we are better off to have material that is unused than be forced to admit that we are ignorant about the respondent's question or point.

It is important to watch the time of our responses. Often, when we are prepared to speak on a topic, we can be caught up in enthusiasm for the subject and end up telling people far more than they ever wanted to hear. When responding to a question, it is best to make our answers brief, no more than a minute or two. If respondents want a fuller answer, they can always request more information.

A good way to phrase longer responses is to compose them as if they were mini-speeches. A sentence or two can provide the introduction. The body of the mini-speech is the answer, divided, if necessary, into points. A summary sentence or two provides a conclusion.

When dealing with interaction, we need to respect the questioner. Some respondents will demonstrate an understanding of our topic and an appreciation of our ideas. Others may ask questions so stupid we wonder if they even listened to what we had to say. When faced with an inappropriate, badly phrased, or ignorant comment, the best recourse is to respond to the best of our ability and politely as possible. As we are all fallible, the time may well come when we ask a stupid question, and when we do, we will appreciate being treated decently. Beyond that, we are more persuasive with considerate responses than with ridicule.

Conclusion

Persuasion is often the goal of public speaking. To compose an effective persuasive speech, we need first to analyze our audience so that we may adapt our message as much as possible to its beliefs and values. In a persuasive speech, we attempt to change the way our audience feels, thinks, or acts. With the presentational speech, we attempt to persuade a decision making body to act on a proposal. The basic organizational pattern for a persuasive speech is the problem-solution pattern. First show that a problem is serious enough to require action, then show that our solution to the problem is the best remedy. The Monroe Motivated Sequence is an elaboration of this basic pattern and involves five steps: attention, need, satisfaction, visualization, and action. To handle interaction with our audience, we should be prepared to present additional information. Throughout the persuasive process, we should establish a sense of identification between our audience and our proposal.

• • • Discussion Questions

1. What situations do you know that would require a presentational speech?

2. Select one of the examples raised by question one. What audience characteristics would be important to the success of the presentational speech?

3. Think of a topic you would use for an informational speech. How would you reword the thesis statement for that speech to make it a persuasive thesis statement?

4. How is the problem-solution pattern used in advertising?

5. What advantages does the Monroe Motivated Sequence have over a simple problem-solution approach?

6. Why is evidence defined as "anything the audience will believe when presented"?

7. In what instance would facts be useful evidence?

8. In what instances would figures—numerical evidence—be effective?

9. In what situations would emotions be effective as evidence?

10. What situations would call for the use of testimonials and expert opinion as evidence?

11. In what instance would a story make good evidence?

12. Why is credibility important in persuasion?

13. How would you foster identification when speaking to a group of college students? Business people? School children? Residents of a retirement community?

• • • Sources and References

Aristotle. *The Rhetoric and Poetics of Aristotle.* Trans. W. Rhys Roberts and Ingram Bywater. New York: The Modern Library, 1954.

Burke, Kenneth. *A Rhetoric of Motives.* New York: Prentice-Hall, Inc., 1958.

Crable, Richard E. "Evidence, Warrants and Beliefs in Public Speaking." *Principles of Human Communication.* 2nd ed. Eds. Barry Brummett, Linda L. Putnam, and Richard E. Crable. Dubuque, Iowa: Kendall/Hunt Publishing Company, 1984. 174–80.

Gronbeck, Bruce E., Douglas H. Ehninger, Raymie E. McKerrow, Alan H. Monroe. *Principles and Types of Speech Communication.* 11th ed. Glenview, Illinois: Scott, Foresman/Little, Brown Higher Education, 1990.

Monroe, Alan H. *Principles and Types of Speech.* Rev. ed. New York: Scott, Foresman and Company, 1939.

Nadeau, Ray E. *A Basic Rhetoric of Speech-Communication.* Redding, Massachusetts: Addison-Wesley Publishing Company, 1969.

Vibbert, Stephen L. "Presentational Speaking as a Communication Skill." *Principles of Human Communication.* 2nd ed. Eds.. Barry Brummett, Linda L. Putnam, and Richard E. Crable. Dubuque, Iowa: Kendall/Hunt Publishing Company, 1984. 238–42.

Name _____ Section _____ Date _____

Composing A Persuasive Speech

1. Why is audience analysis especially important before composing a persuasive message?

   _____

   _____

2. What is the most important thing to determine about an audience before trying to persuade it?

   _____

3. What is a presentational speech?

   _____

   _____

4. What is meant by the phrase, "A presentational speech is interactive?"

   _____

   _____

5. What is unique about the way in which a thesis statement is arranged for a persuasive speech?

   _____

   _____

6. Compose a thesis statement which could be used for a persuasive speech.

   _____

   _____

7. What organizational pattern is preferred for the persuasive speech?

   _____

   _____

8. In what way is the use of the thesis statement different in the persuasive speech than in the informative speech?

   _____

   _____

Why is it used differently?

_____|_____

_____

9. Describe the Monroe Motivated Sequence.

_____

_____

_____

10. What is the satisfaction step?

_____

How does it compare with the problem-solution format?

_____

11. What takes place in the visualization step?

_____

_____

12. Describe the alternatives for presenting the visualization step.

   A. _____

   B. _____

   C. _____

13. What forms the conclusion of the persuasive speech which uses the Motivated Sequence?

_____

14. Define evidence.

_____

15. List three types of material that may comprise evidence and give examples of them.

   1. _____

   2. _____

   3. _____

16. What are some possible sources for facts to use in a persuasive speech?

_____

17. How do testimonials differ from expert opinion?

_____

_____

18. What part does credibility play in persuasive efforts?

_____

_____

19. What is Kenneth Burke's viewpoint regarding persuasion and identification?

_____

_____

20. How can a speaker foster a sense of identification with the audience?

_____

_____

21. How can a persuasive speaker successfully handle interaction with the audience?

_____

_____

Name _____ Section _____

Persuasive Thesis Statement Development Exercise

Provide amplification for the following statements to form a completed thesis statement.

Topic	Position	Amplification
1. Tuition	should be lowered	
2. Vacations	should be extended	
3. Working	can aid time management	
4. Chocolate	is addictive	
5. Writing well	takes practice	

Provide a position and amplification for the following topics.

Topic	Position	Amplification
1. Voting		
2. Running		
3. Alcoholism		
4. Engineering		
5. The economy		

Write five thesis statements below on persuasive topics of your choice.

1.

2.

3.

4.

5.

Name _____Section _____

Evidence Exercise I

Read the account, then determine if the statements following it are:

1. TRUE
2. POSSIBLY TRUE
3. NOT ABLE TO BE DETERMINED or
4. UNTRUE based on the evidence presented.

Be prepared to defend your answer by stating whether the evidence you used in making your evaluation was fact, figure, emotion, testimonial, expert opinion or a story.

Chris and Pat Clements are on trial for the murder of Joseph Brown, owner of a small manufacturing firm. Mrs. Brown found her husband's body in their garage with four cuts on his left hand and three bruises on the head, apparently inflicted by a blunt object. A baseball bat was found near the body. Fibers similar to those in a jacket worn by the victim were identified on Pat Clements' gloves. No fingerprints were found at the crime scene. Chris Clements was named by Mrs. Brown as responsible for her husband's death. The motive was Joseph Brown's refusal to void a contract that limited possible future income for Chris Clements. Pat Clements' help had been solicited by Chris, according to Mrs. Brown.

1. Chris and Pat Clements are related.

2. Pat Clements is on trial for the murder of Joseph Brown.

3. Chris Clements was responsible for the death of Joseph Brown.

4. Joseph Brown died as a result of blows to the head.

5. Joseph Brown was killed with a baseball bat.

6. Fiber samples indicated Pat Clements' involvement in the crime.

7. Chris Clements was angry with Joseph Brown because Brown would not void a contract.

8. Mrs. Brown cooperated in the murder investigation.

9. Joseph Brown was a successful businessman.

10. Mrs. Brown and Chris Clements were having an affair.

Name _____ Section _____

Evidence Exercise II

Which type of evidence—fact, figures, emotions, testimonials, expert opinion, or stories—would be advantageous to use in the following situations? If more than one type of evidence would be appropriate, list the strongest type first, followed by other types in descending order of importance.

1. petitioning the city council for a permit to hold a street dance at the beginning of school

2. asking a parent to borrow the car for a weekend

3. interviewing for an internship

4. requesting a grade change due to multiple correct answer choices on an exam question

5. convincing a police officer not to issue a ticket when you were driving eight miles per hour over the speed limit

6. seeking a full refund for an unsatisfactory product after using it for six months

7. asking someone out for a date

8. urging a client to buy your product

9. soliciting donations for the cancer society

10. running for student body president

Public Service Announcement

The class will be divided into groups. You and your group are to create a thirty second public service announcement. A public service announcement is a presentation offered by a television or radio station for the public good. Public service announcements are usually composed by not-for-profit organizations such as the Red Cross, United Way, American Heart Association, etc.

You may choose your own topic, but you must include in your announcement all the steps of the Monroe Motivated Sequence: attention, need, satisfaction, visualization, and action.

Some suggested topics are:

> donate blood
> buckle up
> contribute to . . .
> have your blood pressure checked
> neuter your pet
> recycle your trash
> don't litter
> register to vote
> don't drink and drive
> use the campus night escort service

After you have written your announcement, you will be asked to present it to the class. One person may read it or members of the group may play different roles in the presentation.

15

Persuasion and Reasoning

Key Concepts

In earlier chapters, we examined the nature of persuasion and the basic principles of constructing an effective persuasive speech. As we have seen, when we attempt to persuade others, we set forth arguments and reasons for the acceptance of our viewpoints. When we use the term "argument" in persuasion, we do not mean "hostility" or "emotionally charged encounters." As one persuasion theorist has pointed out, the matter is more one of "winning belief" than winning quarrels (Simons 178). The object of reasoning in persuasion is not to score points but to bring the persuader and persuadee together in how they view a matter.

This chapter examines some of the ways available to us as we attempt to win belief and to reach accord with those with whom we disagree. Recognizing the techniques of persuasive strategies enhances our abilities as communicators and makes us better "consumers" of persuasion. When we know lines of reasoning, we become more effective in influencing others and better at evaluating the persuasive efforts presented to us.

We will examine lines of reasoning in three ways. First, we will look at some of the patterns of argumentation available to us in responding to situations. Second, we will look at ways we can evaluate ideas presented to us as receivers of communication. Finally, we will look at arguments whose weak points so often outweigh their strong point that they are labelled "fallacies."

Keep in mind that lines of argument are persuasive *strategies*, not persuasive *guarantees*. Lines of reasoning are approaches we can take in communicating with others. They are not magical formulae that will automatically render us successful. Neither are they fixed forms to be used in the same way with all audiences. Effective communicators adapt lines of reasoning from audience to audience and from situation to situation.

The Flow of Reasoning

Effective reasoning and argumentation tend to follow recognizable patterns. In making up our own minds, we usually follow one of two patterns. We begin with ideas we hold and apply them to new situations or we collect observations until their cumulative weight leads us to draw a conclusion that makes sense of the observations.

For example, in speculating about a grade for a class, one could begin with a major idea: "The syllabus says that students achieving 585 points or above will receive an *A*." One then applies that major idea to a specific situation: "My semester score is 593 points. I can expect an *A* in this class." We could also speculate on a grade from the other direction and start by compiling observations: "My quiz grades equal 83 points; my first exam equals 92 points; my second exam equals 87 points; my third exam equals 84 points; my term project equals 137 points; My total points to date are 483." Based on that collection of data, one could then reach some conclusion about the semester grade: "A perfect score, 100 points on the final exam, will still be two points short of an *A*."

The first method of reasoning is known as "deductive reasoning." The second is known as "inductive reasoning." As arguments become more complicated, the number of premises, evidence and conclusions increase, and the relationships between them become more intricate. The basic movements, however, remain the same.

Deductive Reasoning

Patterns of Deductive Reasoning

When we reason deductively, we begin with a certainty, or a very high degree of certainty, and end with a conclusion based on that certainty. We start with an accepted idea or principle, then apply that idea or principle to a specific case. The move is one from the principle to the particular, from idea to application, from the abstract to the concrete.

"Hondas are good cars," thinks a prospective buyer in the showroom, then turns to the sales representative and says, "I want that one."

"The vet said generic dog foods are not good for my pet, so I started buying a higher priced name brand."

Syllogisms

Creating Syllogisms

The best known type of deductive argument is the syllogism. The syllogism is a form of argument that has been discussed by rhetoricians and philosophers for more than two millennia. The classic syllogism contains three parts: a major premise, a minor premise, and a conclusion. The first we have already seen though not in its formal style:

Major Premise: If students achieve 585 or more points in this course, they will receive an *A*.
Minor Premise: I have 593 points.
Conclusion: I will receive an *A*.

Syllogisms can be used to make judgments of value:

Major Premise: Rembrandt was a great painter.
Minor Premise: This painting is by Rembrandt.
Conclusion: This is a great work of art.

Syllogisms can also argue which of two alternatives is the most likely to happen.

Major Premise: For the university to meet its predicted financial needs, the legislature will have to appropriate more funds or we will have to raise tuition.
Minor Premise: The legislature will not appropriate more funds.
Conclusion: We will have to raise student tuition.

While syllogisms can be the subject of detailed discussion and analysis, the basic form is fairly simple. We first make a general statement about a classification or group. The statement should be one accepted or likely to be accepted by our audience. We then place an individual or small group within or without of that classification. Finally, we draw the logical conclusion (Nadeau 40).

If the pattern is not followed, the line of reasoning breaks down. If the minor premise does not fit as a subcategory of the major premise, whatever conclusion the speaker draws will be invalid. Changing the relationship of the major and minor premises changes the acceptability of the arguments.

Major Premise: Students who receive 585 points or more in this communication class will receive an *A*.
Minor Premise: I have 593 points in my biology class.
Conclusion: I will receive an *A* in this communication class.

Major Premise: Rembrandt was a great painter.
Minor Premise: This painting is by Sigmund Freud.
Conclusion: This is a great work of art.

A speaker will also be unsuccessful in using a syllogistic line of reasoning if the audience does not accept the major premise. If the speaker does not gain accord on the major premise, then the audience will be reluctant to grant accord on the minor premise and conclusion.

The syllogism is a widely used line of reasoning, but much of the time it is used in a shortened fashion. The elements are present, but one or two are left unstated, and it is up to the audience to fill in the blanks. Used in this form, it is often referred to as an "enthymeme," another major communication concept from Aristotle's *Rhetoric* (Book II, Chapter 22).

Enthymemes ask the audience to fill in the missing spaces. Rather than presenting a fully blown syllogism and letting the audience play a passive role in the persuasive interchange, the enthymeme calls upon the audience to play an active role. To follow the line or reasoning, the audience must make an effort to connect two thoughts. The involvement involves the audience in the reasoning process and gives the argument added impact.

In a grocery store, we might overhear, "Let's buy this cider. It's Purdue Cider."

In a class, someone might ask the instructor, "Isn't even a unit exam during 'dead week' against university regulations?"

The first example omits both the major premise and the conclusion. If we worked out the syllogistic line of reasoning, it would look like this:

Major Premise: Purdue Cider is excellent cider.

Minor Premise: This is Purdue Cider.

Conclusion: This is excellent cider.

On the basis of the conclusion, the persuader then urges action, buying the cider.

In the second, the major and minor premises are combined while the conclusion is left to the receiver's intuition. Reconstructed, the second enthymeme would look like this:

Major Premise: University regulations prohibit all exams during 'dead week'.

Minor Premise: What you are proposing is an exam.

Conclusion: You should not give us this test.

Weighing Syllogisms

When presented with syllogisms, we can evaluate them by checking them against their basic criteria. The first question we should ask is, "How readily do I accept the major premise?" If the major assumption is one we do not share, then we should reject the argument. If we accept the major premise, be it stated or unstated, then our next task is to judge the acceptability of the minor premise. Does the individual or subgroup fit logically in the larger classification of the major premise? If the fit is a good one, we can look forward to the conclusion. If the fit is a bad one, we should again be skeptical of the argument. Finally, we should judge how readily the conclusion follows from what precedes it. If the conclusion is in line with the major and minor premise, then we will, in all likelihood, accept the speaker's point. If the conclusion does not flow from the preceding statements, then we will reject or be dubious about the final point.

Inductive Reasoning

Patterns of Inductive Reasoning

Inductive reasoning is what one persuasion theorist calls "reasoning from evidence" (Simons 183). Here we begin with the specific and move to the general. We start by collecting observations, and when we have collected a sufficient number, we make a summary statement that makes sense out of what we have observed.

▲ **Figure 15.1.** Understanding patterns of reasoning helps us be better users and recipients of persuasion. (Coyle)

For example, after collecting information on auto accidents at a given campus intersection, we could then make judgments about the relative safety of the intersection.

Note that while deductive arguments begin with certainty and end with a specific conclusion, inductive arguments begin with a number of specifics and end, not in certainty, but in probability. In essence, we make the best guess we can about what the evidence means. For example, after collecting and tabulating data about the intersection, we might discover that the intersection had four accidents for every five million vehicle crossings. Given that the average accident rate is one per five million crossings, we would conclude that the intersection is unusually dangerous (Fricker).

Inductive arguments may take numerous forms. We will examine several of the best known forms.

Arguments from Authority

Creating Arguments from Authority

We argue or reason inductively from authority when we examine respected sources and judge their collective opinions on a matter. Before buying a car, we may consult *Consumer Reports*, *Motor Trend*, *Road and Track*, and other automobile magazines to see what has been said about different brands and models. We talk to physicians about our health. We read guides to universities and colleges before making the choice of which school to attend.

For our arguments from authority to be persuasive, they must meet several criteria. The authorities must be respected by the audience; the authorities must be relevant to the case at hand; and the authorities must be in sufficient numbers.

Weighing Arguments from Authority

As the target of persuasive efforts, we should ask the same kinds of questions about arguments from authority that we ask when preparing the arguments. Do we respect the authorities? Are the authorities relevant? Are they in sufficient number to be convincing?

When deciding whether or not to attend a movie, we might look at what critics—authorities—have said about the film. Whom would you be most likely to believe: one negative report from the film critic, social editor, and press operator of the *Otaska News*, a weekly newspaper published in a town of 1,200 or five positive reports from the film critics in *The New York Times, Film Digest, At the Movies, Newsweek, and Sneak Previews*? While it is possible that the five positive sources from notable publications could be mistaken, most of us would tend to accept them more readily than the one negative response.

Arguments from Statistics or Examples

Creating Arguments from Statistics or Examples

When we argue from examples, we collect enough samples of a given action or condition that we can generalize about the nature of the occurrence or the situation. If a situation is dramatic enough, one example may make the point. Usually, though, several examples will be necessary to support the desired conclusion. When we collect a large number of examples and express our findings numerically, we argue from statistics.

Legal reasoning, for example, is often reasoning from examples (Levi 2; Golding 10). To decide what to do in a given case, people look at what was done in previous similar cases. If someone dies without leaving a formal will but instead a rough draft of a will is found, how

legally binding is that rough draft? The answer will be found in earlier cases that addressed the same problem.

To discover the effectiveness of a new drug, the medicine is tested in a "double blind" experiment. People with a similar ailment are divided into groups. One group will be given the experimental drug. Another group will be given a placebo, something that looks like a drug but has no effect. A third group receives nothing, but its members are monitored as closely as those in the first two groups. The experiment is called a "double blind" because neither the person giving the drug nor the persons receiving the drug know who is receiving the drug and who is receiving the placebo. Experimenters collect numerous observations about the drug, quantify them, study them, and then draw conclusions about the drug's efficacy and applicability.

If we were arguing for better safety lighting in a given part of campus, one of the key points would be the problems created by the existing system. Here reasoning from examples or statistics would be very helpful. Central to the proposal for better lighting would be the number of accidents and assaults occurring in the area. To conclude that the area needed improved lighting, the persuader would need to collect enough examples to reach the conclusion, "This area is a problem sufficient to require action."

Weighing Arguments from Statistics or Examples

"How relevant are the examples?" is a question we should entertain when presented with arguments from examples. Cases of crimes committed in low light areas on other campuses will carry less weight than cases from the home campus.

"What is the scope of the evidence?" and "Do we have sufficient cases to draw an acceptable conclusion?" are questions that apply to both examples and statistics. One of the classic stories of advertising fraud is the aspirin company that advertised that "Three out of four doctors prefer our brand to all others." Investigation revealed that the company had, indeed, asked only four doctors for their opinions. For most of us to accept that argument, the number would have to be much higher and chosen from a true spectrum of doctors.

"How recent are the figures?" is another major question that must be asked of statistical evidence. One could report on the number of people listening to a given radio station, but unless the data are recent, they would be of little persuasive value to an advertiser.

"How fairly are the figures collected?" is another important question to which statistical data should be subjected. One does not obtain an accurate reflection of student drinking habits if the only people polled are those lined up outside bars on Friday nights. To obtain accurate statistics, those selected should be an accurate reflection of the larger group. Furthermore, everyone in the larger group must have an equal chance of being selected for the subject group.

Similarly, one needs to ask, "Who produced the figures?" If the source of the statistics is one whose livelihood or well being is tied to the figures, one should be wary of the evidence. One of the best known examples is the inflated figures produced by the United States armed forces in Vietnam. The Vietnam War was a controversial engagement and support in the United States was limited. To counter arguments against the war, the statistics of casualties, engagements, and losses were exaggerated to maintain the image that our forces were successful (Berman; Karnow; Sheehan). Even if figures are not distorted, they will have more impact coming from a disinterested source rather than one closely aligned with the product or idea.

Statistical evidence is dubious if it fails to use appropriate measures. One of the most common mistakes made in reporting statistics is to presume that the "average" or "mean" is a true reflection of the group being measured.

"The Ajax School Corporation continues to promote academic excellence by encouraging teacher-student interaction in small classes. The average classroom in the system now has twenty-two students."

If one class has thirty-five students and another has nine, their average size is twenty-two. The claim to academic excellence may be di-minished if it turns out that many classes are as high as thirty students while a few very small classes pull the average into the low twenties.

To be an accurate reflection, the statistics would also need to include the *median*, the *mode*, and the *range*. The median is the point on the scale at which half the figures are above it and half below. The mode is the figure occurring most often. The range shows the highest point reached, the lowest, and the distribution of data between those two points.

Arguments from Signs

Creating Arguments from Signs

Reason from signs is a form of reasoning that is derived from indicators. In this method of reasoning, data are not important in themselves but are important for what they point to or indicate. When arguing from signs, the data or pieces of information do not *cause* a condition or set of circumstances but instead *warn* us that the condition or set of circumstances is about to happen. In arguing from signs, a person introduces information, then shows towards what the information points. An argument based on signs uses the signs as a kind of predictor: "Since we see these signs, we can then expect...."

If someone is driving on a trip, glances at the instrument panel and notices the gas gauge is nearing empty, the impact of that indication is clear. The driver needs to refuel soon or run the risk of being stranded. The low reading on the gas gauge is a sign of impending problems. It does not, though, cause the impending problem.

A typical argument from sign would be the forecasts for the national economy based on new housing starts and automobiles sales. These two areas are considered valid indicators of the growth or shrinking or the economy. They are considered important indictors because they require large outlays of money and are the kind of purchases people make when they are affluent. Food purchases, for example, are less valid as indicators since food must be bought no matter what the economy.

Weighing Arguments from Signs

The validity of an argument from signs depends on the relationship between the sign and the conditions which it signals. If the two are closely correlated, the argument will be stronger than a line of reasoning in which the relationship is weak or non-existent.

If you were trying to ascertain the educational level of a person and you knew that person was a public school teacher, you could easily argue from sign to an acceptable conclusion. As a college degree is required of public school teachers, you could argue with a high degree of certainty that the person possesses a college diploma. The sign, "public school teacher," is linked very strongly with the conclusion, "possessing a college degree." You could not use the same sign to argue that the person was, say, an avid birdwatcher. No link exists between the two parts of that argument.

Arguments from Cause and Effect

Creating Arguments from Cause and Effect

Closely linked to reasoning from sign is reasoning from cause and effect. Again, we see a relationship between conditions and an effect. In an argument from sign, the pieces of evidence merely point to the existence of a condition. In an argument from cause and effect, the evidence shows what caused the condition. Reasoning from sign is arguing that something exists or will exist. Reasoning from cause and effect is arguing *why* something exists or will exist (Freely 153).

When using cause and effect reasoning, we can argue in two directions. We can argue from the causes or likely causes to say that the effect will take place, or we may argue from the effect and point to the reasons behind the condition. If one knows the cause, one argues from cause to the inferred effect. If one knows the effect, one argues from the effect back to the inferred cause (Freely 151). To be successful, both methods depend on the persuadee's acceptance of the described relationship. If our audience accepts the link between cause and effect, we can then argue for maintaining or changing the status quo by illustrating how current circumstances give rise to the particular set of causes and effects. Consider the following arguments:

Cause to effect: Tax revenues are down. University expenses are up. Inflation continues at five per cent per year. It easy to see that a tuition increase is inevitable.

Effect to cause: Student tuition has been raised ten per cent. The reasons are clear: tax revenues are down, university expenses are up, and inflation continues at five per cent per year.

Weighing Arguments from Cause and Effect

The success of a cause and effect line of reasoning depends on the strength of the relationship between its two parts. Thus, in evaluating a cause and effect argument, the chief question to be asked is, "How valid is the link between the proposed cause and proposed effect?" Two conditions may exist in close relationship with each other, but that does not mean that one causes the other. For example, a positive correlation exists between the length of people's pants legs and their educational levels. To a point, the more education one has, the longer the person's inseam. The reason is simple. We grow over the span of our education. A high school graduate is considerably taller than a first grader and hence will have not only more education but longer legs as well.

In the 1992 presidential elections, some reasoned that Bush's successful military campaigns and skills in international diplomacy (cause) would lead to his re-election (effect). They did not. Following the election, Clinton's forces argued that his slate of new programs (effect) was prompted by his mandate from the people (cause). If one does not accept Clinton's forty-six percent of the popular vote as a mandate, then the argument is unacceptable.

In addition to judging the existence of a cause-effect relationship, one also needs to ask if other forces were at work in a given situation. What the persuader offers as the chief cause or causes may only be a small part of the larger picture. "What other causes might lead to the same effect?" is another important question that critical audience members should ask.

According to a survey of 123 models of 1988-1990 cars conducted by the Highway Loss Data Institute, the two models with the least injures and collision damage were the Chevrolet

Caprice and the Plymouth Grand Voyager ("How Safe . . . 16–18). The effect is clear. One might even use it to argue that the cars possessed superior designs or safety features or handling capabilities that lead to their impressive standings. The data could be used as selling points for prospective owners: buy one of these and be guaranteed a safer ride.

Upon closer inspection, it turns out that the cause has little to do with design. This model of Caprice did not have airbags, even as an option. Two other factors were probably much more influential. One was weight. Both are large vehicles. In a collision, the larger the car, the less likely it is to be damaged, especially when it collides with a smaller vehicle. The second factor involves who buys and drives theses cars. Both the Caprice and Voyager are vehicles designed to carry a large number of people and are known as "family cars." The drivers and owners are people looking for practicality, not performance. They are likely to be conservative drivers, protective of their passengers. The safety record may be as much a matter of driver caution as it is safety design.

Arguments from Analogy

Creating Arguments from Analogy

Another method of inductive argument is argument from analogy. An analogy is a comparison of two things that are similar in many ways. By understanding the first thing, we come to understand the second. The use of analogies is a common teaching technique. We can, for example, see the three parts of a speech as similar to an airplane flight. The introduction is like the takeoff; the body is like the trip; and the conclusion is like the landing. In a lesson on electricity, an instructor may explain the flow of electricity through a wire by comparing it to the flow of water through a pipe. The key terms in understanding the flow of electricity—volts, ohms, and amps—correspond to three easily understood terms about the flow of water: pressure, resistance, and amount.

When we reason from analogy, we compare two things and on the basis of their similarities presume that their unknown characteristics will also be similar. A popular argument from analogy is the "If it walks like a duck . . ." argument. In attempting to classify a new fowl, we might observe that, "It walks like a duck; it swims like a duck; and it sounds like a duck." The conclusion would be that because the two birds share a significant number of characteristics, they must also share the same classification: the unknown fowl is a duck.

In a more sophisticated fashion, a legislator might argue: "The governor may call his plan an 'income adjustment,' but it is more than that. The adjustment will be paid by all wage earners in the state, just like a tax. The money will be collected by the Bureau of Revenue, just like a tax. The income will become state monies, just like a tax. The 'income adjustment' is nothing more than a new tax and should be treated as such."

One of our major social issues is the problem of health care. In the debate about the best approach to providing health care, we often hear an argument from analogy that compares the Canadian system of health care with the American system. The arguments run like this: "America and Canada face similar situations. Both are big, industrialized countries. Both have a large population, rising health care problems, democratic governments. They have about the same level of taxation. Canada has a workable system of health care. The United States does not. Since the two countries are so alike, the Canadian system would work in the United States."

Weighing Arguments from Analogy

The major factor in the acceptability of an argument from analogy is how readily we, or our audiences, accept the similarities between the two things—objects, cases, situations—being compared. If we readily accept the similarities, then the final conclusion is likely to make sense. If we see significant dissimilarities, then we are likely to reject the argument. The key question is, "How genuine, complete, and significant are the similarities presented to us?"

If one were a gambler, one might be persuaded to put money on a horse in the Kentucky Derby if it could be shown that the animal had the same lineage, training, track record, and jockey as last year's winner. One would be far less likely to bet on a horse just because it was the same color as last year's winner and wore a saddle and bridle like last year's winner.

The argument for a Canadian-style health care plan is effective only if the audience accepts the two countries as being significantly similar. The argument will be rejected if the audience sees the countries as dissimilar in important ways such as available resources or tolerance for governmental control.

If something "walks like a duck . . .," to some it may indeed be a duck. To others, it may be a new species of geese. The conclusion will depend on how well the persuader lines up the similarities.

From the preceding discussion, it should be clear how inductive reasoning leads from particulars to a general conclusion. One examines individual pieces of evidence and based on that collection of evidence reaches a conclusion that binds the separate piece of evidence into a coherent whole. Which method of reasoning is best—deductive or inductive—will depend upon the nature of the issue, the particulars of an audience, the type of evidence available, and the abilities of the speaker.

Fallacies in Arguments

A fallacy is a mistaken idea, an illogical projection from premise to conclusion. Simply put, a fallacious argument is one in which the premises and conclusions do not match up to make good sense. While they may have "the appearance of truth or reasonableness" (Freely 159), they do not stand up to close inspection. To some degree, we have already discussed fallacious arguments when we have pointed out where the above lines of reasoning can go astray and have urged close analysis of arguments offered in support of any proposition.

Beyond those examples, though, we have a group of arguments that stand as a class unto themselves due to their history of misuse. While they may be legitimately applied in some cases, more often than not they are the sign of slick appeals and shallow reasoning. Like the better lines of reasoning, they, too, have been in existence for centuries. Some are even dignified

with Latin names while others have colorful names they have acquired over time.

The *ad hominem* ("to the man") argument is an attack upon a person rather than an attack upon an idea. If one cannot discredit a proposal, then one discredits the person making the proposal. If people can be convinced that the proposer is of dubious character, they may reject the proposal without evaluating it.

The *ad populum* ("to the people") argument is also sometimes called "getting on the bandwagon." The idea comes from earlier times when the circus would parade down the main street of a town. The bandwagon contained, of course, the band, a large group playing as loudly as possible. "Getting on the bandwagon" came to mean joining a large number of people making a lot of noise and a great display while moving toward some goal.

It is an "everybody is doing it" or "everybody wants it" argument. In pressing such an argument, several important ideas may be ignored or glossed over. First, how many people constitute "everybody"? Unless valid statistics can be produced to show a significant number in favor of a proposal, the argument should be rejected. Second, even if a large number favor a proposal, that does not mean the proposal has value. "Everybody" is not always correct.

The "straw man" or "red herring" argument is another line of reasoning designed to lead one away from the central issue of a discussion. Instead of contending with a strong opponent, one creates a figure of little substance or strength, a "straw man," and proceeds to pummel it. If a persuader cannot successfully attack a proposal, then the persuader diverts attention from it by attacking a proposal which is vulnerable. A "red herring" was a smelly fish dragged across a fugitive's trail to divert the pursuing hounds onto a false track.

The "false dichotomy" argument involves presenting an audience only two alternatives when, in reality, a variety of alternatives may be present. "It's us or rust" was the slogan of a national automobile rustproofing company. Despite its catchy rhyme, a car owner had more than the two choices. Other rust proofing companies could be used. The owner could sell the car before rust developed. The car could be stored in the winter and driven only after the salt trucks had quit running. The owner could even move to a warmer climate to avoid winter and salty streets.

"Begging the question" is a kind of circular argument whereby the premises prove the conclusion and the conclusion proves the premises. Begging the question is when one says, "It is what it is because it is what it is." Calvin Coolidge, president of the United States from 1923 to 1929, supposedly provided one of the classic begging the question arguments with a comment on the economy. He stated that "When a large number of people are out of work, you see a rise in unemployment."

Contemporary examples can be found in advertising, among other places. In touting the size of its van, Volkswagen proclaimed, "Eurovan is here! The World's Largest Van For Its Size" ("Selling It" 271). In other words, no other van of the same size is bigger. A box of Swanson Chicken Pot Pie advertises its contents as having "100% More Chicken than Swanson 7 oz. Pies" ("Selling It" 271). The box contains a fourteen ounce pot pie.

Conclusion

In discussing issues and arguing persuasively, we need to be aware of the lines of reasoning available for us to use. The two major methods of reasoning argue in different directions. Deductive reasoning moves from a general idea or principle to specific applications or illustrations. It can also be characterized by a movement from certainty or a high degree of certainty to a conclusion. Inductive reasoning moves from particulars to a general conclusion that combines the particulars into a coherent whole. Its movement is one that begins with evidence and ends with a conclusion based on probability. In addition to logical uses of arguments, fallacious arguments may have the appearance of reason but are severely flawed.

Besides recognizing lines of reasoning, effective argumentation also relies on our adaptation of reasoning to a given situation. Rather than being set patterns of organization, arguments must be adapted to the audience, speaker, topic, and other variables of each speaking situation.

• • • Discussion Questions

1. In terms of reasoning and persuasion, what is an "argument"?

2. Cite an example of a syllogism. What are its major premise, minor, premise, and conclusion?

3. Provide an example of an enthymeme. How does it function as a condensed version of a syllogism? What are its implied major premise, minor premise, and conclusion?

4. What is the difference between deductive and inductive reasoning?

5. Provide examples of the various types of inductive arguments (authority, statistics or examples, signs, cause and effect, analogy).

6. How do we judge the validity of the various inductive arguments?

7. Bring in an ad from a newspaper or magazine. What arguments does the ad make? How valid are the arguments in the ad?

8. What makes a fallacious argument unacceptable?

9. Cite an example of a fallacious argument. What makes the argument fallacious?

• • • **Sources and References**

Aristotle. *Rhetoric.* Trans. W. Rhys Roberts. New York: The Modern Library, 1964.

Berman, Larry. *Lyndon Johnson's War.* New York: Norton, 1989.

Freely, Austin J. *Argumentation and Debate: Critical Thinking for Reasoned Decision Making.* 7th ed. Belmont, California: Wadsworth Publishing Company, 1990.

Fricker, John. Associate Professor of Civil Engineering, Purdue University. Personal interview. 9 June 1993.

Golding, Martin P. *Legal Reasoning.* New York: Alfred A, Knopf, 1984.

"How Safe is Your Car? What Insurance Data Say." *Consumers' Research Magazine.* Nov. 1991: 16–18.

Karnow, Stanley. *Vietnam: A History.* New York: Penguin Books, 1991.

Kirwan, C. A. *Logic and Argument.* New York: New York University Press, 1978.

Lee, Ronald and Karen King Lee. *Arguing Persuasively.* New York: Longman, Inc., 1989.

Levi, Edward H. *An Introduction to Legal Reasoning.* Chicago: University of Chicago Press, 1962.

Missimer, Connie A. *Good Arguments: An Introduction to Critical Thinking.* Englewood Cliffs, New Jersey: Prentice Hall, 1990.

Purtrill, Richard L. *Logic: Argumentation, Refutation, and Proof.* New York: Harper and Row, Publishers, 1979.

"Selling It." *Consumer Reports* April 1993: 271.

Sheehan, Neil. *A Bright Shining Lie: John Paul Vann and America in Vietnam.* New York: Vintage Books, 1988.

Simons, Herbert W. *Persuasion: Understanding, Practice, and Analysis.* 2nd ed. New York: Random House, 1986.

Toulmin, Stephen, Richard Rieke, and Allan Janik. *An Introduction to Reasoning.* New York: Macmillan Publishing Company, Inc., 1979.

Verderber, Richard F. *Essentials of Persuasive Speaking: Theory and Contexts.* Belmont, California: Wadsworth Publishing Company, 1991.

Walton, Douglas N. *Informal Logic: A Handbook for Critical Argumentation.* Cambridge, England: Cambridge University Press, 1989.

Weddle, Perry. *Argument: A Critical Guide to Critical Thinking.* New York: McGraw-Hill, Inc., 1978.

Willard, Charles Arthur. *A Theory of Argumentation.* Tuscaloosa, Alabama: University of Alabama Press, 1989.

Name _____ Section _____ Date _____

Persuasion and Reasoning

1. What is deductive reasoning?

   _____

   _____

2. How is a syllogism constructed?

   _____

   _____

3. What is an enthymeme?

   _____

   _____

4. How is the enthymeme used in persuasive speaking?

   _____

   _____

5. When presented with a syllogism, how can you evaluate it for validity?

   _____

   _____

6. What is inductive reasoning?

   _____

   _____

7. What criteria must be met by arguments from authority in order to be considered persuasive?

   _____

   _____

8. What five questions should you ask regarding examples or statistics before accepting them as valid evidence?

    1. _____

    2. _____

    3. _____

    4. _____

    5. _____

9. How can you determine the validity of arguments from signs?

    _____

    _____

10. What measures the success of an argument based on cause and effect?

    _____

    _____

11. What is an analogy?

    _____

    _____

12. What is a fallacy?

    _____

    _____

13. What is the *ad hominem* (to the man) argument?

    _____

    _____

14. What is the *ad populum* (to the people) argument?

    _____

    _____

15. What is the straw man or red herring argument?

    _____

    _____

16. What is a false dichotomy?

_____

_____

17. What is begging the question?

_____

_____

Sample Exam Questions

1. Which of the following statements BEST illustrates what is meant by "process" in communication?
   a. Process means that communication is a set of standard procedures for accomplishing our goals.
   b. Process is the mixture of communicative styles.
   c. Process means that communication is ongoing and created by the communicating parties.
   d. Process is the forward movement of communication.
   e. Process is the handling of information by the receiving party in a communication transaction.

2. An important factor in persuasive speaking is how the speaker is perceived by the audience. Which term BEST identifies this factor?
   a. charisma
   b. credibility
   c. stature
   d. power
   e. poise

3. "Evidence" is BEST defined as:
   a. the facts and figures you present your audience.
   b. the course of action you want your audience to accept.
   c. the strength of your main ideas.
   d. the collection of visual aids you display to enhance your message.
   e. anything your audience will believe when presented with it.

4. Which statement BEST defines "climate" as it pertains to small groups?
   a. Group climate is the feelings that group members have toward each other.
   b. Group climate is the agenda created for the meeting, a predictable pattern akin to the weather.
   c. Group climate is the temperature and humidity of the group's meeting place which can positively or adversely affect the group.
   d. Group climate is the relatively enduring quality of the group situation that is experienced in common by group members and arises from and influences their interaction and behavior.
   e. Group climate is the positive atmosphere created by the group in its approach to problem solving that allows and encourages the growth of solutions and the proper judgment of solutions.

5. Gary B.'s small group was given the responsibility of selecting a site for an upcoming family reunion. The group came up with various possibilities and discussed them until everyone agreed on the best place for the reunion. Which statement BEST describes the methods of decision making used by the group?
   a. parliamentary procedure
   b. convivial
   c. leader made
   d. democratic
   e. consensus

6. To describe what it was like to attend the Indianapolis 500 with over a half million in attendance, Sherry W. said, "It was as if you were one drop of water in the Mississippi River." Her method of describing is BEST labeled:
    a. description by analogy.
    b. description by providing examples.
    c. description by contrast.
    d. description by poetic language.
    e. description by formula.

7. Which statement BEST describes the first step a problem solving group should take when addressing a problem?
    a. Decide what happens to the group.
    b. Select the best alternative as a solution.
    c. Define the problem.
    d. Investigate the problem situation.
    e. Set criteria for a solution.

8. One method for finding a topic for a speech is to put down a word, then from that word, you create a web of associations. Which term BEST labels this method of finding a topic?
    a. brainstorming
    b. clustering
    c. self exploration
    d. free association
    e. Morgan's speech development technique

9. The three elements of a thesis statement are:
    a. the topic, the argument, the details.
    b. the subject, the ramifications, the solution.
    c. the topic, your position, amplification.
    d. the subject, the verb, the object.
    e. the introduction, the body, the conclusion.

10. Kathy S. is giving a speech on, "How to Raise Delicious Tomatoes." Her three main points are: "preparing the soil," "planting the tomatoes," and "caring for the tomato plants." Which statement BEST describes her method of speech organization?
    a. spatial
    b. structure-function
    c. topical
    d. chronological
    e. problem-solution

Answers for Sample Exam Questions

1. c
2. b
3. e
4. d
5. e
6. a
7. c
8. b
9. c
10. d

Library Research in Communication

Communication is a broad discipline, including research from the fields of psychology, sociology, medicine, linguistics, and many others. Because of its interdisciplinary nature, library research in this field takes on added dimensions. As with any research, one must know how to identify and locate information sources, evaluate the information, and then synthesize it into a well-organized presentation. Knowing some basic procedures and resources will provide you with a good foundation on which to begin your research project.

A universal process of conducting research cannot be prescribed for every topic or every individual. Research is dynamic and individualized, with a great many factors contributing to each person's approach to studying a given topic. However, understanding a basic **research strategy** - a method of identifying, locating, and evaluating information in an organized, logical fashion - will ensure that you have considered your options and found appropriate materials in an efficient manner without neglecting important resources. The following diagram illustrates this process:

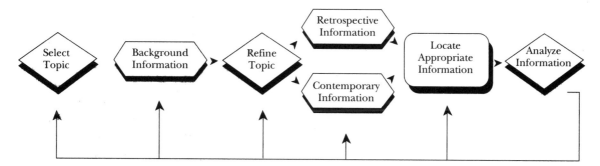

Selecting and Refining a Topic

Finding the right topic for your research can sometimes be the most challenging part of the entire research process. There are a number of important, preliminary considerations which you must make before even beginning to look for your information:

▶ Assess what you already know about the subject.
▶ Determine the perspective from which you will approach the topic.
▶ Determine the discipline(s) that will provide appropriate information.
▶ Articulate your needs and develop a focus.

If you are unclear about how to answer any of these questions, or if you feel you would like additional information about the subject area you have chosen, you may wish to gather some general background information to get an overview. Understanding basic concepts, theories, etc., and putting the topic into an appropriate context may give some direction to your treatment of the subject. Encyclopedias, dictionaries, and handbooks are often good sources for finding general information. They will provide basic, introductory information on a particular topic and offer a broad perspective, summarizing major developments in the field, identifying seminal researchers or other notable individuals, or leading you to important works related to the subject. As you read through some introductory essays, keep in mind how the various elements of the topic relate to each other. Are there approaches to the topic that you have not considered? What discipline(s) are most likely to be writing about these various perspectives? Remember, when using general information sources, you may need to look under broader subjects than the particular topic you have chosen. Your specific topic may be discussed within the context of a related subject. Use the indexes in these sources whenever possible.

While learning about a new subject area, you may come across unfamiliar words or terms, or familiar words used in a context other than what you are familiar with. Dictionaries and encyclopedias—which may be either general or specialized for a specific field or discipline—may offer some clarification. It will be important that you understand how the terms relate to one another. Is one term synonomous with another? Do they convey slightly different meanings? Is one term more specific? Understanding how the concepts within the subject area—hence, the terms that are used—relate to one another is directly related to how you will go about searching in the library for your information. With the increasing proliferation of computerized databases and systems, which allow for greatly enhanced search capabilities, your mastery of these electronic sources will depend largely on how well you understand your topic.

Usually located in the Reference section of the library, general information sources are arranged so that you can find the needed information quickly. A few examples of encyclopedias, dictionaries, and handbooks related to communication are:

- *Dictionary of American English on Historical Principles*
- *Dictionary of the Social Sciences*
- *Encyclopedia of Educational Research*
- *Encyclopedia of Management*
- *Encyclopedia of Philosophy*
- *Encyclopedia of Psychology*
- *Encyclopedia of Sociology*
- *Grove's Dictionary of Music and Musicians*
- *Handbook of Data Communications and Networks*
- *Handbook of Organizational Behavior*
- *International Dictionary of Films and Filmmakers*
- *International Encyclopedia of Communications*
- *McGraw-Hill Encyclopedia of Science and Technology*
- *Oxford English Dictionary*
- *Survey of Social Science: Psychology Series*
- *Taxonomy of Concepts in Communication*
- *World Press Encyclopedia*
- *The Writer's Handbook*

Other general survey sources may be identified by using the library catalog. By looking under the subject heading for the broad discipline that matches your topic, and then looking further for the standard subheading"—Dictionaries," you may locate specialized dictionaries as well as encyclopedias and handbooks in that particular field. For example, searching under the subject heading "communication—dictionaries" in a card or online catalog will help you find encyclopedias, handbooks and dictionaries in the broad field of communication.

In online catalogs, additional search techniques may be used to identify general information sources. Many computerized catalogs allow searching on key words in the bibliographic record. Conducting a keyword search will often result in more entries because the terms may appear in any part of the bibliographic record rather than as subject headings only. For example, the keyword search "k=psychology and dictionaries" will identify any record in the database in which these two words appear. You will find many of the encyclopedias and handbooks in the broad field of psychology with this type of search, but you may also find sources on specific branches of psychology, such as social psychology, experimental psychology, or pathological psychology.

Once you have a basic understanding of the subject area, you can determine the scope of your topic and consider focusing on particular aspects. The information you found from the general sources will help you to determine what particular approach is of most interest to you. It is important to comprehend the many avenues of inquiry that are possible and to make conscious decisions about which one(s) you will choose. Whenever possible, try to relate your topic to your own interests or experiences. Personalizing the topic will make the research more meaningful and relevant. You may wish to consider limiting your topic by such factors as:

▶ Geographic region (i.e. country, state, city)
▶ Time period (i.e. prehistory, 18th century, 1991, 2020)

▶ Population group (i.e. students, accountants, women, minorities)
▶ Other considerations (i.e. cross-disciplinary perspectives, etc.).

Refining your topic into a well formulated research question will provide you with a theme for your research. Having a well-defined focus will help to unify disparate elements, eliminate nonproductive efforts, and save you a great deal of time.

Searching for In-Depth Information

Once you have formulated your research question, you are ready to begin looking for in-depth information, which is more comprehensive and will provide additional detail. This in-depth information may be categorized into two types: retrospective and contemporary. Depending on the nature of your topic, you will need to determine the time frame of materials which will be relevant to your research.

Retrospective information is that which is written after an event or idea occurs. Because a period of time has elapsed between the event and publication, this information often includes historical analysis or evaluation of the topic. This type of information is typically found in books or pamphlets. Many encyclopedia articles will include bibliographies of key works on the subject, which may provide you with some good sources to start with. To locate additional books, however, you must use the library's catalog, which may be in a card catalog format or it may be computerized, in microform, or some other medium.

Regardless of the physical format, the basic principles of using a catalog remain essentially the same. Library catalogs provide access to the collections of a particular library or libraries. Items may be searched by for author, title, subject, and often, by additional options, such as key words in the record or call numbers. Specific search methods (i.e. search commands in computerized catalogs, etc.) may vary from one catalog to another. However, understanding some general fundamentals will provide you with a good foundation in using any library catalog.

Most library catalogs utilize a controlled vocabulary for organizing records by subject. A controlled vocabulary is a pre-determined list of terms used when assigning subject headings to each item in the catalog. In many college and university libraries, the Library of Congress subject headings are used. The listing of Library of Congress subject headings (LCSH) provides you with the exact format of the subject headings that will be used in the catalog. In addition, it may also indicate narrower, broader, or other related terms. It is important that you identify the correct subject headings to use when researching your topic so that you can most efficiently locate the items you need.

How to use Library of Congress Subject Headings

a. Identify term(s) relevant to your selected topic
b. Look up your term(s) in LCSH
c. If your term is in bold-faced print, you have located an acceptable subject heading to use in the catalog. If the library has materials on this topic, they will be listed under this heading.
d. If LCSH indicates that you should USE another term, turn to that heading.
e. Having located an accepted subject heading, LCSH may provide related terms. These related terms will be preceded by **UF**, **BT**, **RT**, or **NT**.

UF   denotes a subject heading *not* used in the catalog.
BT   refers to "broader terms." You may wish to look under this heading, particularly if you looked in the catalog under the bold-faced heading and no items were listed.
RT   refers to "related terms." LCSH is telling you that this term is related to your topic and you may wish to also look under this accepted heading.
NT   refers to "narrower terms." You may wish to use this heading, particularly if you looked in the catalog under the bold-faced heading and a great number of items were listed.

Sample entry from LCSH:

• •

Apprehension   **Perception**
  USE Perception   UF   Apprehension
                                                BT   Intellect
                                                     Thought and Thinking
                                                RT   Intuition (Psychology)
                                                NT   Intersensory effects
                                                     Subliminal perception

• •

Online catalogs often provide additional opportunities to search for information about a topic other than the subject heading approach. The ability to search free-text (which is to say, by any key word in the bibliographic record) offers tremendous capabilities and flexibility. A major concept to understand in online searching is that of Boolean logic, which is a method of combining terms together in specified ways within each record. Boolean logic utilizes operators which instruct the system how to process the resulting combination. The major operators recognized by most online systems are:

AND — narrows a search; requires that *each* term be present in the same record, regardless of their order. Use to find records with several distinct concepts. For example: *perception and children*

OR — broadens a search; requires that either term, or both, be present in the same record. Use it to group similar or related concepts. For example: *perception or intuition*

NOT — narrows a search; requires that the first term be present , but not the second. Use it to exclude records with the specified concept. For example: *perception not subliminal*

Since the search terms may appear anywhere in the bibliographic record (as an author, a word in the title, a word in a subject heading, etc.) and in any context, these searches must be constructed carefully. A clear understanding of the topic and the terminology is critical to effectively utilize the capabilities of these logical operations.

After locating appropriate records in the catalog, be sure to copy all relevant information about each item. All bibliographic information is included—author, title, publisher, date and place of publication—and specific location information, to help you locate the item on the shelf. Many catalog records also provide such additional information as a physical description of the item (number of pages, inclusion of illustrations and bibliographies, etc.) and notes, outlining the contents of the work.

You can use information in a catalog record to evaluate an item's potential usefulness to your research even before you locate it on the shelf. The *publication date* is an important indicator of the appropriateness of information about issues which may have radically changed in recent years. The *publisher* may provide an indication of the authority or perspective of the work: scholarly or university presses tend to treat a topic very differently than a popular publisher. The presence of *bibliographies* and *indexes* can be a useful evaluation tool: bibliographies will help in locating additional information, and often, a bibliography and index indicate a more scholarly approach. The *notes* field may specify the contents of anthologies or collections of essays, stories, or other works. Careful review of catalog records can furnish you with a great deal of information and make your research easier and more efficient.

With the materials you have gathered from your use of the catalog, you may find that you indeed have a solid general background or historical perspective on the topic, but you may be lacking in the recent research, developments, or opinions. Books, by their very nature, cannot report on the most current developments. They have a broader scope and thus take more time to write, and the publication process itself takes considerable time. So, for reports of what may have happened last month, for example, you will need to use some other types of materials.

Contemporary information — that which is representative of the time in which it was written — is typically found in such publications as newspapers, journals and magazines. Collectively, these publications may be referred to as "periodical literature" or simply "periodicals." To help eliminate confusion about the appropriateness of different types of periodicals for your research, some basic criteria have been established to help you determine the purpose and/or level of scholarship of magazines and journals. The nature of your topic will determine, to some extent, the most suitable type of publication.

TYPE OF PUBLICATION CRITERIA	SCHOLARLY JOURNALS	SUBSTANTIAL NEWS/ GENERAL INTEREST	POPULAR	SENSATIONAL
FORMAT	Generally have grave, serious formats.	Attractive in appearance.	Generally slick and glossy with an attractive format.	Often produced in a cheap, newspaper format.
GRAPHICS	Contain graphs and charts, but seldom glossy pages or pictures.	Include photographs, illustrations and graphics to enhance the publication.	Contain photographs, illustrations, and drawings to enhance their image.	Contain melodramatic photographs.
SOURCES	Cite sources with foot-notes and bibliographies.	Occasionally cite sources, but this is the exception .	Rarely cite sources, which may be obscure.	Rarely cite sources of information.
AUTHORS	Written by and for scholars or researchers in the specialty.	Written for an educated, general audience by the magazine's staff, a scholar, or free-lance writers.	Written by the publication's staff or free-lance writers for a broad based audience.	Contain articles written by free-lance writers or the publication's staff for an impression-able readership.
LANGUAGE	Use terminology, jargon and language of the discipline. Reader is assumed to have a similar scholarly back-ground.	Use language appro-priate for an educat-ed reader-ship. Do not emphasize a specialty but assume a basic level of intelligence.	Use simple language to meet a minimal education level. Articles are kept short, with little depth.	Contain language that is simple and easy to read and understand. An inflammatory, sensational style is often used.
PURPOSE	Inform, report or make available origi-nal research or experimentation to the rest of the schol-arly world.	Provide general information to a wide, interested audience.	Designed to enter-tain or persuade. A hidden (or not so hidden) agenda is to sell products or services.	Arouse curiosity and interest by stretch-ing and twisting the truth. Outrageous, startling headlines are used to pique curiosity and gain readership.
PUBLISHERS	Generally published by a professional organization.	Generally published by commercial enter-prises for profit.	Published for profit.	Published for profit.
ADVERTISING	Contain selective advertising.	Carry advertising.	Contain extensive advertising.	Advertising is as melo-dramatic as the stories.
EXAMPLES	*AMERICAN ETHNOLOGIST JOURNAL OF COMMUNICATION JOURNAL OF POLITICS*	*FORBES PSYCHOLOGY TODAY SCIENTIFIC AMERICAN TIME*	*GLAMOUR PEOPLE WEEKLY READER'S DIGEST SPORTS ILLUSTRATED*	*GLOBE NATIONAL ENQUIRER STAR SUN*

Indexes and abstracts will help you to identify appropriate sources of contemporary information. (The basic differences between an index and an abstract is that an abstract provides a summary of the article and is often divided into a separate index section and an abstract section; an index has no summaries and only one section). Each index or abstract covers a select group of periodical titles, which may be determined by the general subject(s) or disciplines covered, or by the type of material. Whereas many indexes are printed in book form, a growing number are becoming available in electronic or computerized formats, such as CD-ROM. As with library catalogs, the actual mechanics of using different indexes may vary from one source or system to another. However, understanding the general function of indexes and realizing that different indexes serve different purposes will provide you with enough information to use them effectively in your research. A selected list of indexes and abstracts appears below:

- *Applied Science and Technology Index*
- *Biography Index*
- *Biological and Agricultural Index*
- *Book Review Index*
- *Business Periodicals Index*
- *Communication Abstracts*
- *Education Index*
- *Film Literature Index*

- *General Science Index*
- *Humanities Index*
- *Medline*
- *New York Times Index*
- *Psychological Abstracts*
- *Readers Guide to Periodical Literature*
- *Short Story Index*
- *Social Sciences Index*

Selecting the appropriate indexes for your research will be determined largely by your approach to the topic. Some topics may require articles from scholarly journals, whereas others may rely more on popular magazines or newspapers. Other topics may be considered from various disciplinary perspectives. Still others may take you into literature written last week or last month, whereas others may require that you find materials written ten, twenty or fifty years ago. Consider the following factors in selecting the indexes and abstracts that will be most relevant to your topic:

▶ **Subject relevancy**—Only with a fairly thorough understanding of the topic can you decide what disciplines are most appropriate for reporting on the research in the specified subject area.

▶ **Time period covered by source**—Be certain that the index or abstract you select covers materials for the appropriate time period for your topic. Many of the computerized databases have been developed only in recent years and may be limited to more recent materials.

▶ **Level of material**—Some indexes, such as *Reader's Guide to Periodical Literature*, focus largely on the popular magazines while others lead to scholarly and technical papers, conference proceedings, manuscript collections, and the like. Your knowledge of the topic will determine what level of materials is most suitable.

▶ **Type of material**—The nature of your topic will be key to determining the type of material to be used in your research. For some topics, magazine and newspaper accounts may suffice; others may require more in-depth analysis, leading to more scholarly research in the field. Some topics may be more appropriately covered in books, which provide a broader, more comprehensive overview of the subject area.

▶ **Breadth of coverage**—Each index and abstract determines its own "universe" of materials to be included. Some features to look for include: comprehensiveness of indexing (i.e., does it index *every* article in each of the magazines, journals, or newspapers it includes, or is it selective?); inclusion of international materials; inclusion of materials written in other languages.

Indexes and abstracts will provide references to articles on your selected topic. Those in the print format are usually arranged alphabetically by subject, though some also list authors and titles. The electronic index databases often provide many of the same search features and functions as the on-line catalogs, providing access to articles by author, title, subject headings, the name of the magazine or journal, date, or any keyword in the record. Oftentimes, the electronic sources provide abstracts, which may also be searchable.

Each entry in an index or abstract is referred to as a "citation." The elements of a citation include: the author(s) of the article; the title of the article; the name of the periodical; the volume number, and sometimes the specific issue number; the pages on which the article appears; and the date of the issue. Be sure to copy all relevant information from the index so that you have complete information when you compile your list of references. The following example illustrates a typical bibliographic citation for a journal article:

> Cappella, J.N. and Palmer, M.T. "The structure and organization of verbal and nonverbal behavior: data for models of reception." *Journal of Language and Social Psychology* 8(3/4):167-192, 1989.

A number of different styles for citing articles are employed throughout the literature. These various styles have been established to best serve the needs of researchers and of scholarly publication in particular fields of study The standard styles used include the MLA (Modern Language Association) style and the APA (American Psychological Association) style, among others. Be sure to use the style appropriate for your research. Manuals explaining each style are available.

Evaluating Information

Once you have identified and located your sources, you begin the task of analyzing, synthesizing and evaluating the information. The process of evaluation is a critical component of the research process. The fact that something appears in print does not necessarily make it true or "correct." It is your responsibility as a researcher to think critically about the information and determine its authority and suitability to your needs. Consider the reliability, credibility, and perspective of the information presented when evaluating your sources.

Reliability

Are the facts accurate? Do they support the thesis? Can you rely on this information? These are some of the questions researchers must ask themselves to determine the reliability of the information presented in any given source. While experts in a subject area may easily judge a work's reliability, it may be more difficult for the novice. One way to determine reliability is to compare the work with other writings on the topic. If you find that it is in conflict with other sources, you should question why there is a discrepancy. It may be that the source in disagreement is in fact the "correct" one or it may be presenting new information or offering a different perspective. In any case, it is important that you check out the differences.

Book reviews offer one source of information on reliability. Often written by other experts in the field, they provide insight on the information presented and may relate it to other works on the topic. Care must be taken, however, to consider the objectivity and authority of the book review itself. Book review indexes are useful in identifying reviews of many books published. Two such indexes are *Book Review Digest* and *Book Review Index*. Each of these sources indexes reviews which have been published in American and English publications.

Credibility

Credibility refers to the authority and/or qualifications of the writer who makes the claims or presents the information in the work. Does the author have the appropriate training, education, or expertise? Are the "authorities" cited by the author qualified to make the claims they are making? Ascertaining the credentials of the author or experts named will help to determine the credibility of the work.

A number of reference works will provide assistance in finding biographical information for many authors and other individuals: *Biography and Genealogy Master Index* serves as an index to many sources which provide biographical information on people from all nationalities, occupations, and time periods; *Current Biography* compiles short articles on individuals of current interest or popularity, from all occupations and of various nationalities; *Contemporary Authors* includes brief entries on writers in fiction, nonfiction, poetry, journalism, television, and other fields; and, *Biography Index* is a guide to biographical material appearing in selected periodicals and books.

Perspective

The perspective of the information presented is very important to consider when evaluating a work. How an author's cultural or experiential background affects the approach he or she has taken may profoundly affect the viewpoints that are expressed or the conclusions reached. It may also determine what information has been included or excluded. Some of the background information found when determining an author's credibility may help in determining one's perspective, as well. Consider the following:

▶ Affiliation of the author(s)—the person's political, professional, social, or economic affiliations may determine the views expressed.

▶ Place of publication—where a publication originates from may serve as a clue to its perspective. For example, information presented in one country may vary greatly from the information presented in another.

▶ Date of publication—perspectives often change over time; you must try to understand why people write what they do in the context of their times.

After evaluating each of your sources and the information contained within them, you may find that you wish to eliminate some of them as inappropriate and find references to other materials that will better support your particular research question. Or you may find that there is not enough evidence available to support the specific view which you had proposed. Following the model research strategy, you may need to go back to the stage of identifying more information sources - either retrospective or contemporary - or perhaps even to the point of refining your topic once again. Wherever it leads you, the objective of your research is to develop a well-formulated adequately supported analysis of your topic, and to present it in an organized fashion.

Conclusion

The basic research strategy presented here is intended to provide a framework for finding information in any subject area, for any information need. Whether you are writing a comprehensive research paper, conducting a five minute speech, or simply wanting to find out about a favorite personality, applying this model will guide you through the steps of gathering the necessary information. At whatever stage of the process, or whatever source you are looking at, making informed decisions to evaluate the usefulness and appropriateness of any information is critical.

As a researcher, you must recognize that information itself does not constitute knowledge. Knowledge refers to an understanding or awareness gained through study or research. In order to effectively engage in that research, you must become "information literate," understanding how to effectively identify, locate, evaluate and communicate information for any given need.

Name _____ Section _____ Date _____

Research Topic Profile

What is your research topic? _____

_____

_____

Into what subject area(s) does your topic fit? (i.e. sociology, history, science)

_____

_____

What general call number(s) correspond(s) to your subject area(s)

_____

Do You Need General Information?

Find an encyclopedia, dictionary, or handbook in your subject area by browsing the call number area(s) in the UGRL Reference Collection. Remember you are looking for general, not specific information. If your topic is cocaine use by athletes, you may want background information on cocaine, as well as drug use by athletes.

1. **List the bibliographic information for the entries you found.**

_____

_____

_____

_____

_____

2. **List any additional titles found in the bibliography of the encyclopedia article or other source.**

_____

_____

_____

Use the *Library of Congress Subject Headings*

1. **List the LC Subject Heading(s) for your topic.**

_____

2. **List additional** *see also* **terms you may wish to use.**

_____

_____

_____

3. **List any broader (BT) or narrower (NT) headings you may wish to use.**

_____

_____

Narrowed Topic _____

Do You Need Retrospective Information?

1. Look under your subject headings in the catalog(s).

Catalog(s) used _____

2. Write down the complete citations and call numbers for all useful books. List additional books on a separate piece of paper.

_____

Location_____

_____

Location_____

Do You Need Contemporary Information?

1. Check the list of abstracts and indexes (listing on p. 406 of this text) for appropriate ones to use. List index/abstract title(s) used:

_____

_____

_____

2. Terms looked under _____

_____

3. Citations found (author(s), title of article, full magazine title, volume, date, page). List additional articles on a separate piece of paper.

_____

_____

_____

_____

_____

_____

_____

4. Look up the magazine or journal title(s) from above the THOR and record the location(s) for each title.

    magazine title _____

    location _____

    magazine title _____

    location _____

    magazine title _____

    location _____

    magazine title _____

    location _____

5. Check NewsBank for your topic. List subject terms investigated, and author, title of article, newspaper, date and NewsBank microfiche category and number.

    _____

    _____

    _____

    _____

    _____

    _____

    _____

    _____

Is there enough information available on your topic to write a good research paper?

_____

If not, how can you broaden or modify your topic?

_____

_____

_____

_____

_____

Index